Taking Sides: Clashing Views in Management, 5/e

Kathleen J. Barnes and George E. Smith

ISBN-10: 1259873455   ISBN-13: 9781259873454

Contents

Detailed Table of Contents

Unit 1: Ethical Issues for Managers

Unit 2: Human Resource Management

Is Social Media a Tool of Expression or Trouble for Businesses?
Yes: Christopher E. Parker, from "The Rising Tide of Social Media," *The Federal Lawyer* (2011)
No: David L. Barron, from "Social Media: Frontier for Employee Disputes," *Baseline* (2012)

Christopher E. Parker argues that the prevalence of social media is quite clear and a useful tool for business. Many employers now routinely use social networking sites in advertising, marketing, communication, and decision making, and to conduct research about the backgrounds of job candidates. David L. Barron argues that employees are increasingly making complaints to human resources departments and management over offensive or harassing statements made online. With the rise of cyber-bullying and "textual harassment," employees must be made to understand that company policies extend into cyber-space and social media forums, and these policies must be followed.

Are Unions Good or Bad for Employees and Corporations?
Yes: Henry Blodget, from "I've Always Hated the Idea of Labor Unions, But It May Be Time to Reconsider," *Business Insider* (2012)
No: Derek Thompson, from " 'Unnecessary' and 'Political': Why Unions Are Bad for America," *The Atlantic* (2012)

Business Insider contributor Henry Blodget lists the reasons he doesn't like unions, but then discusses the extreme compensation inequity that is worse than any time since the late 1920s. Derek Thompson relays *The Atlantic's* readers' responses to the question whether unions were necessary to restore wealth to average American families.

Unit 3: Strategic Management

Is Outsourcing a Wise Corporate Strategy?
Yes: BusinessWeek, from "The Future of Outsourcing: How It's Transforming Whole Industries and Changing the Way We Work," *Bloomberg Businessweek* (2006)
No: Ephraim Schwartz, from "Painful Lessons from IT Outsourcing Gone Bad," *InfoWorld* (2008)

BusinessWeek writers argue that outsourcing is likely to become even more important to corporate America in the near future. Indeed, they suggest that it has the potential to transform whole industries. *InfoWorld* columnist Ephraim Schwartz explores the often-overlooked costs associated with failed outsourcing initiatives. His analysis consists of four brief case studies of outsourcing initiatives that turned out badly.

Will the Use of Reshoring/Insourcing by Corporations Increase?
Yes: Andrew Sikula, Sr., et al., from "Insourcing: Reversing American Outsourcing in the New World Economy," *Supervision* (2010)
No: David J. Lynch, from " 'Reshoring' of Jobs Looks Meager," *Bloomberg Businessweek* (2012)

Andrew Sikula and colleagues discuss reasons why a movement to insourcing is currently occurring. The authors conclude that this movement is going to expand during the next several years in the United States. David J. Lynch observes that many of the jobs a nation (e.g., China) is losing are heading to other low-cost Asian nations. In addition, he observes that while some jobs have returned to the United States, other jobs are still being shipped out of the country.

Does Expanding via Mergers and Acquisitions Make for Sound Corporate Strategy?
Yes: Rosy Kalra, from "Mergers and Acquisitions: An Empirical Study on the Post-Merger Performance of Selected Corporate Firms in India," *The IUP Journal of Business Strategy* (2013)
No: Anand Sanwal, from "M&A's Losing Hand," *Business Finance Magazine* (2008)

Rosy Kalra studied 47 firms listed in Indian stock exchanges which underwent mergers and acquisitions between April 1, 2008 and March 31, 2009. Kalra's study showed there is significant improvement in the liquidity, profitability, operating performance, and financial leverage for a few merged/acquirer firms. Anand Sanwal examines 33 large merger and acquisition (M&A) transactions from Europe, Canada, and the United States. The evidence is that a great number of these M&A transactions have actually destroyed value. He also contends that in many of the transactions that did fare well, luck was often a large factor.

Unit 5: International Management

<u>**Do Unskilled Immigrants Hurt the American Economy?**</u>
Yes: Steven Malanga, from "How Unskilled Immigrants Hurt Our Economy," *City Journal* (2006)
No: Diana Furchtgott-Roth, from "The Case for Immigration," *The New York Sun* (2006)

Steven Malanga believes the influx of unskilled immigrant's results in job loss by native workers and lower investment in labor-saving technology. He also contends that illegal immigration taxes our already-strained welfare and social security systems. Diana Furchtgott-Roth, senior fellow at the Hudson Institute and a former chief economist at the U.S. Department of Labor, points out that annual immigration represents a small portion of the U.S. labor force, and, in any event, immigrant laborers complement, rather than replace, legal American citizens in the workplace.

<u>**Is Economic Globalization Good for Humankind?**</u>
Yes: Paul A. Gigot and Guy Sorman, from "Foreword," The Heritage Foundation (2008)
No: Branko Milanovic, from "Why Globalization Is in Trouble—Parts 1 and 2," *YaleGlobal Online* (2006)

Arguing that globalization is good for humankind are Paul A. Gigot and Guy Sorman. They outline seven ways in which globalization has positively impacted life and what needs to be done to further its advancement. Branko Milanovic, an economist with both the Carnegie Endowment for International Peace and the World Bank, is against globalization. Milanovic addresses several reasons for his views while emphasizing the incompatibility of globalization with the ages-old ethnic and religious traditions and values that characterize much of the world.

<u>**Are Protectionist Policies Beneficial to Business?**</u>
Yes: Ha-Joon Chang, from "Protecting the Global Poor," *Prospect Magazine* (2007)
No: Robert Krol, from "Trade, Protectionism, and the U.S. Economy: Examining the Evidence," The Cato Institute (2008)

In support of the idea that protectionist policies help business, Ha-Joon Chang focuses attention on developing industries in poor countries. Further, he describes and advocates historical protectionist policies from around the world. Robert Krol describes the findings of various economic studies of international trade. The areas that he surveys include the effect of trade on employment and wages as well of the costs of trade restrictions. He concludes that overall the benefits from protectionist policies are overshadowed by their negative effects.

<u>**Is Globalization Beneficial for Society?**</u>
Yes: Stephen A. Baker and Robert A. Lawson, from "The Benefits of Globalization: An Economic Perspective," *Journal of Lutheran Ethics* (2002)
No: Sergio Obeso, from "Globalization and Its Consequences for the Countries and People in Mexico and Latin America, *Kolping International* (Accessed 2012)

Professors Steven A. Baker and Robert A. Larson discuss the benefits of globalization for both developed and developing nations and peoples. While acknowledging that there are imperfections in the approach, they note that globalization can have a positive effect and can help nations and people successfully address the issue of poverty. Sergio Obeso, Archbishop Emeritus of Xalapa, presents his view of globalization's impact on the people of Mexico and Latin America. While he acknowledges that some benefits were derived from these practices and this process, Archbishop Obeso observes that there have been adverse consequences on local and regional cultures as well as other forms of regional and nationalistic expression (e.g., politics, religion, societal values).

Preface

He who knows only his side of the case knows little of that. His reasons may have been good, and no one may have been able to refute them. But if he is equally unable to refute the reasons on the opposite side he has no ground for preferring either opinion.

John Stuart Mill

The United States criminal system is adversarial in nature; two sides with incompatible goals meet in front of a judge and/or jury to determine the fate of an individual charged with a crime. Underlying this process is the presupposition that truth can be reached through the presentation of conflicting viewpoints. *Taking Sides: Clashing Views in Management* is predicated on this presupposition. Each of the debates presented here mimics the courtroom: There are two opposing sides, each vigorously presenting its evidence and questioning its opponent's case; there is a judge—the reader—who considers the relative merits of each side, hopefully maintaining objectivity while searching for truth; and there is a time for rendering a verdict which may signal vindication for one side or perhaps leave the decision open for debate and consideration on another day and time.

This text consists of debates on controversial issues in the field of business management. Each issue consists of opposing viewpoints presented in a pro and con format. It is your role as judge to give each side a fair and unbiased hearing. This will be a difficult task, for the authors of each of the articles is an expert and defends his or her position with great vigor.

To help in this task, we suggest that you ask difficult questions, make notes on troubling points, and interact with the material. If you have a preconceived opinion about an issue, force yourself to look critically at the side you support. This, too, is difficult to do as it's much easier to find the weaknesses in the opposing point of view than in your own. None the less, doing so helps protect against self-deception and, frequently, strengthens your original belief. Perhaps most importantly, it makes you think!

Book Organization

The text is divided into units, each addressing a different aspect of management. At the beginning of each unit is a unit opener that briefly identifies the specific issues in the section. Next are the issues themselves, each of which starts with an introduction that sets the stage for the debate as it is argued in the YES and NO selections. The section following the selections provides some final observations and comments about the topic. The *Exploring the Issue* section contains *Critical Thinking and Reflection* questions, *Is There Common Ground?* and *Additional Resources* and *Internet References* for further reading.

We'd like to make a few observations regarding this new edition. Those familiar with the previous edition will notice that we have made several significant changes in this edition. First, we dropped issues that proved too inaccessible, not particularly controversial, somewhat outdated, or too similar to another topic. Second, of the topics carried over from the previous edition, several have been updated with newer articles by different authors. Finally, and perhaps most significantly, we have added a number of new issues that address some of the many contemporary controversies and discussions existing in management today.

Our overarching goal with this work has been to contribute to the development of critical thinkers who are willing to question their own values and beliefs to get to the "truth" of difficult questions and matters. We hope that this work contributes to that goal and that you find the topics to be not only controversial, but interesting and educational as well. Thank you for your interest in and support of our work!

Editors of This Volume

KATHLEEN J. BARNES is a professor of management and associate dean at William Paterson University's Cotsakos College of Business. She has taught principles of management, human resource management, organizational behavior, organizational leadership, and organizational strategy. Barnes received her PhD from the University at Albany, SUNY. Her current research interests include experiential learning and education, organizational culture, and individual and team empowerment.

GEORGE E. SMITH is an associate professor of management at the University of South Carolina, Beaufort. He has taught principles of management, business, government, and society, human resource management, contemporary business and the capstone course in management. Smith received his PhD from The Rockefeller College of Public Affairs & Policy at the University at Albany, SUNY. His current areas of research interest include experiential learning and education, ethics education, and exploring management history's place in the management/business education curriculum.

Acknowledgments

We extend our heartfelt thanks to our McGraw-Hill editor, Debra Henricks for her professionalism and flexibility in making the completion of this work possible. We'd also like to thank our family and friends for their continued support and encouragement. Thank you!

We dedicate this text to our spouses—JoDee LaCasse and Christine Smith. JoDee's and Christine's support and love helped us become the successful people that we are today.

Editors/Academic Advisory Board

Members of the Academic Advisory Board are instrumental in the final selection of articles for each edition of TAKING SIDES. Their review of articles for content, level, and appropriateness provides critical direction to the editors and staff. We think that you will find their careful consideration well reflected in this volume.

Academic Advisory Board Members

Yoa A. Amewokunu
Virginia State University

Robert Atkin
University of Pittsburgh

Derek D. Bardell
Delgado Community College

Glenn W. Briggs
Webster University

Barry Brock
Barry University

Dennis Brode
Sinclair Community College

Marilyn Brooks-Lewis
Warren County Community

Buck Buchanan
Defi ance College

Kalyan S. Chakravarty
California State University

Bonnie Chavez
Santa Barbara City College

Rachna Condos
American River College

William L. Corsover
Barry University

Dale Cox
Gadsden State Community College

Kevin W. Cruthirds
The University of Texas–Brownsville

Kevin Cruz
University of Texas–El Paso

Anthony D'Ascoli
Miami Dade College

Elizabeth Danon-Leva
University of Texas at Austion

Charles E. Davies, Jr.
Hillsdale College

Miles K. Davis
Shenandoah University

Donald Doty
Northwest University

Karen Eboch
Bowling Green State University

Thomas Eveland
DeVry University

Diane Fagan
Webster University

Jeffrey Fahrenwald
Rockford College

Janice Feldbauer
Schoolcraft College and Macomb Community College

Charles Feldhaus
Indiana University-Purdue University

Martin Felix
Johnson & Wales University

Anthony Fruzzetti
Johnson & Wales University

Karen Gaines
Kansas City Kansas Community College

James Glasgow
Villanova University

Joel Goldhar
Illinois Institute of Technology

David S. Greisler
York College of Pennsylvania

M. Ray Grubbs
Millsaps College

Semere Haile
Grambling State

Jon Harbaugh
Southern Oregon University

Jim Henderson
Alverno College

P. L. "Rick" Hogan
Pierce College

Phillip A. Jeck
University of Central Oklahoma

Masud Kadri
University of Phoenix

James Katzenstein
California State University, Dominguez Hills

Gary F. Kelly
Clarkson University

Carolyn Kelly Ottman
Milwaukee School of Engineering

Jane LeMaster
University of Texas–Pan American

Victor Lipe
Trident Technical College

David Little
High Point University

Nick Lockard
Texas Lutheran University

Jayme Long
Delta State University

Susan Losapio
Southern New Hampshire University

Ed Maglisceau
Santa Fe University of Art and Design

Kenyetta McCurty
Amridge University

Jeanne McNett
Assumption College

Joseph B. Mosca
Monmouth University

Tina Nabatchi
Syracuse University

Don A. Okhomina
Fayetteville State University

David Olson
California State University

Floyd Ormsbee
Clarkson University

Mary Jo Payne
University of Phoenix

Pedro David Perez
Cornell University–Ithaca

Richard J. Pilarski
SUNY Empire State College

Renee Porter
Lindenwood University

Lynn Powell
James Madison University

Michael J. Provitera
Barry University

Eivis Qenani
Cal Poly–San Luis Obispo

Kathryn Ready
Winona State University

Robert K. Rowe
Park University

Raymond Ruetsch
Columbia College

Jean Sampson
McKendree University

Jan Napoleon Saykiewicz
Duquesne University

Calvin Scheidt
Tidewater Community College

Michael Scheuermann
Drexel University

Peter Schneider
U. S. Merchant Marine Academy

Bruce Schultz
Brooklyn College

Anthony W. Slone
Elizabethtown Community and Technical College

Gerald Smith
University of Northern Iowa

Katrina Stark
University of Great Falls

Ira Teich
Lander College for Men

Eric Teoro
Lincoln Christian College

Elionne Walker
University of Saint Thomas

Timothy L. Weaver
Moorpark College

Caroline Shaffer Westerhof
California National University, Kaplan University

Mary I. Williams
College of Southern Nevada–North Las Vegas

Debra D. Woods
Westmoreland County Community College

Mary Wright
Hope International University

Introduction

Controversial Issues in Management

This introduction briefly discusses a different area of business management. Each unit provides important information about a specific management area and sets the stage for the debate topics that comprise this book. This introduction is organized paralleling the debate topics presentation in the text: business ethics-related issues; human resource management-related issues; strategic management-related issues; environment-related; and international management-related issues.

Ethical Issues for Managers

Many business ethics scholars analyze this complex management topic at two levels. The macro-level involves issues broad in nature and relevant for analysis at the organizational level. At the micro-level of analysis, business ethics is concerned primarily with the ethical decision-making process of individuals in the workplace.

Ethical Issues for Managers and Taking Sides

The first unit of this book consists of two debates—one at the macro and one at the micro-levels of analyses. Each topic is in a debate format and presents articles supportive of each side.

The first issue presents the macro-level corporate social responsibility (CSR) versus profit maximization controversy. Advocates of free-market capitalism believe that the only responsibility an organization has is to maximize profits for its shareholders, whereas stakeholder theory states that managers have obligations that go beyond profit maximization since they are concerned with satisfying the needs of all of stakeholders. Thus, those firms that do not place the interests of one set of stakeholders above the rest are acting in a *socially responsible* manner, whereas firms that stick to the traditional emphasis of maximizing profit with disregard of other stakeholder interests are frequently viewed as irresponsible and immoral.

The second issue examines a highly controversial micro-level topic, the issue of executive pay. In recent years, the business and news media have portrayed numerous examples of U.S. CEOs receiving millions of dollars in salary and benefits while their organizations were posting losses, laying off workers, and, in some instances, even declaring bankruptcy. As a result of the public outrage generated by these stories, the question of top-level management compensation has taken on greater significance in the field of management. The specific question addressed in this issue is whether or not CEO pay is just.

Human Resource Management

Human resource management (HRM) is the design and implementation of formal systems that utilize human resources to accomplish organizational goals (http://www.inc.com/encyclopedia /human-resource-management.html). Although the fields of organizational behavior and human resource management are both conducted primarily at the individual level of analysis, HRM is a much more practical area of management characterized by laws, regulations, and formal systems.

Human Resource Management and Taking Sides

The second unit of this book consists of four debates. Each topic is in a debate format and presents articles supportive of each side.

The first issue addresses whether an employer's need to monitor workers trumps employee privacy concerns. The authors in this issue present arguments defending an employer's need to monitor employee behavior and criticizing the practice. One particularly challenging question in this issue is that of the rights of employers and employees when using electronic media such as e-mail and social media tools.

The second topic in this unit asks if workplace drug testing is a wise corporate strategy, particularly in light of the seemingly obvious concerns about privacy rights. This issue examines the benefits and costs of drug testing as well as the rationale for conducting these tests.

The third issue is a brief examination of an issue that extends employee monitoring into a discussion of whether or not social media is a tool of expression for employees or potential trouble for businesses. Social media has become a marketing tool used by many organizations. Today it seems like every company can tweet at will and has a Facebook page and strives to be "liked." The issue here is what are the concerns that social media presents for corporations and how do corporations attempt to negotiate those concerns.

The final issue in this section examines opinions on the contemporary role and place of labor unions. The labor movement that spawned these unions grew out of a need to see that the interests of workers were protected and some of its achievements included better wages, safer work environments, and formal representation in negotiations with management. The authors of these articles debate the merits and need for labor unions in the present business environment.

Strategic Management

While HRM is primarily concerned with understanding, motivating, and managing individual employees in the workplace, the focus of strategic management is on the organization as a whole. The basic unit of strategic management is a *strategy*. A strategy is a plan designed to achieve a specific goal or organizational target. In the business world, strategic management refers to the process of effectively developing and executing the collection of plans designed to achieve the organization's goals. Typically, the goals of the organization reflect the overall purpose of the company as spelled out in the firm's mission statement. In most large companies, top-level executives and managers are responsible for the development of the organization's strategies, while mid-level managers and supervisors are typically in charge of making sure the strategies are implemented successfully. Thus, the executives are involved in *strategy formulation,* while the managers and supervisors are concerned with *strategy implementation.*

Strategic Management and Taking Sides

The third unit of this text contains five issues particularly relevant to the topic of strategic management. United States firms have been adopting the view that reducing costs through labor force reductions—downsizing—should not be reserved only for desperate firms on the edge of bankruptcy. Indeed, many organizations now routinely reduce their workforce even when the firm is profitable and its future prospects appear positive. Closely related to downsizing is the corporate strategy of outsourcing. While moving domestically expensive operational functions to a country with lower wage rates may reduce costs, many have argued that it is an unpatriotic strategy and should not be condoned, particularly when the economy is in bad shape. Interestingly, two of the issues in this section explores corporations' increased use of reshoring (sometimes called "backshoring," which is when jobs that were offshored are brought back onshore) and insourcing (a management decision made to maintain control of critical production processes or competencies) and whether it makes good business (economic) sense to bring manufacturing back to the United States.

Important topics in issue three of this unit are growth and mergers and acquisitions (M&As) as corporate initiatives and whether growth is always an inherent corporate value. Additionally, although M&A as a mode of corporate expansion has been around since at least the Industrial Revolution, it exploded in the early 1980s. Presently, merger activity seems to be continuing unabated as firms seek strength and security in size. Here, inquiry as to whether or not expanding via mergers and/or acquisitions really is wise strategy is explored.

Environmental Management

Over the last quarter century, environmental managerial challenges have grown in importance so dramatically that executives in corporate America have no alternative but to take them into account when formulating organizational strategy. Specifically, United States organizations now face the difficult challenge of maintaining financial success while recognizing obligations to protect and maintain the world's physical environment.

Environmental Management and Taking Sides

An underlying assumption of the environmental movement in the United States and abroad is that the health of the planet is deteriorating and that business activity is primarily responsible. An important idea that emerged in the 1980s in response to this assumption is the concept of sustainable development. This idea, a conceptual child of corporate social responsibility, holds that corporations should conduct their business activities and develop their plans and goals within a framework that recognizes that the earth's resources are limited and must be preserved. Consequently, corporations should take into account the needs of future generations when mapping out future growth strategies. Not surprisingly, however, this concept is controversial to many. Sustainability-related topics and corporate sustainability reporting's practice and value are some of the topics explored. One issue questions the goal of sustainability for business and the potential for creating sustainable businesses. The second issue discusses whether corporations should adopt environmentally friendly corporate sustainability reporting and sustainable development policies. Finally, the last issue in this section examines whether corporate sustainability reporting is a valuable corporate reporting tool.

International Management

In response to the tremendous growth of competition from international firms, corporations all over the world have embraced the idea of globalization by extending sales and/or production operations to markets abroad. Globalization offers firms many advantages: access to new sources of cheap labor; access to new sources of highly skilled labor; access to established markets; and access to emerging markets (e.g., China, Russia, and India). These advantages come at a cost (i.e., globalization, by its very definition means greater competition). Thus, a second critical challenge facing United States managers is responding successfully to the tremendous growth of competition from international firms, both here and abroad.

International Management and Taking Sides

An important and controversial social issues of our time are the growing number of illegal aliens in the United States. This issue poses a serious problem to the nation and is likely to be an important political, social, and economic issue for the foreseeable future. We ask whether United States firms should be allowed to tap into this reservoir of labor legally or whether doing so hurts the American economy. Passions run high when this topic is raised, so it's no surprise that the two articles presented come to completely different conclusions.

A growing number of countries around the world have embraced the idea of globalization as a means of raising the standard of living for their citizens. Despite the fact that much evidence attests to the economic benefits that accrue as a result of globalization, there are those who question whether globalization on the whole is a positive occurrence. The questions, "Is Economic Globalization Good for Humankind?" and "Is Globalization Beneficial for Society?" provide two competing answers. Additionally, there are a growing number of politicians, media pundits, and business experts who are calling for the United States president to help the United States economy by enacting a wide range of protectionist economic policies. On the other hand, the vast majority of economists is skeptical of protectionism and seemingly appears to have much empirical and historical evidence on hand to support their view. This leads to the text's third topic, "Are Protectionist Policies Beneficial to Business?"

Unit 1

UNIT

Ethical Issues for Managers

*A*n *old saying holds that business ethics is an oxymoron. For years, the generally accepted view on morality and business was that they don't mix, that business is a game played by a different set of rules. To act morally was to act weakly. And in the business arena, weak firms were dead firms.*

Things certainly change. In today's business arena, firms are finding that immoral behavior can prove fatal. The financial industry's recent experiences amid the financial meltdown that began Fall 2008 appear to lend credence to those who believe that ethical behavior is an afterthought in corporate boardrooms. Ethical behavior is certainly not an afterthought in this unit, which examines several ethically laden issues of importance to many managers in corporate America.

Selected, Edited, and with Issue Framing Material by:
Kathleen J. Barnes, *William Paterson University*
and
George E. Smith, *University of South Carolina, Beaufort*

ISSUE

Do Corporations Have a Responsibility to Society Beyond Maximizing Profit?

YES: Knowledge@Wharton, from "Why Companies Can No Longer Afford to Ignore Their Social Responsibilities," *Time* (2012)

NO: Milton Friedman, from "The Social Responsibility of Business Is to Increase Its Profits," *The New York Times Magazine* (1970)

Learning Outcomes
After reading this issue, you will be able to:
• Appreciate the conflicts businesses face as they attempt to balance the demands of various stakeholders. • Understand why businesses are expected to do more than simply generate profit. • Explain why businesses may have a limited response in terms of their contributions to society. • Understand the challenge of implementing or practicing corporate responsibility beyond profit generation.

ISSUE SUMMARY

YES: Knowledge@Wharton maintains that companies care about corporate social responsibility because their customers do and ignore it at their own peril.

NO: In his classical defense of the profit motive, Nobel laureate Milton Friedman attacks social responsibility, arguing that spending shareholders' property against their wishes is immoral, illegal, and ultimately unproductive.

Not surprisingly, in the wake of the subprime mortgage, housing-bubble meltdown, and the associated chaos in the financial services industry, attitudes toward U.S. corporations have turned decidedly negative. A 2008 survey conducted by Gallup found that a third of those polled believe that big business represents the single largest threat to our country's future (www.gallup.com/poll/5248/Big-Business.aspx). Additionally, in a Fall 2008 Pew Research Center poll, nearly 6 in 10 respondents (59 percent) indicated that business corporations make too much profit. This survey also reported that 62 percent of those polled believe that financial executives in America are "more greedy than they were in the past" (http://people-press.org/report/7pageicM399). Indeed, at the end of 2008, social commentators and political analysts placed the blame for the debacle on the pursuit of profit.

An interesting outcome of this attention on corporate behavior has been a renewed interest in the question of what the purpose of business is in general. While this is not a new topic, it is one that generates passionate debate. As a result of the renewed interest in defining and understanding corporate responsibility, this issue focuses on examining the question, "Do corporations have a responsibility to society beyond maximizing profit?"

Those who answer in the affirmative usually provide a two-pronged response. The first response is based on stakeholder theory and the second on practical observations and assertions. Stakeholder theory argues that the manager's job is to balance interests among the various groups with a stake in the company's survival. Consequently, management's obligations have been expanded beyond focusing primarily on financial gain for shareholders to include satisfying the needs and concerns of all of its stakeholders. Organizations that recognize this expansion and act on it accordingly are said to be acting in a socially responsible manner, whereas firms that stick to the traditional emphasis of increasing share price as priority one are deemed irresponsible and immoral.

The second prong in the "yes" response consists of more practical arguments. One point often raised is that because corporations are the source of many problems in society—pollution, corruption, discrimination, and so on—they should be required to resolve those problems. After all, the community in which the corporation resides is a legitimate stakeholder of the firm. Also, business organizations are members of society and, as such, should assume the responsibilities of membership. Another argument holds that organizations frequently have a lot of financial resources and, therefore, are in a position to use the money for social good and not just for increasing the power and wealth of the firm and its shareholders.

On the other side of the debate, the strongest and most consistent defender of shareholder theory has been free market economist and Nobel laureate Milton Friedman. In his anti-stakeholder approach, Friedman argues that shareholders—not employees, customers, or suppliers—own the companies in which they invest and, consequently, have the legal right to expect management to comply with their desires (which is usually to maximize the value of their investments). Consider the example of a corporation whose management, without shareholder consent, wants to use some of the company's profits on its local community by contributing to the creation of a park project. If management chooses to reduce profit distribution to its shareholders and spend it on the project, its members have acted both immorally and illegally because they have, in effect, stolen from the shareholders. If they choose to pay shareholders out-of-profit and instead finance the project by reducing labor costs, the employees will suffer. If they choose to

avoid antagonizing shareholders and employees and contribute to the park by raising product prices, they will hurt their customers and possibly price themselves out of the market. Thus according to Friedman, doing anything other than increasing shareholder wealth is tantamount to theft, is immoral, and is ultimately self-defeating for the organization.

The following two selections address the question of whether or not corporations have responsibilities to society that extend beyond profit maximization. The "pro" selection is by Knowledge@Wharton, which focuses on focusing on the many companies that have made corporate social responsibility a priority. More than 8,000 businesses around the world have signed the United Nations Global Compact pledging to show good global citizenship in the areas of human labor rights, labor standards, and environmental protection. Knowledge@Wharton's work is a reminder to management to care about corporate social responsibility because their customers do and ignoring corporate social responsibility at their own peril.

For the "con" side, Milton Friedman's classic anti-stakeholder article was selected. Originally written in 1970, Friedman emphasizes that responsible management seeks to maximize profit. While Friedman doesn't deny that good can be accomplished through profitability—namely via the acts of individuals—he is concerned that any responsibility or expectation beyond the pursuit of profit detracts from the mission of business.

YES

Why Companies Can No Longer Afford to Ignore Their Social Responsibilities?

In 1970, the economist and Nobel laureate Milton Friedman published an article in *The New York Times Magazine* titled, "The Social Responsibility of Business Is to Increase Its Profits." In the article, he referred to corporate social responsibility (CSR) programs as "hypocritical window-dressing," and said that businesspeople inclined toward such programs "reveal a suicidal impulse." Even four decades ago, at a time of growing public concern for the environment, his views represented the general skepticism and contempt with which many in Corporate America viewed CSR.

Times have changed. There remain company chieftains who take a Friedman-esque view, of course, but many more have made CSR a priority. Ten years ago, for instance, only about a dozen Fortune 500 companies issued a CSR or sustainability report. Now the majority does. More than 8,000 businesses around the world have signed the UN Global Compact pledging to show good global citizenship in the areas of human rights, labor standards and environmental protection. The next generation of business leaders is even more likely to prioritize CSR. According to data released this month by Net Impact, the nonprofit that aims to help businesses promote sustainability, 65% of MBAs surveyed say they want to make a social or environmental difference through their jobs.

Today, amid a lingering recession that has dented corporate profits and intensified pressure from shareholders, companies are devising new CSR models. Rather than staffing a modest CSR department—and slapping it on the org chart as a small offshoot of the public relations (PR) or philanthropy division—many companies are instead trying to embed CSR into their operations. Some blue-chip companies, such as Visa, are creating new markets in the developing world by closely aligning social causes with their overarching corporate strategies. Others, such as Walmart, have made ambitious commitments to sustainability as a way to save money and tighten their supply chain.

"CSR is an old-fashioned idea that needs to be upgraded," says Eric Orts, professor of legal studies and business ethics at Wharton and director of the school's Initiative for Global Environmental Leadership. "For companies to take CSR seriously, it has to be integrated into the DNA of the enterprise. Companies need to say: 'We want to make money, sure, but we also care about our effect on society and the environment. And that comes through in the kinds of jobs we provide, the kinds of products we make and the ways in which we use resources.'"

Ignore CSR at Your Peril

One of the biggest criticisms leveled against CSR is that companies only care about it for marketing purposes. CSR is merely a buzzword embraced by corporations because they "should." "For most companies, [CSR] is PR," according to Ian C. MacMillan, professor of innovation and entrepreneurship at Wharton. "It looks good. It sounds good. It's the 'right' thing to do—and it gets the media out of their face."

These days, corporate motivation seems almost beside the point because of the significant business risks to ignoring CSR. Consumers and other companies are likely to shun firms that develop unethical reputations. And arguably, companies that don't pay attention to their ethical responsibilities are more likely to stumble into legal troubles, such as mass corruption or accounting fraud scandals.

Quite simply, companies care about CSR because their customers do. Consumers, by and large, are a self-motivated and self-interested lot. But numerous studies indicate that a company's CSR policies increasingly factor into their decisions. For example, a survey by Landor Associates, the branding company, found that 77% of consumers say it is important for companies to be socially responsible. "There's a heightened awareness of the need to be, and to be seen as, a good corporate citizen," says Robert Grosshandler, CEO of iGive.com, which helps consumers direct a percentage of their online purchases to support charities.

And in the Electronic Age, where information about a given company's environmental record and labor practices is readily available—and readily tweeted and retweeted—companies must pay careful attention to what their customers do and say. "In the Information Age, customers have more access to information," says Grosshandler. "They're more educated. They're no longer hidden from how their food is produced or how their iPods are made. And, because of things like social media, like-minded people more easily find each other, have their say and effect change. There's a level of transparency that wasn't there before."

CSR is also a way to attract and retain talent. In a global workforce study by Towers Perrin, the professional services firm, CSR is the third most important driver of employee engagement overall. For companies in the United States, an organization's stature in the community is the second most important driver of employee engagement, and a company's reputation for social responsibility is also among the top 10. According to a Deloitte survey conducted last year, 70% of young Millennials, those ages 18 to 26, say a company's commitment to the community has an influence on their decision to work there.

"The Millennial generation has seen a lot of natural disasters, political disasters and corporate disasters. They think the world is screwed up," says Kellie McElhaney, who is the faculty director of Haas' Center for Responsible Business. "They feel personally responsible, and they feel empowered to create change."

Bottom of the Pyramid

The global financial crisis has not been kind to CSR departments. While data on precise numbers of CSR positions is hard to come by, sustainability practitioners say that many companies have scaled back in recent years (although CSR has not been cut disproportionately to other cost centers).

Partly as a result of the crisis, some companies have refined their approach to CSR by more closely relating social causes to their core businesses. This approach, according to Jerry (Yoram) Wind, a Wharton marketing professor, interprets CSR as "socially responsible capitalism. . . . At the company level, the business objectives need to be to both maximize shareholder value in the long term and to address society's biggest problems," says Wind, also the director of the school's SEI Center for Advanced Studies in Management." This requires having any CSR initiative be an integral part of the business strategy and not a separate department."

Take the Coca-Cola Company, which recently started a program to empower young women entrepreneurs. The 5×20 program aims to bring five million women in the developing world into its business by 2020 as local bottlers and distributors of Coca-Cola products. Research suggests that such an investment in women can have a multiplier effect that leads not only to increased revenues and more workers for businesses, but also to better-educated, healthier families and eventually more prosperous communities.

Visa is another example. The company has built partnerships with local governments and non-profits focused on financial inclusion. These alliances are already transforming the economic architecture in parts of the developing world by giving financially underserved people a way to pay, get paid and save money, sometimes through electronic and mobile payment systems. Research by the Gates Foundation and others has shown that the usage of these kinds of services enables poor people to better withstand blows to their personal finances, build assets and connect into the wider economy.

Does Coca-Cola benefit from more bottlers? Yes. Does Visa benefit from more people using its services? Absolutely. But these CSR efforts seek to capitalize on "the fortune at the bottom of the pyramid," an idea that C.K. Prahalad popularized in his 2006 book of the same name. Prahalad referred to the largest, but poorest, socio-economic group in emerging economies as seeds for future growth markets.

"There are large numbers of people in the world who have no jobs and who have no hope. They need jobs and more education, better healthcare and food. They need to be self-sufficient, not dependent because some do-gooder gave them a handout," says Wharton's MacMillan. "Companies need to start creating markets in these places."

These new markets represent a long-term investment, he adds. "It's a pattern of enlightened self-interest: The company ends up better off with customers they have seeded who are healthier, better nourished and have more education. And [the company] has residual loyalty because [it] was there first."

Saving Money, Saving the Planet

Other companies are taking a slightly different approach: viewing CSR as a cost-saver. "The downturn has refocused CSR practitioners," says Marcus Chung, vice president of the CSR and sustainability practice at Fleishman-Hillard and former head of CSR at Talbots, the women's apparel chain. "There are more CSR practitioners today whose main job is to find ways to support business strategy and save the company money."

Many CSR professionals serve as internal consultants providing counsel to colleagues and acting as a resource for decisions concerning real estate, supply chain or operations, he adds. "They are helping other departments understand the financial rewards of more sustainable operations. This approach to CSR has become more key in the last few years."

Climate Corps, the Environmental Defense Fund's summer internship for business school students, follows this model. The fellowship places MBA students in Fortune 500 companies, cities and universities to build the business case for energy efficiency. Since 2008, the program has helped organizations cut 1.6 billion kilowatt hours of electricity use and avoid more than one million metric tons of CO_2 emissions annually, and has saved $1 billion in net operational costs.

Walmart is another example. Its social responsibility policy is encompassed by three goals: to be fully supplied by renewable energy, to create zero waste and to sell products that sustain people and the environment. These are lofty targets—and if achieved, ones that ultimately save the company a great deal of money. "The company is not perfect, but it is dealing with sustainability squarely as a business imperative," says Haas' McElhaney, adding that "These are hard-core measurable and reportable goals. The main criticism is that the company is shoving this down the supply chain's throat, but if you're Wal-Mart, that is your leverage."

Nien-hê Hsieh, co-director of the Wharton Ethics Program and a visiting professor at Harvard Business School this year, describes Walmart as a company that complicates the CSR picture. "On one hand, it has been challenged on its labor practices and the Mexican bribery scandal," he says. "But on the other hand, it has had an aggressive sustainability policy. If Walmart does alter its global footprint, it would make a difference in the world."

At the entrepreneurial level, some smaller, niche companies are experimenting with CSR as a mission of the triple bottom line: people, planet and profits. Take, for instance, the advent and gradual spread of so-called B Corporations, which are recognized in seven states, including California and New York. B Corps, as they are known—the "B" stands for beneficial—are a new kind of business entity that by law are required to generate social and environmental advantages.

The designation is only a few years old, but already there are more than 500 certified B Corps across 60 different industries. Companies include Seventh Generation, the maker of natural household and personal care products; Pura Vida, which sells organic, fair trade coffee; Etsy, the online market for handmade goods; and King Arthur Flour. Wharton's Orts calls B Corps "interesting experiments for a more fundamental merging of the goals of traditional profit-making and social responsibility."

The B Corps model of integrating CSR concerns into normal business practices may hold a key for how large publicly traded firms ought to reset their corporate vision and objectives, he says, adding that a "major rethinking of the relationship between Wall Street investors and business management" is in order. The pressure on companies to maximize shareholder returns makes it very difficult for them to undertake long-term investments for the social good if these decisions will drive down their short-term stock prices.

"If there is one thing that the financial crisis and stock market crash of 2008 should have taught us, it is that short-run share prices are an unreliable indicator of long-run business sustainability," says Orts. "The idea that companies don't have any independent ethical responsibility for the consequences of their actions on the environment and society just doesn't make sense. It is an outmoded view to say that one must rely only on the government and regulation to police business responsibilities. What we need is re-conception of what the purpose of business is."

KNOWLEDGE@WHARTON is the online research and business analysis journal of the Wharton School of the University of Pennsylvania.

Milton Friedman    **NO**

The Social Responsibility of Business Is to Increase Its Profits

When I hear businessmen speak eloquently about the "social responsibilities of business in a free-enterprise system," I am reminded of the wonderful line about the Frenchman who discovered at the age of 70 that he had been speaking prose all his life. The businessmen believe that they are defending free enterprise when they declaim that business is not concerned "merely" with profit but also with promoting desirable "social ends; that business has a social conscience" and takes seriously its responsibilities for providing employment, eliminating discrimination, avoiding pollution and whatever else may be the catchwords of the contemporary crop of reformers. In fact they are—or would be if they or anyone else took them seriously—preaching pure and unadulterated socialism. Businessmen who talk this way are unwitting puppets of the intellectual forces that have been undermining the basis of a free society these past decades.

The discussions of the "social responsibilities of business" are notable for their analytical looseness and lack of rigor. What does it mean to say that "business" has responsibilities? Only people can have responsibilities. A corporation is an artificial person and in this sense may have artificial responsibilities, but "business" as a whole cannot be said to have responsibilities, even in this vague sense. The first step toward clarity in examining the doctrine of the social responsibility of business is to ask precisely what it implies for whom.

Presumably, the individuals who are to be responsible are businessmen, which means individual proprietors or corporate executives. Most of the discussion of social responsibility is directed at corporations, so in what follows I shall mostly neglect the individual proprietor and speak of corporate executives.

In a free-enterprise, private-property system, a corporate executive is an employee of the owners of the business. He has direct responsibility to his employers. That responsibility is to conduct the business in accordance with their desires, which generally will be to make as much money as possible while conforming to the basic rules of the society, both those embodied in law and those embodied in ethical custom. Of course, in some cases his employers may have a different objective. A group of persons might establish a corporation for an eleemosynary purpose—for example, a hospital or a school. The manager of such a corporation will not have money profit as his objective but the rendering of certain services.

In either case, the key point is that, in his capacity as a corporate executive, the manager is the agent of the individuals who own the corporation or establish the eleemosynary institution, and his primary responsibility is to them.

Needless to say, this does not mean that it is easy to judge how well he is performing his task. But at least the criterion of performance is straightforward, and the persons among whom a voluntary contractual arrangement exists are clearly defined.

Of course, the corporate executive is also a person in his own right. As a person, he may have many other responsibilities that he recognizes or assumes voluntarily—to his family, his conscience, his feelings of charity, his church, his clubs, his city, his country. He may feel impelled by these responsibilities to devote part of his income to causes he regards as worthy, to refuse to work for particular corporations, even to leave his job, for example, to join his country's armed forces. If we wish, we may refer to some of these responsibilities as "social responsibilities." But in these respects he is acting as a principal, not an agent; he is spending his own money or time or energy, not the money of his employers or the time or energy he has contracted to devote to their purposes. If these are "social responsibilities," they are the social responsibilities of individuals, not of business.

What does it mean to say that the corporate executive has a "social responsibility" in his capacity as businessman? If this statement is not pure rhetoric, it must mean that he is to act in some way that is not in the interest of his employers. For example, that he is to refrain from increasing the price of the product in order to contribute to the social objective of preventing inflation, even though a price increase would be in the best interests of the corporation. Or that he is to make expenditures on reducing pollution beyond the amount that is in the best interests of the corporation or that is required by law in order to contribute to the social objective of improving the environment. Or that, at the expense of corporate profits, he is to hire "hard-core" unemployed instead of better-qualified available workmen to contribute to the social objective of reducing poverty.

In each of these cases, the corporate executive would be spending someone else's money for a general social interest. Insofar as his actions in accord with his "social responsibility" reduce returns to stockholders, he is spending their money. Insofar as his actions raise the price to customers, he is spending the customers' money. Insofar as his actions lower the wages of some employees, he is spending their money.

The stockholders or the customers or the employees could separately spend their own money on the particular action if they wished to do so. The executive is exercising a distinct "social responsibility," rather than serving as an agent of the stockholders or the customers or the employees, only if he spends the money in a different way than they would have spent it.

But if he does this, he is in effect imposing taxes, on the one hand, and deciding how the tax proceeds shall be spent, on the other.

This process raises political questions on two levels: principle and consequences. On the level of political principle, the imposition of taxes and the expenditure of tax proceeds are governmental functions. We have established elaborate constitutional, parliamentary and judicial provisions to control these functions, to assure that taxes are imposed so far as possible in accordance with the preferences and desires of the public—after all, "taxation without representation" was one of the battle cries of the American Revolution. We have a system of checks and balances to separate the legislative function of imposing taxes and enacting expenditures from the executive function of collecting taxes and administering expenditure programs and from the judicial function of mediating disputes and interpreting the law.

Here the businessman—self-selected or appointed directly or indirectly by stockholders—is to be simultaneously legislator, executive and jurist. He is to decide whom to tax by how much and for what purpose, and he is to spend the proceeds—all this guided only by general exhortations from on high to restrain inflation, improve the environment, fight poverty and so on and on.

The whole justification for permitting the corporate executive to be selected by the stockholders is that the executive is an agent serving the interests of his principal. This justification disappears when the corporate executive imposes taxes and spends the proceeds for "social" purposes. He becomes in effect a public employee, a civil servant, even though he remains in name an employee of a private enterprise. On grounds of political principle, it is intolerable that such civil servants—insofar as their actions in the name of social responsibility are real and not just window-dressing—should be selected as they are now. If they are to be civil servants, then they must be selected through a political process. If they are to impose taxes and make expenditures to foster "social" objectives, then political machinery must be set up to guide the assessment of

taxes and to determine through a political process the objectives to be served.

This is the basic reason why the doctrine of "social responsibility" involves the acceptance of the socialist view that political mechanisms, not market mechanisms, are the appropriate way to determine the allocation of scarce resources to alternative uses.

On the grounds of consequences, can the corporate executive in fact discharge his alleged "social responsibilities"? On the one hand, suppose he could get away with spending the stockholders' or customers' or employees' money. How is he to know how to spend it? He is told that he must contribute to fighting inflation. How is he to know what action of his will contribute to that end? He is presumably an expert in running his company—in producing a product or selling it or financing it. But nothing about his selection makes him an expert on inflation. Will his holding down the price of his product reduce inflationary pressure? Or, by leaving more spending power in the hands of his customers, simply divert it elsewhere? Or, by forcing him to produce less because of the lower price, will it simply contribute to shortages? Even if he could answer these questions, how much cost is he justified in imposing on his stockholders, customers and employees for this social purpose? What is the appropriate share and what is the appropriate share of others?

And, whether he wants to or not, can he get away with spending his stockholders', customers' or employees' money? Will not the stockholders fire him? (Either the present ones or those who take over when his actions in the name of social responsibility have reduced the corporation's profits and the price of its stock.) His customers and his employees can desert him for other producers and employers less scrupulous in exercising their social responsibilities.

This facet of "social responsibility" doctrine is brought into sharp relief when the doctrine is used to justify wage restraint by trade unions. The conflict of interest is naked and clear when union officials are asked to subordinate the interest of their members to some more general social purpose. If the union officials try to enforce wage restraint, the consequence is likely to be wildcat strikes, rank-and-file revolts and the emergence of strong competitors for their jobs. We thus have the ironic phenomenon that union leaders—at least in the U.S.—have objected to Government interference with the market far more consistently and courageously than have business leaders.

The difficulty of exercising "social responsibility" illustrates, of course, the great virtue of private competitive enterprise—it forces people to be responsible for their own actions and makes it difficult for them to "exploit" other people for either selfish or unselfish purposes. They can do good—but only at their own expense.

Many a reader who has followed the argument this far may be tempted to remonstrate that it is all well and good to speak of government's having the responsibility to impose taxes and determine expenditures for such "social" purposes as controlling pollution or training the hard-core unemployed, but that the problems are too urgent to wait on the slow course of political processes, that the exercise of social responsibility by businessmen is a quicker and surer way to solve pressing current problems.

Aside from the question of fact—I share Adam Smith's skepticism about the benefits that can be expected from "those who affected to trade for the public good"—this argument must be rejected on grounds of principle. What it amounts to is an assertion that those who favor the taxes and expenditures in question have failed to persuade a majority of their fellow citizens to be of like mind and that they are seeking to attain by undemocratic procedures what they cannot attain by democratic procedures. In a free society, it is hard for "good" people to do "good," but that is a small price to pay for making it hard for "evil" people to do "evil," especially since one man's good is another's evil.

I have, for simplicity, concentrated on the special case of the corporate executive, except only for the brief digression on trade unions. But precisely the same argument applies to the newer phenomenon of calling upon stockholders to require corporations to exercise social responsibility (the recent G.M. crusade, for example). In most of these cases, what is in effect involved is some stockholders trying to get other stockholders (or customers or employees) to contribute against their will to "social" causes favored by the activists. Insofar as they succeed, they are again imposing taxes and spending the proceeds.

The situation of the individual proprietor is somewhat different. If he acts to reduce the returns of his enterprise in order to exercise his "social responsibility," he is spending his own money, not someone else's. If he wishes to spend his money on such purposes, that is his right, and I cannot see that there is any objection to his doing so. In the process, he, too, may impose costs on employees and customers. However, because he is far less likely than a large corporation or union to have monopolistic power, any such side effects will tend to be minor.

Of course, in practice the doctrine of social responsibility is frequently a cloak for actions that are justified on other grounds rather than a reason for those actions.

To illustrate, it may well be in the long-run interest of a corporation that is a major employer in a small community to devote resources to providing amenities to that community or to improving its government. That may make it easier to attract desirable employees, it may reduce the wage bill or lessen losses from pilferage and sabotage or have other worthwhile effects. Or it may be that, given the laws about the deductibility of corporate charitable contributions, the stockholders can contribute more to charities they favor by having the corporation make the gift than by doing it themselves, since they can in that way contribute an amount that would otherwise have been paid as corporate taxes.

In each of these—and many similar—cases, there is a strong temptation to rationalize these actions as an exercise of "social responsibility." In the present climate of opinion, with its widespread aversion to "capitalism," "profits," the "soulless corporation" and

so on, this is one way for a corporation to generate goodwill as a by-product of expenditures that are entirely justified in its own self-interest.

It would be inconsistent of me to call on corporate executives to refrain from this hypocritical window-dressing because it harms the foundations of a free society. That would be to call on them to exercise a "social responsibility"! If our institutions, and the attitudes of the public, make it in their self-interest to cloak their actions in this way, I cannot summon much indignation to denounce them. At the same time, I can express admiration for those individual proprietors or owners of closely held corporations or stockholders of more broadly held corporations who disdain such tactics as approaching fraud.

Whether blameworthy or not, the use of the cloak of social responsibility, and the nonsense spoken in its name by influential and prestigious businessmen, does clearly harm the foundations of a free society. I have been impressed time and again by the schizophrenic character of many businessmen. They are capable of being extremely far-sighted and clear-headed in matters that are internal to their businesses. They are incredibly short-sighted and muddleheaded in matters that are outside their businesses but affect the possible survival of business in general. This short-sightedness is strikingly exemplified in the calls from many businessmen for wage and price guidelines or controls or income policies. There is nothing that could do more in a brief period to destroy a market system and replace it by a centrally controlled system than effective governmental control of prices and wages.

The short-sightedness is also exemplified in speeches by businessmen on social responsibility. This may gain them kudos in the short run. But it helps to strengthen the already too prevalent view that the pursuit of profits is wicked and immoral and must be curbed and controlled by external forces. Once this view is adopted, the external forces that curb the market will not be the social consciences, however highly developed, of the pontificating executives; it will be the iron fist of Government bureaucrats. Here, as with price and wage controls, businessmen seem to me to reveal a suicidal impulse.

The political principle that underlies the market mechanism is unanimity. In an ideal free market resting on private property, no individual can coerce any other, all cooperation is voluntary, all parties to such cooperation benefit or they need not participate. There are no "social" values, no "social" responsibilities in any sense other than the shared values and responsibilities of individuals. Society is a collection of individuals and of the various groups they voluntarily form.

The political principle that underlies the political mechanism is conformity. The individual must serve a more general social interest—whether that be determined by a church or a dictator or a majority. The individual may have a vote and a say in what is to be done, but if he is overruled, he must conform. It is appropriate for some to require others to contribute to a general social purpose whether they wish to or not.

Unfortunately, unanimity is not always feasible. There are some respects in which conformity appears unavoidable, so I do not see how one can avoid the use of the political mechanism altogether.

But the doctrine of "social responsibility" taken seriously would extend the scope of the political mechanism to every human activity. It does not differ in philosophy from the most explicitly collectivist doctrine. It differs only by professing to believe that collectivist ends can be attained without collectivist means. That is why, in my book "Capitalism and Freedom," I have called it a "fundamentally subversive doctrine" in a free society, and have said

that in such a society, "there is one and only one social responsibility of business—to use its resources and engage in activities designed to increase its profits so long as it stays within the rules of the game, which is to say, engages in open and free competition without deception or fraud."

Milton Friedman was the winner of the 1974 Nobel Prize in Economics and is recognized as one of the most important economists of the twentieth century. Friedman was the author of numerous academic publications as well as several highly influential books written primarily from a free-market, pro-capitalism perspective.

EXPLORING THE ISSUE

Do Corporations Have a Responsibility to Society Beyond Maximizing Profit?

Critical Thinking and Reflection

1. What do corporations "owe" society?
2. Does my stake in an organization change my view or outlook on what corporations should do for society?
3. In what types of activities should corporations become more involved? Do corporations possess knowledge, skills, and abilities that could prove beneficial to society?
4. Are there limits that should be placed on corporate involvement in society?
5. Given the power corporations already possess, should they be granted additional power via the corporate responsibility issues discussed in these articles?

Is There Common Ground?

The common ground that exists with this issue is the recognition of business as a powerful societal actor. Both sides of this debate recognize and acknowledge the existence of business or corporate power, but vary in their views of what this power or influence means in terms of corporate responsibility or responsiveness to broader society and societal issues. The crux of this debate being, how much power does society want to give business and what should be the role of business in society?

As evidenced by the original dates of publication of these contrasting works, this is a discussion that has already spanned several decades. In light of contemporary challenges and public sentiment, it is anticipated that this topic will be the subject of continued discussion and debate for decades to come.

Additional Resources

Barro, R.J. (1998). "Milton Friedman: Being Right Is the Best Revenge," *Business Week*, July 13, p. 11.

Freeman, R.E. (2002). "Fixing the Ethics Crisis in Corporate America," *Miller Center Report*, Fall, pp. 13–17.

Hartman, L.P. (2004). *Perspectives in Business Ethics*, 3rd ed., New York: McGraw-Hill.

Mycoskie, B. (2016). "How I did it . . . The Founder of Toms on Reimagining the Company's Mission," *Harvard Business Review,* Ja/Fe, pp. 41–44.

Peloza, J., Ye, C. & Montford, W.J. (2015). "When Companies Do Good, Are Their Products Good for You? How Corporate Social Responsibility Creates a Health Halo," *Journal of Public Policy & Marketing*, 34(1), pp. 19–31.

Wang, H., Tong, L., Takeuchi, R. & George, G. (2016). "Corporate Social Responsibility: An Overview and New Research Directions," *Academy of Management Journal*, 59(2), pp. 534–544.

Internet References . . .

Big Business

www.gallup.com/poll/5248/Big-Business.aspx

Does Corporate Social Responsibility Increase Profits?

http://business-ethics.com/2015/05/05/does-corporate
-social-responsibility-increase-profits/

Making the Case for Social Responsibility

http://culturalshifts.com/archives/181

Milton Friedman Was Right

http://online.wsj.com/article
/SB116432800408631539.html

The Case Against Corporate Social Responsibility

http://www.cis.org.au/images/stories policymagazine
/2001-winter/2001-17-2-david-henderson.pdf

The Inadequacy of Social-Responsibility Programs

http://www.theatlantic.com/business/archive/2015/07
/corporate-social-responsibility/399206/

The Social Responsibility of Profit

www.eco-imperialism.com/content/article.php3?id=242

What Is a Business for?

http://ssrn.com/abstract=932676

Selected, Edited, and with Issue Framing Material by:
Kathleen J. Barnes, *William Paterson University*
and
George E. Smith, *University of South Carolina, Beaufort*

ISSUE

Are U.S. CEOs Paid
More Than They Deserve?

YES: Sarah Anderson et al., from "Executive Excess 2008: How Average Taxpayers Subsidize Runaway Pay," Institute for Policy Studies (2008)

NO: Poonkulali Thangavelu, from "Justifications for High CEO Pay (AAPL, GE)," *Investopedia* (2015)

Learning Outcomes
After reading this issue, you will be able to:
• Understand the positive and negative consequences of executive pay in the workplace.
• Understand how executive pay can be used as a workplace tool.
• Understand policies that might be implemented concerning executive pay.
• Appreciate the legal implications of executive pay's use in the workplace.

ISSUE SUMMARY

YES: Arguing that U.S. CEOs are substantially overpaid in a 2008 study conducted for the Institute for Policy Studies (IPS) are compensation expert and IPS Fellow Sarah Anderson and her colleagues.

NO: Arguing that companies have come up with a number of reasons for the pay differential between CEOs and other workers, but they sometimes seem to be specious, as a CEO's pay is often set by their boards of directors who have every incentive to please them, states respected financial journalist Poonkulali Thangavelu.

O n February 4, 2009, in what must have been a tremendously rewarding moment for those who believe that American CEO pay is out of control, President Obama placed a ceiling on the amount of pay top executives at financial institutions receiving federal bailout funds can receive. Imposing a cap of $500,000 on top executive pay, President Obama stated that Americans are angry "at executives being rewarded for failure." He also pointed out that "For top executives to award themselves these kinds of compensation packages in the midst of this economic crisis is not only in bad taste, it's a bad strategy—and I will not tolerate it as president" (*The Seattle Times,* 2009).

Less than six weeks later, the issue of excessive CEO pay achieved even greater attention when it was reported that senior level executives at AIG, a huge U.S. insurance company based in New York City, doled out more than $160 million in bonuses using funds they received as part of the federal government's massive bailout of the financial industry. Again, Obama expressed outrage, declaring that his administration would "pursue every single legal avenue to block those bonuses and make the American taxpayers whole" (Sweet, 2009).

Clearly, the topic of U.S. CEO compensation is one that invokes much emotion and, if President Obama's behavior is any indication, significant political attention as well. And who doubts that the average American citizen believes that American CEOs are paid more than they deserve? Nevertheless, as is so often the case, closer scrutiny of this topic suggests that things are not so simple. In fact, even in the aftermath of the financial debacle of 2008, many academicians, public intellectuals, and business observers strongly believe that U.S. CEO pay is not excessive. Furthermore, and as you shall soon learn, they have very compelling reasons for advocating this view. As the purpose of this text is to have you decide where you stand on controversial issues in management, let's consider, Are U.S. CEOs paid more than they deserve?

Those who argue that U.S. CEOs are overpaid raise several interesting points in support of their position. One emotionally powerful point involves the apparent irrational act of paying a CEO millions of dollars while her or his firm is simultaneously reducing its workforce via layoffs and downsizing. Why should a CEO be rewarded for cutting the workforce? Additionally, some boards of directors have shown a willingness to award large bonuses not only to high-performing CEOs, but also to CEOs whose organizations were clear under-performers the previous year. Such actions suggest that an individual CEO's pay may not be tied to how well he or she performs, a situation that most would agree is not fair. Perhaps the strongest argument put forth by those who think U.S. CEOs are overpaid is based on a comparison of the CEO pay-to-worker pay ratio in America to that of other industrialized countries. Critics frequently point out that U.S. executives typically make several hundred times more in annual income than the lowest paid employees in their firms. In other countries, however, the ratio is considerably smaller. For example, in Japan the typical CEO makes only about 15 times the lowest worker, and many member countries of the European Union restrict top executive pay to around 20 times the lowest worker's pay.

On the other side of the debate, supporters of current U.S. CEO pay levels argue that CEO pay is, like most jobs in America, subject to labor market influences. Currently, the market for quality CEOs is very tight, and wage increasing bidding wars are the norm. Thus, CEO pay is clearly subject to labor market conditions. In response to the layoff issue, proponents of existing CEO pay levels argue that CEOs are paid to make and execute difficult decisions. They point out that often the alternative to downsizing and staying in business is not downsizing and going out of business entirely. Proponents also point out that U.S. CEOs, in many instances, are actually *underpaid* because U.S. CEOs and their organizations have created an incredible amount of wealth over the past two decades. In other words, when compared to the wealth U.S. CEOs have made for shareholders, their compensation packages typically look very reasonable.

The following selections represent opposite sides of our CEO pay debate. The affirmative position in this debate is provided by a 2008 study conducted for the Institute for Policy Studies by Sarah Anderson and her colleagues. The negative position put forward by Poonkulali Thangavelu, a respected financial journalist, argues that companies come up with a number of reasons for the pay differential between CEOs and other workers, but they sometimes seem to be specious, as a CEO's pay is often set by their boards of directors who have every incentive to please them.

YES

Sarah Anderson et al.

Executive Excess 2008: How Average Taxpayers Subsidize Runaway Pay

Tax Subsidies for Executive Excess

The U.S. tax code currently is riddled with loopholes that allow top corporate and financial leaders to avoid paying their fair share of taxes. Still other loopholes allow corporations to claim unwarranted deductions for exorbitant executive pay. Ordinary taxpayers wind up picking up the bill. That's why this report defines such loopholes as "subsidies for executive excess."

This section focuses on five such subsidies. For each one, analysts have been able to calculate an estimated annual cost to taxpayers. The first three of these subsidies put money directly into executive pockets. The final two give employers an incentive for doling out excessive executive rewards. All five have become targets for legislative reform action.

Estimated Annual Cost to Taxpayers of the Five Most Direct Tax Subsidies for Excessive Executive Pay

1. Preferential capital gains treatment of carried interest	$2,661,000,000
2. Unlimited deferred compensation	$80,600,000
3. Offshore deferred compensation	$2,086,000,000
4. Unlimited tax deductibility of executive pay	$5,249,475,000
5. Stock option accounting double standard	$10,000,000,000
Total	**$20,077,075,000**

Subsidy #1

Preferential capital-gains treatment of carried interest
Annual cost: $2,661,000,000

The top 50 highest-paid private equity and hedge fund managers last year made $558 million on average, according to the business trade journal *Alpha*.[1] The top five each collected over $1 billion. These private investment fund magnates hardly seem to need taxpayer assistance. Yet they get it—in massive amounts. Our current tax code allows top private investment fund managers to pay taxes, as investor Warren Buffett has repeatedly noted, at lower rates than their office receptionists.[2]

This tax loophole plays off the peculiarities of pay practices in the investment fund industry. In a publicly traded corporation, a CEO pay package typically includes salary, bonus, perks, and stock awards of various sorts. Private investment fund managers take their rewards through two distinctly different revenue streams. They first collect annual management fees, usually set at 2 percent of the capital they oversee. But these managers also collect a share of

the profits realized when they sell fund assets. Within the financial industry, this share goes by the label of "carried interest." Private investment fund managers usually claim, for themselves, a 20 percent "carried interest" share.

Fund managers report this carried interest as a capital gain, not ordinary income. This categorization, critics note, distorts marketplace reality. Carried interest, they point out, clearly represents payment for the delivery of a professional service, the managing of other people's money. Such professional fees, everywhere else in the economy, face the same tax rate as ordinary wage and salary income, up to 35 percent for income in the highest tax bracket.

The capital gains tax rate, by contrast, now sits at only 15 percent. On every $1 million pocketed in "carried interest," in other words, an investment fund manager saves about $200,000 in taxes.

KKR: TAX BREAK BONANZA

Corporate buyout king Henry Kravis earned $450 million as the head of the KKR private equity fund in 2006, *Forbes* reports.[3] A labor group, using public documents, has estimated that Kravis saved somewhere between $58.6 million and $96 million in taxes on that income, thanks to the carried interest loophole.[4] *Forbes* currently ranks Kravis as the 178th wealthiest individual in the world, with a net worth of $5.5 billion.[5]

KKR has launched a vigorous lobbying campaign to "defend" the carried interest loophole—and preferential tax treatment for Henry Kravis. In 2007, the fund paid more than $2 million to advance its interests in Congress. Kravis himself went to Capitol Hill to lobby Senators in July 2007, a job he has traditionally left to those further down the totem pole.[6]

KKR is also a key player in an industry lobby group formed principally to protect tax preferences for investment fund managers. The Private Equity Council opened up shop in early 2007 and spent over $2 million on lobbying before the year ended. The Council's member firms, including the high-profile Blackstone and Carlyle investment funds, spent an additional $7.9 million.[7] In the year's first six months alone, Blackstone shelled out what *The Washington Post* subsequently called the "heftiest six-month payment to any lobbyist ever reported."[8]

Pending reform: Subject carried interest to the same tax rate as ordinary income.

Last November, the U.S. House of Representatives passed a tax reform bill that would have closed the carried interest loophole.[9] But an aggressive lobbying campaign by deep-pocketed investment fund industry movers and shakers—current and potential major campaign donors all—halted the initiative in the Senate.[10]

If the reform had been adopted, the Joint Committee on Taxation estimates, the federal government would have garnered an additional $2,661,000,000 in 2008.[11]

Subsidy #2

Unlimited deferred compensation
Annual cost: $80,600,000

The vast majority of CEOs at large companies now legally shield unlimited amounts of compensation from taxes through special deferred accounts set up by their employers.

According to researchers at Equilar, a compensation analytics firm, 83.4 percent of S&P 500 companies offered such accounts for their top brass in 2007.[12] Equilar found that deferred compensation plan balances increased by 54.3 percent last year, to a median value of $4,517,488.

By contrast, ordinary taxpayers face strict limits on how much income they can defer from taxes via 401(k) plans—$15,500 max per year for most workers.

What makes special deferred pay accounts such a desirable perk for top executives? These accounts offer, of course, the standard economic advantage of pretax compounding. Dollars stashed in deferred-pay pots grow and grow, untaxed, until executives start withdrawing from them. Down the road, at that withdrawal time, the executives might just face a lower tax rate than they do now. Today's top executives, after all, have watched top federal marginal tax rates fall sharply since their careers began. These rates, they have reason to hope, could sink even lower.

Executive deferred pay accounts boast another appealing feature. Many corporations guarantee executives an above-market rate of return on the dollars in their deferred pay accounts. American Express CEO Kenneth I. Chenault, the Associated Press notes, collected $1.55 million in above-market returns on his deferred compensation in 2007.[13] Average corporate employees, by contrast, enjoy no guarantees on the dollars in their deferred-pay 401(k)s. The funds in 401(k)s grow and compound taxfree. But if an employee's investment choices go sour, the funds may not grow at all.

Over recent decades, by forcing workers out of traditional "defined-benefit" pension plans into "defined-contribution" plans like 401(k)s, corporations in the United States have shifted the risk of retirement funding onto workers. Increasingly, in our new American economy, only executives rate retirement security.

Tax Benefits of Deferring Compensation

A hypothetical based on two taxpayers in the top income tax bracket:

Taxpayer who *can* defer compensation

1. Receives compensation in the amount of $100

2. Defers compensation for 5 years, earning 10% return on investment each year, for a total of $161.05

3. Amount the taxpayer can pocket after paying a one-time tax of 35%: **$104.68**

Taxpayer who *cannot* defer compensation

1. Receives compensation in the amount of $100

2. Pays a tax of $35, leaving only $65 to invest

3. Amount available to the taxpayer after earning an after-tax return of 6.5% per year (10% return—35% tax on earnings per year) for five years: **$89.06**

Source: Based on analysis by the Joint Committee on Taxation.[14]

TARGET'S TREASURE CHEST

Before retiring in January 2008, Target CEO Robert Ulrich amassed a treasure chest of $140,791,549 in deferred compensation—all of this over and beyond the dollars in his regular pension and 401(k). Last year alone Ulrich contributed $9,511,070 to his pay-deferral pot.

Ulrich can clearly afford to set aside millions in his deferred-pay stash and still easily maintain the style of life to which he has become accustomed. Last year he cashed in $93,497,000 in stock options.[15]

Pending reform: Cap the amount of pay executives can have deferred.

In 2007, Senate Finance Committee chairman Max Baucus (D-Montana) and the panel's ranking minority member, Senator Charles Grassley (R-Iowa), pushed all the way to a House-Senate conference committee legislation that would have limited annual executive pay deferrals to $1 million.[16] This extremely modest cap, if enacted, would have generated an estimated $806 million over 10 years.[17] Attacked fiercely by corporate interests, this proposal did not survive the conference committee deliberations, but Senator Baucus has pledged to revisit it.

Subsidy #3

Offshore deferred compensation
Annual cost: $2,086,000,000

U.S.-based corporations do incur a tax cost when they allow their executives to stash massive sums in deferred accounts. Until executives begin to withdraw from the accounts, the company cannot claim a tax deduction for the executive compensation deferred.

Businesses registered in offshore tax havens, on the other hand, have little or nothing to lose by allowing their employees to accumulate boatloads of compensation in deferred accounts, since registering in such havens allows them to sidestep the U.S. tax liabilities they would otherwise face.

Offshore maneuvering creates particularly lucrative tax-avoidance opportunities for hedge funds, since most of them have already created offshore subsidiaries. Hedge Fund Research, a Chicago-based analyst firm, estimates that of the total $1.86 trillion invested in hedge funds, $1.25 trillion is kept in funds registered offshore.[18] According to the Joint Committee on Taxation on Capitol Hill, 92 percent of offshore hedge funds have situated themselves in the notorious tax havens of the Cayman Islands, the British Virgin Islands, Bermuda, and the Bahamas.[19]

Deferring pay in offshore accounts represents only one way that the wealthy use tax havens to avoid paying their fair share of taxes. The practice of stashing funds in offshore banks, one Senate investigation has found, costs U.S. taxpayers an estimated $100 billion dollars each year.[20] The data so far available do not reveal how many of these billions benefit business executives, the focus of this report, as opposed to other rich tax-dodgers.

CITADEL: PROTECTING PAY FROM TAXES

Kenneth Griffin, the head of Citadel Investment Group, made $1.5 billion in 2007, up from $1.2 billion in 2006.[21] Citadel's largest fund, the Bermuda-registered Citadel Kensington Ltd.,[22] manages about $10 billion in assets and has reported over 20 percent annual gains for the past nine years.[23] Information on Griffin's tax-deferred offshore accounts is not publicly available, and the investment kingpin lustily defends the tax breaks he enjoys.

"I am proud to be an American," he told the *New York Times* last year. "But if the tax became too high, as a matter of principle, I would not be working this hard."[24]

To help maintain Griffin's work ethic, Citadel has spent more than $1.1 million since the beginning of 2007 lobbying to preserve tax loopholes for private investment managers. Griffin is also hedging his political bets. He has hosted fund-raisers for both Senators Obama and McCain and acted as a "bundler" to collect more than $50,000 for each candidate.[25]

Pending reform: Prevent executives from using offshore tax-deferred compensation accounts.

The Joint Committee on Taxation estimates that American hedge fund managers have amassed so much wealth in offshore deferred accounts that if this tax-dodging scheme had been eliminated this year, the federal government would have received an additional $2,086,000,000 in revenue.[26] A bill that would have closed this loophole passed this year in the House, but stalled in the Senate.[27]

Subsidy #4

Unlimited tax deductibility of executive pay
Annual cost: $5,249,475,000

Tax law allows corporations to deduct the cost of executive compensation from their income taxes, as a business expense, so long as this compensation remains "reasonable." But what's reasonable? The IRS has no clear definition.

In 1993, the Clinton Administration sought to provide some guidance here by promoting legislation designed to cap executive pay deductions at $1 million.

But this attempt to define executive pay reasonableness has proved wholly ineffective because the legislation, as enacted, allows an exception for "performance-based" pay. Most companies simply limit top executive salaries to $1 million or so and then add on to that total various assortments of "performance-based" bonuses, stock awards, and other long-term compensation that increases overall executive pay about an average ten times over.

This tax loophole operates as a powerful subsidy for excessive compensation. The more corporations pay out in executive compensation, the less they owe in taxes. And average taxpayers wind up paying the bill.

WAL-MART: "WE DEDUCT FOR MORE"

In 2007, Wal-Mart CEO H. Lee Scott, Jr. made $29,682,000—1,314 times as much as the company's average fulltime workers. The discount giant refuses to disclose pay levels for its thousands of part-time workers, but reports that full-time workers make an average of $10.86 per hour.

If Wal-Mart had been required to pay corporate income taxes on the portion of Scott's compensation that exceeded 25 times the value of the firm's average full-time compensation, the company's tax bill would have increased by $10,191,069 in 2007.[28]

This seems a small price to pay, given that taxpayers have provided billions of dollars in subsidies to Wal-Mart over the years in the form of public assistance for the retailer's poorly compensated employees.[29]

Pending reform: Deny corporations deductions on any executive pay that runs over 25 times the pay of a company's lowest-paid worker.

This legislation, the Income Equity Act, has been pending before Congress since the early 1990s, introduced first by the now retired Martin Sabo (D-Minn.) and currently by Barbara Lee (D-Calif.).[30]

The Income Equity Act would not set a ceiling on, or dictate in any way, how much corporations can pay their executives. The legislation would instead place a cap on the amount of pay that corporations can deduct off their taxes. Corporations could still freely pay their executives outlandishly large sums. But the federal government—and America's average taxpayers—would no longer reward them for their excessive generosity.

The bill could have an important impact on lower-level workers as well. By tying pay at the top of the corporate ladder to pay at the bottom, the Income Equity Act would encourage corporations to raise pay at the bottom, since the greater the pay for a company's lowest-paid worker, the higher the tax-deductible pay for the company's highest-paid executives.

The Income Equity Act would, if enacted, also require corporations to annually reveal the pay gap between their highest-and lowest-paid workers. American taxpayers and consumers currently have no way of knowing exactly how much companies squeeze their least powerful workers to create windfalls for executives at the top.

Government estimates of the tax revenue implications of this bill are not available. The Institute for Policy Studies has calculated a conservative estimate, based on a limited sample of the top five executives at 1,500 U.S. firms. The current subsidy, by these calculations is: $5,249,475,000.[31]

Subsidy #5

Stock option accounting double standard
Annual cost: $10,000,000,000

Stock options—the most lucrative of all executive pay categories—come with a magical accounting and tax double standard that makes them nearly irresistible to both executives and the corporations that employ them.

Current *accounting* rules value stock options on their grant date. The current *tax code* values stock options on the day that executives decide to cash them in. The two numbers rarely match, and in recent years, the actual "inthe-pocket" value has been significantly higher than the grant date estimate. As a result, companies can lower their tax bill by claiming deductions for options-related costs that are much higher than what they report in their financial statements.

At the same time, by reporting a low expense for stock options on financial statements, corporations can show higher quarterly net earnings. That keeps Wall Street investors happy, share prices high, and executive rewards flowing at ever more ample levels.

Internal Revenue Service research shows that corporations claimed 2005 stock option tax deductions that were collectively $61 billion larger than the expenses shown on company books.[32]

"By eliminating this outdated and overly gener-ous corporate tax deduction," notes Senator Carl Levin (D-Michigan), "we would eliminate a tax incentive that encourages corporate boards to hand out huge executive stock option pay which, in turn, fuels the growing chasm be tween executive pay and the earnings of rank and file workers."[33]

UNITEDHEALTH'S STOCK-OPTION SLEIGHT OF HAND

Between 2002 and 2006, a Congressional inquiry has found, UnitedHealth Group, one of the nation's largest health insurance companies, claimed a tax deduction of $317.7 million on 9 million stock options exercised by CEO William McGuire.

In its financial statement, UnitedHealth recorded zero expenses related to those options.[34] The stock option accounting double standard offers all corporations, not just UnitedHealth, an incentive to dole out generous helpings of executive stock options. At UnitedHealth, corporate board members took this doling out to the extreme.

In 2006, the company became one of the top culprits in a rash of stock option backdating scandals after news reports revealed that McGuire and other high-level executives had been allowed to pick the grant dates for their options to maximize payouts.

Continued

"Backdating" itself does not break the law, but improper reporting does. Government investigators nailed UnitedHealth for improperly reporting the real cost of its executive options. As a result, McGuire had to forfeit about $618 million worth of options to help settle shareholder and federal government claims and paid a record $7 million fine to the SEC.[35]

In July 2008, the company announced it was settling one shareholder suit for $895 million and cutting costs by laying off 4,000 employees.[36] McGuire technically "lost" his job, too, but he still retired into the sunset with hundreds of millions in dubiously acquired compensation.

Pending reform: Mandate a single standard for reporting stock options.[37]

Neither the Joint Committee on Taxation nor the Congressional Budget Office has analyzed the revenue implications of this reform. In 2007, Senator Levin cited an estimate of $5 billion to $10 billion in additional revenues that could be generated by eliminating what he calls "unwarranted and excess stock option deductions."

Levin chairs the Senate's Permanent Subcommittee on Investigations, the panel that has led the examination of the stock option accounting double standard. Levin based his estimate on partial-year numbers for 2004 that were considerably lower than the IRS findings for 2005. This report uses the high-end estimate.[38]

Additional Subsidies for Executive Excess

The tax and accounting loopholes noted above actually deliver a relatively small piece of the taxpayer largesse that every year plops into corporate coffers. The federal government also encourages and supports excessive executive pay indirectly, through a variety of supports that range from procurement contracts to handouts that go by the label of "corporate welfare." A recent report revealed that two-thirds of U.S. companies paid no federal income taxes between 1998 and 2005, in part because of tax credits.[39] How much of this taxpayer money winds up in the pockets of top executives? No researchers have yet calculated a specific figure. But the sum likely dwarfs the executive pay subsidies that flow through tax loopholes.

Nearly every major corporation in the United States owes a significant chunk of its profitability to interactions with federal, state, and local governing bodies. Executives regularly claim credit—and huge rewards—for their corporate "performance." Without taxpayer dollars, executives would "perform" nowhere near as well.

That reality creates an opportunity that executive pay reformers have seldom appreciated. Government policies today encourage executive excess. But governments at all levels, if they so chose, could leverage the power of the public purse to discourage such excess and encourage instead the more equitable pay differentials that nurture effective and efficient enterprises and healthy economies.

We describe here a small sampling of today's indirect subsidies for executive excess and the opportunities that ending these subsidies would create for real executive pay reform.

I. Government Procurement and Executive Excess

By law, the U.S. government denies contracts to companies that discriminate, in their employment practices, by race or gender. Our tax dollars, Americans agree, should not subsidize racial or gender inequality. But billions of taxpayer dollars flow annually to companies that increase economic inequality—by paying CEOs hundreds of times more than their workers.

In theory, existing law prevents government contractors from pouring tax dollars, at excessive levels, into executive pockets. Every year, the Office of Management and Budget establishes a maximum benchmark for contractor compensation, $612,196 in FY 2008. But this benchmark only limits the executive pay a company can directly bill the government for reimbursement. The benchmark in no way curbs windfalls that contracts generate for companies and their top executives.

One bill before Congress, the Patriot Corporations Act, would discourage these windfalls.[40] This legislation offers a preference in the evaluation of bids or proposals for federal contracts to companies that meet a series of benchmarks for good corporate citizenship. Among the benchmarks: paying executives no more than 100 times the pay of their lowest-paid employee.

Most top contractors do not currently meet this standard.

The Institute for Policy Studies has analyzed the data available for the top 100 U.S. federal government contractors in 2006. Together, these contractors received over $226 billion in taxpayer-funded contracts.[42] Of these 100 contractors, 47 operate as publicly traded U.S. corporations, a distinction that requires these companies

---

LOCKHEED MARTIN CEO: GETTING RICH ON THE DOLE

Perennial top-ranking defense contractor Lockheed Martin took in $32.1 billion from the federal government in 2006, most of it from the Pentagon. These taxpayer dollars made up more than 80 percent of the aerospace giant's total revenues.

In 2007, Lockheed Martin CEO Robert Stevens took home more than $24 million—787 times the annual pay of a typical U.S. worker ($30,617). That placed the company far over the 100-to-1 standard for good corporate citizenship the pending Patriot Corporations Act proposes.

To make matters worse, at the same time CEO Stevens and his fellow executives were lining his pockets with taxpayer dollars, government auditors were accusing the aerospace firm of more than $8 billion in cost overruns on weapons development projects.[41]

---

to report the annual earnings of their top five executives. In 2006, 40 of the 47 (85 percent) paid their CEOs more than 100 times the pay of a typical U.S. worker.[43]

The privately held U.S. companies on this list have not been required to report their executive pay to the SEC. At an October 2007 hearing, members of Congress pushed the CEO of one of these private contactors, Blackwater's Erik Prince, to disclose his personal compensation. Blackwater has received over $1 billion to provide security services in Iraq and Afghanistan, but Prince refused to give a specific figure for his own compensation, defiantly noting that he collected "more than $1 million."[44]

Congress recently passed legislation, the Government Contractor Accountability Act, which will now require executive pay disclosure of all major contractors that receive more than 80 percent of their revenues from federal contracts.[45]

2. Bailouts and Executive Excess

Shortly after the 9/11 attacks, lawmakers in Congress established an important precedent to limit windfall profit-taking in industries that receive substantial government assistance. The $15 billion airline industry bailout Congress okayed in 2001 required that airline companies accepting bailout dollars ban raises and limit severance

for all executives who had taken home over $300,000 the previous year.

Unfortunately, lawmakers have not applied strict limits on executive pay in other bailout situations.

This year, the Federal Reserve Board has taken aggressive action to prop up the troubled U.S. financial sector, injecting hundreds of billions of dollars of liquidity into the system—with no restrictions whatsoever on pay for the executives who had reaped massive personal gains while engaging in behaviors that created the credit crisis. The Federal Reserve also agreed to buy up to $29 billion in shaky mortgage bonds to facilitate JPMorgan Chase's purchase of beleaguered Bear Stearns, a move that put taxpayers at risk while placing no restrictions on the benefits that executives might reap from the subsidy.[49]

In late July, Congress followed up this Federal Reserve action by passing a rescue package for Fannie Mae and Freddie Mac that contained only loose controls over the executive pay practices of these private sector "governmentsponsored enterprises." The bill created a new regulator for the two mortgage firms and gives this regulator the authority to limit or withhold "golden parachutes" and to ensure that executive pay levels are "reasonable." But the legislation does not define "reasonable," a decision that allows regulators considerable latitude.[50]

FANNIE AND FREDDIE: RISKY FOR TAXPAYERS, NOT CEOS

In 2007, the heads of Freddie Mac and Fannie Mae both earned far more than the average for large company CEOs—despite their utter failure to recognize the housing bubble or avert the mortgage crisis.[46] At Freddie Mac, chief Richard Syron took in nearly $19.8 million, while presiding over a 50 percent drop in the company's stock.[47] Fannie Mae head Daniel Mudd made $13.4 million, 27 percent more than the average for S&P 500 CEOs, according to the Associated Press.[48]

During the debate over a taxpayer bailout for the firms, Senator Bob Casey (D-Pennsylvania) urged the mortgate firms' boards to sue to recover the bonuses that Syron and Mudd pocketed while failing to do their jobs.

Executive Pay Subsidies: What's At Stake?

Fiscal Trade-offs

Our ongoing—and deepening—U.S. economic downturn is forcing governments at every level to make painful choices on which problems to address and which to ignore. In this political climate, taxpayer subsidies for executive excess take on an even greater significance.

All subsidies involve trade-offs. Each time we allow executives and their employers to avoid paying taxes they would otherwise owe, we reduce government's capacity to deliver needed services that taxpayers and their families would otherwise receive.

Tax subsidies for excessive executive pay represent a particularly indefensible waste of government resources. At the moment, no serious observer of the American scene is arguing that top business executives, as a group, earn too little in compensation. So why then

should government, in any manner, be encouraging corporations and investment firms to pay their executives even more?

Those tax dollars that currently go to encouraging and rewarding corporate America's most advantaged could, if redirected, go a long way toward addressing *real* problems.

Consider, for instance, one of America's weakest and most vulnerable populations: children with disabilities and other special needs. In the 2007 fiscal year, the federal government distributed not quite $10.8 billion in state aid for special education.[51] Top business executives this year will enjoy nearly twice that amount in federal subsidies for excessive executive compensation.

Or consider federal support for risk taking. Ample rewards for business executives, defenders of contemporary American executive pay often argue, serve as an important incentive for the risk taking necessary to keep an economy innovative and growing.

CEO PAY AND WORKER RIGHTS: WITHOUT LABOR LAW REFORM, CEO-WORKER PAY GAP LIKELY TO GROW

The divide between CEO and worker pay is on course to grow even wider, since industries projected to have the largest employment growth in the next decade show pay gaps that are far wider than industries that are losing the most jobs. One reason for the

difference: union representation. In the expanding service sectors, only a tiny percentage of workers have the power to bargain collectively for fair compensation.

According to the Labor Department, the top job growth industry, food services, will add over 1 million jobs by 2016. The 9.3 million non-management workers in this sector—only 1.2 percent of whom are union members—earn an average of $18,877 per year.[56] The CEOs of the top 10 firms in this industry—McDonald's, YUM Brands (owner of KFC, Taco Bell, Pizza Hut), and other major employers that set industry-wide pay standards—averaged 354 times that amount in 2007.

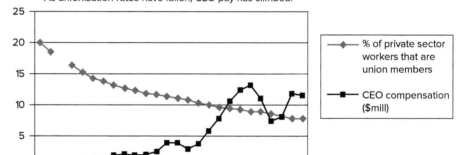

Executive Pay and Unionization, 1980–2005
As unionization rates have fallen, CEO pay has climbed.

In retail, another fast-growing industry with low unionization, the CEO-worker pay gap runs even wider, 453-to-1.

By contrast, in industries like auto parts and pulp and paper, where unionization rates are above 20 percent, CEO-worker pay gaps stand at 173-to-1 and 219-to-1 respectively. These manufacturing workers have used union leverage over the years to bargain for decent compensation. Today, however, "free trade" agreements and other factors are slashing employment in these traditional union strongholds.

Without legislative action to allow more workers the right to organize, the divide between compensation for top executives and the rest of us will only continue to grow.

Chart sources: Unionization: Bureau of National Affairs, Union Membership And Earnings Data Book. CEO pay: *Business Week* and *Wall Street Journal* surveys.[57]

But executives hardly make up the only risk-takers on our economic scene today. Many Americans, every day they walk into work, risk their lives. In 2006, 5,320 private-sector workers died on the job. Nearly half a million more lost workdays to on-the-job falls and back injuries.[52]

What's government doing about this real problem? In 2006, the federal government spent $264 million enforcing workplace safety standards. The government is devoting 75 times more than that $264 million, every year, encouraging higher paychecks for top executives, precious few of whom will ever face real "risk" in the workplace.[53]

Additional Economic Costs of a Pay System out of Control

Subsidies for excessive executive pay don't just involve fiscal trade-offs. These subsidies have deep consequences for the economy as a whole—and the economic well-being of America's families.

Senator McCain has not yet endorsed any of the five. In 2002, he co-sponsored a bill similar to the pending proposed fix for the stock option accounting double standard. But McCain has declined, according to Senator Levin's office, to take a position on the current bill.[54]

In 2007, both candidates voted in favor of a minimum wage bill that included an amendment to cap executive deferred compensation. But neither has spoken out about this measure specifically, and the proposal is still pending, since a House-Senate Conference Committee stripped the deferred-pay limit from the minimum wage bill.[55]

None of these five reforms will, either individually or as a group, fully correct the power imbalances in the American economy that have tilted rewards so far up the corporate ladder. The first step needed to restore some modicum of balance? That would be passage of the **Employee Free Choice Act,** the legislation now pending in Congress that would expand collective bargaining throughout the American economy. Senator McCain opposes this legislation, Senator Obama supports it.

Conclusion

Journalists have been writing about rising executive pay since the early 1980s. Over the past quarter-century, poll after poll has shown widespread public opposition to our contemporary CEO pay levels. Almost every high-ranking political leader in the United States has, at one time or another, expressed dismay over pay at America's corporate summit. Surveys have found that even those individuals directly responsible for setting executive pay levels—the members of corporate boards of directors—feel we have a serious executive pay problem.

Yet, year after year, nothing changes. Executive pay continues to rise much faster than compensation elsewhere in the U.S. economy. Does all this mean that rising executive pay reflects some inexorable natural economic phenomenon? Not at all. Public policies, we have detailed in this edition of *Executive Excess*, have fueled the executive pay explosion. We can change public policies.

Historically, troubled economic times in the United States have helped generate long-overdue public policy reforms. We have now entered troubled economic times, likely our worst since executive pay started ballooning in the 1980s. Ballooning executive pay has helped create our current economic woes. Deflating that excess can help end them.

Notes

1. *Alpha* magazine, April 22, 2008.

2. Buffett disclosed to NBC's Tom Brokaw that he paid 17.7 percent of his income in federal income and payroll taxes. His office employees paid an average of 32.9 percent of their income. Buffett attributed this difference to the special treatment of capital gains income. See: www.cnbc.com/id/21543506/site/14081545/

3. Michael K. Ozanian and Peter J. Schwartz, "Top Guns," *Forbes*, May 21, 2007.

4. Services Employees International Union, "Buyout Industry Tax Loopholes That Cost Billions Should be Closed in 2009," (press release) Apr 15, 2008. See: www.reuters.com/article/pressRelease/idUS218165+15-Apr-2008+PRN20080415

5. "Billionaires 2008," *Forbes,* March 24, 2008.

6. Stephen Labaton and Jenny Anderson, "Mr. Kravis Goes to Washington (Capra Rolls Over)," *New York Times,* July 11, 2007. See: www.nytimes.com/2007/07/11/business/11tax.html?_r=1&pagewanted=print&oref=slogin

7. Richard Rubin and Emily Cadei, "Private Equity's Lobby Shop Ramping Up for Renewed Tax Battle," *Congressional Quarterly Today*, March 28, 2008. See: www.cqpolitics.com/wmspage.cfm?docID=news-000002693578

8. Jeffrey H. Birnbaum, "Wall Street Paying High Price to Keep Cash," Washington Post, August 21, 2007. See: www.washingtonpost.com/wp-dyn/content/artile/2007/08/20/AR2007082001761.html

9. Temporary Tax Relief Act of 2007 (H.R.3996).

10. Charlie Cray and Christopher Hayes, "Executive Excess on Capitol Hill," *The Nation*, November 12, 2007. See: www.thenation.com/doc/20071126/cray_hayes

11. Joint Committee on Taxation, JCX-105-07, October 31, 2007. See: www.house.gov/jct/x-105-07.pdf

12. Equilar, "S&P 500 CEO Compensation Rises 1.3% to $8.8 Million," April 10, 2008. See: www.equilar.com/Executive_Compensation_Knowledge_Center.php.

13. Associated Press, "Clarification: American Express CEO pay story," May 6, 2008. See: http://news.moneycentral.msn.com/provider/providerarticle.aspx?feed=AP&date=20080506&id=8596806

14. Joint Committee On Taxation, "Present Law and Analysis Relating to Tax Treatment of Partnership Carried Interests and Related Issues, Part II," September 4, 2007, p. 8.

15. Target proxy statement, May 22, 2008. See: www.sec.gov/Archives/edgar/data/27419/000104746908004184/a2183269zdef14a.htm

16. The Small Business and Work Opportunity Act (S. 349).

17. Democratic Policy Committee (press release) January 23, 2007. see: dpc.senate.gov/dpc-new.cfm?doc_name=lb-110-1-11. Note: We divided the 10-year projected revenue by 10 to obtain an annual cost to taxpayers.

18. Imogen Rose-Smith, "Offshore Fantasy?" *Alpha*, April 2008.

19. Joint Committee On Taxation, "Present Law And Analysis Relating To Tax Treatment Of Partnership Carried Interests And Related Issues, Part II," (JCX-63-07) September 4, 2007.

20. Permanent Subcommittee On Investigations Issues Report On Tax Haven Banks Hiding Billions From The IRS (press release) July 17, 2008. See: http://hsgac.senate.gov/public/index.cfm?Fuseaction=PressReleases.View&PressRelease_id=c9724a6a-1135-4cb8-9584-d474499e8131&Affiliation=R

21. The 2006 figure is from *Forbes*, May 21, 2007, while the 2007 figure is from *Alpha*, April 22, 2008.

22. See: www.alacrastore.com/storecontent/spcred/575725

23. Marcia Vickers, "A hedge fund superstar," FORTUNE Magazine, April 3 2007. See: http://money.cnn.com/magazines/fortune/fortune_archive/2007/04/16/8404298/

24. Louis Uchitelle, "The Richest Of The Rich, Proud Of A New Gilded Age," *New York Times Magazine,* July 15, 2007.

25. Michael Luo and Kitty Bennett, "McCain Names More Top Fund-Raisers, Including Lobbyists," *New York Times,* July 16, 2008. See: www.nytimes.com/2008/07/16/us/politics/16donate.html

26. Joint Committee on Taxation, JCX-105-07, October 31, 2007. See: www.house.gov/jct/x-105-07.pdf

27. Temporary Tax Relief Act of 2007 (H.R.3996).

28. Formula: $22,589 (annual average pay for fulltime Wal-Mart workers) × 25 = $564,725 (amount above which Wal-Mart could not claim a deduction under the proposed Income Equity Act). $29,682,064 (Wal-Mart CEO pay in 2007)—$564,275 (amount above which Wal-Mart could not claim a deduction under the proposed law) = $29,117,339 (unallowable corporate deduction) × 35 percent (maximum corporate tax rate) = $10,191,069 (taxpayer savings related to CEO's pay)

29. See, for example: Arindrajit Dube, Dave GrahamSquire, Ken Jacobs and Stephanie Luce, "Living Wage Policies and Wal-Mart: How a Higher Wage Standard Would Impact Wal-Mart Workers and Shoppers," UC Berkeley Labor Center, December 2007, and Democratic Staff of the Committee on Education and the Workforce, U.S. House of Representatives, "Everyday Low Wages: The Hidden Price We All Pay For Wal-Mart: Wal-Mart's Labor Record," February 16, 2004.

30. Income Equity Act (H.R. 3876).

31. Methodology: $5.2 billion is the additional revenue that the federal government would have received if a deductibility cap of no more than 25 times a company's lowest-paid worker pay had been in place in 2003 for the companies that comprise the S&P 500, MidCap400, and SmallCap600. Pay figures for the top five executives in each of these groups drawn from Bebchuk and Grinstein, "The Growth of Executive Pay" (2005). Formula: $12,168 (annual pay for full-time minimum wage workers) × 25 = $304,200 (amount above which corporations could not claim a deduction under the proposed Income Equity Act). $4,280,000 (average pay for top 5 execs in S&P 500)—$304,200 (amount above which corporations could not claim a deduction under the proposed law) = $3,975,800 (unallowable corporate deduction) × 35 percent (maximum corporate tax rate) = $1,391,530 (tax payer savings per executive) × 2,500 (5 execs in 500 companies = $3,478,825,000 in total taxpayer savings. (repeated for MidCap400 and SmallCap600). Note: This calculation uses the minimum wage as the lowest-pay rate but the estimate is conservative in that it only applies to 1,500 companies of varying sizes.

32. Senate Permanent Subcommittee on Investigations (press release), April 21, 2008. See: http://levin.senate.gov/newsroom/release.cfm?id=296455

33. Senate Committee on Homeland Security and Governmental Affairs, press release, September 28, 2007. See: http://hsgac.senate.gov/public/index.cfm?Fuseaction=PressReleases.View&PressRelease_id=661bf7cc-b067-4cf4-a02a-136ed7ed 9160& Affiliation=R

34. Hearing Before the Permanent Subcommittee on Investigations of the Committee on Homeland Security and Governmental Affairs, "Executive Stock Options: Should the Internal Revenue Service and Stockholders Be Given Different Information?" June 5, 2007. See: frwebgate.access.gpo.gov/cgi-bin/getdoc.cgi?dbname=110_senate_hearings&docid=f:36611.pdf

35. David Phelps, "McGuire pays again, ends SEC's inquiry," *Star Tribune* (Minneapolis, MN), December 7, 2007.

36. MarketWatch, July 2, 2008.

37. Ending Corporate Tax Favors For Stock Options Act (S. 2116).

38. Senate Committee on Homeland Security and Governmental Affairs (press release), September 28, 2007. See: http://hsgac.senate.gov/public/index.cfm?Fuseaction=PressReleases.View&PressRelease_id=661bf7cc-b067-4cf4-a02a-136ed7ed9160&Affiliation=R

39. Government Accountability Office, "Comparison of the Reported Tax Liabilities of Foreign- and U.S.-Controlled Corporations, 1998–2005," GAO-08-957, July 24, 2008. See: http://gao.gov/docsearch/abstract.php?rptno=GAO-08-957

40. Patriot Corporations of America Act of 2007 (H.R.3319).

41. Government Accountability Office, "Defense Acquisitions: Assessments of Selected Weapon Programs," March 2008, p. 25, Table 5. See: www.gao.gov/new.items/d08467sp.pdf

42. List compiled by OMB Watch: See: www.fedspending.org/fpds/tables.php?tabtype=t2&subtype=t&year=2006

43. CEO pay figures were calculated from information in corporate proxy statements, based on the Associated Press formula for total compensation, which includes: salary, bonuses, perks, above-market interest on deferred compensation and the value of stock and option awards. Stock and options awards were measured at their fair value on the day of the grant. Worker pay is based on U.S. Department of Labor, Bureau of Labor Statistics, Employment, Hours, and Earnings from the Current Employment Statistics Survey. Average hourly earnings of production workers ($17.42) × average weekly hours of production workers (33.8 hours) × 52 weeks = $30,617.

44. Transcript, House Oversight and Government Reform Committee hearing, October 2, 2007. See: http://oversight.house.gov/documents/20071127131151.pdf

45. OMB Watch, August 5, 2008. See: www.ombwatch.org/article/articleview/4324/

46. Dean Baker, "Paying for Fannie and Freddie's mistakes," *The Guardian,* July 21, 2008.

47. Associated Press, "Freddie Mac CEO paid almost $20M last year," July 18, 2008. See: http://money.cnn.com/2008/07/18/news/newsmakers/Freddiemac_CEO.ap/index.htm?section=money_latest

48. AP inter-active compensation survey. See: hosted.ap.org/dynamic/files/specials/interactives/_business/executive_compensation/index.html?SITE=YAHOO&SECTION=HOME

49. Bob David, Damian Paletta and Rebecca Smith, "Amid Turmoil, U.S. Turns Away From Decades of Deregulation," *Wall Street Journal,* July 25, 2008. See: http://online.wsj.com/article/SB121694460456283007.html

50. Housing and Economic Recovery Act of 2008 (H.R.3221).

51. U.S. Department of Education, Fiscal Year 2001–2009 State Tables. See: www.ed.gov/about/overview/budget/statetables/09stbyprogram.pdf

52. Bureau of Labor Statistics, "Injuries, Illnesses, and Fatalities." See: www.bls.gov/iif/home.htm

53. OMB Watch, "Workers Threatened by Decline in OSHA Budget, Enforcement Activity," Jan. 23, 2008. See: www.ombwatch.org/article/articleview/4143 - 1b

54. E-mail communication with Levin aide Elise Bean, August 5, 2008.

55. Voting record on the Fair Minimum Wage Act of 2007: http://www.senate.gov/legislative/LIS/roll_call_lists/roll_call_vote_cfm.cfm?congress=110&session=1&vote=00042

56. Wage and employment: Based on Bureau of Labor Statistics figures. See: www.bls.gov/oes/current/oessrci.htm. Unionization: Bureau of National Affairs, "Union Membership and Earnings Data Book," 2007, p. 54.

57. Sources: Unionization: Bureau of National Affairs, Union Membership And Earnings Data Book, 2007 Edition, Table 1b, p. 12. CEO pay for 1980–2004: Business Week surveys. For 2005: Wall Street Journal survey. (both surveys covered about 350 large companies). Note: The data end in 2005 because SEC reporting changes make subsequent data not directly comparable. Gaps reflect years for which data were not available.

Sarah Anderson is the director of the Global Economy Project at the Institute for Policy Studies and a coauthor of 14 previous IPS annual reports on executive compensation.

John Cavanagh is the director of the Institute for Policy Studies and coauthor of *Development Redefined: How the Market Met Its Match* (Paradigm Publishers, 2008).

Chuck Collins is a senior scholar at the Institute for Policy Studies where he directs the Program on Inequality and the Common Good. He was a cofounder of United for a Fair Economy, and his latest book, the coauthored *The Moral Measure of the Economy,* appeared earlier this year (Orbis, 2008).

Mike Lapham is the project director of the Responsible Wealth program at United for a Fair Economy. Responsible Wealth organizes business leaders and wealthy individuals to raise their voices in support of tax fairness and corporate accountability.

Sam Pizzigati is an associate fellow of the Institute for Policy Studies and the author of *Greed and Good: Understanding and Overcoming the Inequality That Limits Our Lives* (Apex Press, 2004). He edits *Too Much,* an online weekly on excess and inequality.

Poonkulali Thangavelu

NO

Justifications For High CEO Pay (AAPL, GE)

As the pay gap between the average American worker and chief executive officers of public companies becomes larger, people are questioning what's behind this disparity and what drives the pay of CEOs. According to the AFL-CIO, a federation of labor organizations, for instance, the salary of a typical S&P 500 company CEO in 2014 was 373 times the salary of an average rank-and-file worker. In actual figures, average CEO pacakge was more than $22.6 million in 2014, according to Equilar, which researches executive compensation. Certainly, there is a big disparity between CEO pay and the pay of other workers in corporate America, but is there any reason this disparity exists?

An Incentive for Performance

One major justification put forth by corporations about what's behind gargantuan CEO pay levels is that they have to pay big in order to attract the right candidates who will impact the company's performance. That way, the company's shareholders get a better return on their investment. Companies that come up with this justification say that by awarding a big part of an executive's compensation in the form of stock grants, they are providing an incentive for him or her to run the company well and personally benefit, as well as reward shareholders.

The Superstar Theory

Another factor that companies cite for excessive pay is that some CEOs are indispensable and almost inextricable from the companies they lead. For instance, Steve Jobs will forever be linked to Apple, Inc. (AAPL) as the man who led the company as it introduced many of its major innovations and established it as a major force in the market. Similarly, investors tend to associate General Electric Co. (GE) with Jack Welch.

Board Influence

The pay of public company CEOs is normally set by a compensation committee formed of members of its board of directors. And that's another reason behind skyrocketing CEO pay levels, since these directors, though seemingly independent, tend to be nominated for their directorship by company CEOs. Therefore, the members of these compensation committees tend to be the cronies of the CEOs whose pay they set. Naturally enough, they tend to go along with high CEO pay levels as they enjoy the benefits of their own director positions.

Use of Peer Groups for Comparison

The use of peer groups to determine CEO pay has also been cited as a factor for burgeoning CEO pay. The people setting CEO pay are supposed to look to companies in a similar market and of a similar size to set CEO pay in their own company. In practice, however, many company directors tend to look at bigger and more flourishing companies that tend to pay their CEOs more as an aspirational yardstick to set pay.

Are High CEO Pay Levels Justified?

In a capitalistic system, it is justified that CEOs should be paid for superior performance. However, not all CEOs are superstars and a lot of the time CEOs do not add much long-term value. Instead, they have an incentive to focus more on short-term measures that drive up a company's stock price during their tenure. This leads to excessive risk-taking by companies. Of course, there is the occasional exceptional CEO for whom a case could be made for an exceptional premium, but that doesn't justify the sky-high pay levels of every run-of-the-mill CEO.

And while CEOs should be paid a significantly higher salary than rank-and-file employees for running companies, the questions are how high should the differential be and is there any justification for today's extreme differential?

The Bottom Line

CEOs are at the helm of public companies and the role needs to be adequately rewarded so as to attract suitable candidates who will steer their companies well. While that's not at issue, what has become controversial is the exorbitant levels of pay that CEOs command. Companies have come up with a number of reasons for the pay differential between CEOs and other workers, but they sometimes seem to be specious, as a CEO's pay is often set by their boards of directors who have every incentive to please them. And the use of peer groups to set pay is more aspirational than based on a comparison of apples to apples.

POONKULALI THANGAVELU, a freelance writer and editor based in New York's Brooklyn borough, has written on topics ranging from investments and personal finance to mortgages and commercial real estate finance during the course of her financial journalism career.

EXPLORING THE ISSUE

Are U.S. CEOs Paid
More Than They Deserve?

Critical Thinking and Reflection

1. Would guidelines on executive compensation mitigate potential legal challenges?
2. Would different executive compensation packages change executives' behavior?
3. Will an executive compensation control policy spur other methods to compensate executives?
4. Can executive compensation effectively be contained?
5. Should the executive compensation be changed?

Is There Common Ground?

At its core, this is an issue about equity and the perception of what fair outcomes are for varying labor inputs and classes. As with any equity issue, the issue of CEO and executive pay is contentious because all parties can cite data and provide support to justify their position. Those who labor to produce and deliver goods and services for consumers cite the critical importance of their combined efforts in determining corporate success and profitability via sales, service provision, and productivity levels, while those in CEO and other high-level executive positions stress that market forces and in particular the market for labor at these levels creates an environment that rewards them at rates established by the labor marketplace. Thus, executive salaries are "fair" based on the fact that the market is willing to pay them.

The common ground between these sides is therefore arriving at a shared understanding of how pay levels and scales can be set at fair and equitable levels. The challenge for these two sides is to determine the best or most acceptable approach for arriving at this shared understanding. Given the foreseeable difficulty in arriving at

such a shared understanding when approached from the present tone of this debate, it is likely that the topic of executive compensation will continue to be debated for quite some time.

Additional Resources

Bebchuk, L. & Ginstein, Y. (2005). "The Growth of Executive Pay," *Oxford Review of Economic Policy,* Summer, pp. 283–303.

Hayes, R.M. & Schaefer, S. (2009). "CEO Pay and the Lake Wobegon Effect," *Journal of Financial Economics,* November, pp. 280–290.

Jensen, M.C. & Murphy, K.J. (2010). "CEO Incentives—It's Not What You Pay, but How," *Journal of Applied Corporate Finance,* Winter, pp. 64–76.

Morgenson, G. (2013). "That Unstoppable Climb in C.E.O. Pay," *The New York Times,* June 30, p. BU1.

"Neither rigged nor fair; Executive pay," *The Economist,* June 25, 2016.

Internet References . . .

CEO Pay vs. Performance

http://graphics.wsj.com/ceopay-2015/

CEO to Worker Pay Ratios: Average CEO Earns 204 Times Median Worker Pay

https://www.glassdoor.com/research/ceo-pay-ratio/

Don't Cap CEO Pay: End Bailouts

www.aynrand.org/site/News2?page=NewsArticle&id=21359&news_iv_ctrl=2528

Executive Pay Isn't That Excessive and Some CEOs Really Deserve It

www.ibdeditorials.com/IBDArticles.aspx?id=322697364171124

Executive PayWatch

http://www.aflcio.org/Corporate-Watch/Paywatch-2015

Fixing Executive Compensation Excesses

www.businessweek.com/managing/content/feb2009
/ca2009025_072667.htm

Nothing Wrong with CEOs Making Top Dollar

www.reason.org/news/show/122437.html

**Say on Pay Rules Won't Satisfy Public's Salary
Bloodlust**

www.foxbusiness.com/story/markets/industries
/finance/say-pay-rules-wont-satisfy-publics
-salarybloodlust/

Unit 2

UNIT

Human Resource Management

*C*ompanies have the right to protect themselves, their employees, and even their customers from harm and to ensure a safe and drug-free workplace; however, employees also have a right to privacy. Given this conflict, policies such as employee monitoring, drug testing, and the monitoring of social media are under scrutiny. Labor unions have done much historically to benefit and protect employees, but have unions evolved to the point that they have become impediments to employee progress and the corporate success? This unit explores these important human resource management questions for managers.

Selected, Edited, and with Issue Framing Material by:
Kathleen J. Barnes, *William Paterson University*
and
George E. Smith, *University of South Carolina, Beaufort*

ISSUE

Does an Employer's Need to Monitor Workers Trump Employee Privacy Concerns?

YES: The Week Staff, from "The Rise of Workplace Spying," *The Week* (2015)

NO: Caron Beesley, from "Email, Phone and Social Media Monitoring in the Workplace—Know Your Rights as an Employer," U.S. Small Business Administration (2016)

Learning Outcomes

After reading this issue, you will be able to:

- Understand the positive and negative consequences of employee monitoring in the workplace.
- Understand how employee monitoring can be used as an effective workplace tool.
- Understand the policies that might be implemented concerning employee monitoring.
- Appreciate the legal implications of the use of employee monitoring in the workplace.

ISSUE SUMMARY

YES: The Week staff outlines how a growing number of companies are using technology to monitor employee's emails, phone calls, and movements.

NO: Caron Beesley, a Small Business Administration contributor, provides guidelines to employers on how not to violate employees' right to privacy.

O ne of the oldest sources of workplace conflict arises from the need of managers to monitor and control employee behavior at work. The trouble is that employees feel they have legitimate rights to privacy and that these rights are violated when management monitors workplace behavior. Although this issue is not new, over the past couple of decades it has taken on increased importance as a result of advances in electronic technology that allow for much closer monitoring of a much wider range of employee behaviors. Consequently, employees, now more than ever, feel that their rights are being violated. Employers and shareholders respond that their property rights are frequently violated by employees at the workplace. Thus, it is not surprising that they view monitoring employee behavior as a legitimate method of protecting their property.

To those supportive of employee monitoring policies, the results of the American Management Association survey are perfectly reasonable. Beyond the desire to reduce theft and to increase employee productivity, two additional arguments are frequently made in defense of employee monitoring. First is the fact that corporations can be held legally responsible for the behaviors of their employees at work. By way of example, consider an employee who causes an accident while under the influence of drugs at work. The employee not only causes property and human harm, but also puts the organization into a legal bind because the firm can be held legally responsible for the employee's actions. As often noted, businesses react to this threat by monitoring employee behavior via workplace drug testing.

A second argument supporting an employer's right to monitor involves the issue of property rights. As noted earlier, shareholders have property rights in the organization and are legally allowed to defend and protect it. When an employee uses the organization's property (i.e., computers, telephones, etc.) improperly, the employee is not only violating his or her employment contract, but is also essentially stealing from the company. Thus, from the shareholders' perspective, monitoring employee behavior is simply a way of protecting their property.

On the other side of this debate are those who claim that employees have rights in the workplace. These rights include the right to privacy. Advocates of this perspective assert that monitoring all too often goes beyond tracking employee productivity and is used to gather personal information on employees. They point to numerous instances of management spying on employees with video cameras in restrooms and other non-work-related areas in the office. A second argument raised by supporters of employee rights is to note that many studies have shown little or no evidence that monitoring actually results in productivity gains, thereby undermining an important component of the pro-monitoring position. It should be noted, however, that despite the strong emotional appeal of the privacy rights position, it has not held up well in the courtroom. As noted in the "NO" article for this topic, "And yet there are few, if any, legal protections for employees."

YES

The Week Staff

The Rise of Workplace Spying

A growing number of companies are using technology to monitor their employees' emails, phone calls, and movements. Here's everything you need to know:

How Are Employees Being Tracked

In almost every way. If you work on an office computer, your bosses can not only legally monitor your company email and internet browser history, they can also log keystrokes to check your productivity and even see what you type on private services like Gmail, Facebook, and Twitter. If you have a work cellphone, your employer can pinpoint your precise location through GPS. A survey from the American Management Association found that at least 66 percent of U.S. companies monitor their employees' internet use, 45 percent log keystrokes, and 43 percent track employee emails. And office workers aren't the only ones being spied on. In Amazon's warehouses, workers carry tablets that record their speed and efficiency as they retrieve merchandise for shoppers; in hospitals, nurses wear badges that track how often they wash their hands. "Privacy in today's workplace," says Ellen Bayer of the American Management Association, "is largely illusory."

When Did Companies Start Snooping?

Bosses have always kept a close eye on employees. Henry Ford famously paced the factory floor with a stopwatch, timing his workers' motions in a bid for greater efficiency. He also hired private investigators to spy on employees' home lives to make sure personal problems didn't interfere with their work performance. But modern technology has greatly expanded the possibilities for employee analysis. A point-of-sale computer system connected to a McDonald's cash register, for instance, can capture how well a server sells customers on the latest meal deal; at a supermarket, such a device can record how quickly a cashier scans each grocery item. With this information, management can measure how hard each employee works—and how necessary each is to the business.

Does This Boost Efficiency?

Yes, according to the data. A 2013 study of five chain restaurants found that eateries that used point-of-sale surveillance systems saw a 22 percent drop in theft on average, and a 7 percent increase in revenue. In 2009, UPS fitted its delivery trucks with about 200 sensors that track everything from driving speeds to stop times. This allowed the firm to find out which drivers were sneaking breaks, and to determine how many deliveries could be squeezed into one day. Within four years, the company was handling 1.4 million additional packages a day with 1,000 fewer drivers. Employees, of course, resent the relentless monitoring. One UPS driver told *Harper's* that the company used performance metrics like "a mental whip," adding, "People get intimidated and they work faster."

Who Does the Actual Monitoring?

It's all done automatically: Software programs scan employees' email accounts and computer files and alert supervisors to anything inappropriate. What constitutes inappropriate, of course, is up to each company. Alerts will be triggered at some firms if an employee visits a pornographic website; at Goldman Sachs, emails containing certain swear words are flagged and sent to compliance officers. The American Management Association says a quarter of large and midsize firms have fired employees for misusing office email or the internet. But companies aren't only concerned about detecting offensive behavior by employees.

What Else Are They Looking for?

Some companies search for evidence that employees might be thinking about quitting. They check for obvious signs such as Google searches for headhunters and job-listings sites, but also track subtler signifiers of discontent, such as employees who refer to the company as "they" in emails rather than the more inclusive "we." Bosses might then try to entice these employees to stay, or take steps to ensure that if they do leave, they take no confidential data or client lists with them. But it's a tricky balance—if employees discover their boss has been spying on Google searches they thought were private, office morale can plummet. "Right at the heart of all of this is trust," says Ken Oehler of Aon Hewitt, a human-capital consulting firm. "What sort of message does it send that they need to monitor [workers'] desktops?".

Can Employees Stop This Tracking?

Generally, no. Most employee contracts give management free rein to do what it wants with data gathered from office-issued equipment, but some surveilled workers are fighting back. A former sales executive at wire-transfer firm Intermex filed an unfair dismissal lawsuit against the firm earlier this year, alleging that she was fired after she uninstalled an app on her work cellphone that tracked her whereabouts 24/7. Myrna Arias claims her boss even bragged that he could use the app to tell how fast she was driving when she was off duty. But with few legal protections against prying employers, employment experts say workers should avoid doing anything on their company computer or phone that they wouldn't want their superiors to see. "Even if your boss says you're not being monitored," says Nancy Flynn, founder of the Ohio-based consultancy ePolicy Institute, you should "just assume you're being monitored."

Listening in at the Water Cooler

If you find the idea of your boss reading your emails creepy, how about having your location, tone of voice, and conversation length monitored throughout the working day? Boston-based analytics firm Sociometric Solutions has supplied some 20 companies with employee ID badges fitted with microphone, location sensor, and accelerometer. Sociometric Solutions doesn't record conversations or provide employers with individuals' data. Instead, it crunches data and looks at how employee interactions affect performance. At Bank of America call centers, for example, the firm found that workers in tightly knit groups who took breaks together were more productive and less likely to quit. The bank introduced a shared 15-minute coffee break to improve social interaction and saw productivity increase more than 10 percent while turnover plummeted 70 percent. "It's not just a case of saving tens of millions of dollars," says Sociometric Solutions CEO Ben Waber. "I can also point to thousands of people who say they like their job better."

THE WEEK, a weekly British news magazine which also publishes a United States and an Australian edition, offers commentary and analysis of the day's breaking news and current events as well as arts, entertainment, and people.

Caron Beesley

 **NO**

Email, Phone and Social Media Monitoring in the Workplace—Know Your Rights as an Employer

Do you know how much privacy your employees are entitled to? For example, if you feel employees are abusing their work privileges, is it legal to intercept emails or phone conversations to find out what they're up to and confirm your suspicions? Can you ask potential job candidates for their Facebook profile log-on information?

Here are some general guidelines that can help.

Screening Job Candidate's Social Media Profiles

There has been plenty of coverage in the media recently about companies and public sector organizations asking job candidates for their Facebook passwords as part of the employment screening process. Many of the employers who do this are in law enforcement and are on the lookout for potential illegal activity. But businesses have also been known to use this approach to get a better handle on who they are about to hire.

Although there is no federal law prohibiting this, the Department of Justice considers it a crime to violate social media terms of service and enter these sites illegally. Asking an employee or candidate for their log-on information means you and that individual are both in direct violation of Facebook's Terms of Service (link is external) which states the following: *"You will not solicit login information or access an account belonging to someone else"* or *"You will not share your password . . . let anyone else access your account, or do anything else that might jeopardize the security of your account."*

Many states are also now looking to make this practice illegal.

The Bottom Line: Simply asking for access to personal passwords is a clear privacy violation and is both offensive to the candidate and unethical. Employers and managers should also be careful they're not accessing profile information to determine an employee's religious, sexual or political views. If it's determined that you used this information to discriminate against an employee, you may be found in violation of equal employment opportunity and privacy rules.

Monitoring Employee Social Media Activity in the Workplace

A recent report by Gartner suggests that by 2016, up to 60 percent of employers are expected to watch workers' social media use for security breaches. Currently, no specific laws govern the monitoring of an employee's social media activity on a company's computer (employers are on the lookout for unauthorized posting of company content—videos, documents, photos, etc.). However, the U.S. National Labor Relations Act does address employee rights in regard to the use of social media and acceptable social media policy. There has also been a ruling against employers who fired workers for complaining on social media sites about their workplace conditions.

The Bottom Line: Provide employees with a social media policy and be sure to include information about what you consider confidential and proprietary company information that should not be shared. For more tips on social media monitoring do's and don'ts check out this article from Small Business CEO: Considerations for Social Media Use in the Workplace.

Intercepting Email or Phone Conversations

Increasingly sophisticated ways of storing and accessing email have made it easier than ever for employers to monitor email accounts. But is this an invasion of privacy? The law is fuzzy.

The Electronic Communications Privacy Act (ECPA) of 1986 prohibits the intentional interception of "any wire, oral or electronic communication," but it does include a business use exemption that permits email and phone call monitoring.

This exemption often comes under close scrutiny by courts, and includes several elements. Generally, if an employee is **using a company-owned computer** or phone system, and an employer can show a **valid business** reason for monitoring that employee's email or phone conversations, then the employer is well within his or her rights to do so. Likewise, **if employees have consented to email or phone monitoring** (in their contract of employment, for example), then you may monitor their calls or emails.

But here's the rub: the ECPA draws a line between business and personal email content you can monitor—business content is ok, but personal emails are private.

Tip: If in doubt, consult your legal counsel. Develop and share a monitoring policy with employees (for example, in your employee handbook). If possible, get them to agree to it. Courts often look at whether employees were informed that their calls or emails might be monitored in the workplace, whether there was a valid business justification for the monitoring, and whether the employer complied with established policy.

CARON BEESLEY is a small business owner, a writer, and marketing communications consultant. Caron works with the SBA.gov team to promote essential government resources that help entrepreneurs and small business owners start-up, grow and succeed.

EXPLORING THE ISSUE

Does an Employer's Need to Monitor Workers Trump Employee Privacy Concerns?

Critical Thinking and Reflection

1. Would clearer or stricter guidelines on employee monitoring mitigate potential legal challenges?
2. Would different employee monitoring systems change employees' behavior?
3. Can employee behavior be effectively monitored?
4. Should employers monitor employee behavior? If so, under what circumstances or in which situations?

Is There Common Ground?

Both sides of this issue are concerned with protection. From the business or management point of view, employers feel a need to protect themselves from employee theft (physical and intellectual), low productivity, conflicts of interest, corporate liability, misuse and abuse of company-issued devices, and even harm to organizational reputation. The employee point of view is concerned with protection of personal privacy, freedom of expression, and a desire to maintain and augment trust in the workplace. As a result of these contrasting views of protection, in many instances where employee monitoring has been instituted an atmosphere of stress, distrust, and low company loyalty has resulted.

As technology's capability and scope evolves in the workplace, this issue's importance will continue to grow. For example, the growing trend of employees implementing "bring your own device" (BYOD) policies in the workplace has created both opportunities for businesses and employees, but also raised many questions requiring the introduction and revision of policies and even resulted in new legal rulings. While attempts to balance employer demands with legitimate employee privacy concerns have been made, there is consensus that employee monitoring will remain a complex issue that will receive significant attention and debate for quite some time. Ultimately, companies and employees must continue to work together to create an environment that is capable of protecting the interests of business and maintaining the rights of the employees who work within them.

Additional Resources

Boehle, S. (2008). "They're Watching You," *Training*, September, pp. 23–29.

Ciochetti, C.A. (2011). "The Eavesdropping Employer: A Twenty-First Century Framework for Employee Monitoring," *American Business Law Journal*, 48(2), pp. 285–369.

Curran, K., McIntyre, S., Meenan, H., McCloy, F. & Heaney, C. (2004). "Civil Liberties and Computer Monitoring," *American Journal of Applied Sciences*, 1(3), pp. 225–229.

Dupree, Jr, C.M. & Jude, R.K. (2006). "Who's Reading Your Email? Is That Legal?" *Strategic Finance*, April, 45–47.

Katz, L.M. (2015). "Big Employer is Watching," *HR Magazine*, 60(5), pp. 66–74.

Klemchuk, D.M. & Desai, S. (2014). "Can Employer Monitoring of Employee Social Media Violate the Electronic Communications Privacy Act?" *Intellectual Property & Technology Law Journal*, 26(2), pp. 9–13.

Lohr, S. (2014). "Unblinking Eyes Track Employees," *The New York Times*, June 22, A1.

Martin, K. & Freeman, E. (2003). "Some Problems with Employee Monitoring," *Journal of Business Ethics*, 43, pp. 353–361.

Urbaczewski, A. & Jessup, L.M. (2002). "Does Electronic Monitoring of Employee Internet Usage Work?" *Communications of the ACM*, 45(1), pp. 80–83.

Zetter, K. (2007). "Is Your Boss Spying on You?" *The Reader's Digest*, September, pp. 170–177.

Internet References . . .

Balancing Employee Monitoring with Privacy Concerns

http://www.businessnewsdaily.com/6685-employee
-monitoring-privacy.html

Don't Be an Every Minute Manager

http://www.businessweek.com/stories/2005-09-14
/dont-be-an-every-minute-manager

Firms Step up Employee Monitoring at Work

https://www.bostonglobe.com/business/2016/02/18
/firms-step-monitoring-employee-activities
-work/2I5hoCjsEZWA0bp10BzPrN/story.html

Little Brother is Watching You

https://www.scu.edu/ethics/focus-areas/business
-ethics/resources/littlebrother-is-watching-you/

Monitoring Employee Productivity: Proceed with Caution

https://www.shrm.org/hr-today/news/hr-magazine
/pages/0615-employee-monitoring.aspx

Survey: Many Companies Monitoring, Recording, Videotaping—and Firing—Employees

http://www.amanet.org/training/articles/Electronic
-Monitoring-Surveillane-12.aspx

Selected, Edited, and with Issue Framing Material by:
Kathleen J. Barnes, *William Paterson University*
and
George E. Smith, *University of South Carolina, Beaufort*

ISSUE

Is Workplace Drug Testing a Wise Corporate Policy?

YES: Elaine Davis and Stacie Hueller, from "Strengthening the Case for Workplace Drug Testing: The Growing Problem of Methamphetamines," *SAM Advanced Management Journal* (2006)

NO: Emily Gray Brosious, from "Public Schools Spend Major Cash on Ineffective Student Drug Testing Programs," *Extract* (2015)

Learning Outcomes

After reading this issue, you will be able to:

- Understand the positive and negative consequences of drug testing in the workplace.
- Understand how drug testing can be used as an effective workplace tool.
- Understand what policies might be implemented concerning workplace drug testing.
- Appreciate the practical managerial implications of drug testing policies used in the workplace.

ISSUE SUMMARY

YES: Scholars Elaine Davis and Stacie Hueller provide an analysis on how and why businesses should address the growing use of methamphetamines in the workplace.

NO: Sun-Times Network reporter Emily Gray Brosious cites several secondary schools that drug-test their students even in the light of numerous studies that show very little evidence that drug tests are effective.

Substance abuse costs employers tens of millions of dollars every year as a result of the increased levels of absenteeism, work-related accidents, health care costs, and theft. The National Institute on Drug Abuse reports that 75 percent of illegal drug users are employed and approximately 20 percent of 18- to 25-year-olds use drugs at the workplace. It's not surprising, then, that private employers across the country have adopted various types of drug-testing policies as a way of fighting back. The federal government is also involved in the battle, having entered with the passage of the Drug-free Workplace Act of 1988. This act requires all government agencies and firms with government contracts to take action toward eliminating drugs from the workplace.

Despite society's apparent acceptance of drug testing at work, there is considerable resistance to the policy of testing employees. Central to the opposition's position is the issue of employee privacy rights. Notwithstanding the indisputable fact that the corporations have a right to protect themselves, critics of workplace drug testing fear that it infringes on employee privacy rights. Critics also point to studies that call into question the degree to which employee productivity is truly affected by workplace drug-use.

Responses to the employee privacy issue have generally fallen into one of three categories and can be thought of as compromising a continuum of viewpoints. At one end of the continuum are those who are against drug testing in the workplace under any and all circumstances. This group typically invokes a rights-based argument in contending that individual rights always trump organizational rights. America is a country founded on the belief in the supremacy of individual rights and because drug testing violates an individual's right to privacy, organizations should not be allowed to implement them under any condition.

At the opposite end of this continuum reside the protesting advocates. The view here is that organizations are actually a collection of individuals who share common ownership of the firm and have a right to protect themselves and their property. In as much as they can be held accountable for the moral and legal violations committed by their employees, organizations should be allowed to exercise reasonable control over the workplace. Thus, when taking into account the tremendous damage drug abuse can inflict on an organization, workplace drug testing would appeal to be a reasonable managerial policy.

Perhaps the most commonly espoused view, representing the midpoint of our continuum, is that corporations should maintain employee privacy as an important corporate principle. Testing can be done, but all efforts should be made to protect employee privacy throughout the process, and testing should be implemented only in cases where reasonable grounds for suspicion exist. Thus, the determination to test an employee is made only when there is evidence that consumption of these substances results in undesirable behaviors such as lower productivity or increasing the likelihood of safety violations.

Before you read the following selections and develop your own opinion, some facts should be presented. It is important to know that the courts have consistently sided with the rights of corporations to test employees, provided there is no evidence of discrimination in its implementation or unwarranted targeting of specific individuals for testing. Also, courts have been particularly supportive when the job in question is of a sensitive nature.

Indeed, the fact that workplace drug testing is legal is seemingly attributable to its widespread use and practice by employers. Recent surveys of major American corporations indicate that nearly 90 percent of the firms use some type of drug testing. Almost all firms surveyed use tests as part of the applicant process and eliminate from consideration those individuals who fail (Gray & Brown, 2002). Thus, workplace drug testing is both legal and widespread; nevertheless, the question remains, Does that make it good corporate policy?

Supporting the view that workplace drug testing makes business sense are scholars Elaine Davis and Stacie Hueller. They focus attention on the growing number of methamphetamine use in society and in the workplace. After providing background on

the drug and the threat it poses in the workplace, the authors detail appropriate steps management can take to curb its use. Emily Gray Brosious questions the effectiveness of drug tests in deterring drug use. Specifically, she discusses how public schools are spending substantial money to test students participating in extracurricular activities even in light of numerous studies that show that drug tests are ineffective in deterring drug use.

Beyond the right-to-privacy argument, drug-testing opponents have raised a host of concerns. Foremost among these is the accuracy of the tests themselves. Critics point out that the repercussions from inaccurate test scores can be devastating not only to the specific individuals involved, but also to the rest of the workforce. Employee confidence in management's neutrality as well as the appropriateness of testing can be severely eroded if innocent individuals are punished or guilty employees go undetected.

Testing also seems to send a message of distrust from management to employees regardless of whether such a perception is accurate. As Emily Gray Brosious notes in her selection, another important concern is the expense of testing. There is, not surprisingly, a cost/accuracy tradeoff: Cheap tests are notoriously undependable, and highly accurate tests are extremely expensive. Small firms may have little choice but to use inexpensive tests while large firms with thousands of employees might find the costs to be prohibitive. Finally, critics fear that employers will use the information to target employees for dismissal on grounds that are completely unrelated to job performance.

Despite the valid points raised by the opposing side, supporters of drug-testing policies note that, often, those individuals who have a reason to fear drug tests are the ones who are most vocal against their use. By way of illustration of this point, consider the results of an interesting study: Human resource scholars found that students who had never used drugs were much more likely to support workplace drug-testing programs than were students who had used drugs in the past (Murphy, Thornton & Reynolds, 2002).

YES

Elaine Davis and Stacie Hueller

Strengthening the Case for Workplace Drug Testing: The Growing Problem of Methamphetamines

Introduction and Background

According to the National Institute on Drug Abuse (NIDA), an estimated 75% of illegal drug users are employed and one out of five workers in the 18–25 age bracket uses drugs at the worksite. Methamphetamine (meth) use, in particular, is causing growing alarm for employers across the U.S. In a 2004 summary report by Quest Diagnostics Inc. that analyzed all drug test results performed by the company, positive tests for meth increased 68% over a one-year period. The resulting negative workplace behaviors have caused many companies to increase drug screenings. According to Quest Diagnostics, the country's largest drug-testing company, the number of workers and applicants testing positive for meth has been rapidly increasing in the general workforce, led by southeastern states such as Georgia and Alabama. In addition, U.S. police raids of meth labs increased as much as 500%. Police nationwide rank methamphetamine the No. 1 drug they battle today: in a survey of 500 law-enforcement agencies in 45 states released in July of 2005 by the National Association of Counties, 58% said meth is their biggest drug problem. According to the World Health Organization, the drug is more abused worldwide than cocaine and heroin and is increasingly popular with workers in highly industrialized economies. Future projections indicate that meth use will surpass cocaine as the illegal stimulant of choice.

Implications for employers are great. The U.S. Department of Labor estimates annual workplace losses due to drug use of over $100 billion. Meth abuse losses are from accidents, health insurance and medical costs, absenteeism, tardiness, sick leave abuse, grievances, disability payments, lowered productivity, lowered co-worker morale, turnover, equipment damage, damage to public image, threats to public safety, worksite security and theft. According to the U.S. Center for Substance Abuse Prevention, National Clearinghouse for Alcohol and Drug Information (NCADI), drug users consume almost twice the employment benefits as nonusers, are absent 50% more often, and file more than twice as many workers' compensation claims.

The University of Arkansas Center for Business and Economic Research conducted an economic impact study in Benton County, Arkansas. According to the findings, meth use costs employers an estimated $42,000 per methusing-worker each year. This number does not include treatment, law enforcement, or other drug related expenditures. The Center identified five categories in which meth use most notably affects the workplace. The first and largest impact is on employee absenteeism; employees who use meth are five times more likely to miss work than non-using co-workers. Second, meth users are less productive; it takes four meth users to do the job of three non-meth users. Third, employee theft is more likely. Fourth, health insurance premiums are higher with meth users in the workplace. Lastly, employers pay more in workers' compensation costs because meth users are more likely to file claims and the claim is typically more expensive.

Meth use has moved across socio-economic levels. Once exclusively the choice of low-income people, truckers, and bikers, it is now being used by overworked secretaries, stressed teachers, soldiers on long battle missions, attorneys in law firms, and workers in the medical profession, all in attempts to boost concentration, stamina, and deal with the increasing work pressure of longer hours and need for greater productivity. Furthermore, meth is different from other illegal drugs used in the workplace. It causes more damage to the employee's brain, is more likely to cause mental illness in those who are predisposed, including psychosis, and increases the propensity to aggressive behavior and violence.

Alarm over meth use has intensified in the workplace and organizations are struggling with ways to handle the significant risks of employee abuse. This has led many companies that previously did not have drug policies to implement them and those with policies to revisit and clarify them. A drug-free workplace with well thought out drug-testing procedures, supervisor and staff training, and establishment of an Employee Assistance Program are key elements for organizations to ward off meth's effects. Many companies whose drug problems cannot be remedied using drug-free policies alone have enlisted the help of local law enforcement, and some evidence shows this has helped scale back the problem in the workplace.

Methamphetamine Overview

The drug. Use of amphetamines and their methyl subgroup methamphetamines has been widely documented, as early as the first German synthesis in 1887. They were used to treat asthma, low blood pressure, weight loss, depression, and as a stimulant, but over-the-counter sales were banned in the 1970s due to increasing abuses. The more potent meth is a highly addictive synthetic drug that stimulates the central nervous system with effects similar to the drug "speed." Meth can be taken orally, smoked, injected, or snorted. Known by names such as "ice," "Tina," "glass," and "crystal," meth users experience a high immediately after taking the drug, which lasts for 8 to 14 hours. During this time, users exhibit high energy behavior and usually do not eat or sleep. Methamphetamines work by blocking the brain's ability to rid itself of the euphoria-causing neurotransmitter dopamine. Meth is very similar to cocaine, but cocaine is metabolized more quickly in the body. Thus, the high achieved from meth last hours, compared to a cocaine high which lasts only 30–45 minutes; users often identify the long high as its main attraction. The hours-long meth high is also more suitable to people punching time clocks than the 30-minute cocaine high. Workers can't be running to the bathroom every half hour to get high on cocaine; if an employee does meth in the morning, he or she is good until noon. Meth is also often referred to as the "poor man's cocaine."

Short-term effects of meth use include increased attention and decreased fatigue, increased activity, decreased appetite, euphoria or rush, increased respiration, and hyperthermia. While short-term effects are mostly physical, long-term effects are both physical and psychological and include dependence and addiction, psychosis (paranoia, hallucinations, and mood disturbances), stroke, and severe weight loss. Chronic use can result in inflammation of the heart lining, episodes of violent behavior, extreme paranoia, anxiety, confusion, insomnia, and lead poisoning. Acute lead poisoning occurs because production requires lead acetate as a reagent. Errors during production can lead to drug contamination, which inevitably can poison users.

Continued meth use can damage areas of the brain related to cognition and memory which may persist even years after discontinuation of use. Meth addiction causes long-term, sometimes irreversible behavioral, cognitive, and psychological problems that can continue throughout life. According to Paul Thompson, a brain-mapping expert at UCLA, regular meth users lose about 1% of their brain cells every year, which is comparable to the loss experienced by people with Alzheimer's disease, stroke, and epilepsy. The long-term effects of meth are unusually harsh compared with other drugs.

- **Meth crime.** Because meth is relatively easy to make, abusers eventually attempt to make it themselves. With the advent of the Internet, methrecipes and ingredients are very accessible. Labs are typically found in rural areas; close proximity to farms and distant neighbors make obtaining chemicals necessary for production easy and detection less likely. In Minnesota, the Department of Corrections (DOC) reports that compared to other criminal offenses (which tend to be concentrated in large urban areas) meth has been largely a rural phenomenon, with 72% of the meth offenders incarcerated outside metro counties. This rural overrepresentation is even greater for those imprisoned for the manufacture and sale of meth, with 87% of the offenders coming from rural Minnesota. The Minnesota DOC also reports that as of July 1, 2005, meth inmates constituted 49% of drug offenders in Minnesota prisons. Statistics from the Minnesota Department of Public Safety reveal that meth lab seizures rose more than 700 percent between 1998 and 2003. Minnesota's experience is not unlike that of neighboring states, with Iowa particularly hard hit. Missouri tops the list with more than 8,000 labs, equipment caches, and toxic dumps seized between 2002 and 2004.

- **Company culture.** Employees are being asked by their employers to do more, and meth seems to provide a good solution to busy work schedules and demanding bosses. Many occupations demand long hours of repetitive work, such as construction and manufacturing, and, as a result, these are the most common workplaces where employees use methamphetamines. However, methamphetamine is increasingly a white-collar drug as well; its use is growing in the entertainment, sales, retail, and legal professions. The California Bar Association revealed that one in four lawyers who are admitted voluntarily to drug rehabilitation are addicted to methamphetamines.

In pursuit of increased products and profits, it is easy for corporations and managers to remain unaware of methamphetamine abuse. Although the increasing us of meth consistently makes headlines, part of corporate America doesn't recognize it as a serious problem. Researchers, counselors, and government officials say employers have done little to address the erratic behavior, accidents, increased sick days, and health costs attributed to or associated with its use. According to former workers and addicts at a recreational vehicle manufacturing facility in South Bend, Indiana, their employer was aware of the prevalent meth use, but did nothing about it. According to these workers, employers benefit from allowing employees to use meth. It allows them to be more productive by working faster and avoiding accidents because of their increased state of alertness. This contradicts earlier statistics citing the heavy financial cost of meth use.

Further examples of complacent corporations are those with employees known as "maintenance users." Maintenance users are hard to recognize because "many of the drug's initial characteristics, increased concentration and the ability to work longer hours are traits valued by managers and unlikely to be seen as a problem." Initially, the drug does increase performance. In defense of corporations, some users can hide their methamphetamine use for a very long time and not have altered performance.

Prevention and Solutions: Creating a Drug Free Workplace

According to the Department of Labor and the Department of Health and Human Services Drug Free Workplace Guidelines, a drug-free workplace adheres to a program of policies and activities that discourage alcohol and drug abuse and encourages treatment, recovery, and return to work. The Substance Abuse and Mental Health Services Administration (SAMHSA), a division of the Department of Health and Human Services, advocates six components for a drug-free workplace program: assessment, policy, education and training, EAPs, and drug testing. . . .

Needs assessment involves assessing the current state of drug addiction in your workplace, determining areas needing focused attention and the means by which to evaluate any newly implemented programs. Quantifiable measures of success could include lower absenteeism, reduced turnover, and fewer accidents and workers' compensation claims.

Policy development is the foundation of a drug-free workplace. A written policy tells employees the organization's position on drug abuse and explains what will happen if the policy is violated. Consultation with an attorney is warranted to ensure compliance with state and federal law, particularly with nonregulated industries outside the scope of the Drug-Free Workplace Act of 1988, which mandates a drug-free workplace for recipients of federal contracts and grants. Because each state's laws governing drug testing in the workplace are different, establishing a well-written policy will help companies comply with state and federal laws and meet legal challenges.

Employers should determine which types of drugs they will be testing for, since different tests target specific drugs. Employers' policies should also state what will happen to employees or new hires if they test positive for drug use, such as termination or the chance to enter a companysponsored drug treatment program. Some states mandate rehabilitation and do not allow dismissal. Employers in states without such mandates must decide what they are willing to pay for, since meth treatment can last as long as a year and is very costly. In addition, the policy should set limits on when employees are eligible for rehire after drug-related termination. A drug-free policy must be clear to employees and must be applied consistently from executives to entry-level employees. It is also important for U.S. companies that conduct business internationally to have a standard drug testing policy, because other countries are also feeling the effect of methamphetamines in the workplace. . . .

Employee education is vital and must be more than sending an e-mail to all employees outlining the policy and requiring their adherence. Essential education includes the policy, how to get assistance and referrals, how employee performance problems will be evaluated, appeal provisions, procedures of drug testing if testing is included, confidentiality, and other employee protections in the policy. Companies that proactively advertise a drug-free workplace and offer education to employees, can help deter substance abuse in the workplace. Not only does education help employees understand the effects of substance abuse on their company, it also helps employees identify the common signs of abuse. Corporations who sponsor programs for a drug-free workplace will also display goodwill towards their communities in helping the fight against methamphetamines.

Supervisor training is essential so they know the signs and symptoms of meth abuse and know company policy so they can explain it to other employees. They also need to understand their role, which is not to diagnose addiction but to rate employee performance. The quickest way to spot potential problems is to know your employee's performance. If it starts to decline, steps should be taken to find out why. Supervisors should have comprehensive detailed training about the specifics of the policy. They should learn how to assess situations appropriately and act in the event employees violate the policy. The mandatory training should be documented to prove that supervisors attended and the policy was covered in detail.

Employee Assistance Programs (EAP) offer help to employees and their families with drug and alcohol abuse problems, in addition to personal and work-related problems such as health, finances, and marital and social issues. As part of these programs it is important to address the needs of employees who are not abusers themselves but may face these problems due to a loved one's addiction. EAP enrollment has increased steadily over the past 10 years. EAP play a key role in the fight against meth abuse, providing necessary counseling to employees.

Drug testing serves as a deterrent to continued use of illicit substances and provides a means to detect and identify employees or job applicants who are using meth. Through detection and identification, employers may be able to assist employees in recognizing and admitting their abuse problems so that they may obtain necessary treatment. The American Management Association reports that 60% of employers test employees and new hires.

According to the Joseph Rowntree Foundation, the four fundamental reasons for employing drug testing in the workplace are safety, organizational efficiency, reputation risk, and employee welfare. Employees under the influence of meth at work pose a risk to themselves and others, and employers have a duty to their employees to maintain a safe working environment. Drug testing allows organizations to remain efficient by "weeding out" users who are unproductive, have high rates of absenteeism, and cause high turnover rates. Furthermore, some companies drug test solely because they are concerned about potential damage to their reputations by drug users.

Four common programs are used by companies to test current and prospective employees for drug abuse: random testing, reasonable suspicion testing, post-accident testing, and return-to-work testing. Many states discourage or restrict random testing. Employers have the right to test based on reasonable suspicion, but must have documentation supporting their suspicions. They must provide transportation to and from the testing facility to keep the suspected user from driving under the influence. Postaccident testing is common in many workplaces when human error may be the cause of accidents. A positive post-accident test may prevent employees from collecting workers' compensation or unemployment benefits.

Return-to-work testing is often a stipulation for employees after participating in a drug treatment program. Employees often sign "contracts" with their employers outlining the procedures they must follow to return to work. Elements of the contract often include ongoing rehabilitation programs, passing drug tests upon returning to work, and submitting to unannounced, repeated drug testing. The contracts also state that if the employee fails to follow any of the procedures, employment will be terminated.

While urine and blood testing are the most prevalent, they are also the easiest methods for which users can submit fraudulent specimens. Hair, sweat, and saliva cannot be tampered with as easily; however, a simple Web search for "drug testing" lists numerous Web sites touting advice and selling kits to help drug users pass any type of drug screenings. Recent arrests of some high-profile athletes and movie actors have focused attention on The Whizzinator, a product worn inside pants to conceal a tampered urine sample. As companies get more aggressive in their drug testing and enforcement, more products will be marketed to beat the tests.

Examples of companies who are successfully dealing with meth are numerous. Creative Memories, a large scrapbook manufacturer in St. Cloud, Minnesota, became aggressive with drug testing, policy enforcement, and creating a rehabilitation culture that encourages employees to seek help. The company has seen positive results. HR Director Cindy Mason-Sebastian has been so impressed with the results that she now takes one of her employees, formerly addicted to meth, with her to make team presentations to other organizations on how to control meth in the workplace. One employee tells groups that "getting caught by Creative Memories was the best thing that ever happened to me." Matson Navigation Co., a shipping company in Hawaii, added an educational film to their training lineup. It had been made specifically for the shipping industry and showed maritime workers using meth, which is particularly dangerous in that industry. The impact on employees of seeing co-workers on screen was profound.

Alternatives. Although drug testing and drug-free workplace policies are the two most common methods of handling drug use, there are other alternatives. For most companies, policies that include drug testing, education, and training will be comprehensive enough to curtail most of employee drug use. However, some companies find they need stronger measures. A harsher measure for drug prevention is establishing an undercover operation in conjunction with local law enforcement. Such operations are being undertaken by more organizations with systemic meth problems. Although time intensive (nearly 15 months at a plant in Baltimore), undercover operations are often successful, especially when meth use is widespread or sales are occurring on site. An undercover officer applies for a position, typically a janitor or position that allows mobility throughout the workplace, and then infiltrates a group of users or dealers. After building trust and sometimes simulating drug use with the offenders, the officer collects data that eventually lead to arrests. To maintain confidentiality at the company, only corporate security and Human Resource executives are aware of the investigation until completion. At a GM plant in Baltimore, undercover agents worked for 15 months to collect evidence that led to the arrest of 24 people.

Conclusion

Methamphetamine abuse is a growing problem across the United States and has grave implications for companies, especially major employers in rural areas. Employers see their labor pool shrink as potential employees are passed over due to a positive drug test, or existing employees begin using and are fired for excessive absences, low productivity, or other costly behaviors. Employers have been forced to spend thousands of dollars to implement drug testing to maintain a safe environment. Meth abuse brings a multitude of problems to corporations, and their Human Resources departments may the frontlines of this dilemma.

Meth use may continue, but employers, communities, and law enforcement can work collaboratively at least to stop continued growth in usage. To control this increasing problem, companies need to develop a drug-free policy, educate employees, train supervisors, perform drug tests regularly, and assist employees who need help with abuse. Developing a comprehensive drug-free workplace is a huge undertaking, but the costs of not doing so are even greater. Companies cannot afford to be complacent.

ELAINE DAVIS is St. Cloud State University's G. R. Herberger Distinguished Professor of Business and has published over 40 journal articles on human resources topics.

STACIE HUELLER is an accounting instructor at Minneapolis Business College and a certified public accountant.

Emily Gray Brosious

 **NO**

Public Schools Spend Major Cash on Ineffective Student Drug Testing Programs

More Schools Are Drug Testing Students than Ever Before

Between all of the studying, the exams, the social maneuvering and the harsh discipline, high school can be a stressful place for students these days.

Now throw random drug testing in the mix—positive learning environment, right?

Much like the rest of the country's embrace of tough-on-crime policing and sentencing over the past few decades, public schools have also turned toward harsh disciplinary styles and zero-tolerance policies.

Between 2006 and 2012, public high schools with random drug testing programs rose from 14 to 18 percent, and schools across the country are currently considering implementing mandatory drug testing programs, according to *The Washington Post*.

Daily Kos recently reported on a Wisconsin high school in the Crivitz school district that plans to start drug testing students to allegedly "deter" drug abuse.

Regulations prevent the district from drug testing all students, but it can test any student who is involved in extracurricular activities or who parks their car on school property.

Per Daily Kos:

"We have a growing drug problem in Marinette County and in talking with the police force and talking with school administrators and other conference athletic directors, I just felt that as a school we could do something to try to deter students," said Crivitz High School Athletic Director, Jeff Dorschner.

Another recent report from *The Washington Post* tells of a school district in Carroll County Georgia that's implementing a "random drug testing program for their public high school students."

The school plans to test up to 80 students each month, with each drug test costing about $24—that adds up to about $20,000 annually.

Like many schools that drug test, Carroll County's testing will only apply to public high school students who drive to school and students who participate in extracurricular activities.

Nearly one in five public high schools have similar mandatory drug testing policies, according to the Centers for Disease Control & Prevention.

Per *The Washington Post*:

It may seem odd that a school can require your kid to get tested simply for joining, say, the chess club. But the Supreme Court upheld the constitutionality of such programs in 2002. "We find that testing students who participate in extracurricular activities is a reasonably effective means of addressing the school district's legitimate concerns in preventing, deterring and detecting drug use," Clarence Thomas wrote for the 5–4 majority.

But schools are increasingly pushing further. For instance, a nationally-representative survey of 1,300 school districts found that among the districts with drug testing programs, 28 percent randomly tested *all* students—not just ones participating in after-school programs. These schools are opening themselves up to a legal challenge.

Why Do Schools Drug Test Students

Good question. Considering students with hard substance abuse issues are somewhat easy to identify based on academic performance and school behavior alone, it seems like drug testing is a bit of overkill. Unless, of course, the goal is to find out which students are using marijuana, as that may not be readily obvious.

Indeed, critics say such drug testing policies are meant to target those students who use particular substances, like marijuana, "while ignoring steroid use by some athletes," according to Counter Current News.

School districts and administrators typically say drug testing is done to deter drug use, but numerous studies have shown very little evidence that drug tests are effective in this regard.

The Washington Post notes that they don't test for "the one drug that is most favored by high school students, and which is also the most hazardous to their health: alcohol."

There are also plenty of potentially negative impacts that drug testing might have on students and schools:

- Drug testing may cause fewer student to get involved in extracurricular activities.
- Drug tests may violate students' privacy rights by exposing to administrators any medications a student might be taking.
- Drug tests may result in harsh disciplinary action—including suspension and expulsion—that can harm a student's prospects of attending a desired college or university.

- Drug testing programs are expensive for school districts, and the vast majority of students tested do not test positive for drugs. (*The Washington Post* reports it costs about $3,000 for each positive test.)

EMILY GRAY Brosious is a Chicago-based multimedia journalist covering national marijuana news and culture for the Sun Times Network's news vertical site.

EXPLORING THE ISSUE

Is Workplace Drug Testing a Wise Corporate Policy?

Critical Thinking and Reflection

1. Would guidelines on drug testing mitigate potential legal challenges?
2. Would different drug-testing methods change employees' behavior?
3. Will a drug-testing policy spur other ways for employees to use drugs?
4. Can organizations truly monitor and control employee behavior in this arena?
5. What are the ethical issues and limitations of workplace drug testing?
6. Can employees' drug use on their personal time be effectively contained?

Is There Common Ground?

Neither side of this issue appears to negate the notion that employee and customer safety and employee productivity are important outcomes that may be potentially gained through an effective drug-testing program. However, the two sides of this debate disagree on the message that the requirement to take a test sends to employees and the perception of privacy violations. Some employees perceive the testing to be a sign of distrust and feel it to be a clear violation and disregard of personal privacy and individual rights.

As with other issues in this book the issue of equity or fairness also emerges in this issue's discussion. Specifically, the question of how systematic and formalized are the corporate testing processes and procedures. The raising of these issues has led corporations to improve their approaches to drug testing through additional training and education, better explanation of the timing of testing, and greater clarity of the substances being tested for. Furthermore, loopholes in systems that may have allowed some employees to skirt testing have been challenged and come under legal scrutiny and pressure.

If nothing else, there is consensus that workplace drug testing is a highly charged topic. The present movement to legalize previously controlled substances for "recreational use" will continue to fuel this discussion and drive its debate for quite some time.

Additional Resources

Gies, T.P. & Grant, G.D. (2015). "The Legalization of Marijuana: What It Means for Employer Drug Testing," *Employee Relations Law Journal*, 41(1), pp. 35–46.

Glasser, N.M. & Hoerner, J.K. (2016). "The Growing Conflict Between Drug, Employment Laws," *HR Focus*, January, pp. 1–4.

Mathis, R.L. & Jackson, J.H. (2007). *Human Resource Management*, 11th ed., New York: Thompson South-Western.

Tunnell, K.D. (2004). *Pissing on Demand: Workplace Drug-Testing and the Rise of the Detox Industry*, New York: NYU Press.

Weber, L. (2015). "Drug Use Is on the Rise Among Workers in U.S.," *Wall Street Journal*, June 3, 265(128), pp. B1–B7.

References

Gray, G. & Brown, D. (2002). *Perspectives in Business Ethics*, 2nd ed., Laura P. Hartman, ed., New York: McGraw-Hill, p. 433.

Murphy, K.R., Thornton, G.C. & Reynolds, D.H. (2002). *Perspectives in Business Ethics*, 2nd ed., Laura P. Hartman, ed., New York: McGraw-Hill Irwin.

Internet References . . .

Drug Testing in the Workplace

http://workrights.us/?products=drug-testing
-in-the-workplace

Establishing a Drug-Free Workplace

www.businessweek.com/smallbiz/content/aug2007
/sb2007081_883800.htm

National Institute on Drug Abuse

http://www. NIDA.nih.gov

Privacy in America: Workplace Drug Testing

https://www.aclu.org/workplace-drug-testing

Reasons for Drug-Testing

http://workplace.samhsa.gov/DrugTesting/pdf/Reasons
%20for%20Drug%20Testing%20-%20
February%202005.pdf

**Second Federal Court in Two Weeks Halts
Suspicionless Drug Testing of Teachers**

www.aclu.org/drugpolicy/testing/38356prs
20090115.html

The Pointlessness of the Workplace Drug Test

http://www.theatlantic.com/business/archive/2015
/06/drug-testing-effectiveness/394850/

**Why Do Employers Still Routinely Drug-Test
Workers**

http://www.slate.com/articles/health_and_science
/cover_story/2015/12/workplace_drug_testing_is
_widespread_but_ineffective.html

Selected, Edited, and with Issue Framing Material by:
Kathleen J. Barnes, *William Paterson University*
and
George E. Smith, *University of South Carolina, Beaufort*

ISSUE

Is Social Media a Tool of Expression or Trouble for Businesses?

YES: Christopher E. Parker, from "The Rising Tide of Social Media," *The Federal Lawyer* (2011)

NO: David L. Barron, from "Social Media: Frontier for Employee Disputes," *Baseline* (2012)

Learning Outcomes
After reading this issue, you will be able to:
• Understand the positive and negative consequences of social media in the workplace.   • Understand how social media can be used as an effective workplace tool.   • Understand why organizations might implement policies concerning social media.   • Appreciate the legal implications of social media use in the workplace.

ISSUE SUMMARY

YES: Christopher E. Parker argues that the prevalence of social media is quite clear and a useful tool for business. Many employers now routinely use social networking sites in advertising, marketing, communication, and decision making, and to conduct research about the backgrounds of job candidates.

NO: David L. Barron argues that employees are increasingly making complaints to human resources departments and management over offensive or harassing statements made online. With the rise of cyber-bullying and "textual harassment," employees must be made to understand that company policies extend into cyber-space and social media forums, and these policies must be followed.

"Social media" is a broad term that generally includes various electronic and web-based means of disseminating or sharing information. Social media includes Facebook, LinkedIn, Twitter, MySpace, YouTube, blogs, chat rooms, wikis, photo-sharing sites, and more. The use of social media is becoming not only increasingly prevalent in the daily lives of people from all walks of life, but also a greater presence in the daily business of many employers.

With employees using social media more frequently in both their private lives and at their jobs, the lines between appropriate and inappropriate uses of this technology are easily blurred. The utility of social media is not limited to the private lives of individuals as a form of self-expression. Businesses are increasingly using social media in advertising, marketing, communication, and decision making related to employment issues.

There are various social media situations that may create headaches for employers. For example, a supervisor who "friends" subordinates in a discriminatory fashion (e.g., only members of the same race or ethnic group) is running the risk of being perceived as unfair or, even worse, a racist. Managers who hack into or gain access to employees' social media sites in violation of security protections or permissions are doing so at the risk of violating employee privacy. Similarly, texts, tweets, and electronic communications can become the subject of a workplace investigation if a complaint is made. Finally, some postings on social media sites have been deemed by the National Labor Relations Board (NLRB) to be protected activity.

With new technology and communications avenues come new obligations and challenges to police and regulate those avenues in the workplace. Although each workplace is different and there is no one-size-fits-all approach to social media, it is critical for employers to recognize the risks and, at a minimum, provide some reasonable guide-posts for employee conduct.

To mitigate potential issues surrounding social media, companies should strongly consider establishing clear policies regarding the following work-related issues:

- use of the company's hardware, software, and computer systems;
- harassment, including via social media;
- trade secrets of the businesses;
- need for confidentiality, non-compete, and non-solicitation;
- use of social media and electronic communication during nonworking hours; and
- social networking and the Federal Communication Commission's (FCC) requirements.

Our two authors examine the issue of social media in the workplace from different perspectives. Christopher Parker argues that the prevalence of social media is quite clear and a potentially useful tool for business. Many employers now routinely use social networking sites in advertising, marketing, communication, and decision making, and to conduct research about the backgrounds of job candidates. David Barron, on the other hand, argues that employees are increasingly making complaints to human resources departments and management over offensive or harassing statements made online. With the rise of cyber-bullying and "textual harassment," employees must be made to understand that company policies extend into cyberspace and social media forums, and these policies must be followed. Both authors do agree that social media in the workplace is in the midst of a state of growth and flux and employers should thoughtfully identify and implement guidelines needed to avoid potentially costly and damaging lawsuits.

YES

Christopher E. Parker

The Rising Tide of Social Media

Guess what? The manner in which employees communicate, both within and outside the workplace, has changed. It's not just e-mails and text messaging anymore, but a broad category of platforms collectively referred to as "social media." These media are now beginning to influence the workplace—the same workplace where we spend many of our waking hours before adjourning to discuss how this time was spent with our friends, family, and connections in cyberspace (known and unknown). Increased communication brings increased opportunity to offend and breach confidences in ways that may have a significant impact on a business. As with all things new, the courts and administrative agencies are hustling to respond and develop the legal landscape involved in using social media.

"Social media" is a broad term that generally includes various electronic and web-based means of disseminating or sharing information, including Facebook®, LinkedIn®, Twitter®, MySpace®, YouTube®, blogs, chat rooms, wikis, photo-sharing sites, and more. The use of social media is becoming not only increasingly prevalent in the daily lives of people from all walks of life but also a greater presence in the daily business of many employers.

With employees using social media more frequently in both their private life and at their jobs, the lines between the uses are easily blurred. Are an employee's after-hours comments on a workplace incident subject to regulation or discipline? Where does one draw the line when the screen name or identity of the individual posting the message is unknown or difficult to decipher? Does it make a difference if the employee clearly identifies himself or herself with the message? Is there a difference in what is considered an appropriate response to a comment about a co-worker as compared to company management? Some of the answers to these potential dilemmas are seemingly obvious; others are not. Legal issues and challenges concerning social media in the workplace are currently winding their way through the court systems, and the legal outcomes are as uncertain as the myriad of fact patterns that may be presented.

The Use of Social Media

The prevalence of social media is quite clear. Facebook claims to have 500 million active users (www.facebook.com/press/info .php?statistics) and, even though the estimate is impossible to verify, there are over 70 million blogs, with almost 1.5 million being added each day. The utility of social media is not limited to the private lives of individuals. Businesses are increasingly using social media in advertising, marketing, communication, and decision-making related to employment issues.

Many employers now routinely use social-networking sites to conduct research about the backgrounds of job candidates. The information runs the gauntlet of potentially delicate information that is assembled about an applicant as part of the hiring process: alcohol use, social groups, religion, age, sexual preference, and the list goes on and on. To further complicate the issue, employees (or applicants) may feel a false sense of privacy or anonymity about the information they are sharing over the Internet, leading them to share too much information about themselves with their employer or too much information about their employer with others. The informality of social networking undoubtedly contributes to piece-meal bites (or perhaps "bytes") of information that may lead to inaccurate and unfortunate conclusions. Claims of invasion of privacy or unlawful discrimination abound.

Potential Effects of Social Media on the Relationship Between the Employer and the Employee

The terrain for potential claims relating to social media and its impact on the workplace is still in the development stage. The gut-level reaction most frequently observed from employees who learn that their employer has checked them out online is a claim of invasion of privacy. These claims, despite their naïveté when it comes to the Internet, can be (legally) frustrated by an employer's well-drafted policy advising applicants and employees of exactly how publicly accessible information may be used as part of the decision-making process in the workplace. A simple declaration that public sources of information, including social media portals, may be considered in the determination or evaluation of the applicant or employee may help dispel any expectation of privacy on the part of an employee.

Privacy claims are not the only landmine with which employers need to contend. The Stored Communications Act, 18 U.S.C. 2701, protects the privacy of stored Internet communications.

Although the protections do not apply to communications "readily accessible to the general public," the main issue in the context of workplace disputes is how the employer gained access to the information. A case heard by the Fourth Circuit Court of Appeals— *Van Alstyne v. Electronic Scriptorium Ltd.*, 560 F.3d 199 (4th Cir. 2009)— involved an employer who was accused of violating the Stored Communications Act by improperly accessing an employee's personal e-mail account. The employee discovered the e-mail "break-in" only when the employer tried to present the e-mails as evidence against the employee in a sexual harassment claim she had filed. In another case, the New Jersey District Court found that employers had violated the Stored Communications Act—but not the employee's common law right to privacy—by gaining access to the employee's chat group on MySpace without the employee's authorization. The employer gained access to the chat group only after coercing another employee to provide the password. *Pietrylo v. Hillside Restaurant Group*, No. 06-5754 (FSH), 2009 WL 3128420 (D.N.J. Sept. 25, 2009). In both cases, the employer was found to have overstepped legal boundaries by gaining access to information that had been subject to security efforts without proper permission.

The Fair Credit Reporting Act requires the consent of an applicant or an employee before an employer can ask a "consumer reporting agency" or another third party to conduct a background check and produce a "consumer report" or other written report of its findings. Even though employers may use consumer reports that contain information from social-networking sites, they must disclose to their employees that such information was the basis for any adverse actions that may have been taken. The Fair Credit Reporting Act does *not* prevent employers from reviewing social-networking sites themselves; however, the act leaves a loophole for employers to do background checks.

The Electronic Communications Privacy Act makes it unlawful to listen to or observe the contents of a private communication without the permission of at least one party to the communication. In addition, the act prohibits parties from intentional interception, access, disclosure, or use of another party's electronic communications. This law has been interpreted to include e-mail communications and may provide some protections for employees' privacy. There are, however, exceptions that the employer may find helpful.

Potential Discrimination Claims Against the Employer

Even though the possibility of an unfiltered look at a job candidate may be tempting, the employer faces serious risks when using the Internet to investigate employees and job applicants. These risks include the potential of discovering information that the employer is not allowed to ask in person or use in the selection or disciplinary process. Using Facebook as an example, many people have listed

information for their personal profile that reveals their race, political affiliation, age, sexual orientation, national origin, and more. Status updates, tweets, and blogs may also reveal a person's potential disabilities, past medical conditions, or the medical conditions of family members.

Potential Implications of Employees' Postings and Social Media Content on the Employer

Employers must beware of confidential information to which employees have access through their jobs becoming public knowledge through employees' use of social media, even in the apparent context of the employee's role as a private individual. Not only can employees leak confidential information about their companies, they may knowingly or unknowingly publish confidential information about their employers' clients or business associates. For example, if an employee works for a health care provider and later "tweets" about a patient at work, that employee could be disseminating information protected by the Health Insurance Portability and Accountability Act (HIPAA) creating serious liabilities for the employer. Other communications by employees may implicate federal copyright or trademark laws. Although many of these types of communications would be unexpected and subject to monitoring if they occurred within the workplace, the user's theoretical anonymity when using the Internet and social media outlets can lead to unexpected consequences.

Guidelines issued by the Federal Trade Commission regarding endorsements and testimonials in advertising may have serious implications for an employee's online activity. The guidelines require all endorsers, including employees, to disclose "material connections" between the endorser and the product or company about which they comment. Because material connections include employment relationships, if a company's employee enjoys contributing to websites dedicated to product reviews, for example, and discusses a product produced by his or her employer, the employee may be considered an endorser and must then abide by the Federal Trade Commission's guidelines. An employer can be held accountable for an employee's actions every time the employee tweets or changes his or her Facebook status regarding a new product at work. A company may then face liability for any unsubstantiated or false claims made by employees, even if they are not authorized to make such comments.

This example further highlights the importance of having thoughtful technology use and confidentiality policies in place for both on-duty and off-duty use.

Training employees about the potential consequences of their actions and the way to best use—or not to use—social media, even on their own time, may be just as important as properly disseminating a written policy. However, policies governing the use of a company's technology, which include off-duty activities, cannot simply ban social media use in its entirety. As discussed below, overbroad policies dealing with use of technology can create liabilities of their own for employers.

Protected Speech and Activity

When dealing with an employee who is using social media in a way the employer does not like or with which the employer does not want to be associated, many employers would simply prefer to terminate the employee who is using social media in that way. Although termination would often seem to be the ideal resolution for the employer in situations like this, employers must be careful when making this decision. Even though the First Amendment does not protect an employee of a private employer from termination or adverse action because of the content of online postings, the content of the postings and information may invoke other kinds of protection, such as Title VII of the Civil Rights Act of 1964. Depending on the content of the online communication, whistle-blower protections under state and federal laws may also be triggered.

Recently, the National Labor Relations Board (NLRB) issued a complaint after an employee was fired from American Medical Response of Connecticut for posting negative comments about her supervisor on her Facebook page. The employer had a policy prohibiting employees from making disparaging remarks about the company or supervisors and from discussing the company "in any way" over the Internet, including via social networks, without advance permission. The NLRB argued that policies restricting an employee's right to criticize working conditions, including the right to publish such criticisms to co-workers, violates the National Labor Relations Act. Faced with further litigation with the NLRB, the case was settled in early February 2011, with the employer agreeing to refrain from limiting the rights of its employees to communicate on work-related issues away from the workplace.

What Should an Employer Do?

The legal arena surrounding the use of social media in the workplace is in the midst of what may be a lengthy evolution. Employers have to balance their own needs to protect their assets against the legal rights of their employees. Companies should strongly consider establishing clear policies regarding several work-related issues:

- use of the company's hardware, software, and computer systems;
- harassment, including via social media;
- trade secrets of the business;
- need for confidentiality, non-compete, and non-solicitation;
- use of social media and electronic communication during nonworking hours; and
- social networking and the Federal Communication Commission's requirements.

Employers' policies should prohibit employees from discussing, including through social media, company information that is confidential or proprietary; clients', partners', vendors', and suppliers' information that is confidential or proprietary; and information that has been embargoed, such as product launch dates or release dates; and pending organizations. At the same time, employers need to recognize that across-the-board restrictions on communications are subject to challenge. Policies related to use of technology and electronic communication should cover use of the company's intellectual property; sexual references; obscenity; reference to illegal drugs; disparagement of any race, religion, gender, age, sexual orientation, disability, or national origin; and the disparagement of the company's or competitors' products, services, executive leadership, employees, strategy, and business prospects.

One cautionary note must be made: The information provided in this column is intended to apply primarily to employment in the private sector. Employers in the public sector face additional limitations on the potential restraints that can be imposed based on the Constitution. As with all such issues, employment policies and decisions related to new issues raised by the widespread use of social media should be discussed with legal counsel, because the landscape is in a state of growth and rapid change.

CHRISTOPHER E. PARKER is a member in the Atlanta, Georgia office of Miller & Martin PILC and serves as the vice-chair for the firm's labor and employment law practice. He is a former chair of the FBA Labor and Employment Law Section and a past president of the Atlanta Chapter of the FBA. Parker received BS and JD degrees from the Ohio State University.

David L. Barron

Social Media: Frontier for Employee Disputes

Ten years ago, employers struggled to adapt their policies to the Internet and email. Today, the new frontier is social media.

With new technology and communication avenues come new obligations to police and regulate those same avenues in the workplace. Although each workplace is different and there is no one-size-fits-all approach to social media, it is critical for employers to recognize the risks and, at a minimum, provide some reasonable guideposts for employee conduct.

Textual Harassment

No employer wants to be the "Facebook police," but employees are increasingly making complaints to human resources departments and management over offensive or harassing statements made online. With the rise of cyber-bullying and "textual harassment," employees must be made to understand that company policies extend into cyberspace and social media forums, and these policies must be followed.

If an employee makes a complaint about online activity, it should be investigated just like any other complaint of harassment or discrimination. That said, an investigation can often be hampered by the lack of access to social media sites.

Suggestions to work around this problem include requesting that witnesses provide screen shots or copies of offending text messages. The employer can also request that an accused employee provide access to his or her Facebook page for the limited purpose of verifying whether the allegations are true. If such access is refused, consider taking statements from employees who may have seen the relevant statements made on a social media site.

Facebook Perils

It has become clear that real liability issues are associated with managers "friending" subordinates. It's unlawful for a manager to inquire in the workplace about certain personal information that's displayed on social media sites. For example, a manager who discovers on Facebook that an employee has a serious illness may later be accused of unlawful discrimination.

In addition, a supervisor who friends subordinates in a discriminatory fashion (e.g., only members of the same race or ethnic group) is running the risk of being perceived as unfair or, even

worse, a racist. Since friending some supervised employees but not others is a risky proposition that could lead to hurt feelings or lawsuits, many companies have advised supervisors to refrain from friending workers who are in a direct line of supervision.

Employee Privacy

It should go without saying that management must never hack into or gain access to employees' social media sites in violation of security protections or permissions. If a site is viewable by the public, however, an employee has no right to privacy, and no permission is required.

Gray areas arise where a worker who has access to another worker's site brings information to management without the other employee's permission. Most courts agree that employees allow access to their Facebook page at their own peril. If someone shares that information with an employer, that is a risk assumed by the employee who granted the access. Simply put, an employer need not ignore evidence of misconduct because it comes through an indirect source.

Similarly, texts, tweets and electronic communications can become the subject of a workplace investigation if a complaint is made. One thing to keep in mind is that an employer can lawfully search employee-owned cell phones only if the employer provides notice in its policies that employees have no expectation of privacy for information stored on these devices. As long as such notice is provided, an employer has the right to search a cell phone, just as it would to search a vehicle or purse if a violation of policy is suspected.

Other Headaches

There are a number of emerging legal issues that have created headaches for employers. First, some postings on social media sites have been deemed by the National Labor Relations Board to be protected activity.

Firing an employee over an online social media complaint about wages, a "jerk" boss or employment conditions, for example, can lead to a lawsuit. Some states also have laws protecting employees from discipline for lawful offduty conduct. Thus far, it is unclear whether these laws will apply to social media activity.

Also, employers should exercise caution in setting up their own social media pages and allowing nonexempt employees to monitor and update those pages. Blogging, tweeting or posting company-related information online is considered work, and hourly employees must be compensated for this time, including any applicable overtime.

In summary, having a social media policy is no longer relevant only for high-tech companies and large corporations. Employers of all sizes and industries are facing substantial legal risks, and they should review this emerging area to identify what guidelines need to be implemented to avoid lawsuits.

DAVID L. BARRON is a labor and employment attorney at Cozen O'Connor's Houston office.

EXPLORING THE ISSUE

Is Social Media a Tool of Expression or Trouble for Businesses?

Critical Thinking and Reflection

1. Would workplace guidelines on social media mitigate potential legal issues for an employer?
2. Would workplace guidelines on social media affect employee behavior?
3. Will a social media control policy spur attempts to find other ways to obtain information on co-workers and colleagues?
4. Should employers be allowed to prevent employee expression via social media?

Is There Common Ground?

There appears to be a consensus that social media in the workplace is in the midst of a state of growth, evolution, and rapid change. Many employers now routinely use social networking sites in advertising, marketing, communication, and decision making, and to conduct research about the backgrounds of job candidates. Employees are also increasingly making complaints to human resources departments and management over offensive or harassing statements made online. Both authors agree that social media in the workplace are in the midst of a state of growth and rapid change and that organizations should thoughtfully identify and develop guidelines to potentially head off and avoid potential lawsuits and liability.

Additional Resources

Farley, A. (2011). "Building a Social Media Policy," *ABA Bank Marketing*, October, pp. 18–22.

McCarthy, M.P. & Krishna, S. (2011). "Social Media: Time for a Governance Framework," *NACD Directorship*, September, p. 88.

Segal, J. (2012). "Widening Web of Social Media," *HR Magazine*, June, pp. 117–120.

Internet References . . .

Tool or Trouble?

Bednar, J. (2011). "Tool or Trouble?" December 19, pp. 33–36.

http://businesswest.com/

Why You Need a Social Media Policy

Henricks, M. (2011). "Why You Need a Social Media Policy," January 6.

www.entrepreneur.com/article/217813

820,000 Reasons to Have a Social Media Policy

Hyman, J. (2012). "820,000 Reasons to Have a Social Media Policy."

**www.workforce.com/article/20120719
/BLOGS07/120719931/820-000-reasons-to
-have-a-social-media-policy**

Selected, Edited, and with Issue Framing Material by:
Kathleen J. Barnes, *William Paterson University*
and
George E. Smith, *University of South Carolina, Beaufort*

ISSUE

Are Unions Good or Bad for Employees and Corporations?

YES: Henry Blodget, from "I've Always Hated the Idea of Labor Unions, But It May Be Time to Reconsider," *Business Insider* (2012)

NO: Derek Thompson, from "'Unnecessary' and 'Political': Why Unions Are Bad for America," *The Atlantic* (2012)

Learning Outcomes
After reading this issue, you will be able to:
• Define and describe what a labor union is.
• Explain the potential benefits that labor unions can assist their membership with.
• Present and defend competing views on the need for labor unions.
• Develop a personal opinion on the need for labor unions grounded in your understanding of the issue readings.

ISSUE SUMMARY

YES: *Business Insider* contributor Henry Blodget lists the reasons he doesn't like unions, but then discusses the extreme compensation inequity that is worse than any time since the late 1920s.

NO: Derek Thompson relays *The Atlantic*'s readers' responses to the question whether unions were necessary to restore wealth to average American families.

The History of Unions in the United States

Labor unions have existed in one form or another in the United States since the birth of the country. They were created in an effort to protect the working population from abuses such as sweatshops and unsafe working conditions. On the other hand, they have also been accused of crippling industries and consorting with organized crime over the decades. But in one way or another, labor unions have been woven into the political, economic, and cultural fabric of America, and their influence has played a colorful role in its development according to Investopedia.

Origin of Labor Unions

The first hundred years of United States history saw relatively little in the development of labor unions. A few were organized in scattered fashion, but many of those simply disbanded after they had achieved their goals, such as when the printers briefly unionized in New York City in 1778. The first successful strike in building trades took place in 1791 when Philadelphia carpenters campaigned for a 10-hour workday. The need for both skilled and unskilled labor mushroomed during the Industrial Revolution and the Civil War, and the subsequent discontinuation of slavery helped to illustrate the right of workers to receive a fair wage for their labor.

Protecting Worker Rights

The National Labor Union was created in 1866 to convince Congress to limit the workday for federal employees to eight hours, but the private sector was much harder for unions to penetrate. The continual flood of immigrants coming into the country further diluted the workforce, and the price of labor declined as a result. Poor pay and working conditions in the 1890s led the Pullman Railroad workers and United Mine workers to lay down their tools in protest, but both strikes were broken up by the government. The Federation of

Organized Trades and Labor Unions was formed in 1881, and the American Federation of Labor (AFL) was founded five years later. Congress became more sympathetic toward the labor force as time passed, which led to the creation of the Department of Labor. The Clayton Antitrust Act of 1914 allowed employees to strike and boycott their employers and was followed by the Public Contract and the Fair Labor Standards Acts, which mandated a minimum wage, extra pay for overtime work and basic child labor laws.

The Impact of Wartime

Labor unions grew in power and number from the Civil War through World War I, as the need for factory workers and other laborers continued to increase. Unions lost ground during the Roaring 1920s, however, when the economy grew so much the need for unionization seemed irrelevant. The Great Depression quickly reversed this trend and unions grew stronger than ever under Roosevelt's New Deal policies. Union membership grew exponentially as the depression wore on and workers sought employment and protection through their local trade unions.

The power of the labor unions was somewhat curtailed during World War II, however, as some unions, such as those in the defense industry, were forbidden by the government to strike due to the impediment that it would present to wartime production. But the end of the war saw a wave of strikes in many industries and it was at this point that union power and membership reached its zenith. The unions were a controlling force in the economy during the late 1940s and 1950s, and the AFL merged with the Congress of Industrial Organizations (CIO) at this point to spearhead the American labor force.

Decreasing Power

But the strength of the unions during this era led many union leaders into corruption and complacency, and the power of the unions began to decline in subsequent decades. As additional laws were passed outlawing child labor and mandating equal pay for equal work regardless of race or gender, unions became less important to workers who were able to rely on federal laws to protect them.

The Bottom Line

Despite the erosion in their power and influence, labor unions are still proving their importance, as they were instrumental in getting President Obama elected in 2008 and reelected in 2012. The unions hoped that Obama would have been able to pass the Employee Free Choice Act, which is a measure of legislation that will greatly streamline and shorten the process currently in place that unions must use to bring in new members. This act would effectively shift the balance of power in the workplace in the unions' favor and allow their memberships to grow rapidly. Although the possible impact that this could have on the economy is somewhat unclear, unions will continue to play a role in the U.S. labor force for decades to come.

YES

Henry Blodget

I've Always Hated the Idea of Labor Unions, But It May Be Time to Reconsider?

I've always hated the idea of labor unions.

Why?

Several reasons.

- They create an "us versus them" culture within companies, instead of putting everyone on the same team
- They create a culture of entitlement
- They restrict flexibility and hurt competitiveness
- They drive companies to move jobs out of the country, to places where there are no unions
- They often become career employment for their leaders, who pay themselves well (much better than the workers they're representing)
- They maintain ludicrous compensation and benefit levels for jobs based purely on seniority (some bartenders in one of the New York hotel unions, for example, apparently make ~$200,000 a year)
- They force companies to treat all union employees equally, regardless of the relative skill and value of particular employees—thus reducing incentives for people to do a great job
- Etc.

And all those are indeed negatives.

But we've now developed a bigger problem in this country.

Namely, we've developed inequality so extreme that it is worse than any time since the late 1920s.

Contributing to this inequality is a new religion of shareholder value that has come to be defined only by "today's stock price" and not by many other less-visible attributes that build long-term economic value.

Like many religions, the "shareholder value" religion started well: In the 1980s, American companies were bloated and lethargic, and senior management pay was so detached from performance that shareholders were an afterthought.

But now the pendulum has swung too far the other way. Now, it's all about stock performance—to the point where even good companies are now quietly shafting other constituencies that should benefit from their existence.

Most notably: Rank-and-file employees.

Great companies in a healthy and balanced economy don't view employees as "inputs." They don't view them as "costs." They don't try to pay them "as little as they have to to keep them from quitting." They view their employees as the extremely valuable assets they are (or should be). Most importantly, they share their wealth with them.

One of the big problems in the U.S. economy is that America's biggest companies are no longer sharing their wealth with rank-and file-employees.

Consider the following two charts:

1. Corporate profit margins just hit an all-time high. Companies are making more per dollar of sales than they ever have before.
2. Wages as a percent of the economy are at an all-time low. This is closely related to the chart above. One reason companies are so profitable is that they're paying employees less than they ever have before.

When presented with these charts, many people invoke one of two arguments. First, technology is making employees irrelevant. Second, low-skill jobs command low pay.

Both of these arguments miss key points: Technology has been making some jobs obsolete for 200+ years now, but it is only recently that corporate profit margins have gone through the roof. Just because you can pay full-time employees so little that they're below the poverty line doesn't mean you should—especially when retention is often a problem and your profit margin is extraordinarily high.

More broadly, what's wrong with this picture?

What's wrong is that an obsession with a narrow view of "shareholder value" has led companies to put "maximizing current earnings growth" ahead of another critical priority in a healthy economy: Investing in human and physical capital and future growth.

Corporate Profit Margins Business Insider, St. Louis Fed.

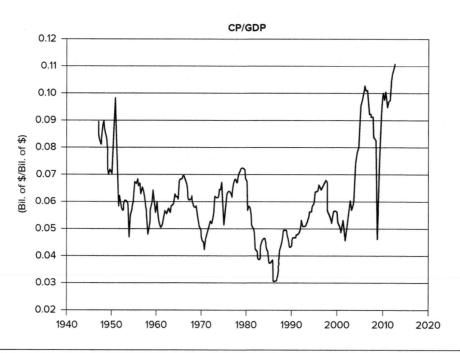

Wages To GDP Business Insider, St. Louis Fed.

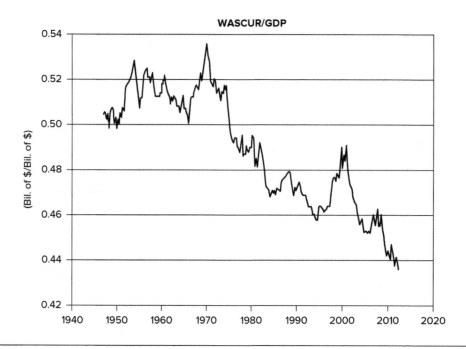

If American companies were willing to trade off some of their current earnings growth to make investments in wage increases and hiring, American workers would have more money to spend. And as American workers spent more money, the economy would begin to grow more quickly again. And the growing economy would help the companies begin to grow more quickly again. And so on.

But, instead, U.S. companies have become so obsessed with generating near-term profits that they're paying their employees less, cutting capital investments, and under-investing in future growth.

This may help make their shareholders temporarily richer.

But it doesn't make the economy (or the companies) healthier.

And, ultimately, as with any ecosystem that gets out of whack, it's bad for the whole ecosystem.

So, for the sake of the economy, we have to fix this problem.

Ideally, we would fix it by getting companies to voluntarily share more of their wealth with their employees. But the "shareholder value" religion has now been so thoroughly embraced that any suggestion of voluntary sharing is viewed as heresy.

(You've heard all the responses: "The only duty of a company is to produce the highest possible return for its owners!" "If employees want to make more money, they should go start their own companies!" Etc. Beyond basic fairness and the team spirit of we're-all-in-this-together, what these responses lack is any appreciation of the value of personal loyalty, retention, respect, and pride in the workforce. People love working for companies that treat them well. And they'll go to the mat for them.)

Anyway, it would be great if companies would start sharing their wealth voluntarily. But, as yet, with a couple of notable exceptions (Apple recently gave its store employees a raise it didn't need to give them), they've shown no signs of doing that.

So if companies can't be persuaded to do this on their own, maybe it's time to rethink our view of labor unions.

Although correlation is not causation, the chart below suggests that labor unions might be able to help induce companies to share their wealth, at least in some industries.

This chart is from EPI. It is based on the work of Piketty and Saez (the deans of inequality research).

The chart shows the correlation between the share of the national income going to "the 1 percent" with membership in labor unions. What it suggests is that, as unions have declined, income inequality has soared.

Again, right now in this country, we have the painful juxtaposition of the highest corporate profit margins in history, combined with one of the highest unemployment rates in history. We also have the lowest wages in history as a percent of the economy.

Income Union Membership EPI, Felix Salmon.

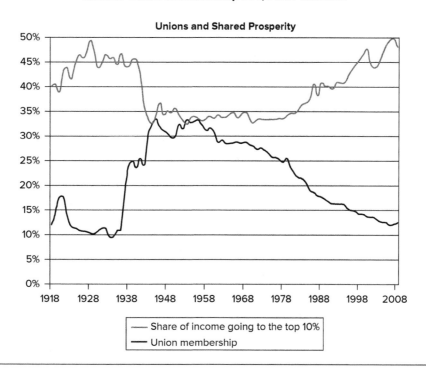

That's not good for the economy . . . because rich people can't buy all the products we need to sell to have a healthy economy (they can't eat that much food or drive that many cars, for example).

And it's also just not right.

Healthy capitalism is not about "maximizing near-term profits." It is about balancing the interests of several critical constituencies:

- Shareholders
- Customers
- Employees
- Society, and
- The Environment

It's time more of our business leaders started to understand that.

HENRY BLODGET is an American businessman, investor, journalist, and author. He is the editor and CEO of *Business Insider,* a business news aggregator site, as well as a host of Yahoo Daily Ticker, a finance show on Yahoo. Blodget is a former equity research analyst who was senior Internet analyst for CIBC Oppenheimer and the head of the global Internet research team at Merrill Lynch during the dot-com era.

Derek Thompson

 **NO**

'Unnecessary' and 'Political': Why Unions Are Bad for America

We asked you to tell us if unions were necessary to restore wealth to average American families. Some of you said yes. Some of you said no. There's a comment section below. Keep talking to us.

I Was in a Union and "Unions Are Unnecessary"

I worked in a unionized refinery and my personal experience has been that unions are unnecessary. As an engineer, I was unable to touch any tools, provide any assistance to our technicians and operators for "taking work away from a union employee." While not always the case, the union gave protection to the laborer to be extremely lazy and unproductive because as long as he showed up to work on time, there was no way he could get fired. The technicians and operators started at $28.00 an hour, which was more than I made as an engineer. Obviously they have a much lower ceiling and top out pretty quickly, but that is an enormous amount of money for someone who can get away with being lazy as he wants. Also, during lead-ups to labor negotiations (there were two big ones while I was there), there was ample evidence of sabotage to the plant while engineers were being trained to operate the refinery in the event of a strike. I cannot for the life of me understand why one would put people at risk in order to protect their job.

There were several unionized technicians and operators that were very pleasant and worked hard when asked to do so, but this was not the norm. Additionally, often the best unionized workers were promoted to management and were no longer protected by the union.

I understand that there was a time in the nation when we had 14-year-old kids working 18 hours a day, but we have long since moved past those days.

I'm all for finding ways to close the income inequality gap (higher taxes, more efficient tax code), but I assure you that unionizing labor will not solve our problem.

"The Right to Leave"

With all this discussion of power, people seem to be missing the biggest bargaining chip of all—the right to leave. An employee has the nearly unfettered right to walk away from a job. Even with noncompete clauses and other employment contracts, there are very, very few cases in which an employee can be forced to work. Conversely, a company has numerous restrictions on when, how, and who they can terminate.

Why Unions Could Increase Unemployment

Consumers will naturally gravitate toward the best value, which is why Wal-Mart has been successful by imparting downward pressure on prices and the cost of living. That you don't like them because it hurts your profit margin selling whatever it is you're selling doesn't change the fact that basic laws of supply and demand have led to consumers getting the goods they want at lower cost. Subsidies impede creative destruction (though maybe you'd rather still be a peasant in the Dark Ages?), and tariffs force up prices for everyone, decrease choice, and increase the cost of living—which particularly hurts the poor. I guess you just don't care about poor people, huh?

By the same token, employees will work for the employer offering the best terms of employment. Right now there are more job-seekers than jobs, so the leverage lies with employers. The opposite is true in a good economy. Making it more difficult for businesses to hire and adapt may mean some people get better terms, but a larger percentage get no job at all.

Why Would a Young Person Join a Union?

I was on the executive board of the Providence Newspaper Guild TNG/CWA Local 31041 from 2005 to early 2007. I think unions are relevant, but are stuck in time. They're relevant because they hope to create fairness in employee pay—a flatter salary system, rather than all the money flowing to the top of the food chain. But, their strategies and focal points were stuck in an era that had no relation to reality. It was like trying to argue for the rotary dial phone. Sure, there is a need for the telephone, but any new ways to use them are forbidden. My experience was baffling and eye opening.

I was the youngest member on the board (32!). We managed over $1 million in dues, about 500 employees, and a handful of lower boards. The average length of employment was over 18 years and like all newspapers, the ProJo was in terrible decline. I remember journalists vehemently protesting the paper's online presence and calling on the union to prevent the company from hiring content producers. It was, to me, out of touch crazy talk. It was like watching an episode of Mad Men, where the vernacular was from an entirely different—and dead—era.

We all had decent pay and a process for employee review, but the union prevented the paper from moving forward. The sales department, I'm not kidding, used a proprietary phone and terminal system from the 1970s and 1980s. Literally these big machines with huge keyboards with weird symbols and codes. The screens were CRTs, with black backgrounds and a green cursor. Parts for these beasts were cannibalized from 10 or so other dead behemoths piled in a closet—they were no longer made.

Why couldn't the sales department upgrade? Training. The employees were essentially in the same position, on the phones taking ads, for an average of over 20 years. No bs. They were older women, and training them would have cost thousands of dollars because the women were too old to learn new technologies. So, the union saw no need for upgrades and blocked it for years.

I ran for the seat after I was denied by my superiors to streamline a work process, one that would have saved the company thousands of dollars immediately. I outlined a plan, including implementation, a management scheme, and-roll out schedule. I even prepared a list of objections, so my pitch would be polished and surely accepted. To my surprise there was unanimous agreement that the plan was effective—no objections but one: it wouldn't work because of union rules.

I did not anticipate that response. Afterward, I had a bizarre conversation with the union steward. He focused on the fact that my innovation "would benefit the company, not employees so it will never work around here."

Stunned, I ran for an open seat to see from the inside why ideas and innovation were frowned upon. Once on the board, I first could not believe that no one was under 45. In fact, most were well into their 50s and 60s. To them, everything was a battle, "us vs. them." Management was Enemy #1, with the internet an emerging threat. Meetings were strategy sessions that focused on two things. First, meeting member needs (these were the good works, like settling discrimination suits for underrepresented workers). The second priority was more energetic, and focused on how to defeat the company. I did not understand the second part, and was assured with a wink and a nod that "it was the right thing to do, just look at history."

I argued with my fellow board members that young people needed to be involved with the union, that they needed a plan to transfer and promote the union to a new generation. I also argued that innovation was stifling employees from being recognized and promoted - to the default, robotic objection of, "seniority trumps all." If anyone wanted a promotion, everyone in the company would have to be notified of the new position with senior employees having more weight on the applications. The whole system was so utterly foreign to me.

Then, I heard from the inside that Belo was about buy out the ProJo. I left in a hurry to avoid a slaughter and went back to school to become a climate change specialist.

Unions may be necessary, but they're killing themselves by sticking to old ideals and arguments that no longer apply to the 21st Century. Why—honestly—any young person would want to join a union, I have no idea.—Michael Cote

"Unions and Government Are a Bad Match"

The difference between public sector and private sector unions is critical. What on earth is the argument for taking gov't action to dismantle the remaining private sector unions? If they are fading on their own, and given that hardly anyone is these days blaming them for the biggest economic problems facing the United States, why put them under attack? I don't think either Republicans or Democrats would contemplate doing that; it doesn't make sense in terms of electoral maps for one thing.

Public sector unions are something different altogether. They seem ill-conceived, and there's nothing like a big financial squeeze in state budgets to shed a light on their dysfunction. Management (whatever that is, presumably the state legislature but arguably the taxpayers) can't pack up the shop or outsource or close down operations or anything that resembles the big cards that management plays in the private sector when negotiating with unions. By the time agreed-to pensions and other expenses come on line and begin to weigh on the state budget, they're just another budget item at the state level and it becomes a question of tax rates and so on, all worked out in arrears. It's just unworkable, untenable. Unions and government are a bad match.—*bystander*

If You Want More Money, "Go Somewhere Else"

You negotiate with your feet. If you are treated worse than market value, you go somewhere else. In times like now when everyone's market value is less, and there are fewer options, you take what you get and you like it. When times get better, that is when you get your due.

Companies that don't pay their people what they are worth go out of business. Companies that pay their people more than they are worth go out of business even faster.

All About Capital-D Democratic Politics

I don't know why, but the U.S. union movement veered in an adversarial direction, probably in the 1950s. The dominant theme of industrial unions in their heyday was a pathological opposition to management that resulted in the death of the heavy industrial companies that employed them. Just consider the ways in which the UAW and auto workers interacted with the big three, which eventually led the biggest and most powerful corporations in the country to bankruptcy in a generation (and not because the product became defunct, as shown by the success of the transplants). It was not so much pay and benefits (although with the big three, it was largely that), but rigid work rules, featherbedding, and a reflexive opposition to anything management wanted to accomplish. I have personally seen AFL-CIO operatives take positions during hearings on OSHA regulations which, if implemented, would clearly result in their members losing their jobs. I can only assume that they testified as they did not to benefit their members but because "management" (industry) was taking the opposite position.

I also suspect that German labor officials are not as self-interested as U.S. labor leadership. For example, I note that you didn't mention such things as Gerald McEntee's seven chartered flights between August and December of 2011 that cost AFSCME $98,115.66.

The main reason many liberals are concerned about this issue is that labor is one of the last reliable conduits of cash and foot soldiers for the Democratic party (through a mandatory tax on their members). This was the real reason for all the consternation about Scott Walker in Wisconsin, not any so-called threat to collective bargaining.

The balance of power in the legal system is also strongly weighted towards the employees. Companies spend tremendous amounts of time and money to ensure compliance with all labor laws. The very threat of a wrongful termination suit has cowed many employers into not exercising their rights to terminate. This isn't a matter of poor employees versus big bad corporations. There are few protections that a union can provide that aren't found in our enormous legal code.

"Young People Do Not Believe Unions Are Providing Services Worthy of Their Cost"

The decline of unions has little to do with political attacks upon them: in our democracy, if 90 percent of the real workforce demanded something, they would get it. It has everything to do with the fact that young people nowadays do not believe that unions are providing services worthy of their cost. They recognize—correctly—that unions harm the hard-working and productive for the benefit of the idle and unambitious, and want no part of it. We can even recognize that unions did provide valuable results in the past—although please miss me with one more iteration of "the guys who brought you the weekend"—without buying the idea that they are due plaudits in perpetuity for pulling kids out of mills a hundred and fifty years ago.—*TheAnonymouse*

Unions Aren't Behind the Fall of the Middle Class

As far as I can tell there are two major causes for middle class woes:

1. The cost of health care. High spending by employers over the past 20–30 years has been all but eaten up by the rising costs of health care. It's only as you get into the upper echelons of income where health care costs become a smaller part of the total pie that people aren't being squeezed this way.
2. Competition from abroad. Free trade grows the world economy and in the long run will benefit America, but all of that capital flowing out of America to other parts of the world sure doesn't help in the short run.

If American workers were really being underpaid, unions would have a lot more sway, simply because employers (whether corporations or state governments) couldn't really afford to alienate unionized workers.

The only places I know of where unions are thriving are in very specific skilled professions where there's a shortage of qualified workers (diesel mechanics, for example).

"Their Unfortunate Demise Is Almost Entirely Their Own Fault"

Unions are a service industry like lawyers and accountants. They sell a service representing and advocating for workers. Their unfortunate demise is almost entirely their own fault. They charge too much for their services through dues and many current members and many more prospective members do not see the value for their dues. Slavishly committed to protecting the very worst employees by making firing almost impossible (think the Rubber Room for NYC teachers), unions have become synonymous with mediocre work and waste. Ignoring the reality that almost all of their employees are now shareholders in corporate America through pension funds and 401k plans, union leadership persists with the dated notion that it is the unions vs. corporations.

Unions are needed more than ever but their message needs to be completely reconsidered. New leadership from outside the ranks is needed that understands that a union is a service. The cronyism that governs the middle levels of leadership needs to be stopped; no one currently respects it. Dues need to be lowered. The product is too expensive.

Most importantly, unions need to recognize that merit is to be rewarded, and poor performance is to be disciplined and even fired—easily. Unions need to sell themselves as a catalyst for upward social mobility, as a service that will permit employees to succeed better than they would otherwise do. Instead of seniority being the principal criterium for everything, merit and education need to dominate their focus. Since the 1930s, "employers" have developed a much healthier (but still imperfect) perspective on the value of employees, dating the original and persistent union mindset of "us vs. them."

Finally, unions need to stop looking outside for blame and to legislatures for help. Tools like "card check" and "closed shops" really lack merit in the eyes of the public. Unions can and must succeed, but only if they repair themselves and start selling a product that both employees and employers see as indispensable.

DEREK THOMPSON is a senior editor at *The Atlantic*, where he writes about economics, labor markets, and the entertainment business.

EXPLORING THE ISSUE

Are Unions Good or Bad for Employees and Corporations?

Critical Thinking and Reflection

1. What is the role of labor unions?
2. Based on the readings presented in this issue, do you believe that labor unions are good or bad for U.S. business interests? Why?
3. Detractors have decried the value of labor unions in terms of present and past performance. How would you respond to their assessment of labor union performance based on what you have read?
4. An article entitled, "Trade Unions—Romance and Reality" was published in the *Harvard Business Review* in 1958 (Selekman, B. M., 36(3), pp. 76–90). Without reading the article, what would you say was the "romance" or were the things that attracted employees to labor unions? What do you believe the "reality" or actual outcome of labor union membership has been for those who were romanced and attracted to labor unions?
5. If you were given the option to become a labor union member or not become a labor union member, which option would you select? Explain why you made your selection.

Is There Common Ground?

It is interesting to observe that the common ground that exists in the two articles framing this issue is the role and place of unions in the lives of their employees. In Donald Myers book *Human Resource Management*, he states that a union is "an organization of employees who have some common interests, like collectively bargaining with their employer over the terms and conditions of employment in such matters as pay, benefits, job security, safety and health" (1992, p. 877). The notion that labor unions give employees a voice in negotiations with organizations and their management is a consistent theme that is examined in books and articles.

The disagreement that has arisen with the passage of time regards the level of success that unions have had in collective bargaining and perceptions of the success or lack of success that they will have in the future. This conflict and debate in the United States is not new. In 1958, Benjamin M. Selekman reflected on the first quarter of a century of unionization. In this work he wrote:

To say that the community is less than happy with unions would surely be an understatement. Labor is now in the doghouse—just as business occupied that unenviable spot in the 1930's. Every time a major negotiation begins, the community is perturbed by the possibility of a strike in a basic industry like steel or automobiles—with all the implications that such a stoppage has for other interrelated businesses. Again, when workers shut down the subways of New York, or immobilize tugboats and harbor shipping, an almost perceptible tremor goes through the nation.

Finally, as a result of successive wage increases and fringe benefits won by unions since the war, the major problem of inflation has been laid at their door.

Indeed, it is probably more accurate to say that a considerable segment of the community—even union sympathizers—are disillusioned, if not shocked by recent developments in unions. ("Trade Unions—Romance and Reality," *Harvard Business Review*, 36(3), p. 770)

To use the sentiment of the title of Selekman's work, there will likely always be a certain "romance" attached to unions especially as they pertain to protecting and ensuring the rights and interests of their members. The actual reality of those outcomes is likely to continue to receive significant attention and ongoing debate in the foreseeable future as labor and management continue to pursue their independent agendas and protect their own interests.

Additional Resources

Boccardy, B. T. (2011). "Public Sector Unions: A Convenient Scapegoat," *Working USA: The Journal of Labor and Society*, 14(3), pp. 411–415

Burliegh, N. (2015). "Sad State of the Union," *Newsweek*, 164(15), pp. 12–15.

Burns, J. (2013). "Labor's Economic Weapons: Learning from Labor History," *Labor Studies Journal*, 37(4), pp. 337–344.

Grossman, R. J. (2013). "Leading from Behind," *HR Magazine*, 58(12), pp. 37–41.

Hodges, A. (2016). "Imagining U.S. Labor Relations without Union Security," *Employee Responsibilities & Rights Journal*, 28(2), pp. 135–145.

Magnani, E. & Prentice, D. (2010). "Did Lower Unionization in the United States Result in More Flexible Industries?" *Industrial & Labor Relations Review*, 63(4), pp. 662–680.

Weber, D. O. (2015). "The State of the Unions," *Physician Executive*, 37(4), pp. 4–15.

Internet References . . .

Farewell to America's Middle Class: Unions are Basically Dead

http://www.theatlantic.com/business/archive/2015/10
/unions-are-basically-dead/412831/

How Unions Help All Workers

http://www.epi.org/publication/briefingpapers_bp143/

Is the U.S. Better Off Without Unions?

https://www.bloomberg.com/view/articles/2014-02-19
/is-the-u-s-better-off-without-unions-

What Have Unions Done for Us?

http://www.cnn.com/2012/09/04/opinion
/brazile-unions/

What Unions Do: How Labor Unions Affect Jobs and the Economy

http://www.heritage.org/research/reports/2009/05
/what-unions-do-how-labor-unions-affect-jobs
-and-the-economy

What's Wrong With Unions?

http://www.economist.com/blogs/freeexchange
/2009/02/whats_wrong_with_unions

Why Unions Are Harmful to Workers

http://www.foxnews.com/opinion/2011/03/17/unions
-harmful-workers.html

Unit 3

UNIT

Strategic Management

*E*xecutives do their utmost to help their firms grow and to increase profits. It seems intuitive that successful firms are growing firms. So why would highly knowledgeable and respected business scholars and observers argue that growth is not necessary for a firm to be successful? Speaking of growth, consider the issue of mergers and acquisitions. Would you be surprised to learn that, frequently, firms that engage in these behaviors actually experience a loss in corporate value? So why are mergers and acquisitions (M&As) so popular? With continued pressure on businesses for profitability, outsourcing and reshoring/insourcing are attractive options for businesses. For answers to these and questions, examine the five topics comprising this unit.

Selected, Edited, and with Issue Framing Material by:
Kathleen J. Barnes, *William Paterson University*
and
George E. Smith, *University of South Carolina, Beaufort*

ISSUE

Is Outsourcing a Wise Corporate Strategy?

YES: BusinessWeek, from "The Future of Outsourcing: How It's Transforming Whole Industries and Changing the Way We Work," *Bloomberg BusinessWeek* (2006)

NO: Ephraim Schwartz, from "Painful Lessons from IT Outsourcing Gone Bad," *InfoWorld* (2008)

Learning Outcomes

After reading this issue you will be able to:

- Describe the positive and negative consequences of outsourcing as a corporate strategy.
- Discuss how outsourcing can be used as an effective corporate strategy.
- Understand what tactics might be used to implement outsourcing as an effective corporate strategy.
- Appreciate the practical implications of outsourcing as a corporate strategy.

ISSUE SUMMARY

YES: *BusinessWeek* writers argue that outsourcing is likely to become even more important to corporate America in the near future. Indeed, they suggest that it has the potential to transform whole industries.

NO: *InfoWorld* columnist Ephraim Schwartz explores the often-overlooked costs associated with failed outsourcing initiatives. His analysis consists of four brief case studies of outsourcing initiatives that turned out badly.

Based on the past presidential elections, it would appear that one of the most contentious issues in American society is the outsourcing question. In 2004, the Democratic nominee, John Kerry, repeatedly expressed his disdain for U.S. firms that "sent jobs overseas" and promised, if elected, to punish those businesses that engaged in outsourcing. In 2008, while on the campaign trail, then-Democratic presidential nominee Barack Obama said, "Unlike John McCain, I will stop giving tax breaks to corporations that ship jobs overseas, and I will start giving them to companies that create good jobs right here in America." (Griswold, 2009). Speaking in front of a joint session of Congress on February 24, 2009, President Obama made this statement: "We will restore a sense of fairness and balance to our tax code by finally ending the tax breaks for corporations that ship our jobs overseas." (Ikenson, 2009).

As Eduardo Porter notes, the political rhetoric noted in the previous paragraph is a ploy taken "from a [political] playbook used repeatedly by politicians of the right and left over the last two decades" ("The Folly of Attacking Outsourcing," *New York Times*,

August 8, 2012, B1). Porter continues by noting some of the recent history of this debate in political circles:

> In 1992, Ross Perot ran for president on the strength of the "giant sucking sound" of jobs going to Mexico. Four years later, Pat Buchanan tried to gain the Republican nomination by promising to repeal the North American Free Trade Agreement and withdraw from the World Trade Organization. In 2004, John Kerry accused George W. Bush of providing tax breaks to outsourcers.

Perhaps part of the reason this topic is so controversial is because it overlaps and is related to several other contentious issues. Some critics claim that outsourcing encourages the development of sweatshops in Third World countries. Proponents of outsourcing often claim that increased competition from globalization virtually requires outsourcing as a business strategy. Depending on which side of the protectionism issue is being considered, outsourcing is presented as either pro-or anti-American. Given the antagonism that exists in the minds of many toward outsourcing, one might reasonably question whether outsourcing is a wise course of action for a firm to follow.

Proponents of outsourcing have strong points on their side of the issue. The call to end outsourcing is, in their view, merely protectionism in disguise, a concept entirely at odds with traditional American political and economic principles. American capitalism and prosperity were built on free trade; forcing American firms to forego cheap overseas labor in the name of patriotism will ultimately cause U.S. firms, and society, to suffer. In terms of the exploitation of foreign labor argument, supporters respond that it is not exploitation at all. Edwin Locke, Dean's Professor of Leadership and Motivation at the University of Maryland and a contributing author to the Ayn Rand Institute, an influential think tank, addresses

> the claim that multinational companies [e.g., American firms] exploit workers in poor countries by paying lower wages than they would pay in their home countries. Well, what is the alternative? It is: no wages! The comparative advantage of poorer countries is precisely that their wages are low, thus reducing the costs of production. If multinational corporations had to pay the same wages as in their home countries, they would not bother to invest in poorer countries at all and millions of people would lose their livelihoods.

Supporters also point out that the United States has the second highest corporate tax rate in the world, thus incentivizing firms to both make investments and move operations overseas.

On the other hand, those who argue that outsourcing is bad business generally rely on several lines of attack. The first and most obvious argument is that outsourcing moves jobs out of America and into foreign countries. Make no mistake, this is no small trend: Millions of jobs have left American shores in recent years, and many millions more are vulnerable. Critics also point to the growth of outsourcing in the service sector as an alarming trend. The historical justification for outsourcing was built on the belief that jobs lost in manufacturing would be replaced by jobs in the service sector as the United States shifted from an industrial to a service-based economy. Because the current outsourcing wave is primarily service based, the concern is that outsourcing will accelerate further as we continue to move toward a service-oriented society. Finally, consistent with our comments earlier about the sweatshop issue, many charge that outsourcing is nothing more than American firms exploiting cheaper labor in other countries to increase profits.

In the selections that follow, both sides of this interesting topic will be discussed. In the first selection, *BusinessWeek* writers argue that outsourcing is likely to become even more important to corporate America in the near future. In contrast to this position, *InfoWorld* columnist Ephraim Schwartz explores the often-overlooked costs associated with failed outsourcing initiatives by analyzing four brief case studies of outsourcing initiatives that turned out badly.

YES ↵

BusinessWeek

The Future of Outsourcing: How It's Transforming Whole Industries and Changing the Way We Work

Globalization has been brutal to midwestern manufacturers like the Paper Converting Machine Co. For decades, PCMC's Green Bay (Wis.) factory, its oiled wooden factory floors worn smooth by work boots, thrived by making ever-more-complex equipment to weave, fold, and print packaging for everything from potato chips to baby wipes.

But PCMC has fallen on hard times. First came the 2001 recession. Then, two years ago, one of the company's biggest customers told it to slash its machinery prices by 40% and urged it to move production to China. Last year, a St. Louis holding company, Barry-Wehmiller Cos., acquired the manufacturer and promptly cut workers and non-union pay. In five years sales have plunged by 40%, to $170 million, and the workforce has shrunk from 2,000 to 1,100. Employees have been traumatized, says operations manager Craig Compton, a muscular former hockey player. "All you hear about is China and all these companies closing or taking their operations overseas."

But now, Compton says, he is "probably the most optimistic I've been in five years." Hope is coming from an unusual source. As part of its turnaround strategy, Barry-Wehmiller plans to shift some design work to its 160-engineer center in Chennai, India. By having U.S. and Indian designers collaborate 24/7, explains Vasant Bennett, president of Barry-Wehmiller's engineering services unit, PCMC hopes to slash development costs and time, win orders it often missed due to engineering constraints—and keep production in Green Bay. Barry-Wehmiller says the strategy already has boosted profits at some of the 32 other midsize U.S. machinery makers it has bought. "We can compete and create great American jobs," vows CEO Robert Chapman. "But not without offshoring."

Come again? Ever since the offshore shift of skilled work sparked widespread debate and a political firestorm three years ago, it has been portrayed as the killer of good-paying American jobs. "Benedict Arnold CEOs" hire software engineers, computer help staff, and credit-card bill collectors to exploit the low wages of poor nations. U.S. workers suddenly face a grave new threat, with even highly educated tech and service professionals having to compete against legions of hungry college grads in India, China, and the Philippines willing to work twice as hard for one-fifth the pay.

Workers' fears have some grounding in fact. The prime motive of most corporate bean counters jumping on the offshoring bandwagon has been to take advantage of such "labor arbitrage"—the huge wage gap between industrialized and developing nations. And without doubt, big layoffs often accompany big outsourcing deals.

The changes can be harsh and deep. But a more enlightened, strategic view of global sourcing is starting to emerge as managers get a better fix on its potential. The new buzzword is "transformational outsourcing." Many executives are discovering offshoring is really about corporate growth, making better use of skilled U.S. staff, and even job creation in the U.S., not just cheap wages abroad. True, the labor savings from global sourcing can still be substantial. But it's peanuts compared to the enormous gains in efficiency, productivity, quality, and revenues that can be achieved by fully leveraging offshore talent.

Thus entrepreneurs such as Chapman see a chance to turn around dying businesses, speed up their pace of innovation, or fund development projects that otherwise would have been unaffordable. More aggressive outsourcers are aiming to create radical business models that can give them an edge and change the game in their industries. Old-line multinationals see offshoring as a catalyst for a broader plan to overhaul outdated office operations and prepare for new competitive battles. And while some want to downsize, others are keen to liberate expensive analysts, engineers, and salesmen from routine tasks so they can spend more time innovating and dealing with customers. "This isn't about labor cost," says Daniel Marovitz, technology managing director for Deutsche Bank's global businesses (DB). "The issue is that if you don't do it, you won't survive."

The new attitude is emerging in corporations across the U.S. and Europe in virtually every industry. Ask executives at Penske Truck Leasing why the company outsources dozens of business processes to Mexico and India, and they cite greater efficiency and customer service. Ask managers at U.S.-Dutch professional publishing giant Wolters Kluwer (**WTKWY**) why they're racing to shift software development and editorial work to India and the Philippines, and they will say it's about being able to pump out a greater variety of books, journals, and Web-based content more rapidly. Ask Wachovia Corp. (**WB**), the Charlotte (N.C.)-based bank, why it just inked a $1.1 billion deal with India's Genpact to outsource finance and accounting jobs and why it handed over administration of its humanresources programs to Lincolnshire (Ill.)-based Hewitt Associates (**HEW**). It's "what we need to do to become a great customer-relationship company," says Director of Corporate Development Peter J. Sidebottom. Wachovia aims to reinvest up to 40% of the $600 million to $1 billion it hopes to take out in costs over three years into branches, ATMs, and personnel to boost its core business.

Here's what such transformations typically entail: Genpact, Accenture (**ACN**), IBM Services, or another big outsourcing specialist dispatches teams to meticulously dissect the workflow of an entire human resources, finance, or info tech department. The team then helps build a new IT platform, redesigns all processes, and administers programs, acting as a virtual subsidiary. The contractor then disperses work among global networks of staff ranging from the U.S. to Asia to Eastern Europe.

In recent years, Procter & Gamble (**PG**), DuPont (**DD**), Cisco Systems (**CSCO**), ABN Amro (**ABN**), Unilever, Rockwell Collins (**COL**), and Marriott (**MAR**) were among those that signed such megadeals, worth billions.

In 2004, for example, drugmaker Wyeth Pharmaceuticals transferred its entire clinical-testing operation to Accenture Ltd. "Boards of directors of virtually every big company now are insisting on very articulated outsourcing strategies," says Peter Allen, global services managing director of TPI, a consulting firm that advised on 15 major outsourcing contracts last year worth $14 billion. "Many CEOs are saying, 'Don't tell me how much I can save. Show me how we can grow by 40% without increasing our capacity in the U.S.,'" says Atul Vashistha, CEO of outsourcing consultant neoIT and co-author of the book *The Offshore Nation.*

Some observers even believe Big Business is on the cusp of a new burst of productivity growth, ignited in part by offshore outsourcing as a catalyst. "Once this transformation is done," predicts Arthur H. Harper, former CEO of General Electric Co.'s equipment management businesses, "I think we will end up with companies that deliver products faster at lower costs, and are better able to compete against anyone in the world." As executives shed more operations, they also are spurring new debate about how the future corporation will look. Some management pundits theorize about the "totally disaggregated corporation," wherein every function not regarded as crucial is stripped away.

Processes, Now on Sale

In theory, it is becoming possible to buy, off the shelf, practically any function you need to run a company. Want to start a budget airline but don't want to invest in a huge back office? Accenture's Navitaire unit can manage reservations, plan routes, assign crew, and calculate optimal prices for each seat.

Have a cool new telecom or medical device but lack market researchers? For about $5,000, analytics outfits such as New Delhi-based Evalueserve Inc. will, within a day, assemble a team of Indian patent attorneys, engineers, and business analysts, start mining global databases, and call dozens of U.S. experts and wholesalers to provide an independent appraisal.

Want to market quickly a new mutual fund or insurance policy? IT services providers such as India's Tata Consultancy Services Ltd. are building software platforms that furnish every business process needed and secure all regulatory approvals. A sister company, Tata Technologies, boasts 2,000 Indian engineers and recently bought 700-employee Novi (Mich.) auto-and aerospace-engineering firm Incat International PLC. Tata Technologies can now handle everything from turning a conceptual design into detailed specs for interiors, chassis, and electrical systems to designing the tooling and factory-floor layout. "If you map out the entire vehicle-development process, we have the capability to supply every piece of it," says Chief Operating Officer Jeffrey D. Sage, an IBM and General Motors Corp. (**GM**) veteran. Tata is designing all doors for a future truck, for example, and the power train for a U.S. sedan. The company is hiring 100 experienced U.S. engineers at salaries of $100,000 and up.

Few big companies have tried all these options yet. But some, like Procter & Gamble, are showing that the ideas are not far-fetched. Over the past three years the $57 billion consumer-products company has outsourced everything from IT infrastructure and human resources to management of its offices from Cincinnati to Moscow. CEO Alan G. Lafley also has announced he wants half of all new P&G products to come from outside by 2010, vs. 20% [in 2006]. In the near future, some analysts predict, Detroit and European carmakers will go the way of the PC industry, relying on outsiders to develop new models bearing their brand names. BMW has done just that with a sport-utility vehicle. And Big Pharma will bring blockbuster drugs to market at a fraction of the current $1 billion average cost by allying with partners in India, China, and Russia in molecular research and clinical testing.

Of course, corporations have been outsourcing management of IT systems to the likes of Electronic Data Systems (**EDS**), IBM (**IBM**), and Accenture for more than a decade, while Detroit has long given engineering jobs to outside design firms. Futurists have envisioned "hollow" and "virtual" corporations since the 1980s.

It hasn't happened yet. Reengineering a company may make sense on paper, but it's extremely expensive and entails big risks if executed poorly. Corporations can't simply be snapped apart and reconfigured like LEGO sets, after all. They are complex, living organisms that can be thrown into convulsions if a transplant operation is botched. Valued employees send out their résumés, customers are outraged at deteriorating service, a brand name can be damaged. In consultant surveys, what's more, many U.S. managers complain about the quality of off-shored work and unexpected costs.

But as companies work out such kinks, the rise of the offshore option is dramatically changing the economics of reengineering. With millions of low-cost engineers, financial analysts, consumer marketers, and architects now readily available via the Web, CEOs can see a quicker payoff. "It used to be that companies struggled for a few years to show a 5% or 10% increase in productivity from outsourcing," says Pramod Bhasin, CEO of Genpact, the 19,000-employee back-office-processing unit spun off by GE last year. "But by offshoring work, they can see savings of 30% to 40% in the first year" in labor costs. Then the efficiency gains kick in. A $10 billion company might initially only shave a few million dollars in wages after transferring back-office procurement or bill collection overseas. But better management of these processes could free up hundreds of millions in cash flow annually.

Those savings, in turn, help underwrite far broader corporate restructuring that can be truly transformational. DuPont has long wanted to fix its unwieldy system for administering records, payroll, and benefits for its 60,000 employees in 70 nations, with data scattered among different software platforms and global business units. By awarding a long-term contract to Cincinnati-based Convergys Corp., the world's biggest call-center operator, to redesign and administer its human resources programs, it expects to cut costs 20% in the first year and 30% a year afterward. To get corporate backing for the move, "it certainly helps a lot to have savings from the outset," says DuPont Senior Human Resources Vice-President James C. Borel.

Creative new companies can exploit the possibilities of offshoring even faster than established players. Crimson Consulting Group is a good example. The Los Altos (Calif.) firm, which performs global market research on everything from routers to software for clients including Cisco, HP, and Microsoft (**MSFT**), has only 14 full-time employees. But it farms out research to India's Evalueserve and some 5,000 other independent experts from Silicon Valley to China, the Czech Republic, and South Africa. "This allows a small firm like us to compete with McKinsey and Bain on a very global basis with very low costs," says CEO Glenn Gow. Former GE exec Harper is on the same wavelength. Like Barry-Wehmiller, his new five-partner private-equity firm plans to buy struggling midsize manufacturers and use offshore outsourcing to help revitalize them. Harper's NexGen Capital Partners also plans to farm out most of its own office work. "The people who understand this will start from Day One and never build a back room," Harper says. "They will outsource everything they can."

Some aggressive outsourcers are using their low-cost, superefficient business models to challenge incumbents. Pasadena, (Calif.)-based IndyMac Bancorp Inc. (NDE), founded in 1985, illustrates the new breed of financial services company. In three years, IndyMac has risen from 22nd-largest U.S. mortgage issuer to No. 9, while its 18% return on equity in 2004 outpaced most rivals. The thrift's initial edge was its technology to process, price, and approve loan applications in less than a minute.

But IndyMac also credits its aggressive offshore outsourcing strategy, which Consumer Banking CEO Ashwin Adarkar says has helped make it "more productive, costefficient, and flexible than our competitors, with better customer service." IndyMac is using 250 mostly Indian staff from New York-based Cognizant Technology Solutions Corp. (**CTSH**) to help build a next-generation software platform and applications that, it expects, will boost efficiency at least 20% by 2008. IndyMac has also begun shifting tasks, ranging from bill collection to "welcome calls" that help U.S. borrowers make their first mortgage payments on time, to India's Exlservice Holdings Inc. and its 5,000-strong staff. In all, Exlservice and other Indian providers handle 33 back-office processes offshore. Yet rather than losing any American jobs, IndyMac has doubled its U.S. workforce to nearly 6,000 in four years—and is still hiring.

Superior Service

Smart use of offshoring can juice the performance of established players, too. Five years ago, Penske Truck Leasing, a joint venture between GE and Penske Corp., paid $768 million for trucker Rollins Truck Leasing Corp.—just in time for the recession. Customer service, spread among four U.S. call centers, was inconsistent. "I realized our business needed a transformation," says CFO Frank Cocuzza. He began by shifting a few dozen data-processing jobs to GE's huge Mexican and Indian call centers, now called Genpact. He then hired Genpact to help restructure most of his back office. That relationship now spans 30 processes involved in leasing 216,000 trucks and providing logistical services for customers.

Now, if a Penske truck is held up at a weigh station because it lacks a certain permit, for example, the driver calls an 800 number. Genpact staff in India obtains the document over the Web. The weigh station is notified electronically, and the truck is back on the road within 30 minutes. Before, Penske thought it did well if it accomplished that in two hours. And when a driver finishes his job, his entire log, including records of mileage, tolls, and fuel purchases, is shipped to Mexico, punched into computers, and processed in Hyderabad. In all, 60% of the 1,000 workers handling Penske back-office process are in India or Mexico, and Penske is still ramping up. Under a new program, when a manufacturer asks Penske to arrange for a delivery to a buyer, Indian staff helps with the scheduling, billing, and invoices. The $15 million in direct labor-cost savings are small compared with the gains in efficiency and customer service, Cocuzza says.

Big Pharma is pursuing huge boosts in efficiency as well. Eli Lilly & Co.'s (**LLY**) labs are more productive than most, having released eight major drugs in the past five years. But for each new drug, Lilly estimates it invests a hefty $1.1 billion. That could reach $1.5 billion in four years. "Those kinds of costs are fundamentally unsustainable," says Steven M. Paul, Lilly's science and tech executive vice-president. Outsourcing figures heavily in Lilly's strategy to lower that cost to $800 million. The drugmaker now does 20% of its chemistry work in China for one-quarter the U.S. cost and helped fund a startup lab, Shanghai's Chem-Explorer Co., with 230 chemists. Lilly now is trying to slash the costs of clinical trials on human patients, which range from $50 million to $300 million per drug, and is expanding such efforts in Brazil, Russia, China, and India.

Other manufacturers and tech companies are learning to capitalize on global talent pools to rush products to market sooner at lower costs. OnStor Inc., a Los Gatos (Calif.) developer of storage systems, says its tie-up with Bangalore engineering-services outfit HCL Technologies Ltd. enables it to get customized products to clients twice as fast as its major rivals. "If we want to recruit a great engineer in Silicon Valley, our lead time is three months," says CEO Bob Miller. "With HCL, we can pick up the phone and get somebody in two or three days."

Such strategies offer a glimpse into the productive uses of global outsourcing. But most experts remain cautious. The McKinsey Global Institute estimates $18.4 billion in global IT work and $11.4 billion in business-process services have been shifted abroad so far—just one-tenth of the potential offshore market. One reason is that executives still have a lot to learn about using offshore talent to boost productivity. Professor Mohanbir Sawhney of Northwestern University's Kellogg School of Management, a self-proclaimed "big believer in total disaggregation," says: "One of our tasks in business schools is to train people to manage the virtual, globally distributed corporation. How do you manage employees you can't even see?"

The management challenges will grow more urgent as rising global salaries dissipate the easy cost gains from offshore outsourcing. The winning companies of the future will be those most adept at leveraging global talent to transform themselves and their industries, creating better jobs for everyone.

BUSINESSWEEK is a weekly business magazine currently headquartered in New York City.

Ephraim Schwartz

 **NO**

Painful Lessons from IT Outsourcing Gone Bad

As companies look to economize in a weak economy worsened by rising energy costs, it may be more tempting than ever to consider outsourcing your IT—whether to a cloud-based provider, to a shop in your town, or to a provider in some far-off land. Certainly, outsourcing has worked well for many companies, but it can also lead to business-damaging nightmares, says Larry Harding, founder and president of High Street Partners, a global consultancy that advises company on how to expand overseas. After all, if outsourcers fail, you're left holding the bag without the resources to fix the problem.

In his consulting, Harding has seen many outsourcing horror stories, from corrupt general managers "with all sorts of conflicts of interest" (such as service providers getting kickbacks from landlords on the leased space) to projects torn apart by huge turnover rates. "You end up with project teams that are hugely inconsistent. You might have a good team in place, but a month later, three-quarters of the team has transitioned," Harding says.

"Only when executed well can it pull out hundreds of millions in cost and transform organizations," says Brian Keane, CEO of Dextrys, an outsourcing service provider that focuses mainly on China.

In the sometimes panicked desire to save money—especially with the powerful lure of "half-price" workers in places like India, China, and the Philippines—good execution flies out the window. And that's where the problems flock in. Outsourcing is not for the faint-hearted or the ill-prepared. It just doesn't "happen."

That's why understanding what can go wrong before you jump into outsourcing is a great way to reduce your risk because then you can approach outsourcing with eyes wide open, Harding notes. The companies who've lived through outsourcing horrors have two things in common: lack of preparedness going into a new relationship and lack of communication once the projects gets under way. Other factors can make these worse, of course.

Outsourcing's Biggest Horror Show

In the pantheon of outsourcing horror stories, the $4 billion deal between the U.S. Navy and global services provider EDS stands out as one of the most horrific. It started back in 2003 when the Plano, Texas, vendor beat out the likes of IBM and Accenture for the contract. The deal was to manage voice, video, networking, training, and desktops for 350,000 Navy and Marine Corps users. But just one year later, EDS was writing off close to $350 million due to its inability to come even close to fulfilling its obligations.

The reasons behind the failure are complex, but suffice it to say that one of the major causes behind the debacle was that EDS, perhaps anxious to win the prize, never realized that the Navy and Marine Corps had tens of thousands of legacy and custom applications for which it was expected to either integrate or rip and replace. An EDS spokesperson said at the time the company's goal was to get the number of legacy apps down to a mere 10,000 to 12,000.

While there was plenty of blame to go around at EDS, the Navy took its share of blame as well. One of the major issues with the Navy was that the buck stopped nowhere. There was no single person or entity that could help EDS determine what legacy applications were needed and what applications could be excised. EDS, for example, found 11 different label-making applications, but there was no one who could say which 10 to eliminate.

Most companies will never face outsourcing problems on the scale of the Navy and EDS. But many will face their own horrors on systems and projects just as critical. Consider these four modern examples and what lessons the companies painfully learned.

Horror No. 1: A Medical Firm's Configuration Management Surprise

When Fran Schmidt, now a configuration engineer with Orasi Consulting, was told at her previous job in the medical industry to head up a team to outsource the existing in-house development and quality assurance IT departments, she faced the usual problems.

"There was one Indian fellow no one could understand over the phone. It took us months to figure out what he was saying," Schmidt recalls with a smile.

That was expected. But what the medical firm didn't count on was that its existing configuration management tool, Microsoft Visual SourceSafe, which worked fine locally, would be a total bust when used collaboratively between two groups 8,000 miles apart. It took the remote teams in India an average of 13 hours to get updates on source code. And with a time difference of about 11 hours, the outsourcers were behind a full day's work.

"When we hit the [Send] button, there was no code done by the previous shift the entire time they were at work," recalls Schmidt.

Not having immediate access to what was previously done the day before caused major problems for in-house developers. "All our progress schedules were behind. It's a domino effect with everyone playing catch-up." And the firm's customers paid the price: They were upset because they were not getting the same level of care that they expected.

The medical firm ultimately switched its configuration management tool to AccuRev, cutting the transoceanic updating from 13 hours to about an hour and a half. All told, it took around six months to recover from the disaster, Schmidt recalls.

The obvious lesson was the need to test your infrastructure before going live in an offshoring scenario. But the medical firm also learned another hard lesson: The desire to save big bucks so blinded the executives that they didn't realize they were replacing a group of people experienced with using a product to a group of people who were looking at it for the first time. "We underestimated the loss of knowledge that would take place during the transition," Schmidt says.

Horror No. 2: Manufacturing Efficiency Doesn't Extend to Marketing

Executives in charge of a small consumer product group at Hewlett-Packard were under the gun. They were told in no uncertain terms to cut all costs related to getting the product into the big-box stores such as Best Buy and Circuit City, recalls Margaret McDonald, then marketing manager for the HP department and now president of her own company, McDonald Wordsmith Communications. (McDonald would not name the product and would only say that it is sold today at places such as Best Buy.)

"We were trying to get as much work as possible over to the Taiwan manufacturer with the goal to get the cost for these products down as low as possible," McDonald recalls. The Taiwanese outsourcer had a great deal of experience in getting the bill-of-materials costs lower, and HP was seeing that benefit. So managers started pushing for more savings elsewhere, insisting that the entire project be handed over to Taiwan—everything from manufacture to writing the instruction manuals to all the marketing materials.

"These execs were being evaluated on cost, not on the quality of the brand," says McDonald. When she tried to tell her managers that what they wanted was unreasonable for an outsourced manufacturer to deliver, they accused her of just trying to hold on to her job.

As she predicted, the project turned out to be a disaster. Take this example of the Taiwan-produced marketing materials: "This glamour of new product will perfectly fit to your daily life from any of locations!" Of course, non-native English prose like that never saw the light of day, but it wasted six months until the higher-ups finally realized what was happening.

McDonald isn't sure her managers learned a lesson. She sees the failure not due to the offshore firm hired or even the miscommunication between the US and Taiwan firms. Instead, she sees the problems as a failure within HP, between its own internal organizations. "The main [HP] branding people had no idea was going on." And the local managers reacted to the extreme cost pressures in a vacuum, with no concern for protecting the brand, McDonald says. The fact that the job was outsourced simply created the right circumstances for these internal flaws to finally become evident.

Horror No. 3: Giant Telecom Stumbles in Transition to Offshore

Steve Martin, a consultant and partner at Pace Harmon, a company that is often called in to help fix outsourcing deals gone bad, recalls the giant telecommunications company headed for disaster: It never considered the fact that although its new offshore provider was good at coding, it did not understand the business side of telecommunications.

The outsourcing project was divided into two phases. In phase one, all the internally managed operations were moved to an outsourced service provider (in this case, based in the United States). The idea was to test and stabilize the outsourcing approach with a local provider first, before taking the riskier step of moving the application development offshore.

The first phase went fairly well, so the telecom initiated phase two, shifting the effort to India. That didn't proceed so smoothly. The Indian provider simply didn't understand the telecom business, so lost in the transition halfway across the globe was all the telecom's inherent knowledge of the business applications—what it is supposed to do and why. "All of that knowledge got left in the US," Martin recalls.

Because the Indian firm didn't understand what it was coding, it took much longer to develop the applications. And they didn't work well, resulting in even more time and effort to figure out where they went wrong and fix them. It got so bad that the telecom canceled the off-shoring midway and brought the effort back home.

Of course, there were lingering problems to resolve, such as how to handle the disputes over tens of millions of dollars in service credits the telecom believed it was due from the Indian outsourcer, which argued that it delivered what it had been asked to do. "An amazingly large amount of costs had to be reconciled," Martin notes. The two companies eschewed a legal battle to avoid the bad publicity, ultimately settling the dispute privately.

What the telecom company learned the hard way was that there is more to a deal than signing the contract. In the original deal, pricing took precedence over every other consideration because the executives wanted to show that they saved millions of dollars. Shortchanged in the process were the details of the transition, the development processes, and the governance. Adequate thought was not given to the obligations of the people who were responsible for executing the transition.

"The contract was executed from a business perspective, where it looked great, but not enough thought was given to how to programmatically move to the new environment," Martin says.

Horror No. 4: Service Provider Blacks Out the Client

James Hills, president of marketing firm MarketingHelp-Net, probably had one of the most terrifying offshore experiences of all. When a dispute between his new company and the Web site developers grew heated, he came into the office one day—only to discover the developers had shut his client's site down.

"I came in and checked e-mail. No e-mail, no Web site. They had simply turned it off. It was all gone," Hills recalls. While he was shocked to discover this, in some ways, he was not surprised. After all, the relationship with the offshore provider had been troubled from the start.

It started when Hills took on an assignment from a major client. Rather than trying to develop Web design skills needed to complete the client's project, Hills decided to farm that part of the job out to an offshore provider in the Philippines, at a savings of half of the cost of working with a local Web site designer, says Hills.

As soon as the offshore provider began sending back completed work, Hills knew there was trouble: "Functionality and community features didn't mesh properly, and the design wasn't what we were looking for." On top of that, the offshore provider continually missed deadlines.

Becoming increasingly frustrated, Hills didn't make the final payment. The result, of course, was a panicked wake-up call from his client telling him there was no e-mail and no Web site.

Looking back, Hills says that if had he to do it over, he would have been more diligent in checking references. He did only a perfunctory check of references, unfortunately taking it for granted that the offshore design firm actually created the Web sites they claimed.

Time differences also played a key role in the soured relationship. "We weren't able to communicate directly, only through IM," Hills says. And as a small startup at the time, he couldn't support multiple shifts at home to get overlap with India, nor ask his staff to work 20 hours a day to cover both time zones. And sending a manager to the Philippines was out of the question, Hills says.

Hills doubts he'll ever outsource again, but if he did, he would insist that the job be done with a US-based company that puts its offshore staff onto the company's payroll. "No contract workers," Hills says tersely.

Ephraim Schwartz is an editor-at-large at InfoWorld.com. He also writes the Reality Check blog at www.inforworld.com/blogs /ephraim-schwarz.

EXPLORING THE ISSUE

Is Outsourcing a Wise Corporate Strategy?

Critical Thinking and Reflection

1. What might be the tactics of an outsourcing strategy?
2. How might an outsourcing strategy be implemented in a corporation?
3. What might be the costs to consumers, corporations, and the nation of corporations committed to an outsourcing strategy?
4. What is the likelihood that an enacted outsourcing strategy will lead to anticipated outcomes?
5. What does the future hold for companies following outsourcing strategies?

Is There Common Ground?

One reason the issue of outsourcing policies is so contentious is that both sides can easily cite data in support of their position.

While finding common ground on basic aspects of this important management topic is difficult, there is consensus that outsourcing policies are an important topic that will be debated for quite some time, especially in certain industries.

Additional Resources

Insinga, R. C. & Werle, M. J. (2000). "Linking Outsourcing to Business Strategy," *The Academy of Management Executive*, November, pp. 58–70.

Kakabadse, A. & Kakabadse, N. (2005). "Outsourcing: Current and Future Trends," *Thunderbird International Business Review*, March/April, pp. 183–204.

Lankford, W. & Parsa, F. (1999). "Outsourcing a Primer," *Management Decision*, pp. 310–316.

Internet References . . .

Customer Disservice? Critics Say the Promised Savings from Offshoring Come at Too Steep a Price, While Companies Say Very Little at All

Alster, N. (2005). "Customer Disservice? Critics Say the Promised Savings from Offshoring Come at Too Steep a Price, While Companies Say Very Little at All," *CFO Magazine, CFO IT*, Fall.

www.cfo.com/article.cfm/4390954

TARP Relief Law Might Discriminate Against Off-Shore Call Centers

Bierce, W. B. (2009). "TARP Relief Law Might Discriminate Against Off-Shore Call Centers," *Outsourcing-law.com*, January 24.

http://blog.outsourcing-law.com/2009/01/tarp-relief - law-might-discriminate.html

Anti-Outsourcing Campaign Renewed by Lou Dobbs

Boyd, R. (2005). "Anti-Outsourcing Campaign Renewed by Lou Dobbs," *The New York Sun*, February 2.

www.nysun.com/business/anti-outsourcing-campaign -renewed-by-lou-dobbs/8635/

Outsource, Outsource, and Outsource Some More

Griswold, D. T. (2004). "Outsource, Outsource, and Outsource Some More," Center for Trade Policy Studies, The Cato Institute, May 3.

www.freetrade.org/pubs/articles/dg-05-03-04.html

Shipping Jobs Overseas or Reaching New Customers? Why Congress Should Not Tax Reinvested Earnings Abroad

Griswold, D.T. (2009). "Shipping Jobs Overseas or Reaching New Customers? Why Congress Should Not Tax Reinvested Earnings Abroad," *Center for Trade Policy Studies*, Free Trade Bulletin, January 13.

www.freetrade.org/node/926

The Outsourcing Canard

Ikenson, D. (2009). "The Outsourcing Canard," Cato at Liberty.org, February 25.

http://www.cato.org/blog/outsourcing-canard

On May Day Celebrate Capitalism

Locke, E.A. (2003). "On May Day Celebrate Capitalism," The Ayn Rand Institute, April 24

www.aynrand.org/site /News2?page=NewsArticle&id=7449

The Folly of Attacking Outsourcing

Porter, E. (2012). "The Folly of Attacking Outsourcing," *New York Times*, August 7.

www.nytimes.com/2012/08/08/business/economy /in-outsourcing-attacks-tired-rhetoric-and-no-political -leadership-economic-scene.html?_r=0

Selected, Edited, and with Issue Framing Material by:
Kathleen J. Barnes, *William Paterson University*
and
George E. Smith, *University of South Carolina, Beaufort*

ISSUE

Will the Use of Reshoring/Insourcing by Corporations Increase?

YES: Andrew Sikula, Sr., et al., from "Insourcing: Reversing American Outsourcing in the New World Economy," *Supervision* (2010)

NO: David J. Lynch, from "'Reshoring' of Jobs Looks Meager," *Bloomberg BusinessWeek* (2012)

Learning Outcomes

After reading this issue, you will be able to:

- Describe the positive and negative consequences of reshoring/insourcing as a corporate strategy.
- Understand what tactics might be used to implement reshoring/insourcing as an effective corporate strategy.
- Appreciate the practical implications of reshoring/insourcing as a corporate strategy.
- Understand what factors are driving insourcing/reshoring.
- Understand whether insourcing/reshoring a fad or a trend that is here to stay.
- Know whether all businesses look to insource/reshore.
- Understand strategically, what are the benefits of insourcing/reshoring versus outsourcing.

ISSUE SUMMARY

YES: Andrew Sikula and colleagues discuss reasons why a movement to insourcing is currently occurring. The authors conclude that this movement is going to expand during the next several years in the United States.

NO: David J. Lynch observes that many of the jobs a nation (e.g., China) is losing are heading to other low-cost Asian nations. In addition, he observes that while some jobs have returned to the United States, other jobs are still being shipped out of the country.

"Insourcing" is when an organization uses internal labor and personnel and other resources to supply the operational needs of its enterprise. Insourcing is a management decision made to maintain control of critical production processes or competencies. Insourcing is the opposite of outsourcing which is the process where firms shift work outside of its borders.

In recent decades of our increasingly global environment and marketplace, insourcing has taken on an expanded definition. It now often means letting work go outside the organization yet keeping it within national boundaries, rather than subcontracting to suppliers overseas. Outsourcing today often is synonymous with "offshoring" or moving work offshore to another country typically overseas.

When the insourcing definition is expanded in this manner, it is an extension of a company's workplace without transferring the project management and decision-making control to an external provider.

There are many reasons why the resourcing pendulum has begun to significantly swing back toward insourcing and away from outsourcing within the United States and elsewhere. The eight factors or determinants of insourcing include (1) communication, (2) employee morale/loyalty, (3) control, (4) security, (5) transportation, (6) innovation, (7) customer satisfaction, and (8) speed to market.

Offshoring is defined as the movement of a business process done at a company in one country to the same or another company in another, different country. Often the work is moved because of a lower cost of operations in the new location, access to qualified personnel abroad, in particular in technical professions, and increasing speed to market. Outsourcing is the movement of internal business processes to an external organizational unit and refers to the process by which an organization gives part of its work to another firm/organization and makes it responsible for most of the applications as well as the design of the enterprise business process. "Reshoring," sometimes called "backshoring," is when jobs that were offshored are brought back onshore.

In the selections that follow, both sides of this interesting topic will be discussed. In the first article, Andrew Sikula and colleagues discuss reasons why a movement to insourcing is currently occurring. The authors conclude that this movement is going to expand during the next several years in the United States. In contrast to this position, David Lynch observes that many of the jobs a nation such as China is losing are heading to other low-cost Asian nations. In addition, he observes that while some jobs have returned to the United States, other jobs are still being shipped out of the country.

YES

Andrew Sikula, Sr., et al.

Insourcing: Reversing American Outsourcing in the New World Economy

Pendulum Swings and Globality

Politics and economics swing like a pendulum. So do life, health and human emotions. What is a popular belief and value during one period of time may not be in another. Even deep-seated religion is subject to fiuctuation. These fiows of nature and humankind apply to the marketplace as well. Abundances and shortages of supply and demand come and go for all goods and services. This phenomenon as it applies to the insourcing vs. outsourcing issue is the subject of this commentary and analysis.

We now live in a new world economy of global interaction and wholeness. Events in any part of the earth can and do almost instantaneously affect all other parts of the globe. High speed digital electronic communications have greatly helped to speed up this interactivity.

For decades now, economists have convinced us that we live in one international marketplace in which global laws of supply and demand determine consumer behavior. Also, increasingly recognized is the fact that politics, culture, ethics and science are now global as well. Mankind, morality, nature and the weather follow certain absolute laws and set patterns. They may be displayed differently in various locations at any point in time, but they are all universals with some common principles. The talk over the last many decades on relationism, situationalism and human specialty and uniqueness has been overdone. In truth, human beings have more in common than they have differences, and different lands and cultures are more alike than disparate.

Having said this about human and geographical similarity, we still need to recognize the pendulum swing between extremes within common production and manufacturing life cycles. This article discusses the human resource pendulum swing between insourcing and outsourcing work effort and accomplishment.

Insourcing Definition

Insourcing is when an organization uses especially internal labor and personnel, but other resources as well, to supply the operational needs of its enterprise. Insourcing is a management decision made to maintain control of critical production or competencies. Insourcing is the opposite of outsourcing which is the process of firms shifting work outside of its borders.

In recent decades in our increasingly global environment and marketplace, insourcing has taken on an expanded definition. It now often means letting work go outside yet keeping it within national boundaries rather than subcontracting to suppliers overseas. Outsourcing today often is synonymous with offshoring or moving work offshore to another country typically overseas. When the insourcing definition is expanded in this manner, it is an extension of a company's workplace and workforce without transferring the project management and decision-making control to an external provider.

Insourcing is akin to the "promotion from within" concept. Labor and personnel still constitute the bulk of both core competencies and operational expenses for most organizations. Keeping employees trained, developed, motivated and happy at work are pivotal characteristics of well-run, successful enterprises. This is often best achieved when workers are given internal opportunities for professional growth and personal advancement. Promotion from within is the manner in which this becomes possible. In-housing promotions and advancements usually make the majority happy. The outside hiring of personnel, especially into key, well-paid organizational positions, often demoralizes loyal staff members who have often waited years for a chance to advance themselves within their current employment structure. Inside promotions usually result in a chain of internal other promotions from within which spread new life, enthusiasm and additional vigor among many dedicated and aspiring current coworkers and colleagues. As an example, Ashland University in Ohio within the last three years has gone inside for most of its key position openings including University President, Seminary President, Provost, Graduate School Dean, Education Dean, Business Vice President and Facilities Vice President.

Insourcing Evolution

Insourcing vs. outsourcing as resource decisions have always been under close examination. However, the last three decades have seen a great expansion of the outsourcing phenomenon. In the early 1980s, organizations in the United States and elsewhere began delegating their non-core functions to external organizations which specialized in providing a particular product, service or function. Initially, outsourcing was done in an attempt to save on labor costs as many unionized companies found it cheaper to produce their products in non-unionized, underdeveloped countries, even though other raw material transportation costs might increase. This first started for unskilled labor jobs but quickly spread to technical labor, white collar positions, and then to professional services. Eventually, sometimes even entire departmental work units were shifted overseas. Areas of organizational operation once thought to be almost sacred, or at least extremely critical, began to appear in India, Indonesia, Japan, Vietnam, the Dominican Republic and elsewhere. Examples include accounts payable, billing, training, engineering, manufacturing, customer service, technical support, sales/ordering, and others. Clothing companies such as Levi Strauss and shoe companies such as Nike and Reebok often have manufacturing, marketing and distribution all done on foreign soil. International call centers now often perform air travel, hotel reservations and tele-marketing. Outsourcing overseas has even spread to highly specialized medical fields including clinical records, disease diagnosis and the reading of x-rays. In the minds of many, the idea that anything and everything can be outsourced became a possibility.

This all began to change around the turn of the millennium and as we entered the 21st Century. Unhappy customers, especially in regard to foreign-based call centers, started the outsourcing reversal. Overseas scandals, global economic recession and terrorism fueled the embers. A lack of control both in terms of company operations and national security strengthened a turn to insourcing. "Speed to market" became a much more important competitive sales advantage as long distances and transportation costs increasingly offset lower labor expense. Also, in the United States, we are beginning to see a resurgence of national pride, an increased concern for safety, and a desire to return to older traditional work patterns and ways of accomplishing tasks. All of these factors have resulted in a new wave of insourcing and a decline in the popularity and practice of outsourcing. Outsourcing is still a robust theme and practice, but it has lost its momentum.

Insourcing Determinants

There are many reasons why the resourcing pendulum has begun to significantly swing back toward insourcing and away from outsourcing within America and elsewhere. We will briefiy mention eight determinants below. They are easy to understand and do not need prolonged elaboration. The eight insourcing factors or determinants roughly in order of importance include (1) communication; (2) employee morale/loyalty; (3) control; (4) security; (5) transportation; (6) innovation; (7) customer satisfaction; and (8) speed to market.

Communication

It is obviously easier to communicate with someone who is nearby rather than far away. Although computers and digital electronics have made it much easier to communicate with distant colleagues and partners, distance still is a significant barrier to communication. Time differences and various time zones are part and parcel of the communication distance problem. Insourcing reduces or eliminates this obstacle. Considerable time saving is achieved when resource supply chain components are local or internal. Since time is money, expenses can be minimized and profits maximized more readily with neighboring or nearby resources. Communicating is a human interaction, and although it can be aided by computers and electronics, most communication is initiated, received and acted upon by human beings. People communicate more efficiently and effectively when geographical space is lessened.

Employee Morale/Loyalty

Worker motivation and dedication are enhanced when employees know that their work efforts are appreciated and rewarded. Keeping work and promotions inside an organization reduces employee turnover and lowers employee training and management development expenses. Promotion from within costs much less than outsourcing in terms of advertising costs, travel expenses for interviewees, and especially in terms of negotiated salaries. People who know that they will have a chance to move ahead professionally and get promotions over time within their own organization can be life-long, productive assets to an organization. On the other hand, letting work that was formally done inside now go outside of company walls almost always will lead to unhappy employees who start to feel that their work careers may be in jeopardy. The fear of losing one's job and economic insecurity result when companies outsource management employment opportunities.

Control

Control is exercising restraint, direction and command over people and resources. Holding things in check and supervision are easiest to achieve and maintain when production and distribution factors or inputs are nearby. Work products or services need to be regulated and quality checked, and insourcing makes such requirements easier to achieve than does outsourcing. Administration and guidance can be better accomplished and more economically implemented, especially in regard to human oversight, if managers are local instead of regional, national and/or international.

Security

Security is an extension and expansion of control. Security involves safety and freedom from danger and risk. Security eliminates doubt and anxiety and brings about protection and confidence. Security involves precautions taken to guard against crime, theft, attack, sabotage and/ or espionage. Security enhances assurance and attempts to guarantee against loss. Security is vital at the personal, corporate and national levels. Insourcing helps bring about security to societal levels and becomes more difficult as resource supply chains are outsourced. Security is becoming more important at all social strata, as we now live in an increasingly insecure world, where violent terrorist attacks are daily events throughout the world. Homeland security is currently viewed as the number one priority for our national government by most Americans.

Transportation

Goods and services must be delivered to customers. With goods, and with services to a lesser degree, physical distance separates where a product is made from where it is consumed. This space interval may be thousands of miles, especially when offshoring is involved. Even domestic conveyance of items may involve long transport. For example, the average distance a food item purchased in the USA travels between production and consumption is 1,500 miles. The transfer of items across seas can be extremely expensive, and now foreign piracy has become an additional expense and concern. Insourcing can significantly reduce product transportation delivery problems and costs.

Innovation

Innovation is the introduction of new products, services and methods. Innovation involves novel conception, design, creation and invention. It was once thought that this research and development (R&D) requirement for sustained business advantage could best be achieved using an array of employed international professionals. Some evidence suggests otherwise. Today, most business experts believe that insourcing R&D produces better results than outsourcing same. The United States has always been the leader in introducing new products and services to the world, and this is still the case. Although foreign countries may more cheaply copy, produce and improve American invented products, the USA still retains an edge in innovation and creating new things.

Customer Satisfaction

U.S. employers sometimes have had to learn the hard way that happy customers are often more concerned about quality rather than the price of goods and services. This is especially true of services, but it applies to products or goods as well. For example, many companies have seen a big increase in unhappy customers as a result of outsourcing technical services, often to India. Especially in regard to call centers, such corporations have underestimated the negative impact that customer dissatisfaction can have on the bottom line. Also, there is a movement to "Buy American" products, and this movement has both formal organizational bodies as well as unorganized individuals supporting the "made in the USA" purchasing philosophy.

Speed to Market

Price and quality are not the only factors affecting buying decisions. Increasingly important is speed to market or how quickly one might have a purchased good or service in hand. In many cases, speed to market is more important than price and/or quality. Common examples are pharmaceutical purchases. However, sometimes even very big ticket items are involved. Immediate occupancy can affect a home purchase, and the delivery date of a new car often determines who gets the sale. We live in an egocentric world where immediate gratification and current pleasure are important considerations for many overeager consumers. Insourcing enhances the speed to market consumption criterion because it helps eliminate delivery delays.

Outsourcing Weights

There are, of course, also reasons why companies have used outsourcing in the past and will continue to utilize it. We will next list the eight main determinants of outsourcing decisions, again in an estimated descending order of importance. These are easy to comprehend and they do not need individual commentary. Eight outsourcing factors or determinants are (1) labor cost; (2) management delegation; (3) simplicity; (4) expertise; (5) competition; (6) quality; (7) adaptability; and (8) tax advantages.

A few general comments about these eight variables should suffice. Both management delegation and simplicity involve the belief that some unskilled and other professional personnel labor can be performed more economically by workers in undeveloped or underdeveloped countries where wages and salaries are considerably lower than in the United States. There is also the belief, which is erroneous, that this delegation of work elsewhere will make domestic operational matters easier or simpler to manage. Combine these considerations with the often mistaken idea that increased competition will result in hiring the most expert resource suppliers who will produce a better product and service—and presto, you have a rationale for outsourcing. And if things do not go well, you can change the whole thing or arrangement tomorrow or next year (the adaptability advantage). Also, there are both legitimate tax advantages for outsourcing as well as (many believe) other hidden or illegal monetary gains to be had when offshoring activities are involved. . . .

In reality, insourcing vs. outsourcing is neither an either/or nor a black/white decision. It is not necessary to do only one or the other. An organization can insource and outsource at the same time. By insourcing and outsourcing simultaneously, an enterprise can have the best of what both offer in an attempt to obtain a sustainable competitive advantage. We might appropriately label this combination of insourcing and outsourcing as "rightsourcing". However, it is nonetheless true that organizations collectively are seeing a trend away from outsourcing and back to insourcing as the resource supply pendulum shifts to the other direction from where it has been for the last three decades.

Insourcing Examples

Americans and others are experiencing a return to the insourcing of supply chain resources. Internal suppliers of goods and services have come about, especially during the last eight years plus, because of declining economic conditions worldwide and a growing concern for homeland security caused by terrorism throughout the world. We will give some examples of enhanced resource insourcing at the personal-individual, professional-institutional, and governmental-national levels.

Personal-Individual

In an effort to reduce spending, Americans are doing a lot more for themselves now rather than relying so much on outside service providers. More child and elder care is being done by family members and/or close friends rather than by day care and nursing home agencies. Since WalMart has doubled the cost of an oil/filter change from $15 to $30, many men today are now doing this chore of maintenance on family automobiles. Netfiix is booming as people watch more movies at home and fewer in theatres. Fancy restaurant dinners have been cut back as family members eat more meals at home. Haircuts, exercising and alcoholic consumption at home are recently more commonplace. Home elder care is up and hospice residences now typically involve only the last couple days of life. Much of this has been made possible by the high unemployment rate with many people no longer having regular work to occupy their time.

Professional-Institutional

Even professional work is now being performed by regular folk trying to save a buck. Paying a plumber $75 an hour has incentivized many men and women to fix their own leaky faucets and toilets. Home remodeling is often now done by residents rather than by skilled construction tradesmen. Turbo Tax has enabled many households to prepare their own tax returns rather than rely on outside experts to do the work. Legal Zoom has enabled anyone and everyone to now prepare their own wills, trust, advance directives, power of attorney, and other legal documents without the exorbitant fees of an attorney.

Not just individuals but institutions have also turned to insourcing rather than outsourcing to save money. For example, within healthcare, the hospitalist movement is replacing the need for external physicians to make so many in-hospital patient rounds. Doctors and hospitals now hire other doctors who work full time within a hospital to make patient calls converting former travel time to patient care oversight involvement. Universities are using overtime, graduate assistants, adjuncts, full-time temps, term contracts, electronic course delivery, and interims to fill faculty and staff position more as tenured and tenuretrack faculty positions decline appreciably in number. Hourly billing by lawyers and accountants is used less today and may become a relic of history

as legal insourcing takes hold. Prepaid legal service providers are available today for both individuals and institutions.

Governmental-National

At the national level as well, there is evidence of a move away from outsourcing and toward insourcing. Much of this movement is related to U. S. over-reliance on foreign crude oil produced by countries that are anti-American. The American expansion of natural gas capacity and usage is one such happening. So is the whole Going Green movement as solar, wind and water power are being har- nessed more. Recycling is a form of insourcing. Using the National Guard for border patrol and emergency response are governmental-national insourcing examples. Using prison inmates to clean up road sides and fight fires are other government insourcing examples. AmeriCorps and its various internal service projects illustrate national insourcing. And indeed, the whole movement toward more volunteerism and service assistance to those in need is becoming increasingly organized today and is now supplementing our traditional national and governmental insourcing assistance organizations such as the Red Cross, Salvation Army, Goodwill, Meals on Wheels, veteran service organizations, homeless shelters, et al.

The Future of Insourcing

Insourcing is going to expand during the next several years in America, especially at the governmental-national level. In fact, in the minds of many, an overabundance of insourcing at the governmental-national level will cause more problems than it will solve because of high debt financing and the loss of individual freedom issues. Whether or not this will happen remains to be seen, but we are moving in this direction.

Uncle Sam is the biggest employer in the United States. There are 1.8 million federal employees. If you add in military and civilian Department of Defense employees, the number jumps to 4.8 million. During years of Republican rule, there was an effort to move many government jobs to the private sector. This is changing rapidly under President Obama. This past July, the Director of the Office of Management and Budget issued a memo to all Executive Branch departments strongly suggesting that it would be better to have more federal employees and fewer private contract workers. Accordingly, the Department of Defense is planning to reduce outside contractors and boost internal personnel by 33,400 civilian employees. Intelligence agencies have insourced thousands of contractor jobs already. The Department of Defense is planning to insource 3,200 formerly contracted positions.

Some have said that the government, and especially the military in recent years, has had a research supply chain management mentality of "just in case," while the private sector believes in and practices a "just in time" philosophy. Clearly, politicians of both parties have committed us and our offspring to more government than we can afford. With President Obama's call for public service and the current economic downturn, there has never been a better time to attract people into federal work positions. However, a rush to insource thousands of positions while trying to take on more and more government programs can end in disaster. Government control of banking, the auto industry, insurance, education and health care is moving forward. Government agencies should approach insourcing with a clear plan of action focusing on inherently governmental positions (such as defense), key mission critical roles (such as economic stability), and core competencies (such as leadership). It must be remembered and should be practiced that government can best go about the people's business by largely staying out of it. The dilemma is obvious. Yes, there is a reversing trend toward more insourcing and less outsourcing, and this is a good movement in the right direction. But it is a move that should predominantly be featured within our culture at the personal-individual and professional-institutional levels and not at the governmental-national one. Otherwise, the uniqueness and promise of our great experience and investment in democracy will be at risk.

ANDREW SIKULA, SR., is a professor at Marshall University.

CHONG W. KIM is a professor at Marshall University.

CHARLES K. BRAUN is a professor at Marshall University.

JOHN SIKULA is vice president for Regional Centers and Outreach at Ashland University.

David J. Lynch

 **NO**

'Reshoring' of Jobs Looks Meager

This spring, President Obama said he had "good news" to report: Lost American jobs are returning to the U.S. "For a lot of businesses," the president told a crowd in Albany, N.Y., on May 8, "it's now starting to make sense to bring jobs back home." In trumpeting this "reshoring" of jobs from abroad, the administration points to employers, including General Electric (GE) and Caterpillar (CAT), that have shifted some manufacturing to the U.S. The president also cited an April online survey by Boston Consulting Group showing that 37 percent of manufacturers with sales of more than $1 billion and almost half of those with more than $10 billion "plan to or are actively considering bringing back production from China to the U.S."

Yet there's little data to back up claims of a reshoring rush. For every company Obama praises for coming back home, there are others still shipping jobs out of the country. Honeywell International (HON) in Acton, Mass., plans to eliminate 23 positions by yearend when manufacturing of the company's stainless steel products moves to Nanjing, China. Boston Scientific (BSX) let go about 1,100 workers when the company moved production of its medical stents from Miami to Costa Rica.

The net effect of this two-way traffic on the labor market has been "zero," says Michael Janssen of the Hackett Group (HCKT), a business consulting firm that released a contrarian report on reshoring in May. "Some of these jobs that are coming back get a lot of press," he says. "There are just as many that get no press coverage still going offshore."

The White House stresses that manufacturers have added 495,000 jobs since January 2010, when factory employment bottomed out at almost 6 million below the 2000 level. Nearly 40 percent of those jobs were lost to other countries, either directly or because consumers chose imports over American-made products, says Robert Scott of the Economic Policy Institute in Washington. Now, a combination of rising wages for Chinese workers, a strengthening Chinese currency, and a new appreciation of the virtues of domestic production—including low-cost natural gas—has sparked a return to U.S. manufacturing, the administration says.

No one knows how many of the manufacturing jobs created since 2010 actually made a round trip from the U.S. to a foreign address and back. And if jobs are returning, they're doing so slowly. At the current pace of recovery, it will take 25 years for the U.S. to regain all the factory jobs lost since 2000.

China's cost advantage is gradually eroding. In 2005 production in China was 31 percent cheaper than in advanced nations, according to the Hackett Group's calculations. By 2013 the gap will be down to 16 percent, small enough for U.S. production to make sense in some cases, says the study. Likewise, Hal Sirkin, who wrote a 2011 Boston Consulting Group report that's optimistic about a U.S. manufacturing comeback, estimates that over the next eight years 2 million to 3 million jobs could result from improved U.S. competitiveness. "A significant chunk will be jobs that went to other countries and came back," he says.

So far, many of the jobs China is losing aren't heading to the U.S. but to other low-cost Asian nations. Rising wages in China led Coach (COH) to start looking for alternate places to make its wallets and handbags. By 2015 the company aims to reduce China's share of its production to about 50 percent from almost 80 percent today. New orders will be sent to factories in Vietnam, Indonesia, Thailand, and the Philippines. Reshoring to somebody else's shores will be more common in coming years than jobs returning to the U.S., says Tim Leunig, who teaches economic history at the London School of Economics: "The next president of the United States, whoever he is, will end his term with fewer Americans working in manufacturing than he inherited."

The bottom line: *Though manufacturers have created 495,000 jobs since 2010, there's little evidence it's because of a reshoring surge.*

DAVID J. LYNCH *is a reporter for Bloomburg News in Washington, DC.*

EXPLORING THE ISSUE

Will the Use of Reshoring/Insourcing by Corporations Increase?

Critical Thinking and Reflection

1. What might be the tactics of a reshoring/insourcing strategy?
2. How might a reshoring/insourcing strategy be implemented in a corporation?
3. What might be the costs to consumers, corporations, and the nation of corporations committed to a reshoring/insourcing strategy?
4. What is the likelihood that an enacted reshoring/insourcing strategy will lead to anticipated outcomes?
5. What does the future hold for companies following reshoring/insourcing strategies?

Is There Common Ground?

One reason the issue of reshoring/insourcing is so contentious is that both sides of this issue can cite data and provide examples in support of their position. For example, during times of high unemployment in a nation or region, society would seek opportunities for employment by reshoring or insourcing work back to that nation or region. In contrast, the argument can be made that the costs of operation and production might be lower when offshoring or outsourcing policies and practices are utilized. Thus, these practices may have either positive and/or negative effects on a corporation's bottom line or both. While finding common ground on basic aspects of this important management topic is difficult, there is consensus that reshoring/insourcing policies are an important topic that will be debated for quite some time.

Additional Resources

Cable, C. (2010). "Making the Case for Made in America," *Industry Week*, April, p. 56.

Cancino, A. and Jackson, C.V. (2012). "More Man-ufacturing Work Returns to U.S. Shores," *Chicago Tribune*, March 27.

DePass, D. (2012). "For Some Companies, 'Reshoring' Jobs Gains Appeal," *The Dallas Morning News*, August 11.

Free, M. (2012). "Is the Re-shoring of Manufacturing a Trend or a Trickle?" *Forbes*, June 27.

Kettl, D. F. (2012). "Insourcing Jobs Can Only Happen with States' Help," *Governing*, April.

Moser, H. C. (2012). "U.S. Manufacturing: Forgotten Wisdom from 1791," *Manufacturing Engineering*, March, p. 176.

Murphy, T. (2003). "Insourcing," *WARD'S AutoWorld*, May, pp. 44–48.

Quinn, J. B. & Hilmer, F.B. (1994). "Strategic Outsourcing," *Sloan Management Review*, Summer, pp. 43–55.

Internet References . . .

A New Chinese Export—Jobs

Knowledge@Wharton. (2012). "A New Chinese Export—Jobs."

http://business.time.com/2012/04/12/a-new-chinese-export-jobs/

Re-Shoring: Manufacturers Make a U-Turn

Morris, C. (2012). "Re-Shoring: Manufacturers Make a U-Turn."

http://www.cnbc.com/id/47535355//

Selected, Edited, and with Issue Framing Material by:
Kathleen J. Barnes, *William Paterson University*
and
George E. Smith, *University of South Carolina, Beaufort*

ISSUE

Does Expanding via Mergers and Acquisitions Make for Sound Corporate Strategy?

YES: Rosy Kalra, from "Mergers and Acquisitions: An Empirical Study on the Post-Merger Performance of Selected Corporate Firms in India," *The IUP Journal of Business Strategy* (2013)

NO: Anand Sanwal, from "M&A's Losing Hand," *Business Finance Magazine* (2008)

Learning Outcomes

After reading this issue, you will be able to:

- Define mergers and acquisitions.
- Explain both positive and negative consequences of corporate mergers and acquisitions.
- Discuss the potential risks of mergers and acquisitions.
- List the known "best practices" for mergers and acquisitions.

ISSUE SUMMARY

YES: Rosy Kalra studied 47 firms listed in Indian stock exchanges which underwent mergers and acquisitions between April 1, 2008 and March 31, 2009. Kalra's study showed there is significant improvement in the liquidity, profitability, operating performance, and financial leverage for a few merged/acquirer firms.

NO: Anand Sanwal examines 33 large merger and acquisition (M&A) transactions from Europe, Canada, and the United States. The evidence is that a great number of these M&A transactions have actually destroyed value. He also contends that in many of the transactions that did fare well, luck was often a large factor.

Banks, cars, pharmaceuticals, phones, and beer—what do all these have in common? If you said "abundant merger and acquisition (M&A) activity in their industries," you are absolutely correct. Keep in mind that these are by no means the only industries to experience M&A transactions. For example, when looking in current business periodicals it doesn't take long to learn about the latest M&A transactions and deals. Indeed, mergers (two firms joining together to become one) and acquisitions (one firm buying another) are common means of expansion for many firms. They're also common means of expansion across industries, particularly when firms are looking to move into new business areas.

Firms undertake M&As for many, varied reasons. Among other things, the mergers and acquirers feel that they can increase revenues or cut costs through marketing activities such as cross-selling or bundling products together from the two firms. These companies may also believe that they can share various administrative duties, thus reducing costs further. Other firms undertake M&As as a means of obtaining valuable technology or critical skills that the target may possess. Still others try to diversify business activities to help control their exposure to risk. Sometimes activity is even triggered by other M&A activities, almost as if companies simply don't want to be left behind when an M&A wave is happening. Regardless of the reasons driving M&As, one thing seems evident, M&A transactions are not going away. All of this activity, however, hides an important, seldom-asked question: In reality, do M&As actually generate the value that is expected?

Contrary to those advocates that view M&A activity as a good expansion vehicle, many people argue that past M&A activity has actually destroyed value—so much so, in fact, that it suggests that it may not be sound corporate strategy. Although actual failure rates for M&A transactions depend upon a variety of variables (e.g., timeframe examined, measures used, etc.), it is not uncommon to see estimates stating poor performance or failure for M&As in the range of one-half to two-thirds of all such activity (Vaughn, 2008). Reasons for failures can be numerous. They range from not being able to integrate opposing corporate cultures to failing to capture the synergies that were expected to emerge from the combined entities. Not surprisingly, given these risks, internally generated growth initiatives are often advocated over attempting M&As. Author John Cummings notes that this may be particularly Salient, given the current market conditions: "With debt financing likely scarce for the foreseeable future, the only way forward for most growth-minded organizations is via internally generated profitable revenue expansion—the organic route" (Cummings, 2008, pp. 12–17).

In the "YES" side selection, author Rosy Kalra examined 47 firms listed in Indian stock exchanges which underwent mergers and acquisitions April 1, 2008–March 31, 2009 and captured the impact of mergers and acquisitions on liquidity, profitability, operating performance, and leverage of sample merged/acquirer companies. The study concluded that the Indian corporate firms over a period of April 2008–March 2009 have a significant impact on the liquidity, profitability, operating performance, and financial risk position of acquirer forms in India.

The "NO" side of this debate is presented in Anand Sanwal's article where he provides evidence suggesting that a great number of recent large transactions have actually destroyed value. Additionally, he contends that many transactions that did fare well were often successful because of luck, rather than skill in managing the transaction. Although Sanwal discusses some factors that may increase the success of large M&As, he qualifies this discussion by noting that ". . . . all the research in the world won't change the fact that people like headlines and deals are going to happen." As you read through the selections, ask yourself if these M&A deals are the result of corporate executives chasing headlines or if they represent strategically sound corporate transactions.

YES ←

Rosy Kalra

Mergers and Acquisitions:
An Empirical Study on the Post-Merger
Performance of Selected Corporate Firms in India

Introduction

An entrepreneur can grow his business either by internal expansion or by external expansion. In the case of internal expansion, a firm grows gradually over time in the normal course of the business through acquisition of new assets, replacement of the technologically obsolete equipments and the establishment of new lines of products. But in external expansion, a firm acquires a running business and grows overnight through corporate combinations. These combinations are in the form of mergers, acquisitions, amalgamations and takeovers and have now become important features of corporate restructuring. They have been playing an important role in the external growth of a number of leading companies the worldover.

The primary motives of almost all M&As are congruent with the main purpose for the existence in the business as well as maximizing the shareholders' value. But the question often arises whether all the firms that are merged/acquired are ending up with maximization of profits and shareholders' value? In some cases, the shareholders' wealth gets reduced after a firm is merged/acquired. Hence, the present study is carried out to seek answers to the stated question by evaluating the pre- and post-merger performance of the selected companies considering three years period before and after the process of M&A.

Literature Review

There are a number of studies on the subject; however, there are not many conducted in the Indian context.

Harris *et al.* analyzed the impact of horizontal mergers of US hospital's technical efficiency pre- and post-merger. By using DEA approach, they found a positive impact on hospital's level of efficiency. Constant returns-to-scale model indicated an overall reduction in input utilization after merger as compared to variable returns-to-scale model. Sydney and Jerayr examined positive and negative transfer effects in acquiring an organization. The study was carried out on data obtained from 96 organizations. The results suggested that the routines and practices established in prior situation transfer to new situations and that the effect of such transfer depends on the similarity of industrial environments. Dash analyzed the financial impact of mergers on the shareholders of the acquirer firms. The study found that on an average mergers lead to value destruction, irrespective of their pattern over a long period of time and the destruction is relatively greater in the case of unrelated mergers. Moeller *et al.* analyzed the performance of acquirer firms through two major merger waves that occurred during the period of 1998 to 2001. It was found that even when the target shareholder benefits were taken into account, net impacts still fell by $134 bn. Jarrod *et al.* used semi-structured interviews to identify the relation between corporate strategic planning and M&A strategy, examined the due diligence process in screening a merger or acquisition and evaluated previous experience in successful M&As. The study found that there was a clear alignment between corporate and M&A strategic objectives but that each organization had a different emphasis on individual criterion. Due diligence was also critical to success, and its particular value lay in removing managerial ego and justifying the business case. Finally, there was mixed evidence on the value of experience with improved results from using a flexible framework of assessment. David analyzed the prices paid by foreign firms for acquisitions in the US relative to the price paid by the US firms for mergers. The findings indicate that foreign firms do pay more for the US acquisitions, and that this does result in significantly lower returns on M&As investment in the US by foreign firms. Pramod and Vidvadhar analyzed the impact of mergers on the operating performance of acquiring corporate in different industries by calculating various financial ratios on the selected firms during the period of 1991 to 2003. It was found that mergers had a slightly positive impact on profitability of firms in the banking and finance industry, whereas the pharmaceuticals, textiles and electrical equipment sectors had a negative impact on the operating performance.

Isabel and Susana analyzed family versus non-family firm returns under different legal environments when an M&A is announced. The findings show that family ownership has a significant positive influence on acquirer shareholder M&A valuation. However, a major shareholder ownership of 32% has a negative impact.[1]

Indhumathi *et al.* also analyzed the performance of the acquirer and target corporate firms before and after the period of mergers by calculating various ratios and also applied *t*-test to compare the performance during the study period. The study found that the acquirer corporate firms improved their financial performance after the merger.

Objective of the Study

- To study the impact of M&As on the liquidity, profitability, operating performance and leverage of merged/acquirer companies.

Hypotheses

Based on the objective of the study, the following hypotheses are developed:

H_1:   *There is no significant improvement in the liquidity of merged/acquirer firms.*

H_2:   *There is no significant improvement in the profitability of merged/acquirer firms.*

H_3:   *There is no significant improvement in the operating performance of merged/acquirer firms.*

H_4:   *There is no significant decline in the financial risks of merged/acquirer firms.*

Data and Methodology

The study includes companies which have undergone merger in the period April 1, 2008-March 31, 2009. The study is based on the secondary data taken from the Centre for Monitoring Indian Economy (CMIE) business beacon database, annual reports of selected units, investment websites like moneycontrol.com, indiainfoline.com, websites of the BSE and NSE. Convenience sampling has been employed to select the sample companies for the study. The sample consists of 47 selected merged and acquirer companies listed in BSE or NSE, whose asset worth is more than ₹ 500 cr and for which data was available for the entire period (Table 1). The financial data has been collected for seven years from 2006–2012. The merger completion year 2009 was denoted as year 0. Years 2006, 2007 and 2008 are considered as pre M&A deal years, whereas year 2009 is considered as M&A deal year and years 2010, 2011, 2012 are considered as post deal years.

The pre and post-merger averages for a set of key financial ratios have been computed for 3 years prior to and 3 years after the year of merger completion. To study the impact of M&As on the overall performance of merged/acquirer firms, the analysis focuses on four elements, viz., liquidity, profitability, operating performance and financial risks or leverage. The financial ratios used in the study are Current Ratio, Quick Ratio, Gross Profit Ratio, Net Profit Ratio, Return on Assets, Return on Capital Employed, Debtors Turnover Ratio, Fixed Assets Turnover Ratio, Total Assets Turnover Ratio,

Table 1

Industrial Classification of Selected Companies

Sl. No.	Industry	No. of Companies M&A	No. of Companies Selected
1.	Chemicals and Pharmaceuticals	37	10
2.	Construction and Real Estate	14	6
3.	Finance and Investments	25	3
4.	Food and Beverages	11	3
5.	Machinery	8	3
6.	Metals and Metal Products	21	6
7.	Non-Metallic Mineral Products	10	3
8.	Services	54	7
9.	Textiles	9	2
10.	Transport Equipment	9	4
11.	Electricity	5	0
12.	Mining	3	0
13.	Miscellaneous	11	0
	Total	**217**	**47**

Mergers and Acquisitions: An Empirical Study on the Post-Merger Performance of Selected Corporate Firms in India

Debt Equity Ratio and Interest Coverage Ratio. The post-merger performance has been compared with the pre-merger performance and tested for significant differences using paired '*t*' test at confidence level of 0.05.

Results

The performance of the selected acquirer firms in respect of their liquidity, operating performance, profitability and leverage after merger has been compared to that before merger using *t*-test, and the results of the analysis are presented.

Impact of Merger on the Liquidity of Acquirer Firms

The liquidity ratios used for studying the impact of merger are Current Ratio (CR) and Quick Ratio (QR).

Current Ratio

The CR is the most commonly used ratio for measuring the liquidity position of firms which is also called 'working capital ratio'. It expresses the relationship between current assets and current liabilities.

CR is increased after merger for 29 acquirer firms. From p-values, it is inferred that the CR of Cadila Healthcare Ltd., Reliance Industries Ltd., Tata Chemicals, Siemens Ltd., Sterlite Industries (India) Ltd., and Exide Industries Ltd. increased significantly after M&A process. Overall, it is found that the liquidity position in of CR has improved for six firm after merger.

Quick Ratio

QR shows the relationship between quick or liquid assets and quick liabilities.

It is clear that QR is increased after merger for 22 acquirer firms. QR of Cadila Healthcare Ltd., HDFC Bank, Sterlite Industries (India) Ltd., and HCL Infosystems Ltd. increased significantly after M&A process. Overall, it is found that the liquidity position in terms of QR has improved for four firms after merger.

Impact of Merger on Profitability of Acquirer Firms

The profitability measures considered for the analysis are: Gross Profit Ratio, Net profit Ratio, Return on Assets and Return on Capital Employed.

Gross Profit Ratio

Gross Profit Ratio (GPR) establishes a relationship between gross profit and income.

GPR increased after merger for 20 acquirer firms. GPR of E I D-Parry (India) Ltd. and Gitanjali Gems Ltd. increased significantly after M&A process. Overall, it is found that the profitability in terms of GPR has improved for two firms after merger.

Net Profit Ratio

Net profit ratio establishes a relationship between net profit (after tax) and income. It indicates the overall efficiency of the firms. If the profit is not sufficient, the firm will not be able to achieve satisfactory *ROI*.

Net Profit Ratio increased after merger for 11 acquirer firms. Net Profit Ratio of Cadila Healthcare Ltd. increased significantly after M&A process. Overall, it is found that the profitability in terms of NPR has improved for one firm after merger.

Return on Assets

Return on Assets, popularly known as ROA, is the relationship between net profits after interest and taxes and its total assets. This ratio is an indicator of how profitable a company is in relation to its total assets. It is calculated by dividing a company's annual earnings by its total assets. Sometimes, this is referred to as 'return on investment'.

ROA increased after merger for 33 acquirer firms. ROA of Aarti Industries Ltd., Jubilant Life Sciences Ltd., Dabur India Ltd., Tata Chemicals, Berger Paints India Ltd., Asian Paints Ltd., Gammon India Ltd., State Bank of India, A K Capital Services Ltd., United Spirits Ltd., Kirloskar Brothers Ltd., Steel Authority of India Ltd., Asian Star Co. Ltd., Gitanjali Gems Ltd., HCL Infosystems Ltd., Idea Cellular Ltd., Gati Ltd., Educomp Solutions Ltd., Bombay Rayon Fashions Ltd. and Amtek Auto Ltd. increased significantly after M&A process. Overall, it is found that the profitability in terms of ROA has improved for 20 firms after merger.

Return on Capital Employed

Return on Capital Employed is the primary ratio and is used to measure the overall profitability and efficiency of a business. It increased after merger for 13 acquirer firms. From p-values, it is inferred that the ROCE of all 13 companies increased insignificantly after M&A process. Overall, it is found that the profitability in terms of ROCE has not improved for any company after merger.

Impact of Merger on the Operating Performance of Acquirer Firms

In order to analyze the impact of merger on the operating performance of merged/acqirer firms, three measures are used, viz.; Debtors' Turnover Ratio (DTR), Fixed Assets Turnover Ratio (FATR) and Total Assets Turnover Ratio (TATR).

Debtors Turnover Ratio

Debtors Turnover Ratio (DTR) is an accounting measure used to quantify a firm's effectiveness in extending credit as well as collecting debts. DTR measures how efficiently a firm uses its assets. This ratio is an indication of the number of times debtors' turnover on an average in each year.

DTR increased after merger for 15 acquirer firms. DTR of Asian Paints Ltd. and Bharti Airtel Ltd. increased significantly after M&A process. Overall, it is found from the comparison of DTRs between pre- and post-merger periods that the operating performance in terms of DTR has improved for two firms after merger.

Fixed Assets Turnover Ratio

Fixed Assets Turnover Ratio (FATR) establishes the relationship between fixed assets and net sales, indicating how efficiently they have been used in achieving the sales. A high ratio indicates efficient utilization of fixed assets and a low ratio indicates inefficient utilization.

FATR increased after merger for 15 acquirer firms. FATR of Lupin Ltd., Tata Chemicals, E I D-Parry (India) Ltd. and

HCL Technologies increased significantly after M&A process. Overall, it is found from the comparison of FATRs between pre- and post-merger periods that the operating performance in terms of FATR has improved for four firms after merger.

Total Assets Turnover Ratio

The financial analysts normally like to compute the total assets turnover in addition to or instead of the fixed assets turnover. This ratio shows the firm's ability to generate sales from all financial resources committed to total assets. Total Assets (TA) include Net Fixed Assets (NFA) and Current Assets (CA), (TA = NFA + CA).

The Total Assets Turnover Ratio (TATR) increased after merger for 15 acquirer firms. TATR of Lupin Ltd., Asian Star Co. Ltd. and HCL Technologies increased significantly after M&A process. Overall, it is found that the operating performance in terms of TATR has improved for three firms after merger.

Financial Risk of Acquirer Firms After Merger

In order to study the impact of merger on financial risk of the acquirer firms, two measures, namely, ratio of debt to equity (DER) and interest coverage ratio have been used.

Debt Equity Ratio

This is a measure of a company's financial leverage calculated by dividing its total liabilities by stockholders' equity It indicates what proportion of equity and debt the company is using to finance its assets.

DER increased after merger for 24 acquirer firms. DER of Gammon India Ltd., Jaiprakash Associates Ltd. and Steel Authority of India Ltd. increased significantly after M&A process. Overall, it is found from the comparison of DERs between pre- and post-merger periods that the financial leverage in terms of DER has improved for 3 firms after merger.

Interest Coverage Ratio

Interest Coverage Ratio (ICR) indicates the number of times interest is covered by the profits available to pay the interest charges. Long-term creditors of a firm are interested in knowing the firm's ability to pay interest on their long-term borrowing. Generally, the higher the ratio, the safer are the long-term creditors because even if the earnings of the firm fall, the firm shall be able to meet its commitment of fixed interest charges. But a too high ratio may not be good for the firm because it may imply that the firm is not using debt as a source of finance in order to increase the Earnings Per Share (EPS).

ICR is increased after merger for 11 acquirer firms. ICR of Lupin Ltd. and Exide Industries Ltd. increased significantly after M&A process. Overall, it is found that the financial leverage in terms of ICR has improved for two firms after merger.

Discussion

- The merger activity has had a significant impact on liquidity. The liquidity position in terms of CR and QR has improved for 2 and 4 firms respectively, after merger.
- The merger activity has a significant impact on profitability. The profitability in terms of GPR, NPR, ROA and ROCE has improved for 2, 1, 20 and 0 firms respectively, after merger.
- The merger activity has a significant impact on operating performance. The operating performance in terms of DTR, FATR and TATR has improved for 2, 4 and 3 firms respectively, after merger.
- The merger activity has a significant impact on financial leverage. The financial leverage in terms of DER and ICR has improved for 3 and 2 firms respectively, after merger.

Conclusion

In the context of introduction of large-scale deregulatory policy measures in the 1990s in general and three important amendments made to the Indian Patent Act (1970) in 1999, 2002 and 2005 in particular, the present paper makes an attempt to evaluate the pre- and post-merger performance of the merged/acquirer companies to measure shareholders value-addition and to examine the impact of M&A on the post-merger performance of corporate firms in India. A merger can be termed as an investment alternative in the context of scarce fund resources. The financial characteristics of a firm have a critical role in the merger decision process. They are either explicit decision variables or directly reflect the nonfinancial reasons for acquisition characteristics. The present study measured the financial performance of sample firms from the viewpoint of liquidity, profitability, operating performance and financial risks. It is concluded that the M&As in the Indian corporate firms over a period of April 2008-March 2009 have a significant impact on the liquidity, profitability, operating performance and financial risk position of acquirer firms in India. The type of industry does seem to make a difference to the post-merger performance of acquiring firms. The results of this study show that management cannot take it for granted that synergy will be generated and profits will increase simply by going for mergers and acquisitions. However, it should be tested with a bigger sample size before coming to a final conclusion.

Limitations

- There are certain other factors like change in industry, economy and stock market which can have an impact on the financial performance of merged company, but has not been covered by this study.
- This study is based only on secondary data. Moreover, it is limited to the merger of some selected companies, and the findings of the study cannot be generalized to the whole industry.

- There are many approaches to measure the impact of merger on the financial performance of the company. There is no unanimous opinion among the experts.

Scope for Further Study

- Studies with similar objectives could be attempted with reference to other sectors.
- The study with similar objectives could be made from time-to-time covering a lengthy period.
- The stock index price improvement could be analyzed for pre-merger and post-merger periods.
- The study has assessed success or failure of mergers in financial terms. The human aspect of mergers has not been touched. Gauging the success of mergers through this aspect could be another area of research.

Note

1. http://www.biblioferrersalat.com/media/docurnentos/Fusiones_Requejo. pdf

Rosy Kalra is an Assistant Professor and Head of Department of the Finance Department at Amity University, Noida, Uttar Pradesh, India.

Anand Sanwal

 **NO**

M&A's Losing Hand

It's been an absolutely ugly October in global financial markets, and all indications point to continued uncertainty and volatility for the foreseeable future. Most CEOs and CFOs of public companies are looking dejectedly at company share prices that are a fraction of what they were just a year ago. For companies that are weathering the current storm, the question that progressive CEOs and CFOs will soon begin to consider, as they should, is where do we need to take our business in order to begin delivering shareholder value and returns once again?

Considering this question will require the crafting of a compelling narrative and strategy that these senior leaders can communicate to their employees, customers, and shareholders about what's next—i.e., where is the company's future profitable growth going to come from?

One of the often-used vehicles to achieve growth, in theory, has been mergers and acquisitions (M&A); however, current market conditions make M&A a dicey or even impractical option. The unavailability of credit and increasingly expensive short-term refinancing rates, coupled with the economic downturn and depressed equity prices, have all served to make M&A difficult to accomplish. This has resulted in a spate of dead deals in recent weeks.

According to Deal Logic, the first 13 days of October witnessed 49 deals valued at $57.6 billion pulled, after $62.8 billion worth of deals were pulled in September. Acquirers that were hit by M&A travails include the BG Group, Waste Management, Bristol-Myers Squibb, HSBC Holdings, Dubai World, Xstrata, and Walgreen, to name a few. From this list, it is obvious that the M&A downturn is hitting companies in a diverse array of sectors, industries, and geographies.

How should CEOs, CFOs, and shareholders react to the M&A malaise? Contrary to popular belief, and especially so for those considering a large M&A transaction, they should pop open a bottle of champagne and celebrate. Why? Because according to our research, "megadeals"—those in which the target's value exceeds $10 billion—more often than not destroy shareholder value.

This is the underlying conclusion of our study in which we evaluated all megadeals from 2002 to 2007. We examined 33 M&A megadeals from Europe, Canada, and the USA in which the acquirers were strategic buyers—not financial or private equity concerns. (Please note that because some data were unavailable, in some instances our results do not reflect all 33 deals; see the [box] to get a list of the evaluated deals.)

In what was arguably one of the greatest bull markets we've ever seen, we observed that megadeals actually destroyed value over 60 percent of the time. On average, transactions resulted in negative cumulative excess beta returns (-4.03 percent) in the year after their announcement. (See the sidebar for insights into the research methodology.)

Even among the handful of deals that generated positive returns, we found that success was more often than not attributable to macroeconomic factors beyond the control of the acquirer. So it seems that it is often better to be "lucky than good" or "in the right place at the right time" when undertaking large M&A transactions. Furthermore, the data show that many of the deals, whether successful or not, increased the beta of the acquirer. Higher-risk profiles resulted in a higher cost of capital for the company post-acquisition, making such deals "costlier" in ways that can be very damaging to the larger entity over the longer term.

Following the quantitative analysis of all of the megadeals, we also sought to determine what lessons we could take away from the good, the bad, and the ugly so that future M&A megadeals can avoid past pitfalls and replicate elements of the few successful ones. However, before we do so, it is important to reiterate that our research showed few to no valid reasons to engage in megadeal M&A unless the desire is to redistribute shareholder money to needy investment bankers and lawyers. This being said, all the research in the world won't change the fact that people like headlines, and deals are going to happen. Armed with this level of pragmatism, we developed a set of dimensions that should be considered when engaging in megadeal M&A.

Peeling Back the Findings

Regarding measures that you can control, here are some observations about how you can increase a deal's chances of success:

- **It's important not to overpay.** This is straight from the "master of the obvious" file, but it's clear that disciplined buyers outperform loose spenders. Evidence suggested that premium and performance are inversely correlated, meaning that the greater the premium, the worse the performance. By way of example, Boston Scientific's acquisition of Guidant involved a bidding war with Johnson & Johnson that resulted in Boston Scientific paying a handsome $80 per share as opposed to their original offer of $72. In the case of the Sprint Nextel deal, Nextel took advantage of Sprint's insecurity regarding its ability to compete against other carriers and as a result secured an excellent exit price. Both of these deals resulted in miserable excess returns.

In other cases such as Bank of New York's acquisition of Mellon Financial Corp., a very low premium was involved, as was the case in the CVS-Caremark and Manulife–John Hancock deals, which both did well. Price is not the only consideration, of course, but higher premiums generally make it more difficult for buyers to achieve high returns. The challenge ultimately is that when an acquirer pays a high premium, its shareholders get diluted or it uses cash to prevent dilution. The only way ultimately for the firm to get that cash back is to reengineer expenses out of the combined company. The synergies needed to pay for premium and the excess premium make this impossible. Moreover, the need to significantly reduce expenses can mean cutting muscle, not just fat, resulting in weakened competency and poor morale.

- **Acquiring a faster-growth target is looked upon favorably.** When companies acquire targets with higher growth expectations than their own, it appears that the market supports the acquisition. In contrast, when companies acquire targets that are underperforming and whose growth expectations are lower than their own, acquisitions tend to fail. In cases where both companies underperform and a transaction occurs, postdeal performance tends to be quite lackluster, as such an M&A is used as a poor replacement for an inability to generate organic growth. Unfortunately, combining two cubic zirconias rarely results in a real diamond.
- **Mergers of Equals outperform outright acquisitions.** To determine the effect that the relative size of the buyer to the target has on M&A performance, we found that in general, acquisitions that fell in the Merger of Equals category performed better than those that fell into the outright Acquisitions category. Originally, this seemed slightly counterintuitive; however, a closer look at some of the best-in-class examples shows that in Mergers of Equals, both companies tend to have a fair amount of interest in deal success and thus are more collaborative. In Mergers of Equals, both companies often bring different strengths to the table and thus allow the whole to be greater than the sum of the parts. For example, when Manulife Financial Corporation acquired John Hancock Financial Services, the former provided strong brand recognition, while the latter offered strong access to capital markets, and both presented distinct distribution channels.

M&A Megadeal Success

Through research tied to individual transactions, we determined that high-performing deals considered the following dimensions and questions.

Practical Considerations

- **Macroeconomic and industry factors.** Am I appropriately considering macroeconomic factors on the upside and downside that could impact the industry and/or competitive landscape? Are my expectations for future growth of the target reasonable, and is the deal worthwhile even in a worst-case scenario?
- **Timing.** Are there internal concerns that should take managerial priority?
- **Price.** Am I being disciplined in my determination of the price?
- **Cost savings and revenue synergies.** Am I comfortable that the deal is attractive even if estimated cost savings or opportunities for revenue from the combined company are less than I expect?

Strategic Considerations:

- **Branding, distribution, and scale.** Does the deal provide the potential combined company with greater economies of scale, increased distribution channels, or stronger branding?
- **Organic growth.** Does the deal hamper the potential combined company's potential for organic growth?
- **Integration.** Have we properly accounted for managerial, technological, and cultural integration issues?
- **Geographic and product expansion.** Is there significant overlap between the potential combined companies' geographic and product markets, and will the deal provide an opportunity for expansion?

Our findings suggest in no uncertain terms that firms should be wary of undertaking M&A megadeals. If shareholders who are reeling from the last several months of performance can take solace in one fact, it is that the ability to do M&A may be hampered, at least in the short to medium term, by the economy and credit conditions.

However, these types of exogenous pressures on M&A will ultimately subside, and when this occurs, investment bankers and a host of others will come running back with suggestions for large M&A deals. They will also come equipped with facts and figures showing extensive strategic benefits and magnificent projections about cost and revenue synergies.

Oftentimes, they will paint a picture of market leadership, industry transformation, a bold new vision for the combined entity, and amazing shareholder returns. When this time comes, CEOs and CFOs must resist many elements of these "compelling"

A CLOSER LOOK: RESEARCH METHODOLOGY

For each of the megadeal transactions evaluated (all of which took place between 2002 and 2007), data were collected and analyzed as follows:

- **Data were collected from 60 business days prior to announcement until two years after close.**
- **Most of the analysis was conducted on data from 60 days prior to announcement until 265 days after announcement** (slightly over a year) in order to put all of the deals on the same time scale. This was a sufficient time span because on average the deals closed within 121 days and most companies' excess returns displayed discernible patterns by the end of this time period.
- **Excess beta return was used as the primary metric for financial success** because it measures how much the individual stock's excess return varies in comparison with the market as a whole. The cumulative excess beta return was calculated by zeroing out the returns at the day before announcement (day–1) and then aggregating the returns for each successive day while holding day–1 as the base.
- **Each acquirer's returns were also compared to the company's specific sector index,** in order to account for macroeconomic factors or market trends that may have affected individual segments.
- **Each deal was analyzed on an individual basis** using financial data, company reports and presentations, and media reports and news surrounding each deal.

About the Deals Analyzed

- **The deals spanned all nine of the S&P 500 sectors.**
- **The Financials sector was particularly well represented,** owing to the fact that several financial institutions were engaging in aggressive geographic and market expansion during the time span covered.

M & A Megadeals Evaluated

Acquirer	Target
Capital One	North Fork Bank
Wachovia	South Trust
Regions Financial	AmSouth Bancorp
General Growth Properties	Rouse Company
Wachovia	Golden West Financial
Bank of America	MBNA
JPMorgan Chase	Bank One
Manulife Financial	John Hancock Financial Services
Bank of America	FleetBoston Financial Group
Travelers Companies	Travelers Property Casualty
National Grid	Lattice Group
Harrah's Entertainment	Caesar's Entertainment
Sears Holdings	Sears Roebuck
SUPERVALU	Albertsons
P&G	Gillette
Anadarko Petroleum	Kerr-McGee
ConocoPhillips	Burlington Resources
Chevron	Unocal
Duke Energy	Cinergy
AstraZeneca	Medimmune
CVS	Caremark Rx
J&J	Pfizer Consumer Healthcare
Thermo Fisher Scientific	Fisher Scientific International
Boston Scientific	Guidant
Pfizer	Pharmacia
Symantec	Veritas Software
Sprint Nextel	Nextel Communications
Freeport-McMoRan	Phelps Dodge
Barrick Gold	Placer Dome

- **Deals were categorized as either a "Merger of Equals" or as an "Acquisition."** For the purposes of this study, a "Merger of Equals" was defined as a deal in which the market capitalization of the buyer was less than or equal to 1.5 times the market capitalization of the target at 60 days prior to announcement. All others were considered "Acquisitions."
- **The majority of the deals were from the United States and Canada** simply because of the greater amount of information that was available; however, a few European deals were also included.

narratives, which we readily admit have a seemingly magnetic pull.

Instead, if—as stewards of shareholder money—they take a dispassionate view of the transaction in question, remember the abysmal historical track record of large M&A deals in the past, and also recognize the outsized role that luck plays in successful deals, the decision to say "no deal" should be quite easy.

ANAND SANWAL is a managing director at Brilliont, a firm specializing in corporate portfolio management, innovation, and reengineering. He is the former vice-president, corporate portfolio management and strategic business analysis at American Express.

EXPLORING THE ISSUE

Does Expanding via Mergers and Acquisitions Make for Sound Corporate Strategy?

Critical Thinking and Reflection

1. What can be done to protect the interests of customers and other stakeholders during mergers and acquisitions?
2. How quickly will or should the success (or failure) of a merger or acquisition be known or shown?
3. How might global mergers and acquisitions differ from mergers and acquisitions conducted within a single nation?
4. How would you measure the success or failure of a merger or acquisition?
5. Why do firms merge or acquire one another?
6. What role, if any, does corporate culture play in the merger and acquisition process?

Is There Common Ground?

The common ground that exists in this issue is that there is risk involved in the merger and acquisition process. This observation is made by the authors on both sides of this issue in their respective articles. However, despite the inherent risk, corporations have decided to continue to pursue a course of economic behavior and practice that includes mergers and acquisitions.

The underlying debate that exists here is whether or not the risk is worth the potential payoff. Given the documented high rate of failure and frequent inability of mergers and acquisitions to consistently return anticipated gains and expected benefits, this issue is one that will continue to be discussed and receive additional scrutiny by corporate practitioners and observers for many years to come.

Additional Resources

Brouthers, K. D., van Hastenburg, P. & van den Ven, J. (1998). "If Most Mergers Fail Why Are They So Popular," *Long Range Planning,* June, pp. 347–353.

Cummings, J. (2008). "Why Organic Is Better," *Business Finance,* 14(12), December, pp. 12–17.

Epstein, M. J. (2005). "The Determinants and Evaluation of Merger Success," *Business Horizons,* January–February, pp. 37–46.

Gadiesh, O. & Ormiston, C. (2002). "Six Rationales to Guide Merger Success," *Strategy & Leadership,* 30, pp. 38–40.

Goldberg, S. & Godwin, J.H. (2001). "Your Merger: Will It Really Add Value?" *The Journal of Corporate Accounting & Finance,* January/February, pp. 27–35.

Jackson, S. E. (2007). "Creating Value Through Acquisitions," *The Journal of Business Strategy,* 28(6), pp. 40, 41.

Kroll, K. (2008). "Deals in the Downturn," *Business Finance,* 14(5), May, pp. 20, 22, 24, 25.

Marks, M. L. (2000). "Mixed Signals," *Across the Board,* May, pp. 21–26.

Marks, M. L. & Mirvis, P. H. (2011). "Merge Ahead: A Research Agenda to Increase Merger and Acquisition Success," *Journal of Business Psychology,* 26, pp. 161–168.

Ruquet, M. E. (2008). "Cultural Fit Helps Drive Merger Success," *National Underwriter,* P&C, 112(33), pp. 19, 25, 26.

Sinkin, J. & Putney, T. (2009). "Keeping It Together," *Journal of Accountancy,* 207(4), pp. 24–28.

Trautwein, F. (1990). "Merger Motives and Merger Prescriptions," *Strategic Management Journal,* May/June, pp. 283–295.

Vaughn, R. (2008). "Navigating a Successful Merger," *Risk Management,* 55(1), pp. 36–38, 40, 41.

Vazirani, N. (2015). "A Literature Review on Mergers and Acquisitions Waves and Theories," *SIES Journal of Management,* 11(1), pp. 3–9.

Internet References . . .

20 Key Due Diligence Activities in a Merger and Acquisition Transaction

http://www.forbes.com/sites/allbusiness/2014/12/19/20
-key-due-diligence-activities-in-a-merger-and-acquis
ition-transaction/#14f35f03c40a

2015: A Merger Bonanza

http://www.theatlantic.com/business
/archive/2016/01/2015-mergers-acquisitions/423096/

Demystifying the Merger and Acquisitions Process

http://www.cio.com/article/2904046/mergers
-acquisitions/demystifying-the-merger-and
-acquisition-process.html

Does Your M&A Add Value?

www.ft.com/intl/cms/s/0/7bfb1e10-f256-11dd-9678
-0000779fd2ac.html#axzz2EjgAxm20

Mergers and Acquisitions: Understanding the Essentials of Strategy and Execution in the M&A Ecosystem: Part 1 of 4

http://www.vistage.com/blog/growth-strategy/mergers
-and-acquisitions-understanding-the-essentials-of-strategy
-and-execution-in-the-ma-ecosystem-part-1-of-4/

What Should Everyone Know About Mergers and Acquisitions?

http://www.forbes.com/sites/quora/2013/05/23
/what-should-everyone-know-about-mergers-and
-acquisitions/#5ed791b9345b

Selected, Edited, and with Issue Framing Material by:
Kathleen J. Barnes, *William Paterson University*
and
George E. Smith, *University of South Carolina, Beaufort*

ISSUE

Are Trade Agreements Good or Bad for the U.S. Economy?

YES: Ana I. Eiras, from "Why America Needs to Support Free Trade," The Heritage Foundation (2004)

NO: Robert E. Scott, from "Free Trade Costs American Jobs," *Newsweek* (2015)

Learning Outcomes

After reading this issue, you will be able to:

- Explain the rationale behind engaging in free trade.
- Present arguments against pursuing free-trade agreements.
- Formulate a position either for or against the practice of free trade.
- Identify major U.S. free-trade agreements.

ISSUE SUMMARY

YES: Ana I. Eiras, Heritage Foundation's International Economics Senior Policy Analyst, discusses the classic argument of how free trade is an essential pillar of U.S. economic power and prosperity and outlines reasons to support free trade.

NO: According to Robert E. Scott, the Economic Policy Institute's Director of Trade and Manufacturing Policy Research, several U.S. trade partners managing the value of their own currencies for competitive gain vis-à-vis the United States are the most important barrier to U.S. export success.

The Office of the United States Trade Representative (USTR) website states that trade agreements can create opportunities for Americans and help to grow the U.S. economy. To illustrate this point, the U.S. Chamber of Commerce reported the following outcomes of international trade on its website:

- More than 41 million U.S. jobs are dependent on trade.
- More than $1.4 trillion worth of manufacturing exports in 2014.
- Approximately 6 million factory jobs in the United States, roughly half of all manufacturing employment, directly supported by exports.
- U.S. service providers exported $716 billion worth of services in 2015 (https://www.uschamber.com/international /international-policy/benefits-international-trade-0).

During the 2016 U.S. Presidential campaign, the issue of free trade and trade agreements emerged as one of the several themes. One presidential candidate decried the nation's involvement in these agreements, going so far as to state, "I will never pledge to ever sign any trade agreement that hurts our workers, or that diminishes our freedom and independence" (http://thehill.com/policy/finance/288812 -trump-vow-to-overhaul-us-trade-policy). The candidate's rival who had a lengthy history of supporting and promoting free-trade agreements originally supported the Trans Pacific Partnership (TPP) and stated that "if implemented and enforced, [it] should benefit American businesses and workers" (http://time.com/4426483/dnc -hillary-clinton-trans-pacific-partnership/) only to reverse position as the campaign progressed.

The United States is a member of the World Trade Organization (WTO), and the Marrakesh Agreement establishing the World Trade Organization (WTO Agreement) which sets out rules governing trade among the WTO's 154 members. The United States and other WTO members are currently engaged in Doha Development Round of world trade talks, and a strong, market-opening Doha agreement for both goods and services would be an important contribution to addressing the global economic crisis and helping to restore trade's role in leading economic growth and development.

At present, the United States has free-trade agreements (FTAs) in effect with 20 countries. These FTAs build on the foundation of the World Trade Organization (WTO) Agreement, with more comprehensive, specific, and stronger provisions than the WTO Agreement. Many of the United States' FTAs are bilateral agreements between two governments. These Bilateral Investment Treaties (BITs) help protect private investment, develop market-oriented policies in partner countries, and promote U.S. exports. Other FTAs, like the North American Free Trade Agreement (NAFTA) and the Dominican Republic-Central America-United States Free Trade Agreement (CAFTA-DR), are multilateral agreements among several parties and were entered into with the hope of promoting strong economic growth and prosperity for those in their membership.

As you read and review the articles included in this issue, you will be exposed to thinking that supports and derides the value of free-trade agreements. Ultimately your challenge will be to determine your own position and develop a rationale in defense of that position on this controversial issue.

YES ↵

Ana I. Eiras

Why America Needs to Support Free Trade?

Free trade is again under attack, despite having been, for over a century, the basis of America's wealth. Some groups in the United States blame free trade for the loss of manufacturing jobs, while others blame it for exposing some U.S. producers to foreign competition.

Free trade, however, is good for America, and for a very simple reason: It allows American workers to specialize in goods and services that they produce more efficiently than the rest of the world and then to exchange them for goods and services that other countries produce at higher quality and lower cost.

Specialization and free trade allow the U.S. to become more competitive and innovative. Innovation constantly provides new technologies that allow Americans to produce more, cure more diseases, pollute less, improve education, and choose from a greater range of investment opportunities. The resulting economic growth generates better-paying jobs, higher standards of living, and a greater appreciation of the benefits of living in a peaceful society.

New technologies bring about change, which, as U.S. economic history shows, benefits society as a whole. In the process, however, some sectors suffer until they can adapt to the new changes and begin to benefit from them. Today, Americans are experiencing some of that "suffering" because new technologies are challenging old methods of production.

This change is especially visible in the manufacturing sector, just as it was in the agricultural sector 100 years ago. But in the same way that it adapted then to a new, more industry-based society, America will adapt again to a new, more knowledge-based society.

The Bush Administration should support free trade by all means at its disposal. Keeping America free of protectionism and special favors helps to generate opportunities and fosters economic growth. Economic growth is of particular importance today because eliminating the large federal budget deficit requires either growth to generate tax revenues or something even harder to come by—the political will to cut spending.

To promote economic growth, the Administration should advance more free trade agreements and lead negotiations at the World Trade Organization to eliminate agricultural subsidies, antidumping measures, and other protectionist policies that benefit a very small group of Americans at the expense of most other citizens. In addition, instead of threatening to impose barriers against inexpensive imports, the Administration should lower the tax and regulatory burden on U.S. companies so that they can be more competitive. Moving toward greater, not less, economic freedom benefits all Americans.

Five Reasons to Support Free Trade

For over a century, free trade has been one of the most important determinants of America's wealth and strength. There are at least five important reasons for continuing to support free trade.

REASON #1: Higher Standard of Living

The most compelling reason to support free trade is that society as a whole benefits from it. Free trade improves people's living standards because it allows them to consume higher quality goods at less expensive prices. In the 19th century, British economist David Ricardo showed that any nation that focuses on producing goods in which it has a comparative advantage will be able to get cheaper and better goods from other countries in return. As a result of the exchange, both trading parties gain from producing more efficiently and consuming higher quality goods and services at lower prices.

Trade between nations is the same as trade between people. Consider what the quality of life would be if each person had to produce absolutely everything that he or she consumed, such as food, clothing, cars, or home repairs. Compare that picture with life as it is now as individuals dedicate themselves to working on just one thing—for example, insurance sales—to earn a salary with which they can freely purchase food, a car, a home, clothing, and anything else they wish at higher quality and lower prices than if they had done it themselves.

It simply makes sense for each person to work at what he or she does best and to buy the rest. As a nation, the United States exports in order to purchase imports that other nations produce more skillfully and cheaply. Therefore, the fewer barriers erected against trade with other nations, the more access people will have to the best, least expensive goods and services in the world "supermarket."

Producers benefit as well. In the absence of trade barriers, producers face greater competition from foreign producers, and this increased competition gives them an incentive to improve the quality of their production while keeping prices low in order to compete. At the same time, free trade allows domestic producers to shop around the world for the least expensive inputs they can use for their production, which in turn allows them to keep their cost of production down without sacrificing quality.

In the end, the results benefit both producers—who remain competitive and profitable—and consumers—who pay less for a good or a service than they would if trade barriers existed.

America as a whole is better off with free trade; but with new technologies evolving continuously at home and abroad, open economies are constantly challenged to change the way they do business. In the process of adapting to change, some sectors suffer until they can adapt to the new changes and begin to benefit from them. For example, during the Industrial Revolution, workers in the agricultural sector had to adapt to the "new industrial economy," competing with machines that could do the same work more efficiently. Eventually, the agricultural workers trained themselves to use machinery and seized the opportunity to be part of the new industrial economy.

Today, America again faces major economic changes. The U.S. economy is moving from an industry-based to a knowledge-based model. For example, the U.S. textile industry gradually disappeared during the past two decades because it became increasingly less competitive vis-à-vis the lower cost of labor in foreign countries. As a result, many U.S. textile factories shut down their operations.

South Carolina was one of the states most affected by the shutdown of textile factories. South Carolinians, however, did not become permanently unemployed, because other industries moved to the state to take advantage of a trained labor force.

In 2000, BMW leased a research facility at Clemson University's automotive research campus to train engineers to sustain BMW's growth. IBM and Microsoft each contributed to this project with the idea of creating high-paying jobs tied to knowledge. Through this project, BMW "invested $2.5 billion at the plant, and now employs 4,700 people, with most production workers making $24 per hour."[1]

BMW's investment illustrates the process of adjustment in an economically open society. In order to remain competitive and benefit from the economic evolution brought about by the new knowledge-based technological change, South Carolina's workers trained themselves to seize the higher-paid job opportunities. The adjustment brought better-paying jobs and, with them, the possibility of raising the living standard of all those involved in the process of change.

REASON #2: Competition and Innovation

Innovation is the basis of progress, and competition is the best incentive to innovate. The challenge of having others producing similar products or offering similar services motivates businesses to find new technologies and better ways to provide what they produce. The need to remain competitive forces businesses to strive constantly to innovate. As a result, new technologies are born.

America is perhaps the world's best example of how competition fosters innovation. Although at times the United States has become somewhat protectionist, its economy has been built primarily on the principles of a free market, private enterprise, and competition.

In such a competitive environment, new technologies, from computers to medicines to machinery, have helped the economy to become increasingly more productive per unit of labor and machinery employed in the production process. Since 1948, according to the Bureau of Labor Statistics, multifactor productivity—a ratio of output to combined inputs—in the U.S. private business sector has more than doubled.[2] Productivity has fostered economic growth and, by lowering production costs, has given ordinary Americans the opportunity to raise their standard of living.

The U.S. economy is replete with illustrations of how competition fosters innovation. For example:

- In the 1980s, personal computers were very expensive, few people owned them, and those they did own handled only word texts and a few calculations. Due to increased competition, by 2002, 65.9 percent of people living in the United States owned a personal computer that handled text, calculations, graphics, media, Internet access, and many other functions.[3]
- In 1975, the airline industry carried about 200 million passengers; now, due to competition and lower costs, it carries almost 600 million passengers a year.
- In 1987, only 0.3 percent of Americans owned mobile phones. By 2002, 50 percent owned one. Similarly, in 1975, only 37.3 percent of people had a telephone mainline; now 64.6 percent have one.
- The percentage of people who own a television set soared from 48.6 percent in 1975 to 93.8 percent in 2001.

These are just a few examples of the millions of products and services made available to increasing numbers of people, thanks to the opening of trade and to the freedom of the U.S. economy.

America's ability to compete and innovate derives from its open markets and from the continual search for new markets through the expansion of free trade. Goods and services flowing across borders foster new ideas and allow U.S. producers to learn about the market through the failure and success of traded products. As they learn more, they are able to innovate to remain competitive.

Scottish moral philosopher Adam Smith had observed this simple truth already in 1776, when he wrote in *The Wealth of Nations*:

> When the market is very small, no person can have any encouragement to dedicate himself entirely to one employment, for want of the power to exchange all that

surplus part of the produce of his own labour . . . for such parts of the produce of other men's labour as he has occasion for. . . . As by means of water-carriage [at the time, a means to expand trade] a more extensive market is opened to every sort of industry than what the land-carriage alone can afford. . . . [As a result,] industry of every kind naturally begins to subdivide and improve itself. . . .[4]

Smith was even more of a visionary than Ricardo, for he understood that labor specialization is something that constantly changes and that gaining a comparative advantage requires open borders and the ability to adapt to continuous change. It was free trade that continuously challenged local merchants to improve their products and therefore fostered innovation. Consumers benefited as well because, in an attempt to capture a greater share of the market, producers offered consumers the best possible products in the world at the lowest possible prices.

Protectionist policies have the opposite effect. They give advantages to a very small group of producers that do not want to compete. Tens of millions of consumers, as well as smaller producers buying goods and services from the protected few, bear the cost of such protection by paying higher prices for lower-quality products.

For example, U.S. citizens currently pay higher prices for SUVs, textiles, sugar, agricultural products, lumber, peanuts, orange juice, and many other products than they would if there were no trade protections in place. Removing those protections would allow the market to keep prices low and would encourage protected businesses either to find new technologies in order to compete or to shift operations to a more competitive industry. The result would be greater growth for the economy.

REASON #3: Economic Growth

Economic freedom is essential to economic growth, and the true measure of economic freedom involves more than just the question of whether tariff and non-tariff trade barriers are present. It involves other barriers to commerce such as inflationary pressures, regulations that make it more difficult to do business, restrictive banking systems, whether or not property rights are protected, and the fiscal burden of government.

The data presented over the past seven years in the annual Heritage Foundation/Wall Street Journal *Index of Economic Freedom* show clearly that the economies of countries that open their markets grow at a faster pace than the economies of countries that open their markets less or not at all. Of the 142 nations whose economies have been observed during this seven-year period, those that opened their markets the most grew twice as fast as those that opened them the least.

A growing economy increases the demand for goods and services, and as demand increases, more businesses start and expand their operations. Such expansion leads to the creation of more, better-paid jobs. The same is true when the market expands beyond borders. Gaining free access to other markets opens up new business opportunities, encouraging investment and fostering job creation.

REASON #4: Stronger Institutions and Infrastructure

Free trade also fosters the strengthening and development of institutions that safeguard economic freedom and development. Facing new opportunities to sell and purchase goods and to open all sorts of trade-related businesses, individuals have a strong incentive to create mechanisms and institutions to seize those opportunities. Adam Smith observed this phenomenon in the 1770s, especially in Italy and Switzerland:

> Commerce and manufacturers gradually introduced order and good government, and with them, the liberty and security of individuals, among the inhabitants of the country, who had before lived almost in a continual state of war with their superiors. This, though it has been least observed, is by far the most important of all their effects.[5]

The *rule of law* is the first and most important institution fostered by free trade. In order to enforce contracts, prevent merchandise robbery and damage, and protect ships and their crews, trading countries need to establish a framework of objective rules under which free trade will be conducted. At the same time, those countries need to have a *law enforcement* mechanism to apply those rules, such as a police force and an independent judicial system. The proper functioning of these two institutions encourages individuals to initiate businesses and to sell, buy, and seize to the maximum extent the economic opportunities of free trade.

A third institution fostered by free trade is the *banking and financial system*, which gives individuals access to credit and a place to save and keep their earnings. At the same time, financial instruments, like checks and money wiring, lower the transaction costs associated with trade. Today, the Internet and other telecommunication technologies have significantly reduced the cost of trading worldwide. The result is that more and more people are able to reap the benefits of trading with any nation around the world.

Equally important is the function of *insurance companies*, through which individuals can reduce the cost of damage and robbery to their merchandise. This enables parties to a contract to preserve what is established in that contract at a lower cost than if the insurance did not exist.

Free trade also promotes the *improvement and expansion of infrastructure*. The construction of ports, where ships and airplanes can arrive and safely unload and load merchandise, must expand to accommodate free trade. Hangars and other types of barns located at ports offer the opportunity to store merchandise temporarily. At the same time, free trade fosters the construction and preservation of roads for trucks and automobiles to transport merchandise safely to its final destination.

Likewise important is the *development of all sort of new businesses* to support free trade, including hotels, restaurants, law firms, packaging and delivery services, software development companies, automobile factories, construction businesses, among many others.

REASON #5: Peace

Free trade fosters an enormous chain of economic activity, the benefits of which culminate in a social desire to be at peace with neighboring and even faraway nations with which trade is conducted or might be conducted in the future. When individuals see how beneficial it is to live in an economically free society; when they see how freedom allows them to improve their lives and those of their families; when they can create new businesses, engage in commerce, or work for a decent salary or wage, adding dignity to their lives, they want peace to preserve all these good things.

By contrast, when people live under economic oppression and are at the mercy of a small ruling authority that dictates every aspect of their lives and limits their ability to realize their potential, they resent the life they have and learn to hate better lives elsewhere. If they cannot enjoy the fruits of their efforts and cannot realize their potential; if they cannot feel free to do business, work freely, and trade freely; if they do not have anything to gain or to lose, they begin to feel that any change—even war—might be better. They have no incentive to desire peace with their neighbors.

For this reason, the areas of greatest conflict in the world also happen to be those that are economically repressed. The Economic Freedom Map, drawn annually from the *Index*, shows, for example, that countries that are the most economically repressed have also suffered civil wars and unrest.

- The areas of the Middle East in which civil wars and terrorist havens abound are both economically repressed and mostly unfree.
- North Korea, a country plagued by starvation and poverty, is repressed.
- Brazil, Argentina, parts of Africa, and some former Soviet republics—all mostly unfree—have high levels of poverty and periodically suffer political and economic crises.

Free trade and economic freedom set the process of growth, innovation, and prosperity in motion. In that process, individuals support the creation of institutions that are conducive to growth and that preserve peace and prosperity. The greater the level of prosperity, the greater the likelihood of peace.

The Question of "Fair Trade"

Politicians, opinion makers, journalists, and businessmen commonly talk about the need to support "fair trade." Seldom, however, does anyone explain either what fair trade is or—even more to the point—to whom trade should be fair. In the name of fairness, different groups advocate different protections for their specific industries and call the comparative advantage of other countries "unfair."

For example, U.S. manufacturers think it is unfair that labor in China is cheaper than labor in the United States, and therefore ask for tariffs against Chinese products. But those tariffs would, in reality, be unfair to millions of U.S. consumers and producers who would be forced to pay higher prices for locally manufactured goods. "Fairness" assumes a dubious character in policies that pick and choose whom to treat "fairly."

Others argue that America needs to enact barriers to free trade in order to strengthen national defense. For example, a tariff to protect steel would be justified because we need our own steel to support the construction of tanks, missiles, and arms. This argument is built on the faulty assumption that America's wealth is at least constant. But a constant level may imply that the U.S. is falling behind other nations in relative terms. The strongest national defense depends on a relatively strong economy, and a strong economy is possible only with economic freedom.

As the *Index* demonstrates, once economic barriers begin to emerge, a nation's wealth begins to decline. America's relative economic freedom and wealth have already begun to decline. In fact, according to the *Index*, the United States has lost considerable ground in economic freedom (declining from 4th freest economy to 10th freest in 2004), which means it has also lost more and more opportunities to increase wealth.

The only form of fair trade—if such thing exists—is free trade. When facing competition from Chinese manufacturing, U.S. manufacturers have two options: either adopt new technologies to cut costs and become more competitive or shift the focus of their operations to different areas in which they can be more competitive. Neither of these two options harms consumers, since they will continue to have access to the least expensive, best-quality products.

Most workers benefit as well. For some people, free trade requires change, but they also now have opportunities to use their skills in more efficient, advantageous, and productive ways that are created by the innovation and prosperity that competition promotes. Likewise, for a strong national defense, America needs the resources, innovation, and income that are derived from the absence of barriers to trade and investment.

What the Bush Administration Should Do

The Bush Administration should support free trade by all means at its disposal. Keeping America free of protectionism and special favors will foster economic growth. To that end, the Administration should:

- **Advance as many free trade agreements as possible.** So far, the Administration has advanced free trade agreements with Chile and Singapore and has completed negotiations with Central America, Australia, and Morocco. It should continue to negotiate free trade agreements with other countries around the world.
- **Eliminate agricultural subsidies, antidumping measures, and other protectionist policies.** Subsidies and special protections benefit small economic interests or sectors at the expense of millions of consumers and producers. They translate into higher prices, the impact of which is felt primarily by poor Americans.

The Bush Administration should advance an agenda to eliminate agricultural subsidies at the World Trade Organization. It should take advantage of Europe's recent proposal to put the Doha round back on track by ending agricultural export subsidies, and it should encourage Japan to eliminate agricultural export subsidies as well. It is equally important to engage developing nations so that they eliminate convoluted business regulations, corruption, and weak rule of law. By encouraging these steps, the Administration will help these countries to provide a more business-friendly environment that attracts both foreign and domestic investment.

Conclusion

Free trade is an essential pillar of U.S. economic power and prosperity. It encourages labor force specialization and the exchange of goods and services that other countries do better and at lower cost. Specialization leads to competition and innovation, providing new technologies that allow Americans to produce more goods and services, cure more diseases, pollute less, get better education, and choose from a wider range of investment options. As the economy grows, people enjoy higher standards of living and gain a greater appreciation of the benefits of living in a peaceful society.

Competition, innovation, and new technologies also bring about changes that challenge some sectors to adapt themselves to those new trends and reap their benefits. Changes currently taking place in the U.S. manufacturing sector illustrate the process by which a growing society changes from a more industry-based to a more knowledge-based society. Those businesses and entrepreneurs who seize the opportunity to profit from this change will survive and, in surviving, will provide more and more Americans with the opportunity to increase their standard of living.

The Bush Administration should keep America free of protectionism and special favors. To that end, it should advance more free trade agreements and lead negotiations at the World Trade Organization to eliminate agricultural subsidies, antidumping measures, and other policies that benefit selected groups at the expense of millions of Americans and undermine the nation's ability to grow.

Instead of threatening to impose barriers to inexpensive imports, the Administration should lower the tax and regulatory burden on U.S. companies so that they can be more competitive. The more America moves toward economic freedom, the more it will foster its own prosperity, the prosperity of other nations, and ultimately the cause of liberty around the world.

Notes

1. Jim DuPlessis, *TheState.com*, as quoted by National Association of Seed and Venture Funds (NASVF), at *www.nasvf.org/web/allpress.nsf/pages/7945*.

2. In multifactor productivity measures, output is related to combined inputs of labor, capital, and intermediate purchases. Labor is measured by the number of hours of labor expended in the production of output. Capital includes equipment, structures, land, and inventories. Intermediate purchases are composed of materials, fuels, electricity, and purchased services.

3. World Bank, *World Development Indicators*, 2003, on CD–ROM.

4. Adam Smith, *The Wealth of Nations* (New York: Prometheus Books, 1991), pp. 24–25.

5. As quoted in Nikolaus Piper, "Trade, Globalization and Integration: Some Lessons from Hamburg's History," paper presented at the Mont Pelerin Society meeting, Hamburg, Germany, April 3–6, 2004.

ANA I. EIRAS is Senior Policy Analyst for International Economics in the Center for International Trade and Economics at The Heritage Foundation.

Robert E. Scott  **NO**

Free Trade Costs American Jobs

Recently, the president claimed that critics who say that the Trans-Pacific Partnership (TPP) "is bad for working families . . . don't know what they are talking about."

Skeptics would respond, "Show me the money. Show me the jobs and wages you're going to generate for working Americans. Explain how the TPP is going to be different from the lousy trade deals we've had since the North American Free Trade Agreement (NAFTA) was signed into law in 1993."

The White House Council of Economic Advisors released a report touting the benefits of the TPP in pulling down barriers to U.S. exports abroad, but the report fails to mention the most important barrier to U.S. export success: several major trade partners (including TPP partners) managing the value of their own currencies for competitive gain vis-à-vis the United States. Yet the Obama administration has refused to even discuss the currency issue in the TPP negotiations.

One problem with trade and investment deals, especially with lower-wage countries like South Korea and China, is that they often result in growing trade deficits and job losses. In 2011, President Obama claimed that the Korea-U.S. free trade agreement (KORUS) would "support 70,000 American jobs" because the agreement would "increase exports of American goods by $10 billion to $11 billion."

He failed to say anything about rising imports, which will put Americans out of work. Looking only at exports is like counting only the runs by the home team. It might make you feel good, but it doesn't tell you the outcome of the game—it doesn't tell you whether your team won or lost.

Since KORUS took effect in 2012, exports to Korea have increased by less than $1 billion. Meanwhile, U.S. imports have surged more than $12 billion, resulting in a net loss of 75,000 U.S. jobs.

Similarly, Bill Clinton claimed that NAFTA would create 200,000 jobs in its first two years and a million jobs in five years. Instead, between 1993 (before NAFTA) and 2013, the U.S. trade deficit with Mexico and Canada increased from $17 billion to $177.2 billion, displacing more than 850,000 U.S. jobs.

And then there's Permanent Normal Trade Relations with China and China's admission to the World Trade Organization (WTO), which led to an explosion of imports and the loss of more than 3 million jobs, mostly in manufacturing and mostly in occupations that paid more than the jobs created in exports industries, and much more than jobs in non-traded industries.

While trade and investment deals have eliminated millions of good jobs, that's only the most visible part of their corrosive effect on working Americans. Growing trade with low-wage countries has also driven down the wages of most American workers, especially those without college degrees.

My colleague Josh Bivens has shown that expanded trade with low-wage countries has reduced the annual wages of a typical worker by $1,800 per year. Given that there are roughly 100 million non-college-educated workers in the U.S. economy (about 70 percent of the labor force), the scale of wage losses suffered by this group translates to roughly $180 billion.

Trade deals such as KORUS (completed by President Obama), and the agreement to bring China into the WTO (negotiated by President Clinton), have contributed to these losses. It's not surprising that one commentator concluded that "the Trans-Pacific Partnership trade deal is an abomination," because of its impacts on "low-skilled manufacturing workers and income inequality."

The leading cause of growing U.S. trade deficits is currency manipulation, which distorts trade flows by artificially lowering the cost of U.S. imports and raising the cost of U.S. exports. More than 20 countries, led by China, have been spending about $1 trillion per year buying foreign assets to artificially suppress the value of their currencies. Ending currency manipulation can create between 2.3 million and 5.8 million jobs for working Americans.

Several well-known currency manipulators—including Japan, Malaysia, and Singapore—are members of the proposed TPP, and others—including Korea, Taiwan, and China—have expressed interest in joining the agreement.

Unless there is a strong currency provision in the TPP, reductions in the U.S. trade deficit—the most promising route back to sustainable full employment—will be harder to obtain following its passage. Without a currency provision, the TPP is likely to lead to growing trade deficits and job losses.

If Obama is concerned with working families, he should focus on stopping currency manipulation.

ROBERT E. SCOTT is a Senior Economist and Director of Trade and Manufacturing Policy Research at the Economic Policy Institute (EPI).

EXPLORING THE ISSUE

Are Trade Agreements Good or Bad for the U.S. Economy?

Critical Thinking and Reflection

1. What benefits can nations derive from entering into trade agreements?
2. What are some of the potential costs or risks of entering into a trade agreement?
3. How would you propose to measure the success or failure of a trade agreement? What factors or metrics might you consider?
4. Is it possible for a trade agreement to be viewed as both a success and a failure? Why?
5. If you were consulting with government leaders on trade agreements, what advice would you provide them with?

Is There Common Ground?

The common ground that exists among these competing views on trade is that both sides of the debate are concerned about the economy and its impact on its citizens. Both positions in this argument view the issue as one that affects both the present and future strength and vitality of the United States economy. One side of the debate is focused on consumer benefits (e.g., greater variety, availability, affordability, and choice), economic efficiencies achieved through specialization, and innovation outcomes derived from trade agreements. Meanwhile the opposing view fears that the agreements have weakened and will continue to weaken the nation's economic strength (e.g., reduced manufacturing and related jobs), increase dependence on foreign nations in key and critical industries, and subject the country to trade inequities and inequalities.

It is unlikely that the United States will end its involvement in and with trade agreements. In fact, as the manuscript for this edition was being prepared, the Trans-Pacific Partnership (TPP), a proposed 12-nation deal spanning the Pacific Rim from Japan and Australia to Chile, was receiving significant scrutiny. Because of this pending agreement, and anticipation of future agreements, the debate over the benefits and costs of trade agreements is likely to continue.

Additional Resources

Black, T. & Costa, I. (2016). "A Tale of Two NAFTA Towns," *Bloomberg BusinessWeek,* April 11, pp. 12–13.

Hills, C. A. (2014). "NAFTAs Economic Upsides," *Foreign Affairs,* 93(1), pp. 122–127.

Irwin, D. A. (2016). "The Truth About Trade," *Foreign Affairs,* 95(4), pp. 84–95.

Matthews, C. (2016). "The Tide that Sinks All Boats," *Fortune,* 174(4), pp. 12–14.

Powell, B. (2016). "Are Free Trade Deals Bad for America?" *Newsweek,* 166(24), pp. 12–15.

Schulz, J. D. (2015). "Easing Cross-Border Complexities," *Logistics Management,* 54(6), pp. 36–39.

Internet References . . .

Are Trade Agreements Good for Americans?

http://www.nytimes.com/roomfordebate/2016/03/17
/are-trade-agreements-good-for-americans

Do Trade Agreements Kill Jobs?

http://www.forbes.com/sites/stevedenning/2016/03/08
/should-we-blame-trade-agreements-for
-loss-of-jobs/#2e7caad94320

**Free Trade Agreements Seen as Good for U.S.,
but Concerns Persist**

http://www.people-press.org/2015/05/27/free-trade
-agreements-seen-as-good-for-u-s-but
-concerns-persist/

Free Trade: Good or Bad for America?

http://www.chicagotribune.com/business/sns
-201603301700--tms--retiresmctnrs-a20160330
-20160330-story.html

**Lost Jobs? Deficits? Not so Fast—Trade
Agreements are Still a Roll of the Dice**

https://www.theguardian.com/business/2015/jun/18
/tpp-us-economy-free-trade-agreements
-are-a-roll-of-the-dice

**Phillips: The Insanity of "Free Trade"
Agreements**

http://www.washingtontimes.com/news/2014/mar/17
/phillips-the-insanity-of-free-trade-agreements/

**The Benefits of Free Trade: Addressing Key
Myths**

http://mercatus.org/publication/benefits-free
-trade-addressing-key-myths

**The Open Door of Trade: The Impressive
Benefits of America's Free Trade Agreements**

https://www.uschamber.com/sites/default/files/open
_door_trade_report.pdf

Selected, Edited, and with Issue Framing Material by:
Kathleen J. Barnes, *William Paterson University*
and
George E. Smith, *University of South Carolina, Beaufort*

ISSUE

Does It Make Good Business (Economic) Sense to Bring Manufacturing Back to the United States?

YES: Thomas Roemer, from "Why It's Time to Bring Manufacturing Back Home to the U.S.," *Forbes* (2015)

NO: Sita Slavov and Ben Ho, from "Stop Wishing for the Return of Manufacturing Jobs," *U.S. News & World Report* (2014)

Learning Outcomes
After reading this issue, you will be able to:
• Explain why a business may choose to bring its manufacturing operations back to the United States.
• Describe why a manufacturer may choose to take its manufacturing operations to a country outside of the United States.
• Formulate an opinion regarding the future pattern of manufacturing's return to the United States.
• Share with others your reasoned opinion of what the future will hold in terms of manufacturing's return to the United States.

ISSUE SUMMARY

YES: MIT Sloan School of Management Senior Lecturer and MIT Leaders for Global Operations program Executive Director Thomas Roemer discusses five factors for the shift to bring manufacturing back to the United States.

NO: Sita Slavov and Ben Ho discuss how many politicians emphasize the importance of manufacturing, but this reflects a fundamental misunderstanding of the United States' service-based economy.

Manufacturing in the United States is a vital sector, although its importance to the U.S. economy has been declining for the past 40 years according to the International Trade Administration.

Major increases in the construction, finance, insurance, and real estate, and services industries have played a significant role in reducing manufacturing's impact on overall U.S. production. In 1990, service production and delivery surpassed manufacturing as the largest contributor to overall private industry production. A year later, in 1991, the finance, insurance, and real estate sector also surpassed manufacturing. Since the beginning of the 2007 economic downturn, only computer and electronic products, aerospace, and transportation have seen increasing production levels.

The United States was the world's second largest manufacturer, with a 2010 industrial output of approximately $1696.7 billion. In 2008, its manufacturing output was greater than that of the manufacturing output of China and India combined, despite manufacturing

being a very small portion of the entire U.S. economy, as compared to most other countries' economies.

The largest manufacturing industries in the United States by revenue include petroleum, steel, automobiles, aerospace, telecommunications, chemicals, electronics, food processing, consumer goods, lumber, and mining. The United States leads the world in airplane manufacturing. American companies such as Boeing, Cessna, Lockheed Martin, and General Dynamics produce the vast majority of the world's civilian and military aircraft in factories stretching across the United States. If the top 500 U.S.-based manufacturing firms were counted as a separate country, their total revenue would rank as the world's third-largest economy.

A total of 3.2 million—one in six U.S. factory jobs—have disappeared since the beginning of 2000. The manufacturing sector of the U.S. economy has experienced substantial job losses over the past couple decades. In January 2004, the number of such jobs stood at 14.3 million, down by 3.0 million jobs, or 17.5 percent, since July 2000 and about 5.2 million since the historical peak in 1979. Employment in manufacturing was its lowest since July 1950. The United States produces approximately 21 percent of the world's manufacturing output, a number which has remained unchanged for the last 40 years. The job loss during this continual volume growth is explained by record-breaking productivity gains. In addition, growth in telecommunications, pharmaceuticals, aircraft, heavy machinery, and other industries along with declines in low-end, low-skill industries such as clothing, toys, and other simple manufacturing have resulted in U.S. jobs being more highly skilled and better paying.

YES

Thomas Roemer

Why It's Time to Bring Manufacturing Back Home to the U.S.

In the last decade, we've lost millions of manufacturing jobs to outsourcing. According to *U.S. News and World Report,* there are now 5.1 million fewer American manufacturing jobs than in 2001. The lure of low wages, tax advantages, and other cost savings has made for a seemingly straightforward calculus, and manufacturer after manufacturer, supported by intricate spreadsheets, has abandoned ship, until offshoring has become the emerging mantra of the new millennium. U.S. companies that still manufactured locally have slowly become outliers.

Interestingly, this dynamic now seems to be changing, as we're beginning to see more manufacturing in the U.S. Total output from American manufacturing relative to gross domestic product is back to pre-recession levels, with more than half a million new jobs. According to the Reshoring Initiative, 15% of this job growth results from reshoring alone. There are many reasons for this shift back to the U.S.

More Bang for the Buck

The first has to do with cost. It used to be cheaper to manufacture outside the U.S.; now the costs are now converging. In the manufacturing sector, the U.S. is still among the most productive economies in the world in terms of dollar output per worker. To be more specific, a worker in the U.S. is associated with 10 to 12 times the output of a Chinese worker. That's not a statement about intrinsic abilities; it merely reflects the superior infrastructure of the United States, with its higher investments in automation, information technology, transportation networks, education, and so on. And even though this relative advantage is slowly shrinking thanks to Chinese investment in such infrastructure, the wage gap between Chinese and U.S. workers is shrinking at a much faster rate. The net effect is that overall manufacturing in the U.S. is becoming more attractive again, leading to domestic growth and reshoring.

As productivity rises and automation increasingly replaces manual labor, the returning manufacturing jobs will require a higher degree of technological sophistication from the workforce, and this unfortunately may leave behind those who are unable to adapt. Moreover, while these jobs will be more rewarding and better paid, they will restore only a fraction of the number of jobs lost. Political rhetoric that proclaims a manufacturing renaissance a panacea for lagging job markets is thus misleading and is limited to imagining the future merely as a reflection of the past.

Immediate Gratification

The second reason to manufacture in America involves lead times. Customers have come to expect short delivery windows. With services like Amazon Prime, consumers are accustomed to delivery within one or two days, if not the same day. Offshore manufacturers need to store disproportionally large amounts of inventory to accommodate these expectations. But keeping inventory is costly—it requires space, energy, and labor; it gets lost, stolen, spoiled, and damaged; and, in the case of technology or fashion, it may become obsolete within weeks. Right now, the U.S. stores about $1.7 trillion in inventory, which means annual inventory carrying costs of between $300 billion and $500 billion—roughly the gross domestic products of Denmark and Norway, respectively. Manufacturers with onshore facilities can cut those costs dramatically. However, these indirect costs of offshoring are much harder to quantify than direct manufacturing costs, and they were frequently ignored in the initial rush to offshore.

THOMAS ROEMER is a senior lecturer at the MIT Sloan School of Management and the executive director of the MIT Leaders for Global Operations program.

Sita Slavov and Ben Ho

 **NO**

Stop Wishing for the Return of Manufacturing Jobs

Lawmakers need to embrace the service economy.

In his State of the Union address, President Obama celebrated "a manufacturing sector that's adding jobs for the first time since the 1990s," emphasizing the importance of "[beating] other countries in the race for the next wave of high-tech manufacturing jobs." The president is certainly not along among politicians in emphasizing the importance of manufacturing. In a 2013 speech, House Speaker John Boehner asserted that "America's greatness has always rested on our ability to build and produce things."

The basic assumption underlying these sentiments is that reversing the decline in manufacturing jobs is a good policy goal. In other words, both Obama and Boehner think the U.S. needs to make more "stuff."

But this policy goal reflects a fundamental misunderstanding of the nature of the U.S. economy. More than 70 percent of the wealth created in the U.S. today comes from providing services, a 33 percent increase since 1950. The shift from goods to services is likely to continue. In other words, our future prosperity is not going to come from buying more stuff, but from doing more for each other.

If we want to encourage Americans to make more stuff, then we have to figure out who's going to buy it. Obviously we—and the rest of the world—need a certain amount of stuff, but our current manufacturing sector is perfectly adequate to the task. Manufacturing jobs have declined not because of neglect, but because the U.S. has become really good at manufacturing. America's manufacturing output has increased steadily for the past half century; we just need fewer people to produce that output.

Americans already have plenty of stuff. Think for a second about what you spend your money on, and what you wish you had more of. Food? Televisions? Mobile phones? Cars? In a largely obese nation, we probably don't need more food. We need higher quality food, better prepared food, tastier food, healthier food—but not more food. We have more televisions, mobile phones and cars in this country than we know how to use. We don't need more devices. We need better content on those devices.

Recent research in psychology shows that for most Americans, spending money on experiences leads to greater happiness than spending money on material goods. As we get richer as a nation, therefore, growth in the economy will not be driven by more stuff, but by better health care, more education, more travel and better entertainment.

Some might argue that we could make stuff to sell to other countries. And it's true that outside the U.S. material deprivation is still common. But the trend toward a service economy is universal, and as other countries grow in wealth, their demand for services will increase as well. The U.S. should play to our strengths, a concept economists call comparative advantage. Services like education and entertainment, where we have a significant advantage over the rest of the world, already account for one-third of our exports.

In the post-war years, manufacturing offered a reliable path to the middle class that didn't require a college degree. But there is no reason why service jobs cannot offer the same in today's economy. Not long ago, nearly everyone in the United States was employed in agriculture. Today, just 2 percent of U.S. workers produce enough food to feed the U.S. and much of the rest of the world. Manufacturing is going the same way. According to the Bureau of Labor Statistics, nearly all of the 30 fastest growing jobs over the next 10 years are in services. These include jobs that range from physical therapy assistant, to home health aide, to dental hygienist, to medical secretary, all of which offer a path to a meaningful middle-class career. Many of these jobs do require some training beyond high school. But policy makers would do well to try to improve access to education instead of focusing on preserving manufacturing jobs.

Many politicians are fond of claiming that America is losing its edge. But when they follow up these claims with proposals to promote manufacturing, they are taking a step backwards. Does this mean that services are definitely the future of the American economy? We don't know. A good rule of thumb for economic policy making is that governments should not—and typically cannot—pick winners. However, no good policy can arise without recognition of what our economy has become: a service economy not a manufacturing one.

Sita Slavov is a professor of public policy and the director of the public policy PhD program at George Mason University's Schar School of Policy and Government. She is also a faculty research fellow at the National Bureau of Economic Research and a visiting scholar at the American Enterprise Institute.

Ben Ho is an associate professor of behavioral economics at Vassar College who applies economic tools like game theory and experimental design to understand social systems such as apologies, identity, fairness, and attitudes about climate change.

EXPLORING THE ISSUE

Does It Make Good Business (Economic) Sense to Bring Manufacturing Back to the United States?

Critical Thinking and Reflection

1. When might it make sense to return a company's manufacturing to the United States?
2. Why could you argue that manufacturing overseas or outside of U.S. borders makes sense?
3. If you had to explain this issue to a classmate or friend, how would you present the two sides of the issue to that classmate or friend?
4. What criteria would you give to help a classmate or friend develop their own opinion regarding outsourcing or manufacturing in the United States?
5. Based on your reading of this issue, what do you think the future holds for returning manufacturing? Are you optimistic that this trend will continue and grow? Why or why not?

Is There Common Ground?

Despite what appears to be polar differences in positions, the reality is that both sides of this issue are ultimately concerned with the cost of doing business and seeking the means to enhance profitability. One side argues that the best way to control costs and drive profit is seeking out and leveraging foreign manufacturers who may be able to provide similar services at lower cost compared to U.S. manufacturers. The opposing side, in turn, argues that costs can be controlled and profits driven by bringing manufacturing back to the United States, which, in turn, allows for more oversight of the manufacturing process that may decrease the cost of defective or deficient products and the costs associated with replacement and repairs.

The ultimate common ground to this issue may lie in the simple recognition that in reality both sides are correct with regard to their positions on outsourcing and reshoring. In other words, there will be times when it makes sound business sense to return production to United States' manufacturers and manufacturing. Alternatively, there may well be products and services that lend themselves to being produced where the labor markets and costs of production are the cheapest.

What remains to be seen is whether the reshoring or return of manufacturing is a temporary fad or an ongoing and consistent trend. At this point, it is clear that some businesses see value in returning their manufacturing to United States' locations while others seek to control their costs abroad. It is unlikely that this dialog will ever end as businesses are constantly seeking to enhance their profitability.

Additional Resources

(2016). "The Mythical Decline of U.S. Manufacturing," *ISE Magazine*, 48(7), p. 12.

Forbes, K. (2004). "U.S. Manufacturing: Challenges and Recommendations," *Business Economics*, 39(3), pp. 30–37.

Immelt, J. R. (2012). "The CEO of General Electric on Sparking an American Manufacturing Renewal," *Harvard Business Review*, 90(3), pp. 43–46.

Koenig, K. M. (2014). "Made in America 2014: Production is Growing," *Wood Products*, 119(6), pp. 37–42.

Pickett, L. (2015). "The Case for Reshoring," *Quality*, 54(10), pp. 42–46.

Internet References . . .

Companies Tiptoe Back Toward "Made in the U.S.A."

> http://www.wsj.com/articles/companies-tiptoe-back
> -toward-made-in-the-u-s-a-1421206289

"Good" Jobs Aren't Coming Back Manufacturers Bringing the Most Jobs Back to America

> http://www.usatoday.com/story/money
> /business/2016/04/23/24-7-wallst-economy
> -manufacturers-jobs-outsourcing/83406518/

Why Donald Trump is Wrong About Manufacturing Jobs and China

> http://www.newyorker.com/business/currency
> /why-donald-trump-is-wrong-about-manufacturing
> -jobs-and-china

Why Some Manufacturers are Returning to the U.S.

> http://www.pbs.org/newshour/bb/manufacturers
> -returning-u-s/

Unit 4

UNIT

Environmental Management

*W*ith intensified global pressure from non-governmental organizations (NGOs) and concerned citizens to protect the environment, governments are enacting policies to protect and preserve natural resources and companies are seeking ways to create more sustainable business models. This unit examines whether corporations should adopt environmentally friendly policies of corporate social responsibility (CSR) and sustainable development. Additionally, the unit questions whether it is possible for companies to create sustainable businesses and questions if corporate sustainability reporting is a valuable corporate reporting tool in encouraging stewardship for the earth's natural resources.

Selected, Edited, and with Issue Framing Material by:
Kathleen J. Barnes, *William Paterson University*
and
George E. Smith, *University of South Carolina, Beaufort*

ISSUE

Should Corporations Adopt Environmentally Friendly Policies of Corporate Social Responsibility (CSR) and Sustainable Development?

YES: Sierra Club, from "From the Current Articles of Incorporation & Bylaws, June 20, 1981," Sierra Club (2006)

NO: Paul Driessen, from "Roots of Eco-Imperialism," Free Enterprise Press (2003)

Learning Outcomes

After reading this issue, you will be able to:

- Understand the positive and negative consequences of environmentally friendly corporate social responsibility and sustainable development policies.
- Understand how environmentally friendly corporate social responsibility and sustainable development policies can be used as effective marketing tools.
- Understand and identify policies that might be implemented concerning environmentally friendly corporate social responsibility and sustainable development.
- Appreciate the ethical and legal implications of environmentally friendly corporate social responsibility and sustainable development.

ISSUE SUMMARY

YES: The Sierra Club is a leading environmentalist organization and has consistently advocated for the implementation of CSR policies in the workplace. The selection presented here provides insight into their philosophy and expectations as they relate to corporate behavior and its impact on the natural environment.

NO: Paul Driessen, trained in environmental science and a major advocate for the world's poor, writes a blistering attack on CSR and its constituent policies. He argues that these policies bring misery and death to the world's poor and act as camouflage for the environmentalist's anticapitalism, pro-statism agenda.

Virtually every introductory-level management textbook includes a chapter examining the impact corporate business activities have on the earth's environment. Usually the discussion blames business for much of the damage done to the environment. For example, a typical comment: "For years, businesses conducted their operations with little concern about environmental consequences . . . [businesses were] responsible for consuming significant amounts of materials and energy and causing waste accumulation and resource degradation . . . Businesses would look the other way . . ." (Carroll and Buchholtz, 2009).

Generally, these texts prescribe the adoption of corporate social responsibility (CSR) initiatives to ensure greater acceptance of the needs of the natural environment. Beyond the ubiquitous advocacy of CSR, an increasing number of textbooks—reflecting not just the views of business academia but those of social commentators, environmental nongovernment organization (NGO) activists, and government leaders across the globe—argue that corporations need to adopt policies of "sustainable development," a concept that emphasizes restricting economic growth to levels that won't outstrip the replenishment rate of our natural resources (Carroll and Buchholtz, 2009).

Interestingly, both the concept of CSR and the birth of the modern environmentalism movement were products of the 1960s. Many scholars and social historians argue that the development of

CSR was primarily due to the environmental activism of the 1960s successfully raising social awareness of the negative impact of corporate activity on the earth's environment (Horner, 2007). Thus, it is not surprising that the strongest force advocating CSR today is the environmentalism movement itself.

From an environmental perspective, the way to understand CSR is to view it as an umbrella concept under which a collection of related ideas fulfill specific roles in promoting responsible corporate behavior. *Stakeholder theory*, widely accepted in corporate America and the default approach for almost all business schools, argues that the traditional corporate concern for the creation of shareholder wealth first and foremost is misguided. A CSR/stakeholder approach suggests that all parties with a stake in a company's existence are entitled to input in determining the firm's activities, including the allocation of its revenues and profits. At present, amid the political and social atmosphere, it is the environmental stakeholder that is receiving increased attention and pressure in the corporate boardroom.

Sustainable development (SD) is another CSR-related, environmentally driven concept. SD came to prominence in the 1980s and has been very successful in raising awareness of the impact of corporate activity on the finite natural resources of the planet. As noted earlier, the key aspect of SD is concern for the natural resource needs of future generations. To this end, corporations should develop and implement business plans only after accounting for their potential long-term impact on the earth's natural resource base. The *precautionary principle* (PP) is frequently invoked by environmentalists as a means of alerting the public to possible environmental harm, primarily from the implementation of new technology. As the name suggests, it represents a defensive, assume-the-worst-until-proven-otherwise posture. In a very real sense, it is a guide for regulation.

The last three decades have seen the emergence of *socially responsible investing* (SRI) around the world. The idea behind SRI is to promote social acceptance of the environmentalist agenda by encouraging investment in firms or financial products that specifically reinforce pro-environmental corporate conduct. Taken together, the four concepts discussed here comprise the environmentalist's CSR agenda.

Here then, is your chance to examine this issue from both sides, as we ask you to decide whether or not corporations should adopt enviro-friendly CSR policies. Those who are adamantly against these enviro-friendly CSR policies, as illustrated in Paul Driessen's pointed attack on environmentalism-driven CSR, reject blind acceptance of ideas such as the precautionary principle. Driessen maintains that acceptance and practice of these ideas can be just as damaging as the corporate actions the ideas are designed to restrain. The PP, for example, has dominated public discussion since its adoption by the environmentalists and has played a large role in the numerous laws and regulations that affect virtually every aspect of corporate behavior, not to mention personal lives. However, as Driessen and a rapidly growing number of critics have pointed out, in many instances, this view is much worse than a carelessly optimistic belief that there are no environmental problems at all.

Consider the case of the corporate average fuel economy (CAFÉ) ratings for automobiles. To address smog pollution and the widely accepted perception that worldwide oil supplies were running out, the federal government passed a law in 1975 establishing fuel-efficiency requirements for all cars. The problem is that, over time, these standards have forced automakers to make smaller, lighter, less safe cars. How unsafe? Two reputable studies (i.e., 1989 Harvard University and Brookings Institution study; 2001 National Academy of Sciences) concluded that the CAFÉ standards result in 1,200–3,900 additional deaths every year (Bidinotto, 2004, p. 4). "In the trade-off between saving gasoline and saving lives, the government rules willingly sacrifice lives" (Bidinotto, 2004, p. 4).

Given this finding, it is no surprise that large, safe SUVs are popular with the public; nor is it surprising that SUVs are viewed by environmentalists as a major factor to the depletion of fossil fuels and to global warming. The point of this example is that it is just as dangerous to err on the side of extreme pessimism about the environment as it is to be in a state of unfounded optimism. Further, business executives would be wise to refrain from engaging in unquestioned acceptance of CSR policies, particularly given the increasingly skeptical attitude of both the scientific community and the general public regarding the veracity of the man-made global warming position.

YES

Sierra Club

From the Current Articles of Incorporation & Bylaws, June 20, 1981

The purposes of the Sierra Club are to explore, enjoy, and protect the wild places of the earth; to practice and promote the responsible use of the Earth's ecosystems and resources; to educate and enlist humanity to protect and restore the quality of the natural and human environment; and to use all lawful means to carry out these objectives.

Beliefs about Environment and Society—Developed by Planning Committee and Printed in Sierra Club Goals Pamphlet, 1985–1989, with Board Knowledge, but Not Formally Adopted by It

Humans have evolved as an interdependent part of nature. Humankind has a powerful place in the environment, which may range from steward to destroyer. We must share the Earth's finite resources with other living things and respect all life-enabling processes. Thus, we must control human population numbers and seek a balance that serves all life forms.

Complex and diversified ecosystems provide stability for the Earth's life support processes. Development and other human activities can simplify ecosystems, undermine their dynamic stability, and threaten these processes. Wildness itself has a value serving all species, with too few remaining. We have more to fear from too little wildness than from too much.

Genetic diversity is the product of evolution acting on wildness, and is important because it is biological capital for future evolution. We must preserve genetic diversity in wild tracts and gene pools. No species should be hastened into extinction by human intervention.

The needs of all creatures must be respected, their destinies viewed as separate from human desires, their existence not simply for human benefit. All species have a right to perpetuation of the habitat necessary and required for survival. All creatures should have freedom from needless predation, persecution, and cruel or unduly confining captivity. We must seek moral restraints on human power to affect the well-being of so many species.

Humans must exercise stewardship of the Earth's resources to assure enough for other creatures and for the future. Thus, resources should be renewed indefinitely wherever possible, and resource depletion limited. Resources should be used as long as possible and shared, avoiding waste and needless consumption. We must act knowledgeably and take precautions to avoid initiating irreversible trends. Good stewardship implies a shared moral and social responsibility to take positive action on behalf of conservation.

The enjoyment of the natural environment and the Earth's wild places is a fundamental purpose of the Club, and an end in itself.

Ideal Goals (Summary)—for Environment and Society

To sustain natural life-support systems, avoid impairing them, and avoid irreversible damage to them.

To facilitate species survival; to maintain genetic diversity; to avoid hastened extinction of species; to protect prime natural habitat.

To establish and protect natural reserves, including representative natural areas, wilderness areas in each biome, displays of natural phenomena, and habitats for rare and endangered species.

To control human population growth and impacts; to limit human population numbers and habitat needs within Earth's carrying capacity; to avoid needless human consumption of resources; to plan and control land use, with environmental impact assessment and safeguards, and rehabilitation of damaged sites.

To learn more about the facts, interrelationships, and principles of the Earth's ecosystems, and the place and impact of humans in them; to understand the consequences of human activities within the biosphere.

To develop responsible and appropriate technology matched to end-uses; to introduce sophisticated technology gradually after careful assessment and with precautionary monitoring.

To control pollution of the biosphere; to minimize waste residuals with special care of hazardous materials; to use the best available control technology at sources; and to recycle wastes.

To manage resources soundly; to avoid waste with long-term plans; to sustain the yield of living resources and maintain their productivity and breeding stocks; to prolong availability of nonliving resources such as fossil fuels, minerals, and water.

To impart a sense of social responsibility among consumers, developers, and public authorities concerning environmental protection; to regulate threats to public health; to avoid private degradation of public resources; to minimize impacts on innocent parties and future generations.

For The Sierra Club Organization

To acquire the knowledge, skills, resources, and energy to accomplish the Club's goals for environment and society.

To render service through ability to promote societal well-being; through improving environmental conditions and maintaining environmental quality; through equipping members with understanding, training, and motivation to be effective in improving environmental quality; to advance public education; to foster appreciation of outdoor experience and responsible outdoor behavior.

To have the following characteristics: to be energetic, actively moving projects to completion, catalyzing action, and using the most modern and efficient tools available; to be effective, able to achieve results in a knowledgeable and responsible manner; to possess a breadth of interest and vision encompassing any problem of the physical environment; to be willing to take risks; to be persistent in pursuit of Club causes; to see the Club itself as making history, and thus take a long view; to be cooperative with all who are working toward the same ends; to reflect excellence in Club publications; to be innovative in exploring new means toward Club goals.

To be constituted to reflect a carefully balanced and integrated variety of approaches—democratic, grassroots, decentralized—yet with a strong central core; to foster flexibility, initiative, and collaboration within a central framework of cohesiveness; to respect expertise of its various entities; to consult broadly among its entities

and decide consensually but promptly, with decisions reflecting thorough and serious deliberation; while being basically a membership organization of volunteers, to work closely with professional and support staff; to define the roles of volunteers and staff clearly; to enhance effectiveness through enjoyment of social interaction between volunteers and staff; to be modern while retaining traditions and a sense of the past; to provide an example of good conduct and high standards for the Club and society.

To assure that the public perceives the Club as "the guardian of the environment"; as a leading force in key struggles for the environment in every area; as a powerful force which energizes campaigns and achieves its goals; and as a constructive force with a positive sense for meeting society's needs.

To obtain the necessary and sufficient resources to fulfill the Club's purposes, including:

1. To have a membership large enough to fulfill the Club's purposes and be credible in comparison with other organizations which aspire to be social forces, and large enough to be taken seriously by leaders in national political life; to develop wide-ranging competence among its members on issues; to generate a leadership capable of acting effectively on a great many issues; to produce annual revenues and net worth sufficient to meet its goals; to have geographical distribution of members; to have member representation in political units in the United States and Canada; to have members of varied ages, interests, and backgrounds; to have members who can provide expertise to address diverse issues, with widely varied professional and technical backgrounds and experience.

2. To have a staff large enough and with sufficient professional capacity to provide services to support member operations, and undertake specific staff programs such as lobbying, publications, and outings; staff should share the Club's basic values and assist volunteers in the pursuit of Club goals.

3. To have financial resources to finance the Club's operations at all levels; to have income from diverse sources; to build a net worth sufficient to allow financing of annual operations without borrowing, and ultimately representing at least half the annual operating budget.

4. To have the best possible information resources and systems available to guide and support Club actions; to have information which is sophisticated, current, accurate, in context, and accessible; to have a mix of news, intelligence, fundamental knowledge, theory, and plans; to maintain the institutions necessary to collect and disseminate this information, including a library, newsletters, various communications mechanisms, and links to existing information networks.

Vision Statement for the Sierra Club's Second Century, Board of Directors, September 16–17, 1989

The Challenge

We are facing a global environmental crisis that grows more urgent every day. Threats that were once inconceivable—such as massive oil spill disasters, global climate change, and the poisoning of our air, land, and water—are becoming common events. Species are being annihilated and wilderness is being destroyed at an alarming and accelerating rate.

We live each day knowing that in a few generations—unless humankind takes drastic steps to protect our planet—it is possible that the Earth will hurtle around the Sun devoid of life as we know it.

There is no priority more urgent than saving the Earth.

Our Vision

For nearly 100 years, Sierra Club members have shared a vision of humanity living in harmony with the Earth.

We envision a world where wilderness areas and open spaces are protected habitats sustaining all species . . . a world where oceans and streams are clean and the air is pure . . . a world where a healthy biosphere and a nontoxic environment are inalienable rights. In short, we envision a world saved from the threat of unalterable planetary disaster.

To save our planet, we must change the world—

Priorities must change: People must learn to live in ways that preserve and protect our precious resources.

Policies must change: Our institutions must abandon practices that recklessly endanger the environment.

Values must change: Progress must be measured by its long-term value to living systems and creatures rather than its short-term value to special interests or the economy.

To achieve this vision, people across the nation and around the world must speak out with a powerful voice that cannot be ignored. Aggressive grassroots action on an unprecedented scale is essential to protect our environment and our species. There is no other choice. It will require leadership that is visionary, experienced, and strong.

Our Role

The Sierra Club is uniquely qualified to lead this grassroots action to save the Earth. We are America's largest and most effective grassroots environmental organization—anexperienced, respected, and committed fellowship of citizen activists. Within our ranks lie the expertise, wisdom, and vitality to find the new directions needed to meet the challenges of the future.

We offer proven ability to influence public policy and empower individuals to confront local, national, and global problems. From town halls to our nation's capital to global institutions, Sierra Club activists are scoring enormous victories for the environment through personal action, education, litigation, lobbying, and participation in the political process.

As the Sierra Club prepares for its second century, we offer to America and the world our vision of humanity living in harmony with nature. We dedicate ourselves to achieving this vision as we reaffirm our passionate commitment to explore, enjoy, and protect the Earth.

Statement of Purposes, Development by the Planning Committee in 1985; amended by the Board of Directors, May 5–6, 1990

For purposes of planning, the Sierra Club's purpose, thus, is to preserve, protect, and enhance the natural environment.

The mission of the Sierra Club is to influence public, private, and corporate policies and actions through Club programs at the local, state, national, and international levels.

The strategy of the Sierra Club is to activate appropriate portions of a network of staff, members, and other concerned citizens, using legislative, administrative, electoral, and legal approaches, and to develop supporting public opinion.

Strategic Goals, Board of Directors, May 1–2, 1993

The following goals guide the Club's work:

I. Enhance public perception of "environment" (overcome the perception of limits):

   A. Develop pressure by consumers for green products.
   B. Educate public that strong environmental protection creates jobs.
   C. Reduce consumption levels in the United States through increasing efficiency, recycling, producing more durable goods, and by making waste and nonessential products and packaging socially unacceptable.

II. Build upon and develop new forms of political leverage:

   A. Mobilize market incentives to induce corporate environmental change.
   B. Develop hybrid or "coordinated campaigns," targeting multiple levels of decision making.

C. Work to make existing institutions more responsive and accountable to community and environmental needs.

D. Create new vehicles for responsive institutions of government.

E. Develop unconventional alliances to overcome legislative obstacles.

III. Integrate concerns for environmental protection and social justice to strengthen the environmental movement:

A. Develop more effective means for communicating through race, class, age, and cultural barriers.

B. Re-position the Sierra Club as more visibly concerned about threats to community and workplace environments.

C. Encourage more extensive coalition work between local Sierra Club entities and environmental justice groups.

D. Develop a stronger capacity to influence state and local regulatory and land-use actions (particularly as these relate to pollution threats to vulnerable groups in our society and land uses they find unacceptable).

IV. Enhance the Club's position of leadership within the environmental movement:

A. Continue to develop programs to cultivate and train new leaders.

B. Nurture a culture within the Club that encourages cooperation and collaboration, and that rewards innovative ideas and contributions.

C. Significantly enhance our ability for "quick responses" to issues and challenges.

D. Strengthen the Club's public affairs capacity for "telling our story."

Sierra Club Promise, Board of Directors, November 20–21, 1993

As a Sierra Club member you are empowered to help save the Earth and enjoy the natural world around you.

JOIN OUR CRUSADE

Get involved

Help resolve . . . critical community, national and global environmental challenges.

Philosophy of Service and Stewardship, Board of Directors, September 16–17, 1995

To achieve its mission, the Sierra Club has organized persons of shared environmental concerns into a powerful and effective force for protecting the natural environment. As a grassroots-based organization, we rely on individuals for our resources, talent, and energy. Our members are our most important assets.

We are the Sierra Club. We are members helping other members. We trust and respect members and acknowledge their full range of contributions.

Good Stewardship is:

• providing members with a supportive environment that allows them to determine their relationship with the Club.

• facilitating each member's involvement in the organization at the level the member desires.

• entailing the wise and careful use of the member's time, energy, and resources.

• providing Club members with the materials, information, expertise, and other resources that will strengthen their relationship with the organization.

• creating the foundation that makes it possible for the Club to fulfill its mission now—and in the future.

Sierra Club "Premise" Poster, presented to the Board November 13–14, 1999, by the Communication & Education GovCom

This is not about getting back to nature. It is about understanding we've never left.

We are deep in our nature every day. We're up to our ears in it. It is under our feet, it is in our lungs, it runs through our veins. We are not visitors here. We weren't set down to enjoy the view. We were born here and we're part of it—like any ant, fish, rock, or blade of grass.

This connection is as personal as it is fundamental. It can't be proved with theorems and diagrams. You either feel it or you don't. Sierra Club members feel it.

Maybe it came to you on a mountain trail, or on a river bank, or at a windowsill watching a spider's unthinking intelligence unfold. Simply put, it's the sudden conviction that there is something out there, something wonderful. And it is much, much bigger than you.

A revelation like this could easily overwhelm a person. We choose to let it inspire us. Nature, vastly complex and infinitely subtle, is our perfect metaphor. Related to everything, signifying everything, it is the spring where we go to renew our spirit. And it, in turn, asks something of us. It compels us to take responsibility and then to take action.

Look, there is nothing inevitable about the future of our environment. A poisoned stream can get worse, stay the same, or get better. It depends largely on what we choose to do. That simple belief, backed by 100 years of effort and result, is what drives the Sierra Club.

So, forget the grim cliché of the selfless environmentalist. When you accept your connection to nature, suddenly you can't look at the world without seeing something very personal in it. You are part of it, and you work for the planet because it gives you joy to do so.

You work for the planet because you belong to it.

Organizational and Issues Goals, Board of Directors, November 19–20, 2005

Organizational

In order to build grassroots power in our communities for achieving the Club's objectives related to our conservation initiatives, the Board of Directors adopts the following capacity-building priorities for 2006–2010. The Board asks all Club entities to contribute to the development of these capacities, not exclusively, but as top priorities identified through the Summit Direction Setting Process. The Board further directs staff and Governance Committees to work with grassroots activists to develop appropriate tools and support to:

1. *Seek new allies and build coalitions* to bring different perspectives together around common interests, and build political and community momentum around shared concerns and values.
2. *Create media visibility* through reporters, editors, and news coverage, visibility events, advertising, and other media access and outlets that put our point of view in the public eye and public debate.
3. *Organize people in our communities to take action together* in their neighborhoods and homes, through local networking, groups, and gatherings that build our activist numbers, strength, and diversity.
4. *Enlist public support with messages framed around solutions.* Take our message out to people in our communities with materials, presentations, and public education framed around solutions that the public can understand, relate to, and act on.

The Board of Directors affirms its commitment to the proposition that a key way the Sierra Club can fulfill its national purpose at this point in time is to invest its financial, staff, and moral resources in developing the capacity of its leaders, enhancing its organizational capacity, and conducting programs of effective local action—rekindling the movement that the Sierra Club played such a key role in launching. We affirm that development of the Club's volunteer leadership and the chapters and groups they lead is a critical investment in the strength of the organization as a whole and the environmental movement more broadly.

In order to build grassroots power for achieving the Club's objectives related to our Conservation Initiatives, the Board of Directors identifies four groups of priority decision-makers for 2006–2010. We wish to grow our capacity to influence (1) voters, (2) state officials, and (3) local officials, and maintain our present capacity to influence (4) federal officials.

Issues

The Board of Directors adopts three long-term National Conservation Initiatives for 2006–2010. They are: (1) Smart Energy Solutions, (2) Safe and Healthy Communities, and (3) America's Wild Legacy.

These three Conservation Initiatives will be the centerpieces of our national conservation agenda for the next five years. The single most important goal of this agenda will be to advance a smart, safe, clean energy future in the next decade.

To maximize success, the Conservation Governance Committee and the staff should seek out and give preference to projects and programs that overlap and provide synergy between these three initiatives.

These Conservation Initiatives represent the national conservation agenda that the Sierra Club Board has chosen for focused work over the next five years. They were selected after reviewing the Sierra Summit and pre-Summit direction setting process results from the grassroots leadership and the Summit delegates.

Each initiative will eventually have specific goals, values, action objectives, and public policy outcomes selected to implement them. All Governance Committees and national staff are encouraged to work together to implement these Conservation Initiatives.

Clarification of Conservation Initiatives and their Emphases for 2006–2010, Board of Directors, March 4–5, 2006

The Sierra Club's 114-year history reflects a rich blend of activism and unifying campaigns. Over the last decades, periods of mobilization and focus have represented some of the Club's finest moments, and yielded some of our proudest victories: the Alaska Lands Act, Wild Forest campaign, the replacement of James Watt, the Superfund battle of 1986, California Desert Protection Campaign, the defeat of Newt Gingrich's Contract with America, and our 26-year long defense of the Arctic Refuge.

Now, we have the opportunity to distinguish ourselves again and to lead once more.

2006–2010 Conservation Initiatives

In November 2005, the Board of Directors adopted three long-term conservation initiatives for the Sierra Club—Smart Energy Solutions, America's Wild Legacy, and Safe and Healthy Communities.

Two of these three—America's Wild Legacy and Safe and Healthy Communities—have been part of the Sierra Club's priority conservation work for decades. In adopting them as Conservation Initiatives for 2006–2010, the Board declared its commitment to our continued leadership in these areas.

In contrast, the Sierra Club has not historically made broad energy policy a national priority campaign. Energy, historically, has been a less central and more episodic Club focus. But the times demand that we meet the challenge to move beyond a fossil fuel world and that the Club lead society through one of the largest transformational moments in American history.

The Club's leadership role in confronting global warming and transforming our energy economy advances not only the Club's Smart Energy vision, but our work for America's Wild Legacy and Safe and Healthy Communities as well. The Club must lead America in this moment; there is no other organization with the history, vision, and presence at the community level to play that role.

At the same time, the Club's highest priority for the next decade as an institution is to build its capacity and focus on Smart Energy Solutions. This is the Conservation Initiative where our existing capacities and abilities are least well developed. As a result, we want to identify those opportunities that address the threats from climate change and can contribute to effective solutions where our members live. In building support for this priority, we want to be promoting Smart Energy Solutions in our trainings, communications channels, fundraising, political work, activist outings, and other available opportunities. We ask and encourage all to participate in an early opportunity around Earth Day 2006. It will be our first opportunity to showcase, for example, our Cool Cities program around the country.

Engaging Our Members and Programs in Our Conservation Initiatives

The Board of Directors reaffirms the importance of all three Conservation Initiatives, and the need for the Club to provide support for volunteers and staff working on the Areas of National Concern in all three of these initiatives.

The Board, therefore, requests its Governance Committees, their sub-entities, all programs, and chapters and groups to assess and enhance their readiness to meet our new challenges, especially that of Smart Energy Solutions. The Board further encourages these same entities, as well as members, to join us at this critical time to build public sentiment to achieve all of our conservation initiatives.

In going forward, we are requesting staff and volunteer leaders at all levels to make available the Club's time, expertise, and resources in a way that supports the successful implementation of our Smart Energy Initiative as a truly powerful, effective, and fully integrated campaign, while retaining the Sierra Club's engagement and involvement across the full range of our Conservation Initiatives.

Sierra Club is America's largest and most influential grassroots environmental organization.

Paul Driessen

 **NO**

Roots of Eco-Imperialism

Like a mad scientist's experiment gone terribly awry, corporate social responsibility has mutated into a creature radically different from what its original designers envisioned. It now threatens to cause a moral meltdown, to spawn a system in which the most far-fetched worries of healthy, well-fed First World activists routinely dominate business, economic, technological, scientific and health debates—and override critical concerns of sick, malnourished people in poor Third World countries.

This mutant version of corporate social responsibility demands that businesses and nations conduct their affairs in accord with new "ethical" codes that derive from several intertwined doctrines of social and environmental radicalism.

- **Stakeholder participation** theory asserts that any group that has an interest in, or could arguably be affected by, a corporate decision or the outcome of a public policy debate has a right to pressure the decision makers until they accede to the activists' demands.
- **Sustainable development** (SD) says companies must minimize the extraction and use of natural resources, because corporate activities must "meet the needs and aspirations of the present without compromising the ability of future generations to meet their needs."
- **The precautionary principle** (PP) holds that companies should halt any activities that might threaten "human health or the environment," even if no clear cause-and-effect relationship has been established, and even if the potential threat is largely (or entirely) theoretical.
- **Socially responsible investing** (SRI) insists that pension funds and individual investors should purchase shares in companies that have pledged to conform their corporate policies and actions to sustainability, precautionary and responsibility ideologies.

There is a certain allure to these doctrines—reinforced by news stories and reports extolling the concepts and asserting their widespread acceptance. However, neither the terminology nor its constant repetition represents a groundswell of actual public support or obviates fundamental problems with these precepts. The language might sound clear at first blush. But it is highly elastic and can easily be stretched and molded to fit a wide variety of activist claims, causes and agendas.

As a consequence, the doctrines are the subject of deep concern and passionate debate, as thoughtful people struggle to assess the risks posed for corporations, investors, employees, creditors, and customers—for scientific, economic, and technological advancement—and for people whose hope for a better future depends on ensuring plentiful supplies of affordable electricity, conquering disease and malnutrition, and having unencumbered access to modern technology and greater economic opportunity. As the debate rages, it is becoming increasingly obvious that the doctrines solve few problems and, instead, create a vast multitude of new difficulties.

At their root is the fact that these intertwined CSR doctrines primarily reflect the concerns, preferences, and gloomy worldview of a small cadre of politicians, bureaucrats, academics, multinational NGOs, and wealthy foundations in affluent developed countries. These self-appointed guardians of the public weal have little understanding of (and often harbor a deep distaste for) business, capitalism, market economies, technology, global trade, and the vital role of profits in generating innovation and progress.

Yet, it is they who proclaim and implement the criteria by which businesses are to be judged, decide which of society's goals are important, determine whether those goals are being met, and insist that countervailing needs, viewpoints, and concerns be relegated to secondary or irrelevant status. In so doing, they seek to impose their worldview and change society in ways, and to degrees, that they have not been able to achieve through popular votes, legislation, treaty, or even judicial decisions.

Inherent in the doctrines are several false, pessimistic premises that are at the core of ideological environmentalism. Eco activists erroneously believe, for example, that energy and mineral resources are finite, and are rapidly being exhausted. That activities conducted by corporations, especially large multinational companies, inevitably result in resource depletion, environmental degradation, impaired human and societal health, social harm, and imminent planetary disaster. And that it is primarily profits, not societal or consumer needs and desires—and certainly not a desire to serve humanity—that drive corporate decision-making.

In a nutshell, CSR doctrines are rooted too much in animosity toward business and profits, too much in conjectural problems and theoretical needs of future generations—and too little in real, immediate, life-and-death needs of present generations, especially billions of poor rural people in developing countries. The mutant doctrines give radical activists unprecedented leverage to impose the loftiest of developed world standards on companies, communities, and nations, while ignoring the needs, priorities, and aspirations of people who struggle daily just to survive.

Actually implementing the doctrines requires significant centralized control of land and energy use, economic production and consumption, corporate innovation and initiative, markets, transportation, labor, trade, housing, policy making processes, and people's daily lives. Under the activists' agenda, control would be monitored and enforced through United Nations, European Union, U.S., and other government agencies. All this is the antithesis of the private property rights, capitalism, and freedom of nations, communities, companies, and individuals to make their own decisions, in accord with their own cultural preferences and personal or societal needs—and thereby generate innovation, prosperity, human health, and environmental quality.

The ideological version of corporate social responsibility thus stands in direct opposition to the systems that have generated the greatest wealth, opportunities, technological advancements, and health and environmental improvements in history. Its real effect is to cede decision-making to a few; reduce competition, innovation, trade, investment, and economic vitality; and thereby impair future social, health, and environmental improvements.

According to activist theology, adherence to CSR concepts generates a "triple bottom line" (economic, social, and environmental) that companies should meet in judging "true" profitability and citizenship, David Henderson notes in *Misguided Virtue: False Notions of Corporate Responsibility*. Only by measuring their costs, benefits, and profits against all three standards can businesses meet "society's expectations," earn their "license to operate," and "give capitalism a human face," claim the activists.

But CSR's supposedly equal emphasis on all three components of the triple bottom line is typically skewed so that environmental considerations trump all others. This happens even where people's lives are put at risk, as in the case of strident activist opposition to pesticides despite widespread malaria, or to biotechnology despite rampant malnutrition and starvation.

Mutant CSR also enables countries to impose "legal" barriers to keep foreign goods out and protect domestic businesses and interests—typically through the use of malleable precautionary and sustainability rules that make it easy to cite far-fetched, unproven health or environmental risks, so as to justify heavy-handed actions.

Stakeholder dialogue, according to the World Business Council for Sustainable Development, is "the essence of corporate social responsibility." However, many of the "stakeholders" who seek "dialogues" are actually well-funded activist groups that assert a "right" to participate in corporate and government decision-making, simply because they have a passionate devotion to their cause.

Some stakeholders are "shareholder activists," who own substantial shares in a company—or just enough to qualify them to introduce resolutions at annual meetings, demanding that a company adopt their positions and agendas on sustainable development, global warming, the precautionary principle, or "human rights." Others may be politicians, bureaucrats, and other elites in developing countries, whose personal careers and interests are advanced substantially by being aligned with these causes. That the lives of poor people in these countries might thereby be put at greater risk is often only a secondary consideration.

According to the *Boston Globe, Sacramento Bee,* Capital Research Center, and others, the U.S. environmental movement alone has annual revenues of some $4 billion, primarily as a result of contributions from foundations, corporations, unions, trial lawyers, and taxpayer-funded government agencies. The international green movement's budget has been estimated to be well in excess of $8 billion a year.

As a result, well-organized, media-savvy pressure groups have unprecedented power to promote their agendas, define "society's expectations," and influence public perceptions, corporate decisions, and legislative and regulatory initiatives.

In the international arena, they frequently play a prominent role in negotiations, equal to or more dominant than many multinational companies and even some countries, especially Third World nations. Not surprisingly, the NGOs' agendas frequently conflict with and override the most pressing needs and concerns of people who are struggling to overcome widespread poverty and malnutrition, devastating epidemics, and a virtual absence of electricity and economic opportunity.

Corporate social responsibility, argues Gary Johns, can easily become "an assault on the interests and rights of 'real' stakeholders, those who have invested in or are creditors of corporations. It occurs when managers bow to pressure from interests that have no contract with the corporation, whether by way of employment, or supply of goods or services, or through ownership.

"CSR is also an assault on the interests of the electorate. It occurs by undermining the formal democratic consensus as to what constitutes reasonable business behavior. It also occurs when governments grant NGOs such status that it enables them to set themselves up as judges of corporate behavior," or of national decisions on critical health, economic, and environmental concerns.

In many cases, the activist groups' cumulative membership might be less than 0.01 percent of a community's or country's population. No one elected them as stakeholders. No plebiscite was held to make their narrow definitions and agendas the arbiter of what is moral or in the broader public interest. No election, adjudication, or even United Nations resolution gave them the authority to exclude other stakeholders from debates and decision-making processes—including entire nations and billions of destitute people, who are being denied the benefits of global trade, economic development, abundant affordable energy, and informed use of resources, pesticides, and biotechnology.

And yet, the activists define what is responsible, sustainable, or sufficiently cautious, often in a way that blocks any development which conflicts with their agendas. That other people might be adversely affected—or the world's most destitute citizens might remain mired in chronic hunger, poverty, disease, and despair—enters only superficially into their calculations.

In asserting their demands, they downplay the complex needs and circumstances that confront companies, communities and nations. They ignore the science-based regulatory systems that already protect citizens from actual risks, and raise public fears of far-fetched risks to justify endless delays or outright bans.

Businesses, elected officials, and citizens should take a leadership position on these issues, contest the demands of anti-business activists, challenge their motives, and dispute their underlying premises. As Johns suggests, they need to "make the NGOs prove their bona fides." They need to "question the extent to which [the activists] represent anyone or anything; question the size of their membership; question the source of their funds; and question their expertise. In other words, question their standing and their legitimacy."

Instead, too many businesses, community leaders, and citizens pursue a strategy of appeasement and accommodation, ceding moral authority to unelected NGOs, bureaucrats, "ethical" investor groups, and other activists. Some have actually endorsed the activists' demands and collaborated closely with them, despite serious adverse impacts on the world's poor.

❧⟨◉⟩❧

As a result, says University of Houston economics professor Thomas DeGregori, developed country activists are often able to co-opt local movements, hijacking them to radical agendas, brushing aside legitimate local concerns, and leaving the indigenous people worse off than before.

When India's impoverished Chipko people initiated a movement to build a road and gain access to Himalayan forest resources, to create a small wood products industry, First World environmentalists took it over. The voices of real local stakeholders were all but silenced, says Australian professor Dr. Haripriya Ragan, and their struggle for resources and development were sacrificed to global environmental concerns. Leading the assault were radical

anti-technology activist Vandana Shiva and groups that "tacitly support coercive conservation tactics that weaken local claims to resource access for sustaining livelihoods."

In other cases, "stakeholder involvement" becomes a form of extortion, in which "corporate greed" is replaced by "agenda greed." In 1995, Shell Oil was preparing to sink its Brent Spar offshore oil storage platform in the deep Atlantic, under a permit granted by the UK Environment Ministry. However, Greenpeace launched a vicious and sophisticated $2-million public relations assault that falsely accused the company of planning to dump tons of oil, toxic waste, and radioactive material in the ocean. Shell's timid and unimaginative response to the ensuing media nightmare got the company nothing but a bigger black eye, and it was forced to spend a fortune dismantling the platform onshore.

A year later, Greenpeace issued a written apology, effectively admitting that the entire campaign had been a fraud. There had been no oil or wastes on the structure. Of course, the admission got buried in the business pages or obituaries. Flush from their victory, the Rainbow Warriors went on to shake down other companies and promote bogus claims about chemicals, wood products, and genetically modified "Frankenfood."

Embarrassed by its stinging defeat, Shell tried to refurbish its reputation and learn from its mistakes. Apparently, the company's execs never actually graduated from the School of Hard Knocks. A few years later, when complaints alone failed to garner enough media attention to embarrass Shell over its alleged "failure to protect Nigeria's Ogoni people," Oxfam and Amnesty International hooked up with radical greens, to hammer the company for complicity in an "environmental catastrophe."

It turned out the catastrophe was caused by tribesmen sabotaging oil pipelines, says Dr. Roger Bate, a visiting fellow with the American Enterprise Insitute, to get gullible journalists to write stories that enabled Ogoni leaders to extort huge monetary settlements from the company. But Shell paid up anyway, in hopes that the problem would go away. Meanwhile, the rights groups and media ignored the racketeering, effectively aiding and abetting the tribal leaders, and setting the stage for future blackmail.

❧⟨◉⟩❧

Sustainable development, as defined by environmental activists, focuses too little on fostering sustained economic development, and too much on *restricting* development—typically in the name of protecting the environment. It also reflects their erroneous doctrine that we are rapidly depleting our natural resources and destroying the planet. The putative welfare of "fragile ecosystems" again trumps even the most obvious welfare of people, frequently leading desperate people to wreak havoc on the very ecosystems the activists claim to be protecting.

Leon Louw, executive director of South Africa's Free Market Foundation, refers to sustainable development as "voodoo science." It never asks "sustainable for how long: 10, 200, 1000, a million years? For whom? Advanced people with unknowable future technology, needs and resources? For how long must we conserve so-called 'non-renewables'? Must our descendants, by the same twisted logic, do likewise? Forever?"

Not one person alive at the dawn of the twentieth century could have envisioned the amazing technological feats of that era, its changing raw material needs, or its increasing ability to control pollution. In 1900, coal and wood provided heat. Air pollution and diseases we no longer even hear about killed millions. Telephones, cars and electricity were novelties for the rich. Common folk and freight alike were hauled by horses, which left behind 900,000 tons of manure a year in New York City alone. The Wright brothers still made bicycles. Air conditioners, radios, televisions, plastics, antibiotics, organ transplants and computers could not even be imagined.

Today, the pace of change is exponentially faster than 100 or even 50 years ago. To define sustainability under these conditions is impossible. To suppose that anyone could predict what technologies will exist, what pollutants will be a problem, what fuels and minerals we will need—in what quantities—is to engage in sheer science fiction. Or in the most deceitful public policy scam.

In short, the fundamental problem with "sustainable development," says Oxford University economist Dr. Wilfred Beckerman, is its demand that radical prescriptions be followed to achieve narrowly defined ends, determine which trade-offs should be emphasized, and decide which trade-offs are to be ignored. Here the concept has nothing to add. "Indeed, it subtracts from the objective of maximizing human welfare, because the slogan of sustainable development seems to provide a blanket justification for almost any policy designed to promote almost any ingredient of human welfare, irrespective of its cost and hence irrespective of the other ingredients of welfare."

⤙◈⤚

Precautionary theories likewise promote agendas set by eco-centric activists in developed countries. They ignore countervailing interests and needs of developing nations, such as: creating economic opportunity, ensuring adequate and reliable supplies of affordable energy, alleviating poverty, malnutrition and disease—and ultimately improving environmental quality and ensuring more sustainable practices. It gives CSR, SD, and PP precepts credit for any potential public health and environmental risks they might reduce, public policy analyst Indur Goklany points out, but imposes no "discredit" for risks, injuries, or deaths that they might generate.

Precautionary doctrines hold that, if anyone raises doubts about the safety of a technology, the technology should be severely restricted, if not banned outright, until it is proven to be absolutely safe. But improved safety resulting from introducing the new technology is typically ignored or given short shrift. The precautionary principle also holds that the more serious the theoretical damages, the more society should spend on precautionary measures, or be willing to sacrifice in opportunities foregone. Moreover, say its proponents, the inability to prove how much society might gain or lose from taking those measures should not stand in the way of extreme caution.

The net result is that the precautionary principle repeatedly stifles risk-taking, innovation, economic growth, scientific and technological progress, freedom of choice, and human betterment. Had it governed scientific and technological progress in past centuries, numerous historic achievements would have been limited or prevented, according to 40 internationally renowned scientists who were surveyed by the techno-whiz-kids at *Spiked,* in advance of its May 2003 London conference, "Panic Attack: Interrogating Our Obsession with Risk."

The experts listed modern marvels from A to Z that the precautionary principle would have stopped dead in their tracks: airplanes, antibiotics, aspirin, and automobiles; biotechnology, blood transfusions, CAT scans, and the contraceptive pill; electricity, hybrid crops, and the Green Revolution; microwaves, open heart surgery, and organ transplants; pesticides, radar, and refrigeration; telephones, televisions, water purification, and x-rays—to name but a few.

Imagine what our lives would be without these technological miracles. As Adam Finn, professor of pediatrics at Bristol University's Institute of Child Health observed, "pretty much everything" would have been prevented or limited under this stifling principle, because "there is nothing we do that has no theoretical risk, and nearly everything carries some risk."

Had today's technophobic zealots been in charge in previous centuries, we would have to roll human progress back to the Middle Ages—and beyond, since even fire, the wheel, and organic farming pose risks, and none would have passed the "absolute safety" test the zealots now demand. Putting them in charge now would mean an end to progress in the developed world, and perpetual deprivation and misery for inhabitants of developing nations.

⤙◈⤚

Socially responsible investing (SRI) has become another major driving force behind today's CSR movement, courtesy of a growing coterie of activist pension funds and "ethical" investor advisory firms. They claim to represent people who "want to retire into a clean, civil, and safe world." On this basis, pension fund directors pressure CEOs and shareholders to meet "acceptable standards" of precaution, sustainable development, social responsibility, and societal expectations.

Now, prevailing notions of corporate social responsibility may bring about a cleaner, safer, more civil world for the activists and pensioners, at least in the short run. But what about for the poorest citizens of Africa, Asia, and Latin America? Or even the poorest citizens of the United States, Europe, Canada, Australia, and Japan?

As to "societal expectations"—don't African and Asian societies have a right to expect that they will be protected against malaria, malnutrition, and dysentery? That they will not be told by rich First World foundations, government agencies, and pressure groups how they may or may not respond to lethal threats, including those the developed countries have already eliminated?

To suggest that "socially responsible investors" should have free rein to ignore the conditions and needs of desperate people in the Third World is incomprehensible. But that is often the effect of CSR and SRI policies, as the following chapters demonstrate.

⋅⦿⋅

Corporate social responsibility may, as its advocates constantly assert, be based on a noble quest to improve society and safeguard humanity's and our Earth's future. This is a fundamental justification for modern ideological environmentalism. Of course, similar claims were made on behalf of other coercive, central-authority "isms" of the twentieth century.

However, debates over corporate social responsibility, stakeholder involvement, sustainable development, the precautionary principle, and socially responsible investing have in far too many instances allowed science and logic to be replaced by pressure tactics, political expediency, and a new form of tyranny. In the process, they have left many urgent questions unanswered.

- Are the asserted risks real? Do the benefits outweigh the risks? Will the radical policy proposals improve poor people's lives—or result in more poverty, misery, disease, and death for those most severely and directly affected by the decisions?
- Why have other stakeholders—such as the rural poor in developing countries—had only a limited role or voice in this process? Why are *their* interests not reflected in CSR and precautionary definitions or applications?
- Why have some companies, foundations, and nations collaborated so closely with NGO and government activists in promoting these mutant concepts?
- What is the source of the activists' supposed moral and legal authority for determining what is "ethical" or "socially responsible" or in accordance with "society's expectations"? Who elected them "stakeholders," to sit in judgment over what is or is not an "acceptable risk," or what costs, benefits, and health or economic priorities must be considered (or ignored) in making this determination?

James Shikwati, director of Kenya's Inter-Regional Economic Network, raises additional questions that weigh heavily on the minds of people in his part of the world.

- "Why do Europe's developed countries impose their environmental ethics on poor countries that are simply trying to pass through a stage they themselves went through?
- "After taking numerous risks to reach their current economic and technological status, why do they tell poor countries to use no energy, and no agricultural or pest-control technologies that might pose some conceivable risk of environmental harm?
- "Why do they tell poor countries to follow sustainable development doctrines that really mean little or no energy or economic development?"

Most of these questions might be unanswerable. But they certainly merit careful reflection. For in its most insidious role, corporate social responsibility—as currently defined and applied—ignores the legitimate aspirations and needs of people who have not yet shared the dreams and successes of even lower and middle income people in the developed world. It should come as no surprise that the poor people in developing countries increasingly view CSR, not as a mechanism to improve their lives, but as a virulent kind of neo-colonialism that many call eco-imperialism.

As corporate executives are frequently reminded, nobody cares how much you know, until they know how much you care. It might be appropriate to suggest that ideological environmentalism should devote as much attention to Third World babies, as it does to adorable harp seal pups.

Television, email, websites, satellite transmissions, and even old-fashioned newspapers have enabled well-financed activists to concoct, exaggerate, and spread public anxiety over a seemingly endless parade of theoretical risks. Even for Americans—who live in the safest nation on earth and are unfazed by traffic and numerous other dangers that pose far greater risks than those trumpeted by precautionary propagandists—the constant drumbeat of doom is hard to ignore.

To suggest that the mutant version of corporate social responsibility doctrines represent progress, "environmental justice," or ethical behavior stretches the meaning of those terms beyond the breaking point. In the end, what is truly not sustainable are the human and ecological tolls exacted by the callous policies of radical environmentalism.

Perhaps nowhere is that more apparent than in the arenas of energy, malaria control, malnutrition, and trade.

Paul Driessen is senior policy adviser for the Committee for a Constructive Tomorrow (CFACT), which is sponsoring the All Pain No Gain petition against global-warming hype. Driessen is also a senior policy adviser to the Congress of Racial Equality and author of *Eco-Imperialism: Green Power, Black Death*.

EXPLORING THE ISSUE

Should Corporations Adopt Environmentally Friendly Policies of Corporate Social Responsibility (CSR) and Sustainable Development?

Critical Thinking and Reflection

1. Would guidelines on corporate social responsible and sustainable development policies mitigate potential shareholder legal challenges?
2. Would different corporate social responsible and sustainable development programs change shareholders' view of a company?
3. Can a company's corporate social responsibility and sustainable development's effectiveness be effectively measured?
4. Should a company's corporate social responsibility and sustainable development be measured?
5. What role does a corporation's board of directors play in determining a corporation's level/commitment to social responsible practices?

Is There Common Ground?

Both sides of this debate have powerful arguments to draw on. Should the only purpose of an organization be to maximize profit, or do other stakeholders have a legitimate claim on the fruits of the organizations' success? It's a difficult situation for managers: Don't act in a socially responsible manner and run the risk of community alienation or act in a socially responsible manner and potentially create an atmosphere of stress, distrust, and alienation from shareholders. While there has been no attempt to balance shareholder and environmental demands, there is consensus that corporate social responsibility and sustainable development is a complex issue that will continue to be discussed for many years.

Additional Resources

Bidinotto, R. J. (2004). "Death by Environmentalism," *The Navigator*, The Objectivist Center, March, p. 4.

Carroll, A. B. and Buchholtz, A. K. (2009). *Business and Society: Ethics and Stakeholder Management*, South-Western Cengage.

Horner, C. (2007). *The Politically Incorrect Guide to Global Warming and Environmentalism*, Regnery Publishing.

Milloy, S. (2009). *Green Hell: How Environmentalists Plan to Control Your Life and What You Can Do to Stop Them*, Regnery Publishing.

Spencer, R. (2008). *Climate Confusion: How Global Warming Hysteria Leads to Bad Science, Pandering Politicians and Misguided Policies That Hurt the Poor*, Encounter Books.

Internet References . . .

Why Our Economy Is Killing the Planet and What We Can Do About It

New Scientist. (2008). "Why Our Economy Is Killing the Planet and What We Can Do About It," *New Scientist Special* Report, October 16.

http://business.highbeam.com/137753/article -1G1-188584009/why-our-economy-killing -planet-and-we-can-do

Danger in the Nursery: Impact of Tar Sands Oil Development in Canada's Boreal on Birds

Wells, J., Casey-Lefkowitz, S., and Chavarria, G. (2008). "Danger in the Nursery: Impact of Tar Sands Oil Development in Canada's Boreal on Birds," Natural Resources Defense Council, November.

www.nrdc.org/wildlife/borealbirds.asp

Selected, Edited, and with Issue Framing Material by:
Kathleen J. Barnes, *William Paterson University*
and
George E. Smith, *University of South Carolina, Beaufort*

ISSUE

Is Corporate Sustainability Reporting a Valuable Corporate Reporting Tool?

YES: Brian Ballou, Dan L. Heitger, and Charles E. Landes, from "The Future of Corporate Sustainability Reporting: A Rapidly Growing Assurance Opportunity," *Journal of Accountancy* (2006)

NO: Jeff Leinaweaver, from "Is Corporate Sustainability Reporting a Great Waste of Time?" *The Guardian* (2015)

Learning Outcomes

After reading this issue, you will be able to:

- Understand what corporate sustainability reporting is.
- Explain why corporations choose to report on their sustainability.
- Describe the reported limitations and strengths of contemporary sustainability reporting.
- Understand and explain the monitoring and audit process of corporate sustainability reporting

---

ISSUE SUMMARY

YES: Brian Ballou, Dan L. Heitger, and Charles E. Landes note that corporations have come to the realization that there is value to reporting on sustainability issues and note that this trend is increasing the number of reports published annually. The article also discusses some steps for improving the existing processes that are focused on the G3 Reporting Initiative and auditing.

NO: Jeff Leinaweaver, Global Zen Sustainability principal, warns that companies are wasting time and money creating sustainability reports that aren't effective.

According to the Global Reporting Initiative (GRI), a sustainability report is a report published by a company or organization about the economic, environmental, and social impacts caused by its everyday activities. A sustainability report also presents the organization's values and governance model, and demonstrates the link between its strategy and its commitment to a sustainable global economy.

Sustainability reporting can help organizations to measure, understand, and communicate their economic, environmental, social and governance performance, and then set goals, and manage change more effectively. A sustainability report is the key platform for communicating sustainability performance and impacts—whether positive or negative.

Sustainability reporting can be considered as synonymous with other terms for non-financial reporting; triple bottom line

reporting, corporate social responsibility (CSR) reporting, and more. It is also an intrinsic element of integrated reporting; a more recent development that combines the analysis of financial and non-financial performance.

Building and maintaining trust in businesses and governments is fundamental to achieving a sustainable economy and world. Every day, decisions are made by businesses and governments which have direct impacts on their stakeholders, such as financial institutions, labor organizations, civil society and citizens, and the level of trust they have with them. These decisions are rarely based on financial information alone. They are based on an assessment of risk and opportunity using information on a wide variety of immediate and future issues.

The value of the sustainability reporting process is that it ensures organizations consider their impacts on these sustainability issues, and enables them to be transparent about the risks and opportunities they face. Stakeholders also play a crucial role in identifying these risks and opportunities for organizations, particularly those that are non-financial. This increased transparency leads to better decision making, which helps build and maintain trust in businesses and governments.

Sustainability reports are released by companies and organizations of all types, sizes, and sectors, from every corner of the world.

Major providers of sustainability reporting guidance include:

- GRI (GRI's Sustainability Reporting Standards)
- The Organisation for Economic Co-operation and Development (OECD Guidelines for Multinational Enterprises)
- The United Nations Global Compact (the Communication on Progress)
- The International Organization for Standardization (ISO 26000, International Standard for social responsibility)

YES ↵

Brian Ballou, Dan L. Heitger, and Charles E. Landes

The Future of Corporate Sustainability Reporting: A Rapidly Growing Assurance Opportunity

Faced with increased pressure from internal and external stakeholders, more organizations are measuring and reporting on their social and environmental performance as well as the usual financial reporting measures. Stakeholders have been pressing companies to publicly report this information either in annual financial reports to shareholders or in voluntary corporate performance reports. The worldwide growth of socially responsible investment funds, investment rating systems such as the Dow Jones Sustainability Index and investment policy disclosure requirements also have put financial pressures on companies to make these kinds of nonfinancial disclosures.

As this trend grows, so, too, will the role of accountants and auditors. CPAs within organizations will play a key role by providing and measuring the social and environmental information, using their skills to improve its quality and facilitate its use to make sound business decisions in areas such as investment appraisal, budgeting and strategic planning. Auditors also will have a significant role in verifying the accuracy of the reported information as well as the systems and practices from which it is derived. This article provides all CPAs with an overview of corporate sustainability reporting and the role it may play in businesses worldwide.

Beyond the Bottom Line

Organizations have come to realize that meeting stakeholder expectations is as necessary a condition for sustainability as the need to achieve overall strategic business objectives. While maximizing shareholder value continues to be an overriding concern, companies will not be able to do that over the long term if they don't meet other key stakeholder interests. According to a PricewaterhouseCoopers report, *The Value Reporting Revolution: Moving Beyond the Earnings Game,* "to create long-term economic value for society—shareholders and other stakeholders alike—sustainability says that companies must also create social and environmental value." To create transparent reports that provide accurate and reliable data, as well as a fair picture of overall performance, many companies are now reporting results across the "triple bottom line" of economic, environmental and social performance.

Triple-bottom-line reporting, also known as corporate sustainability reporting (CSR), involves reporting nonfinancial and financial information to a broader set of stakeholders than just shareholders (see exhibit 1). The reports inform stakeholder groups of the reporting organization's ability to manage key risks. Because these interests vary, the type of information varies; however, much of it has to do with the company's economic, operational, social, philanthropic and environmental objectives.

A number of companies—DuPont, Mobil, Allstate, Gap Inc. and British Petroleum-Amoco among them—recognize the potential comparative advantages of publicly disclosing their goals related to nonfinancial and financial performance measures and then reporting on how well they achieve them. To better understand the pressure to be transparent about a broad number of issues, consider that Wal-Mart's annual revenues exceed the gross domestic product (GDP) of Austria; Exxon-Mobil's revenue is greater than the GDP of Argentina or Turkey; and General Motors' revenue is more than the combined GDP of Columbia and the Philippines. All of them are among the world's 50 largest countries.

Criteria for Preparing Sustainability Reports

Reports on corporate sustainability generally are prepared based on reporting criteria established by an outside organization or the company's internal guidelines. The most dominant reporting regulations are those of the Global Reporting Initiative (GRI). Launched in 1997 with the goal of "enhancing the quality, rigor, and utility of sustainability reporting," the GRI began to develop criteria that could eventually serve as the basis for generally accepted reporting standards. The GRI has received active support and input from numerous groups—including businesses, not-for-profit organizations, accounting regulatory bodies (including the AICPA), investor organizations and trade unions—to build reporting guidelines that are accepted worldwide. In October 2006 it released its second comprehensive set of reporting guidelines—called the G3 Reporting Framework.

The rapid increase in the number of companies around the world adopting GRI standards and issuing corporate sustainability reports, along with the fact that the GRI works closely with the

Exhibit 1

Typical Stakeholders for U.S. Publicly Owned Organizations

Financial stakeholders

- Shareholders (institutions, hedge funds, employees and individuals)
- Bond holders
- Banking institutions
- Employees (including unions)
- Other sources of capital (venture capitalists)

Supply chain stakeholders

- Customers
- Alliance partners
- Direct suppliers
- Upstream suppliers
- Contractors

Regulatory stakeholders

- Securities and Exchange Commission
- Internal Revenue Service
- Occupational Health and Safety Administration
- Food and Drug Administration
- Environmental Protection Agency
- Accounting standard setters (FASB, IASB, PCAOB)
- Federal Communications Commission

Political stakeholders

- Federal government (lawmaking and court decisions, for example)
- State governments
- International governments
- United Nations
- European Union
- OPEC
- NATO

Social stakeholders

- Local communities
- General public
- Academia
- Charitable organizations funded by companies
- Environmental and social organizations

United Nations, gives its reporting criteria the credibility necessary to be considered generally accepted. Overall, the number of organizations reporting under GRI guidelines has grown exponentially since 2000. As of October 2006, nearly 1,000 international companies from more than 60 countries had registered with the GRI and were issuing corporate sustainability reports using some or all of its standards. (See exhibit 2 for a list of the 100 U.S. companies.)

Companies can use GRI guidelines in several ways with varying degrees of stringency. For example, they may elect to use them for informal reference or to apply them incrementally. Or they may decide to report their corporate sustainability information based on the more demanding *in accordance* level. The move from *informal* to *in accordance* under GRI standards occurs through enhancements of transparent reporting, reporting coverage across the company and

EXECUTIVE SUMMARY

- **To satisfy the information needs** of external and internal stakeholders, more organizations are measuring and reporting on their social and environmental performance. CPAs can play an important role in providing the needed information and helping to verify its accuracy.
- **Corporate sustainability reporting (CSR)** involves reporting financial and nonfinancial information to key stakeholders on the company's operational, social and environmental activities and its ability to deal with related risks.
- **The most dominant CSR regulations** are those of the Global Reporting Initiative (GRI), which issued its first comprehensive reporting guidelines in 2002 and its G3 Reporting Framework in October 2006. As of October 2006, more than 1,000 international companies had registered with the GRI and issued corporate sustainability reports using its standards.
- **An opportunity exists for CPAs** to audit the information companies present in corporate sustainability reports. As of yet interested parties have not fully agreed on what information can and should be audited. Concern exists about the suitability of the criteria used to prepare the reports and what performance and reporting standards the auditor should use.
- **A joint task force of the AICPA** and the Canadian Institute of Chartered Accountants (CICA) concluded the 2002 GRI standards had not yet reached a point where they were suitable criteria to be considered generally acceptable and allow a set of generally accepted assurance standards for CSR reports to be developed. Two exposure drafts offered by accountants in the Netherlands on assurance engagements related to sustainability reporting are currently under review by international accounting organizations including the AICPA.

---

reporting structure (see www.globalreporting.org/services/report/inaccordancechecks for more information). As of July 2006, just over 20% of the organizations issuing CSR reports using GRI guidelines did so at the *in accordance* level. This percentage has been increasing since 2002, suggesting organizations issuing CSR reports recognize an increasing market value for *in accordance* reports. The new G3 Reporting Framework is designed to improve the process whereby organizations become *in accordance*.

Opportunities to Provide Assurance for CSR

As with any information an organization reports, the lack of an accompanying independent assurance report reduces the quality and informational usefulness of a CSR. (See "Fraud Risk in CSR.") Consider the reaction should public companies begin to issue unaudited financial statements. Aspects of CSRs are auditable because they are quantitative and verifiable. However, the current lack of reliable metrics for all stakeholder measures results in many qualitative statements about risk management and performance and quantitative measures that are not reliable enough to audit. Thus, the reports that are audited generally are limited in scope (a report might be accompanied by a legend stating which measures are audited).

The GRI's new reporting framework addresses the issue of assurance for CSRs. Exhibit 3 provides details on the framework's choices on assurance. In 2005 KPMG reported that accounting firms prepared more than 50% of the assurance reports for CSRs.

Exhibit 4 shows the CSR audit opinion for Royal Dutch/Shell's 2003 fiscal year. It was jointly audited by PricewaterhouseCoopers

LLP (London) and KPMG LLP (The Hague). The opinion points out that only certain measures in the report were audited and describes the type of procedures performed. The last statement in the scope paragraph provides negative assurance for the remainder of the corporate sustainability report (the accounting firms read that part of the report and noted no material inconsistencies).

The majority of information on which assurance currently is being provided is nonfinancial, quantitative performance measures. For example, PricewaterhouseCoopers and KPMG provided assurance on these performance measures in the Shell report:

- Global warming potential.
- Energy efficiency.
- Total spills.
- Flaring in exploration and production activities.
- Fatal accident rate.
- Injury frequency.
- Carbon dioxide release.
- Methane release.
- Regulatory, health, safety and environmental fines.

While there are many other performance measures in the report, their auditability was not at the level the firms could audit with a high enough level of assurance to provide an opinion.

Other assurance approaches that accounting firms use include a review level engagement or limited assurance based on the policies in place and the results of evidence-gathering procedures, as well as verification reports that refer to existing international assurance and attestation standards. For example, exhibit 5 contains the independent auditors' report for Starbucks' 2005 CSR. Moss

Exhibit 2

U.S. COMPANIES REGISTERED WITH THE GRI FOR CORPORATE SUSTAINABILITY REPORTING

3M	Ecolab	Nike
Abbott Labs	EDS	Office Depot
AMD	Exxon Mobil	Pepsico
AES Corporation	Ford	Pinnacle West Capital
Agilent	Freescale Semiconductor	Plan A
Alcoa	GAP	Polaroid
Allegan	Genecor	Procter & Gamble
Alliant Energy	GE	R J Reynolds
Amerada Hess	GM	Reebok
American Standard Companies	Georgia-Pacific	Rio Tinto Borax
Anheuser-Busch	Gillette (now P&G)	SC Johnson & Son
Applied Materials	Green Mountain Energy	Seventh Generation
Avon Products	Haworth	Smithfield Foods
Bank of America	Heinz	Staples
Baxter	Hewlett-Packard	Starbucks
Ben & Jerry's	Intel	State Street
Bristol-Myers Squibb	IBM	Sunoco
Brown & Williamson	International Finance	Target
Calvert Group	International Paper	Temple-Inland
Cascade Eng.	Johnson & Johnson	Texas Instruments
Catholic Healthcare West	Kimberly Clark	Timberland
CH2M Hill	Louisiana Pacific	Time Warner
Chevron	Lucent	Tyco
Chiquita Brands	Masco	Tyson Foods
Cinergy (now Duke)	Mattel	UPS
Cisco Systems	McDonald's	United Technologies
Citigroup	MeadWestvaco	Visteon
Coca-Cola Enterprises	Merck	Wells Fargo
Cummins	Microsoft	Weyerhaeuser
Dell	Mirant	Wisconsin Energy
Dow Chemical	Motorola	World Bank Group
Dow Coming	National Grid	Wyeth
Du Pont	Newmont Mining	YSI Incorporated

Source: As of October 2006, www.globalreporting.org.

Adams LLP issued it as being prepared using international standards approved by the IAASB and issued in 2005 as a guideline. The firm's conclusion says Starbuck's CSR was prepared consistent with its internal policies and report information was reasonably supported by documentation, internal processes and activities, and information provided by external parties. This type of report, while only referring to established criteria (standards approved by the IAASB) still improves the quality of information for external users.

Shell's 2005 CSR report was ranked no. 1 by Pleon's 2005 Global Stakeholder Report (www.pleon.com), which asked stakeholders worldwide to give examples of companies that do a good job of CSR reporting. Interestingly, Shell changed its approach for its 2005 report from using independent accounting firms to an independent panel of experts who reviewed the CSR and offered praise and criticism (see exhibit 6 for excerpts from the panel's report). While this change does not mean the independent accounting firms were ineffective, it suggests organizations should consider a range of methods for providing assurance about the information in the CSR. If accountants fail to act on the opportunity to provide assurance, companies will begin to adopt other, less rigorous, means.

Exhibit 3

ASSURANCE GUIDANCE IN THE GRI G3 REPORTING FRAMEWORK

Assurance

Choices on assurance

Organizations use a variety of approaches to enhance the credibility of their reports. Organizations may have systems of internal controls in place, including internal audit functions, as part of their processes for managing and reporting information. These internal systems are important to the overall integrity and credibility of a report. However, the GRI recommends the use of external assurance for sustainability reports in addition to any internal resources.

A variety of approaches are currently used by report preparers to implement external assurance, including the use of professional assurance providers, stakeholder panels, and other external groups or individuals. However, regardless of the specific approach, it should be conducted by competent groups or individuals external to the organization. These engagements may employ groups or individuals that follow professional standards for assurance, or they may involve approaches that follow systematic, documented, and evidence-based processes but are not governed by a specific standard.

The GRI uses the term *external assurance* to refer to activities designed to result in published conclusions on the quality of the report and the information contained within it. This includes, but is not limited to, consideration of underlying processes for preparing this information. This is different from activities designed to assess or validate the quality or level of performance of an organization, such as issuing performance certifications or compliance assessments. Overall, the key qualities for external assurance of reports using the GRI Reporting Framework are that it:

- Is conducted by groups or individuals external to the organization who are demonstrably competent in both the subject matter and assurance practices;
- Is implemented in a manner that is systematic, documented, evidence-based, and characterized by defined procedures;

- Assesses whether the report provides a reasonable and balanced presentation of performance, taking into consideration the veracity of data in a report as well as the overall selection of content;
- Utilizes groups or individuals to conduct the assurance who are not unduly limited by their relationship with the organization or its stakeholders to reach and publish an independent and impartial conclusion on the report;
- Assesses the extent to which the report preparer has applied the GRI Reporting Framework (including the Reporting Principles) in `the course of reaching its conclusions; and
- Results in an opinion or set of conclusions that is publicly available in written form, and a statement from the assurance provider on their relationship to the report preparer.

As indicated in Profile Disclosure 3.13, organizations should disclose information on their approach to external assurance.

Source: www.globalreporting.org.

Fraud Risk in CSR

Thomas Golden is one of the leading forensic accounting partners at PricewaterhouseCoopers. He believes individuals who perpetrate financial reporting fraud generally fit one of two profiles. The first is otherwise honest individuals who misrepresent the numbers by rationalizing that what they are doing is best for the company. The second group is individuals who are well aware of what they are doing and who are attempting to attain goals dishonestly. Golden says such individuals exhibit a "rampant disregard for the truth." With either pattern, the pressure to misrepresent information is not entirely alleviated by the Sarbanes-Oxley Act or any other act by a government agency or regulator.

In fact, Golden believes that in the case of financial statement reporting, the rules put in place by Sarbanes-Oxley are analogous to squeezing a balloon. Although they make misrepresenting a company's financial reports more difficult (it's harder to "cook the books"), the pressure on the organizational balloon to perform well remains intense and causes misrepresentations to pop out in other areas.

One rather obvious area where this misinformation can pop out is through largely unaudited reports containing mainly nonfinancial information about an organization, such as the success of a company's new drug in Southeast Asia or the number of subscribers in its system. While the auditor reads communications such as press releases, letters to shareholders and the management discussion & analysis section of annual reports for consistency with the financial statements, nonfinancial information in these communications, as well as corporate sustainability reports, provide tempting opportunities for misrepresentations because they are unaudited.

Another intriguing example Golden offers is that of certain prisoners who, even in solitary confinement, have successfully continued to run their gang's activities on the outside. Unfortunately, these prisoners don't stop communicating illegal and dangerous

(Continued)

information to individuals willing to listen. Instead, they adapt to their situation in solitary, which might be difficult at first but becomes easier with practice.

In much the same way, a fraudster might no longer be able to manage earnings or misapply GAAP as easily as before Sarbanes-Oxley, but he or she can find other ways to accomplish the same objectives. And these methods will get easier over time with practice. The use of unaudited communications that contain nonfinancial and other operations data in a misrepresentative manner might be challenging at first, but that will become easier with practice, too.

Golden says that as long as there is an abundance of investors with too much money chasing too few investment opportunities offering high returns, the temptation to misrepresent a company's performance or future prospects based on nonfinancial and other information will be too great to ignore. He says this is a huge hole in the corporate reporting process and if the accounting profession fails to take a leadership role in plugging it, a new market entrant could emerge to capitalize on providing assurance services for corporate sustainability reports.

"Individuals and firms in our profession need to realize they are in the 'assurance,' not simply the 'auditing' business," Golden says, "and investors need assurance on nonfinancial as well as financial data."

Exhibit 4

INDEPENDENT AUDITORS' REPORT FOR ROYAL DUTCH/SHELL 2003 CORPORATE SUSTAINABILITY REPORT

Assurance report

To: Royal Dutch Petroleum Company and the "Shell" Transport and Trading Company, p.l.c.

Introduction

We have been asked to provide assurance on selected data, graphs and statements of the Royal Dutch/Shell Group of Companies (the "Group") contained in The Shell Report 2003. The Shell Report is the responsibility of management. Our responsibility is to express an opinion on the selected data, graphs and statements indicated below based on our assurance work performed.

Assurance work performed

For the safety and environmental parameters identified with the symbol ● on pages 22 to 26, we obtained an understanding of the systems used to generate, aggregate and report the data for these parameters at Group, Business, Zone and Operating Unit level. We assessed the completeness and accuracy of the data reported in respect of 2003 by visiting Operating Units to test systems and review data. We assessed date trends in discussion with management. We tested the calculations mode at Group level. We also completed assurance procedures on the Refinery Energy Index and reported our findings to management.

For the Sakhalin Location Report on pages 16 and 17 we visited the location to inspect documentary evidence and held interviews with Business and in-country management and with three mojar Russian contracting companies to understand and test the systems, procedures, and evidence in place supporting the assertions and matters discussed within this Location Report. We also performed assurance procedures in relation to China West-East pipeline project and reported our findings to management.

We read the whole Report to confirm that there are no material inconsistencies based on the work we have performed.

Basis of opinion

There are no generally accepted international environmental, social and economic reporting standards. This engagement was conducted in accordance with the International Standards for Assurance Engagements. Therefore, we planned and carried out our work to provide reasonable, rather than absolute, assurance on the reliability of the selected data, graphs and statements that were subject to assurance. We believe our work provides a reasonable basis for our opinion.

Considerations and limitations

It is important to read the data and statements in the context of the basis of reporting provided by the management as set out below and the notes below the graphs. Environmental and social data and assertions are subject to more inherent limitations than financial data, given both their nature and the methods used for determining, calculating of estimating such data.

Our assurance scope is limited to those specific matters mentioned in our opinion below. We have not provided assurance over the contents of the entire Shell Report 2003, nor have we undertaken work to confirm that all relevant issues are included. In addition, we have not carried out any work on financial and economic performance data and data reported in respect of future projections and targets. Accordingly, no opinion is given in respect of them. Where we have not provided assurance over previous years' data this is clearly disclosed. We have not performed work on the maintenance and integrity of information from The Shell Report published on the Group's website.

(Continued)

To obtain a thorough understanding of the financial results and financial position of the Group, the reader should consult the Group's audited Financial Statements for the year ended 31 December 2003.

In our opinion:

—The safety and environmental historical data and graphs (together with the notes) on pages 22 to 26, marked with the symbol●,

properly reflect the performance of the reporting entities for each of these parameters;

—The assertions and matters discussed in the Sakhalin Location Report, on pages 16 and 17, are fairly described and supported by underling documentary or other evidence.

22 May 2004

Source: The Shell Report 2003, Royal Dutch/Shell Group of Companies, www.shell.com.

Exhibit 5

AUDITORS' REPORT OF STARBUCKS CORPORATION SUSTAINABILITY REPORT

To the Stakeholders of Starbucks Coffee Company:

We have been engaged to provide assurance on the Corporate Social Responsibility ("CSR") Fiscal 2005 Annual Report (the "Report") of Starbucks Coffee Company ("Starbucks"), for the fiscal year ended October 2, 2005. We have performed evidence-gathering procedures on the following subject matter:

- Key Performance Indicators Summary and Fiscal 2005 Highlights;
- Information and data provided in each area of focus of the Report (World of Products, Society, Environment, and Workplace); and
- The management and reporting for the preparation of this information and data.

We have considered the subject matter against the following evaluation criteria:

- The procedures by which the CSR information and data were prepared, collated and compiled internally; and
- The control environment over the quality of the information and data.

Our statement should be considered in conjunction with the inherent limitations of accuracy and completeness for CSR data, as well as in connection with Starbucks internal reporting guidelines.

The Board of Directors of Starbucks is responsible for both the subject matter and the evaluation criteria.

Our responsibility is to report on the internal reporting processes, information and data for CSR based on our evidence-gathering procedures. Currently there are no statutory requirements or generally accepted verification standards in the United States of America that relate to the preparation, presentation, and verification of CSR reports. There are international standards for the CSR reports that were approved by the International Auditing and Assurances Standards Board (IAASB) in January 2005. Using the IAASB approved standards as a guideline, we planned and performed evidence-gathering procedures to provide a basis for our conclusion. However, we have not performed an audit in accordance with the International Standards on Auditing. Accordingly, we do not express such an opinion.

Our evidence-gathering procedures included, among other activities, the following:

- Testing the effectiveness of the internal reporting system used to collect and compile information on each area of focus in the Report;
- Performing specific procedures, on a sample basis, to validate the CSR data;
- Visiting Starbucks coffee buying operations in Switzerland;
- Visiting Starbucks corporate headquarters in Seattle, Washington;
- Interviewing partners responsible for data collection and reporting;
- Interviewing partners at retail locations;
- Assessing the information gathering and compiling process of each area of focus in the Report;
- Reviewing relevant documentation, including corporate policies, management and reporting structures; and
- Performing tests, on a sample basis, of documentation and systems used to collect, analyze and compile reported CSR information and data.

(Continued)

In our opinion, based on our work described in this report, the CSR information contained in the Report gives a fair representation of CSR performance and activities of Starbucks Coffee Company for the fiscal year ended October 2, 2005. Statements, assertions and data disclosed in the Report are reasonably supported by documentation, internal processes and activities, and information provided by external parties.

Moss Adams LLP
Seattle, Washington
January 27, 2006

Source: Starbucks 2005 Corporate Social Responsibility Report, www.starbucks.com.

Exhibit 6

EXPERT PANEL REPORT FOR SHELL GROUP 2005 CORPORATE SUSTAINABILITY REPORT

Panel of Experts:

Margaret Jungk, Business Department Director, Danish Institute For Human Rights

Dr. Li Lailai, National Programme Director, Leadership For Environment And Development (Lead)—China: Director, Institute For Environment And Development, Beijing

Jermyn Brooks (Review Committee Chair), Board Member, Transparency International

Roger Hammond, Development Director, Living Earth

Jonathan Lash, President, World Resources Institute.

Shell invited us to assess on two counts. Firstly, does it contain the right information about the full range of issues that Shell stakeholders care most about? Secondly, how well does it reflect understanding of stakeholders' expectations? We were guided in our appraisal by the AA1000 Assurance Standard, an independent standard for evaluating sustainability reports against three basic principles: materiality, completeness and responsiveness to stakeholders. We met twice during the final stages of Shell's report drafting process. We interviewed senior Shell staff, including the Chief Executive, and individuals involved with the biggest projects and issues in the Report. In recognition of our time and expertise, an honorarium was offered, payable to us individually or to the organisation of our choice. This is our assessment of the *2005 Shell Sustainability Report,* unedited by Shell. We speak here as individuals, not for our organisations.

Shell's Sustainability Reporting

Since 1998, Shell's reporting has been judged by many external experts as among the best in its sector and overall. Shell has made a serious effort to compile a full and informative report that responds to the needs of the company's international stakeholders, while keeping it concise and readable. The Report's combination of descriptions of the energy challenge and Shell's business strategy, along with environmental and social performance data, documents Shell's concern with sustainability issues and performance. The Report is frank and honest. The company discusses successes as well as challenges and mistakes made (for example, in the accounts of the Corrib and Sakhalin projects).

[*Detailed Comments on Specific Sections Excluded—see Shell.com for complete report*]

We suggest the following ways Shell might improve future Sustainability Reports:

- In selecting subjects for inclusion in the Report, Shell prioritises issues which have the greatest impact on Shell and are highlighted by pressure groups. These measures may fail to take sufficiently into account impacts on wider society, that are not currently the subject of pressure group or media campaigns, but where the company has a substantial and sustained impact. We recommend that these be considered as key selection criteria in future Reports.
- Shell is increasing the number of upstream projects. It is important for the company to comment on how the Shell Project Academy and biodiversity knowledge management system will contribute to the capture and transfer of project experience and skills. Emphasis should be on stakeholder dialogue and conflict-management skills.

(Continued)

- Key performance indicators are presented in the data section of the Report. We believe they could be improved by inclusion of additional metrics, for example relating to pay discrepancies between nationals and non-nationals, the average number of hours worked annually, and the use of hotlines to report breaches of Shell's General Business Principles.
- The annual spend on researching and developing renewables would be more helpful than cumulative figures for the last five years.

Conclusion

We want to thank Shell for its commitment to reporting and its willingness to seek external review of the results. We are impressed by the Report's quality and the care with which it has been compiled. Our critical comments in no way diminish this. We are unanimous in encouraging Shell to make progress on this path.

The Hague, April 3, 2006

Source: The Shell Report 2005, The Shell Group, www.shell.com.

Challenges of Providing Auditor Assurance

There are two major challenges in providing a sustainability report with auditor assurance: the suitability of the criteria management uses to prepare its sustainability report and the performance and reporting standards the auditor uses. International and national standard setters should not let these challenges deter them from seeking a solution—there is need for these reports, as well as to protect the public through auditor verification.

While the GRI appears to have the most commonly adopted criteria for sustainability reporting and is the organization likely to evolve as providing generally accepted CSR guidelines, it has yet to be recognized in this role by a regulatory body. One reason GRI standards are not generally accepted is the nature of the measures included in its earlier 2002 reporting guidelines, which faced issues associated with relevance, reliability, auditability and the like. The GRI says one of its goals in issuing the new G3 guidelines was to improve the relevance and auditability of measures.

In 2002 the AICPA and the Canadian Institute of Chartered Accountants (CICA) formed a joint task force on sustainability reporting. While the task force concluded in 2003 that the GRI had not yet developed to a point where its criteria were suitable, it also recognized the importance of working with the GRI and international standard setters to develop performance and reporting criteria. The task force took an important step in the United States by developing the first attestation engagement on environmental reporting. With the approval of the AICPA Auditing Standards Board, the task force issued Statement of Position 03-2, *Attest Engagements on Greenhouse Gas Emissions Information.* The AICPA also is participating in the Enhanced Business Reporting Consortium (www. ebr360.com), which is examining how to improve information for public company stakeholders.

In January 2005 the professional body of accountants in the Netherlands published two exposure drafts—ED 3410, *Assurance Engagements Relating To Sustainability Report,* and ED 3010, *Practitioners Working With Subject Matter Experts From Other*

Disciplines On Non-Financial Assurance Engagements (presumably referenced in the Starbucks CSR assurance report). These documents were built on International Assurance Standards, which are similar to the attestation standards the ASB issues. In response the International Audit and Assurance Standards Board (IAASB) formed a sustainability advisory expert panel (which includes members from the AICPA/CICA task force) to review the EDs and provide comments and suggestions to the Netherlands. The EDs and the IAASB comment letter can found at www.ifac.org.

The letter focused on several key aspects of the EDs that needed refinement before they would be acceptable to the IAASB and ASB. Those include

- Judgments around the suitability of criteria decision.
- The use of experts in performing these types of engagements.
- The work effort necessary to distinguish between reasonable or high assurance vs. limited or moderate assurance.
- Materiality factors to consider in planning the scope of the engagement and when deciding on the type of report to issue.
- The completeness of the sustainability report.

Adding further to the auditor's challenge is the realization that the information in such reports usually is generated by a diverse set of measurement techniques. Information may be gathered from various sources, some of which are outside the reporting organization because of the specialized expertise required to accurately measure certain items. These circumstances may require the auditor to become familiar with the measurement procedures, management practices, systems and integrity of the other organization(s), in addition to those of the reporting organization. As Shell notes in its 2003 CSR, "environmental and social data and assertions are subject to more inherent limitations than financial data, given both their nature and the methods used for determining, calculating or estimating such data."

An alternate set of assurance standards has been developed by AccountAbility, which has no relationship with the

AICPA, IFAC or other well-established assurance organizations. In 2002 AccountAbility issued its AA1000Assurance Standards, which represented the first assurance standard covering sustainability reporting and performance based on principles of materiality, completeness and responsiveness (www.accountability.org.uk). Some 120 organizations used the AA1000 standard in 2004.

Growth Opportunity

Corporate sustainability reporting is a rapidly growing way to address stakeholder demands for risk management and more performance measurement information. There are tremendous opportunities for CPAs in industry to be involved with the preparation and disclosure of these reports. The GRI G3 Reporting Framework might emerge as the one most likely to be generally accepted. With organizations issuing corporate sustainability reports at a rapid rate using GRI guidelines, stakeholders for all public companies will come to expect these reports at some point in the future.

There also are tremendous opportunities for CPAs in public practice to provide independent assurance on these reports. However, they face several challenges, including the development of performance and reporting standards. The ASB is supportive of and is working with the IAASB to develop international standards that can be tailored for U.S. auditors. Addressing these challenges will satisfy the growing needs of investors who are demanding the information and who would benefit from auditor assurance. In the 2005 Pleon report, researchers Thomas Lowe and Jens Clausen said CSR report credibility is best achieved by external accountants providing formal external report verification. However, as Shell's change to an expert panel illustrates, accountants might only have a finite amount of time to step forward and provide the expected assurance.

Brian Ballou is an associate professor of accounting at Miami University (OH, USA) and co-director of the Center for Governance, Risk Management and Reporting at the Richard T. Farmer School of Business.

Dan L. Heitger is an assistant professor of accounting at Miami University (OH, USA) and co-director of the Center for Governance, Risk Management and Reporting at the Richard T. Farmer School of Business.

Charles E. Landes is vice-president AICPA professional standards and services.

Jeff Leinaweaver

 **NO**

Is Corporate Sustainability Reporting a Great Waste of Time?

What could be less sustainable than reams of reporting that no one reads? That's the concern voiced in a recent report by strategic thinktank and consultancy SustainAbility, which warns that companies are wasting time and money creating sustainability reports that aren't effective.

"We've seen things plateau, and while the reports are doing many good things, they could be doing so much more, adding much more value," says report author and SustainAbility manager Margo Mosher.

After analysing over 50 interviews with its own professional stakeholder network, and a survey of nearly 500 sustainability experts and thought leaders, SustainAbility concludes that sustainability reporting has stalled.

Others throughout the sustainability reporting industry have come to similar conclusions. "Of the companies that are already reporting, I do believe sustainability reporting is stalled, but there's a ton of room for growth. The reason it's plateaued is basically a marketing problem. People write these giant reports, plagued by special language and catch-all-categories, and don't think about the audience," says Kevin Wilhelm, CEO of Sustainability Business Consulting.

Changes in new media may also be detracting from reporting's impact. "The stakeholders who were initially the audience for sustainability reporting are finding other sources of information, including social media," says Suzanne Stormer, vice-president of Corporate Sustainability at Novo Nordisk.

Many companies are producing reports that fail to connect with a broadening audience. "Many of the intended stakeholders have quite specific interests," Stormer says. "For example, issue-interested NGOs. Their information needs may be more specific than what is conveyed in a sustainability report that, by default, will have to paint a picture in broad strokes." Carrie Christopher of Albuquerque-based consulting company Concept Green agrees, saying many reporting companies "have lost their way ," producing reports "written for everybody and nobody at the same time."

So while the drive for corporate credibility and transparency has accelerated the sustainability reporting movement, SustainAbility argues that it's time to take a step back and revisit the reporting agenda. The report says it's not about how to "increase reporting," or how to "make sure more people read sustainability reports," but to focus on using the reports to drive better decision-making and thereby improve business performance towards sustainability.

To reinvigorate corporate sustainability reporting, and add more value to the process, companies need to "zero in on what's important to the key stakeholders," Mosher says. That can be done by integrating the most important materiality issues into the corporate transparency strategy, valuing the business' externalities and looking at the unintended consequences of not taking issues such as resource scarcity more seriously.

"Resource scarcity is a huge driver, not only for valuing externalities and managing risk, but because many companies may not realize they even have a resource dependency," Mosher says. "It's the underlying driver of why we are all worried, and why sustainability is so important."

Christopher and Wilhelm both argue it's less about the issue of transparency performance and more about what the business is actually doing in the world. "It's not about your story; it's about your impact," says Christopher.

Muddied Materiality

While many agree that something is "off" about the efficacy of sustainability reports, it may in part be due to a confusing glut of standards and frameworks, such as the Global Reporting Initiative (GRI), the International Integrated Reporting Council (IIRC), and the Sustainability Accounting Standards Board (SASB). These frameworks, and others, each have their own approach to how an organization's materiality should be determined, reported, and assessed.

Even more confusing is when one framework, such as SASB, which is a compliance-driven approach to materiality based on the United States Security and Exchange Commission, contradicts principle-driven approaches to materiality focused on a global framework, such as the GRI or IIRC. Among the ranks of sustainability reporters, there is a growing sense of framework fatigue.

It's clear that, as part of the transparency process, sustainability reporters will need to justify their framework and approach and why it's important to the business.

As an example, Novo Nordisk has chosen to no longer follow the GRI, the de facto global standard, and instead focus on integrated reporting. "We recognize that SASB, IIRC and GRI each have their rationales, and that the three are not necessarily compatible. We would definitely prefer (and expect) that ultimately we will have one international standard for corporate reporting, " says Novo Nordisk's Stormer. "We use the integrated reporting approach because it is the best way to reflect how we manage our business."

Mark Weick, director of sustainability programs at Dow Chemicals, on the other hand, defends his company's choice to adhere to the new GRI G4 standard. He says: "Common global standards are helpful for both companies and their stakeholders because standards enable fair and transparent data comparisons. We believe the GRI set of metrics is very sound." Dow published a comprehensive 2013 GRI G4 report last year.

As a data partner for the GRI, Lou Coppola, Executive Vice President at the Governance & Accountability Institute, predicts that 2015 will see companies grappling to allow disparate players to "co-exist and integrate in a way that is beneficial for companies, investors and all stakeholders." Ultimately, his position is an optimistic one: "As different players come into the landscape of reporting frameworks we do see some confusion from reporters. In our opinion these facts demonstrate further growth, sophistication, focus and maturing of sustainability reporting."

JEFF LEINAWEAVER is the principal of Global Zen Sustainability, a sustainability practice focused on strategic CSR, organizational storytelling, and social performance. He is also a member of the graduate faculty for Bainbridge Graduate Institute's MBA program in sustainability.

EXPLORING THE ISSUE

Is Corporate Sustainability Reporting a Valuable Corporate Reporting Tool?

Critical Thinking and Reflection

1. What could be done to improve the reporting process?
2. Are the reports really valuable?
3. From a corporate perspective, what do the reports represent, especially given their present state and format?
4. What should a CSR report consist of?
5. Who should monitor and verify the information contained in these reports?
6. Should corporations have to respond to and report on nonfinancial factors?

Is There Common Ground?

Both sides of this debate recognize that the trend for reporting on sustainability issues is on the rise and the demand for these reports does not appear to be weakening as governing bodies and NGOs continue to exert pressure for greater transparency and insight into business processes, practices, and outcomes.

The disagreement at the heart of this issue, however, lies in the value and relevance of the details or content of these reports. Specifically, what information should be included, how should it be reported, and should there be any auditing or formal assessment of these reports. Given the evolutionary nature of this type of reporting, it is anticipated that these discussions and this debate will continue well into the subsequent decade.

Additional Resources

Aras, G. & Crowther, D. (2008). "Corporate Sustainability Reporting: A Study in Disingenuity," *Journal of Business Ethics*, Spring, pp. 279–288.

Bebbington & Brendan O'Dwyer (Eds.), *Sustainability Accounting and Accountability,* London, UK: Routledge, pp. 57–69.

Buhr, N. (2007). "Histories and Rationales for Sustainability Reporting," in Jeffrey Unerman, January.

Hess, D. (2008). "The Three Pillars of Corporate Social Reporting as New Governance Regulation: Disclosure,

Dialogue, and Development," *Business Ethics Quarterly,* 18(4), pp. 447.

Kolk, A. (2004a). "A Decade of Sustainability Reporting: Developments and Significance," *International Journal of Environment and Sustainable Development,* 3(1), pp. 51–64.

Kolk, A. (2004b). "More Than Words? An Analysis of Sustainability Reports," *New Academy Review,* 3(3), pp. 59–75.

MacLean, R. & Rebernak, K. (2007). "Closing the Credibility Gap: The Challenges of Corporate Responsibility Reporting," *Environmental Quality Management,* Summer, pp. 1–6.

Nickell, E. B. & Roberts, R. W. (2014). "The Public Interest Imperative in Corporate Sustainability Reporting Research," *Accounting and the Public Interest,* 14, pp. 79–86.

Pounder, B. (2011). "Trends in Sustainability Reporting," *Strategic Finance,* December, pp. 21–23.

Reilly, A. H. (2009). "Communicating Sustainability Initiatives in Corporate Reports: Linking Implications to Organizational Change," *SAM Advanced Management Journal,* Summer, pp. 33–43.

Sherman, R. W. (2012). "The Triple Bottom Line: The Reporting of 'Doing Well' & 'Doing Good'," *The Journal of Applied Business Research,* July/August, pp. 673–681.

Internet References . . .

Carrots and Sticks: Promoting Transparency and Sustainability

www.globalreporting.org/resourcelibrary/Carrots-And
-Sticks-Promoting-Transparency-And-Sustainbability.pdf

Does Corporate Social Responsibility Increase Profits?

http://business-ethics.com/2011/05/12/doescorporate
-social-responsibility-increase-profits/

Global Reporting Initiative

www.globalreporting.org/reporting/Pages/default.aspx

Mandatory Social Responsibility

www.forbes.com/2010/05/04/corporate-socialrespons
ibility-csr-business-oxford.html

New Group Aims to Set Sustainability Reporting Standards

http://business-ethics.com/2012/10/01/1750-newgroup
-to-set-sustainability-standardsfor-business

The Future of Corporate Social Responsibility Reporting

www.bu.edu/pardee/files/2011/01/PardeellB
-019-Jan-2011.pdf

The Rising Global Interest in Sustainability and Corporate Social Responsibility Reporting

http://sustainability.thomsonreuters.com

Selected, Edited, and with Issue Framing Material by:
Kathleen J. Barnes, *William Paterson University*
and
George E. Smith, *University of South Carolina, Beaufort*

ISSUE

Is It Really Possible to Create Sustainable Businesses?

YES: Chris Boyd, from "Sustainability Is Good Business," *The OECD Observer* (2001)

NO: Auden Schendler and Michael Toffel, from "Corporate Sustainability Is Not Sustainable," *Grist Magazine* (2013)

Learning Outcomes

After reading this issue, you will be able to:

- Describe barriers to sustainability practices in corporations.
- Discuss potential opportunities afforded by a sustainability agenda and strategy.
- Explain what sustainability is and means to supporters of corporate sustainability.
- Appreciate the challenge of building and operating a sustainable business.

ISSUE SUMMARY

YES: Chris Boyd argues that there "is no fundamental contradiction between concern for the environment or social responsibility and the profit motive" and that "it is good business for companies to act in a more sustainable way."

NO: Auden Schendler and Michael Toffel relay that most green scorecards, corporate strategies, media, and shareholder analyses of business focus almost entirely on operational greening activities and policies, and don't actually measure sustainability. These authors then outline five characteristics of a meaningful corporate sustainability program.

In an October 2011 *Harvard Business Review* article on sustainability, Chouinard, Ellison, and Ridgway explain:

No one these days seriously denies the need for sustainable business practices. Even those concerned about only business and not the fate of the planet recognizes that the viability of business itself depends on the resources of healthy ecosystems—fresh water, clean air, robust biodiversity, productive land—and on the stability of just societies. Happily, most of us also care about these things directly (Chouinard, Ellison, and Ridgway, 2011).

The sentiment conveyed in this quotation illustrates the importance that is being given to sustainability and sustainable business. In trying to define and frame the issue of sustainability, the following information can be found on an MIT Sloan Management Review web page (http://sloanreview.mit.edu /what-is-sustainability/).

What Does Sustainability Mean?

Depends on whom you ask. (Debates about it can get warm.) But at root it's the idea that systems—including natural and human ones—need to be regenerative and balanced in order to last. We believe that means all kinds of systems: economic, environmental, societal, and personal. The sustainability question is: How can we design and build a world in which the Earth thrives and people can pursue flourishing lives?

Are There Other Definitions?

Yes—too many to count. Some focus on environmental impact alone, or emphasize the idea of the triple bottom line (measuring performance of organizations or communities on separate economic, environmental, and social dimensions). One of the best-known general definitions emerged from a 1987 United Nations report about sustainable development "meeting the needs of the present without compromising the ability of future generations to meet their own needs." Increasingly, attempts at definition are recognizing that the needs of natural, economic, and social systems are so interdependent that [they] have to be considered in an integrated way.

Based on this information, sustainable businesses then are those that seek to address the needs of business, society, and the environment in the present without adversely impacting the future. These corporations are concerned with conservation, minimizing their "environmental footprints," and becoming responsible stewards of the resources they have been provided. In building on this idea, many organizations have adopted and are adopting "green policies" to reduce waste, make better use of energy, and limit their impact on the environment that will ultimately be left to and passed on to future generations.

The articles included in this issue seek to examine the issue of developing and maintaining a sustainable business. First, Chris Boyd presents his view that sustainability is good business. In his opinion, "there is no fundamental contradiction between concern for the environment or social responsibility and the profit motive." He views the pursuit of sustainability and sustainable business practices as being strategic concepts and issues that businesses should account for and include.

Mr. Schendler and Professor Toffel relay that most green scorecards, corporate strategies, media, and shareholder analyses of business focus almost entirely on operational greening activities and policies, and don't actually measure sustainability. These authors then outline five characteristics of a meaningful corporate sustainability program.

YES ⬅

Chris Boyd

Sustainability Is Good Business

Sustainability, the triple bottom line of economic profitability, respect for the environment and social responsibility: these are the new buzzwords of many a corporate annual report. Global companies everywhere are falling over themselves to declare their adherence to the principles of sustainable development. Is this a new moral crusade on the part of big business, or simply the result of pressure from demonstrators like those in Seattle and Genoa?

For some, either of these arguments may be true, but on the whole, sustainability is largely a question of good business. In fact, there is no fundamental contradiction between concern for the environment or social responsibility and the profit motive that has largely created the developed world as we know it today. In short, greed is still good for you.

Not that unrestrained market forces will deliver sustainability. There is clearly a role for government in setting the right framework for markets to deliver those broader based outcomes we all want for our planet. On the environment side, there are externalities—costs not borne by the polluter—that are excluded from influencing the market at present. This has occurred for various reasons, but mainly because resources, like fresh air and clean water, were simply treated as costless until recently. Historically, we have seen examples of such externalities being successfully internalised—the bringing of common grazing lands into private ownership, thereby creating the incentive to conserve, is one case—though not without conflict. Greenhouse gas emissions that cause global warming are an obvious environmental externality that we now know needs to be internalised. Only in a few countries are emissions regulated or taxed in some way. In most countries, it is "costless" for firms to emit CO_2, so of course there is little incentive for them to change their behaviour unless governments act. Indeed, many companies support efforts to reach worldwide agreement on combating climate change in order to make the necessary economic adjustments in an orderly fashion.

Governments also have a crucial role to play in setting the right framework for markets to function in socially responsible ways. Tax and spending policies should be set in ways that complement the market economy by providing public goods efficiently. More controversially perhaps, governments are mainly responsible for ensuring human rights and fighting corruption, although companies, especially large global ones, cannot and do not ignore these issues.

However, it is good business for companies to act in a more sustainable way, even where the market does not yet provide the appropriate signals. Take climate change as an example. The cement industry is a significant producer of CO_2, the principal greenhouse gas, causing about 5% of the world's emissions. As the world's largest cement producer, Lafarge has an interest in reducing its carbon intensity, not only to prepare itself for a future carbon-constrained world, but also to help avoid rushed and poorly designed legislation. Not only Lafarge in the cement industry, but also companies such as BP and Shell in the oil industry, TransAlta in the power sector and Dupont in chemicals have a similar view of climate change.

On the social side too, our concern for sustainability is grounded in good business reasons. Our cement plants and our quarries often dominate other industries in their local communities. Lafarge has learned over its almost 170 years of existence that the implicit "license to operate" from local communities, gained through actions coming out of dialogue and transparency, is as important as the regulatory permits from the authorities. Without the support and understanding of local communities, changes such as quarry extensions or fuel switches to use waste fuels like used tires, which reduce costs and save fossil fuels, would be more difficult if not impossible to obtain. Our business would become precarious and less flexible.

Acting in a sustainable way can make firms more competitive, more resilient to shocks, nimbler in a fast-changing world, more unified in purpose, more likely to attract and hold customers and the best employees, and more at ease with regulators and financial markets.

Financial markets are beginning to notice these positive effects. Between 1 January 1999 and 30 June 2000, the Dow Jones Sustainability Group World Index—composed of sustainability-driven companies including Lafarge—outperformed the Dow Jones Global World Index by 127 basis point in US dollar terms. The index consists of the top 10% of companies seen as leaders in sustainable development. Their value advantage held in both bull and bear markets.

A Strategy That Pays

The main business drivers of sustainability for manufacturing firms make a good strategic concept for improving business performance:

- Eco-efficiency: Reducing inputs of limited natural raw materials or fuel consumption, reducing waste production and utilising by-products from other industries, allow firms to cut costs;

- Improving product added value: With a sustainability approach, firms expect to be able to expand their product lines to sell more complex and technological products, with more value added (licenses, exclusive technology, etc.). Links with customers and users will become closer and better established in the long term and loyalty will be improved;

- Creating new market opportunities: A sustainability policy should facilitate firms' expansion into new countries or regions through more sensitive and proactive methods of integration and an enhanced environmental approach. New products will allow firms to respond better to the emerging expectations of their customers;

- Strengthening socially responsible management: Such a policy will strengthen corporate culture, help firms to maintain the loyalty of their employees and attract high-potential new employees;

- Improving reputation: A proactive strategy will help firms keep their "license to operate," and improve their corporate image in order to maintain brand value, as well as their relationships with local authorities and communities. This helps to reduce the prospect of inappropriate new taxes and regulations and avoid crises.

Smart Markets

Given the right framework, competitive and open markets are the right way to move towards sustainability. Markets, with all their imperfections, are nevertheless the best means that man has found to produce innovation and efficiency. By rewarding success, markets harness creative energy. It is difficult to imagine that government officials, however well-meaning or efficient, will be better at organising a route to sustainability than the market mechanism, as long as this is properly framed to encourage sustainability.

Certainly, sustainable development should not become an excuse for governments to impose yet more heavy-handed regulation and yet more taxes. Just look at the French government's attempts to impose sustainability reporting by law with over thirty indicators proposed in the social field alone or the US Superfund legislation, which benefits mostly lawyers. More energy should be spent on getting the price and other signals right so that markets work in a more sustainable fashion. This means convincing, not coercing. After all, sustainability will not progress if those that are meant to implement it are alienated from the concept. It also means that governments should take a comprehensive approach. Sustainable development is by its very nature not amenable to the partial, unco-ordinated methods that different government departments tend to employ. An example is the enormous subsidies still paid to fossil fuels in many countries, which conflict with climate change concerns.

No one has a monopoly of knowledge on how to progress towards sustainability. Dialogue and partnership, between governments and civil society in general on the one hand and business on the other, is the way forward. Who knows exactly what will emerge in terms of agreements and initiatives? But what is clear is that markets can and must be made to work for the benefit of all. Without them progress towards global sustainable development will be much more difficult, if not impossible, to achieve.

References

Forum: "OECD Guidelines for Multinational Enterprises," series of opinion articles, in *OECD Observer*, No. 225, March 2001. Also see Policy Brief at www.oecd.org/publications/Pol_brief/

Schmidheiney, Stefan, *Changing Course: A Global Perspective on Development and the Environment*, Business Council for Sustainable Development, MIT Press, Cambridge, 1992.

Sustainable America, The President's Council on Sustainable Development, US Government Printing Office, Washington D.C., 1996.

Witherell, B., Maher, M., "Responsible corporate behaviour for sustainable development," *OECD Observer* No. 226/227, Summer 2001. See www.oecdobserver.org

---

Chris Boyd is senior vice-president of environment and public affairs at Lafarge. Lafarge is a world leader in building materials with 85,000 workers employed in 75 countries.

Auden Schendler and Michael Toffel

 **NO**

Corporate Sustainability Is Not Sustainable

Green initiatives are ubiquitous these days, implemented with zeal at companies like Dupont, IBM, Walmart, and Walt Disney. The programs being rolled out—lighting retrofits, zero-waste factories, and carpool incentives—save money and provide a green glow. Most large companies are working to reduce energy use and waste, and many have integrated sustainability into strategic planning. What's not to like?

Well, for starters, these actions don't meaningfully address the primary barrier to sustainability, climate change. According to the International Energy Agency, without action, global temperatures will likely increase 6 degrees C by 2100, "which would have devastating consequences for the planet." This means more super droughts, floods, storms, fires, crop failures, sea-level rise, and other major disruptions. "Sustainability" simply isn't possible in the face of such a problem, as Superstorm Sandy demonstrated.

So despite perceptions that "sustainable business" is up and running, the environment reminds us we're failing to deal with the problem at anywhere near sufficient scale. Because climate change requires a systemic solution, which only governments can provide, firms serious about addressing it have a critical role well beyond greening their own operations. They must spur government action. But few are.

"Green business" as currently practiced focuses on limited operational efficiencies—cutting carbon footprint and waste reduction—and declares victory. But these measures fail to even dent the climate problem. And the proof is easy: Greenhouse gas emissions continue to rise. Last month, we hit 400 parts per million atmospheric CO_2 for the first time in 3 million years. Worse, though, such small-ball initiatives are a distraction: We fiddle around the edges thinking we're making a real difference (and getting accolades), while the planet inexorably warms.

The reality is that even if one company eliminates its carbon footprint entirely—as Microsoft admirably pledged to do—global warming roars on. That's because the problem is too vast for any single business: Solving climate change means we must switch to mostly carbon-free energy sources by 2050 or find a way to affordably capture carbon dioxide emissions, both monumental tasks.

Even several very large companies cannot, on their own, get us there. In fact, historically, no big environmental problem—from air and water pollution to acid rain or ozone depletion—has ever

been solved by businesses volunteering to do the right thing. We ought not presume that voluntary measures will solve this one.

But nobody seems to have noticed. Most green scorecards, corporate strategies, media, and shareholder analyses of businesses focus almost entirely on operational greening activities and policies, but not on whether companies can continue on their current course in a climate-changed world. In other words, such analyses don't actually measure sustainability.

So what does a meaningful corporate sustainability program look like in the era of climate change?

First, corporate leaders need to directly lobby state and national politicians to introduce sweeping, aggressive bipartisan climate legislation such as a carbon fee-and-dividend program. Strong policy in G8 nations is all the more important because it removes excuses for inaction by China, India, and other countries with rapidly growing carbon footprints.

Second, CEOs should insist that trade groups prioritize climate policy activism and withdraw from associations that refuse to do so, like when Pacific Gas & Electric, Apple, and Nike left the U.S. Chamber of Commerce over its opposition to regulating greenhouse gas emissions.

Third, businesses should market their climate activism so that customers and suppliers appreciate their leadership, understand what matters, and follow suit. Such marketing is also education on one of the key issues of our time.

Fourth, companies should partner with effective nongovernmental organizations such as the Coalition for Environmentally Responsible Economies, the Natural Resources Defense Council, 350.org, Protect Our Winters, and Citizen's Climate Lobby to support their work, become educated on climate science and policy solutions, and understand effective lobbying.

Fifth, managers should demand that suppliers assess their climate impact and set public targets to reduce greenhouse gas emissions. But companies that are multiplying their influence in supply chains—like Dell and Walmart—must not miss the larger and more important opportunity to change the rules of the game through activism.

Even in the United States, a climate laggard, some companies are already responding to climate change in the appropriate way.

Nike, for example, moved beyond operational greening by helping to create BICEP (Business for Innovative Climate and

Energy Policy), which brings its members to Washington, D.C., to lobby for aggressive energy and climate legislation.

Starbucks has also taken out full-page ads in major newspapers to raise public awareness about the importance of climate action and has lobbied the U.S. Congress and the Obama administration to explain the threat climate poses to coffee.

These companies are the exception. Unfortunately, even businesses that are sustainability leaders—like clothing manufacturer Patagonia, a business we admire—don't recognize the primacy of climate change. Instead, it includes climate in a basket of equally weighted issues, like protecting oceans, forests, or fisheries. But that's misguided: Climate vastly trumps (and often includes) those other environmental concerns.

Businesses that claim to be green but aren't loudly making their voices heard on the need for government action on climate change are missing the point. They are not just dodging the key challenge of sustainability; they are distracting us from what really matters.

AUDEN SCHENDLER is vice president of sustainability at Aspen Skiing Company, author of Getting Green Done, and a board member of Protect Our Winters.

MICHAEL TOFFEL is an associate professor at Harvard Business School, where he specializes in business and environment issues.

EXPLORING THE ISSUE

Is It Really Possible to Create Sustainable Businesses?

Critical Thinking and Reflection

1. In what ways are customers benefited by sustainable business practices?
2. How do businesses benefit from pursuing corporate strategies focused on sustainability?
3. Will customers send market signals to businesses engaged in sustainability that will reward those efforts? Why or why not?
4. How could the degree of a business's commitment to sustainability be measured?
5. Are there corporate stakeholders that could assist businesses in pursuing sustainability?

Is There Common Ground?

The common ground on this particular issue appears to be the recognition that businesses need to consider new models that will protect the environment and society in their pursuit of profit. There is a growing commitment to the idea that the environment businesses operate and exist in has a finite set of resources, and responsible use of those resources should be taken into account as businesses develop and execute their strategies.

The challenge embedded here is the viability of these ideas for sustaining business. On one hand, there are those who view things as Boyd does and believe that sustainability should be an integral part of a business's strategy and that sustainability practices reward businesses, especially in the long run. Contrary to this view are those who align themselves with the view held by Schendler and Toffel who observe that most green scorecards, corporate strategies, media and shareholder analyses of business focus almost entirely on operational greening activities and policies, and don't actually measure sustainability.

Given these contrasting viewpoints and contemporary society's desire to protect and preserve the environment and its resources,

it is likely that the issue of business sustainability will continue to receive attention and be a topic of discussion and debate for some time to come.

Additional Resources

Chouinard, Y., Ellison, J. & Ridgeway, R. (2011). "The Big Idea: The Sustainable Economy," *Harvard Business Review*, October, http://hbr.org/2011/10/the-sustainable-economy/ar/1

Crew, D. E. (2010). "Strategies for Implementing Sustainability: Five Leadership Challenges," *SAM Advanced Management Journal*, Spring, pp. 15–21.

Haanaes, K., Balagopal, B., et al. (2011a). "First Look: The Second Annual Sustainability & Innovation Survey," *MIT Sloan Management Review*, Winter, pp. 77–83.

Haanaes, K., Balagopal, B., et al. (2011b). "New Sustainability

Study: The 'Embracers' Seize Advantage," *MIT Sloan Management Review*, Spring, pp. 23–35.

Internet References . . .

10 Sustainable Business Stories that Shaped 2015

https://hbr.org/2015/12/10-sustainable-business-stories
-that-shaped-2015

Like It or Not, Sustainability Is Now Core to Your Business

http://fortune.com/2015/09/24/sustainability-practices
-in-business-intel-unilever-wal-mart-dupont/

Ten Steps to Sustainable Business in 2013

http://iveybusinessjournal.com/publication
/ten-ways-to-help-companies-become-sustainable
-in-2013/

The 7 Fundamentals of Sustainable Business Growth

https://www.fastcompany.com/3049856/the-7-fund
amentals-of-sustainable-business-growth

What Is Sustainability?

http://sloanreview.mit.edu/what-is-sustainability/

Unit 5

UNIT

International Management

*G*overnments of many countries are enacting protectionist economic policies as a means of helping their domestic economies. According to many economists, however, both theory and practice strongly indicate that protectionist actions do more harm than good. Nevertheless, political leaders appear to be receptive to protectionist promptings, leading many intellectuals and social commentators to wonder if such policies might actually be beneficial to United States business interests. Newsworthy and important issues facing many managers and executives today are discussed in this unit.

Selected, Edited, and with Issue Framing Material by:
Kathleen J. Barnes, *William Paterson University*
and
George E. Smith, *University of South Carolina, Beaufort*

ISSUE

Do Unskilled Immigrants Hurt the American Economy?

YES: Steven Malanga, from "How Unskilled Immigrants Hurt Our Economy," *City Journal* (2006)

NO: Diana Furchtgott-Roth, from "The Case for Immigration," *The New York Sun* (2006)

Learning Outcomes
After reading this issue, you will be able to:
• Understand the positive and negative consequences of unskilled immigrants on the American economy.
• Explain how unskilled immigrants can be used as an effective workplace tool.
• Understand the policies that might be implemented concerning unskilled immigration.
• Appreciate the practical implications of unskilled immigrants use in the workplace.

ISSUE SUMMARY

YES: Steven Malanga believes the influx of unskilled immigrants results in job loss by native workers and lower investment in labor-saving technology. He also contends that illegal immigration taxes our already-strained welfare and social security systems.

NO: Diana Furchtgott-Roth, senior fellow at the Hudson Institute and a former chief economist at the U.S. Department of Labor, points out that annual immigration represents a small portion of the U.S. labor force, and, in any event, immigrant laborers complement, rather than replace, legal American citizens in the workplace.

In April 2010, Arizona Governor Jan Brewer signed the "Support Our Law Enforcement and Safe Neighborhoods Act" (SB1070). While many decried the signing of this act by Governor Brewer and raised issues regarding the potentially discriminatory actions of the law, the underlying intent of the act was to impose additional controls on immigration in the state of Arizona beyond those performed by the federal government. Despite the fact that parts of the Arizona act have been struck down in court, 36 additional states have followed Arizona's lead in proposing similar laws. In 31 instances the states rejected or refused to advance the bills. In five states—Utah, Indiana, South Carolina, Georgia, and Alabama—those bills have been voted into law and in many cases have been observed to mirror or even surpass the Arizona law. Some observers believe that this current trend—the passing of immigration law—will continue in the future. This issue focuses on examining the question of whether or not unskilled immigrants threaten the U.S. labor force and ultimately harm the American economy.

According to the Cato Institute, over the past 200 years, the United States has welcomed more than 60 million immigrants to its shores (www.freetrade.org/issues/immigration.html). Although the vast majority of those immigrants entered the country legally, in recent decades, the number of people entering the country illegally has grown tremendously. Estimates currently put the number of illegal immigrants in the United States somewhere between 10 and 15 million. Regardless of the actual figure, there is no question that the continued growth of illegal aliens has important ramifications both politically and socially; indeed, one need only observe the behaviors of the two political parties to verify the truth of this statement.

Of particular importance to this text is the impact of the growth of illegal aliens on the American workplace. Those that believe the overall effect of these unskilled workers is generally beneficial to the U.S. economy provide numerous points in support of their position. They point, for example, to research showing that immigrants and natives frequently do not compete for the same jobs. Interestingly, in areas where demand for labor is high relative to supply, hiring immigrants results in a complementary outcome rather than a competitive situation. Thus, supporters contend the view that illegal aliens and other immigrants take jobs from native workers is simple-minded. An often-overlooked fact is that many immigrants arrive in the United States with strong skill sets and a burning desire to make something of themselves. Indeed, many employers have found that there is a large degree of overlap between the characteristics of an individual willing to accept the risks and dangers of relocating to a foreign land to make a better life for him(her)self and the characteristics of a loyal, dependable, and driven employee. Finally, supporters note that illegal aliens contribute mightily to our economy in ways beyond their physical labor: As a group, they contribute billions of dollars to social security through payroll taxes. For example, *The Washington Post* estimated that during the period from 1990 to 1998, illegal aliens paid more than $20 billion in payroll taxes (Washingtonpost.com). However, owing to fears of being caught and deported, few actually collect payments, thus providing the social security program with a huge net gain.

On the other side of the debate are those who are against corporations being allowed to hire illegal aliens because of the detrimental effects doing so may have on the American labor force. Central to their position is the argument that illegal immigration disproportionately affects poor American natives because the immigrants are willing to work the unskilled jobs typically held by poor Americans and do so for much less pay. They further argue that from this perspective, firms that hire illegal aliens are anti-American because they are effectively displacing legitimate American citizens from these jobs. Another charge frequently leveled at supporters is the negative impact on the economy due to illegal immigration, particularly in the area of taxes. On the one hand critics point out, states lose billions of dollars each year in the form of unpaid taxes. On the other, states are faced with growing demands for governmental services driven by the increase in their populations, some of which is the result of illegal immigration. The net result? States have to raise taxes to meet these needs; thus, the law-abiding American citizen foots the bill for the illegal immigrants. It's hard to see how this outcome can be viewed as anything but harmful to the U.S. economy.

Thus, the question posed here is whether the U.S. economy suffers when American businesses hire unskilled illegal aliens. Answering in the affirmative is columnist Steven Malanga. He believes the influx of unskilled immigrants results in job loss by native workers and lower investment in labor-saving technology. Arguing the other side of the debate is Diana Furchtgott-Roth, a senior fellow at the Hudson Institute and a former chief economist at the U.S. Department of Labor. She points out that annual immigration represents a small portion of the U.S. labor force and immigrant laborers complement, rather than replace, legal American citizens in the workplace.

YES ↰

Steven Malanga

How Unskilled Immigrants Hurt Our Economy

The day after Librado Velasquez arrived on Staten Island after a long, surreptitious journey from his Chiapas, Mexico, home, he headed out to a street corner to wait with other illegal immigrants looking for work. Velasquez, who had supported his wife, seven kids, and his in-laws as a *campesino,* or peasant farmer, until a 1998 hurricane devastated his farm, eventually got work, off the books, loading trucks at a small New Jersey factory, which hired illegals for jobs that required few special skills. The arrangement suited both, until a work injury sent Velasquez to the local emergency room, where federal law required that he be treated, though he could not afford to pay for his care. After five operations, he is now permanently disabled and has remained in the United States to pursue compensation claims. . . .

Velasquez's story illustrates some of the fault lines in the nation's current, highly charged, debate on immigration. Since the mid-1960s, America has welcomed nearly 30 million legal immigrants and received perhaps another 15 million illegals, numbers unprecedented in our history. These immigrants have picked our fruit, cleaned our homes, cut our grass, worked in our factories, and washed our cars. But they have also crowded into our hospital emergency rooms, schools, and government-subsidized aid programs, sparking a fierce debate about their contributions to our society and the costs they impose on it.

Advocates of open immigration argue that welcoming the Librado Velasquezes of the world is essential for our American economy: our businesses need workers like him, because we have a shortage of people willing to do low-wage work. Moreover, the free movement of labor in a global economy pays off for the United States, because immigrants bring skills and capital that expand our economy and offset immigration's costs. Like tax cuts, supporters argue, immigration pays for itself.

But the tale of Librado Velasquez helps show why supporters are wrong about today's immigration, as many Americans sense and so much research has demonstrated. America does not have a vast labor shortage that requires waves of low-wage immigrants to alleviate; in fact, unemployment among unskilled workers is high—about 30 percent. Moreover, many of the unskilled, uneducated workers now journeying here labor, like Velasquez, in shrinking industries, where they force out native workers, and many others work in industries where the availability of cheap workers has led businesses to suspend investment in new technologies that would make them less labor-intensive.

Yet while these workers add little to our economy, they come at great cost, because they are not economic abstractions but human beings, with their own culture and ideas—often at odds with our own. Increasing numbers of them arrive with little education and none of the skills necessary to succeed in a modern economy. Many may wind up stuck on our lowest economic rungs, where they will rely on something that immigrants of other generations didn't have: a vast U.S. welfare and social-services apparatus that has enormously amplified the cost of immigration. Just as welfare reform and other policies are helping to shrink America's underclass by weaning people off such social programs, we are importing a new, foreign-born underclass. As famed free-market economist Milton Friedman puts it: "It's just obvious that you can't have free immigration and a welfare state."

Immigration can only pay off again for America if we reshape our policy, organizing it around what's good for the economy by welcoming workers we truly need and excluding those who, because they have so little to offer, are likely to cost us more than they contribute, and who will struggle for years to find their place here.

Hampering today's immigration debate are our misconceptions about the so-called first great migration some 100 years ago, with which today's immigration is often compared. . . . If America could assimilate 24 million mostly desperate immigrants from that great migration—people one unsympathetic economist at the turn of the twentieth century described as "the unlucky, the thriftless, the worthless"—surely, so the story goes, today's much bigger and richer country can absorb the millions of Librado Velasquezes now venturing here.

But that argument distorts the realities of the first great migration. . . . Those waves of immigrants—many of them urban dwellers who crossed a continent and an ocean to get here—helped supercharge the workforce at a time when the country was going through a transformative economic expansion that craved new workers, especially in its cities. A 1998 National Research Council report noted "that the newly arriving immigrant nonagricultural work force . . . was (slightly) more skilled than the resident American labor force": 27 percent of them were skilled laborers, compared with only 17 percent of that era's native-born workforce.

Many of these immigrants quickly found a place in our economy, participating in the workforce at a higher rate even than the native population. Their success at finding work sent many of them quickly up the economic ladder: those who stayed in America for at least 15 years, for instance, were just as likely to own their own business as native-born workers of the same age, one study found. . . .

What the newcomers of the great migration did not find here was a vast social-services and welfare state. They had to rely on their own resources or those of friends, relatives, or private, often ethnic, charities if things did not go well. That's why about 70 percent of those who came were men in their prime. It's also why many of them left when the economy sputtered several times during the period. . . .

Today's immigration has turned out so differently in part because it emerged out of the 1960s civil rights and Great Society mentality. In 1965, a new immigration act eliminated the old system of national quotas, which critics saw as racist because it greatly favored European nations. Lawmakers created a set of broader immigration quotas for each hemisphere, and they added a new visa preference category for family members to join their relatives here. Senate immigration subcommittee chairman Edward Kennedy reassured the country that, "contrary to the charges in some quarters, [the bill] will not inundate America with immigrants," and "it will not cause American workers to lose their jobs."

But, in fact, the law had an immediate, dramatic effect, increasing immigration by 60 percent in its first ten years. Sojourners from poorer countries around the rest of the world arrived in ever-greater numbers, so that whereas half of immigrants in the 1950s had originated from Europe, 75 percent by the 1970s were from Asia and Latin America. And as the influx of immigrants grew, the special-preferences rule for family unification intensified it further, as the pool of eligible family members around the world also increased. Legal immigration to the U.S. soared from 2.5 million in the 1950s to 4.5 million in the 1970s to 7.3 million in the 1980s to about 10 million in the 1990s.

As the floodgates of legal immigration opened, the widening economic gap between the United States and many of its neighbors also pushed illegal immigration to levels that America had never seen. In particular, when Mexico's move to a more centralized, state-run economy in the 1970s produced hyperinflation, the disparity between its stagnant economy and U.S. prosperity yawned wide. Mexico's per-capita gross domestic product, 37 percent of the United States' in the early 1980s, was only 27 percent of it by the end of the decade—and is now just 25 percent of it. With Mexican farmworkers able to earn seven to ten times as much in the United States as at home, by the 1980s illegals were pouring across our border at the rate of about 225,000 a year, and U.S. sentiment rose for slowing the flow.

But an unusual coalition of business groups, unions, civil rights activists, and church leaders thwarted the call for restrictions with passage of the inaptly named 1986 Immigration Reform and Control Act, which legalized some 2.7 million unauthorized aliens already here, supposedly in exchange for tougher penalties and controls against employers who hired illegals. The law proved no deterrent, however, because supporters, in subsequent legislation and court cases argued on civil rights grounds, weakened the employer sanctions. Meanwhile, more illegals flooded here in the hope of future amnesties from Congress, while the newly legalized sneaked their wives and children into the country rather than have them wait for family-preference visas. The flow of illegals into the country rose to between 300,000 and 500,000 per year in the 1990s, so that a decade after the legislation that had supposedly solved the undocumented alien problem by reclassifying them as legal, the number of illegals living in the United States was back up to about 5 million, while today it's estimated at between 9 million and 13 million.

The flood of immigrants, both legal and illegal, from countries with poor, ill-educated populations, has yielded a mismatch between today's immigrants and the American economy and has left many workers poorly positioned to succeed for the long term. . . . Nearly two-thirds of Mexican immigrants, for instance, are high school dropouts, and most wind up doing either unskilled factory work or small-scale construction projects, or they work in service industries, where they compete for entry-level jobs against one another, against the adult children of other immigrants, and against native-born high school dropouts. Of the 15 industries employing the greatest percentage of foreign-born workers, half are low-wage service industries, including gardening, domestic household work, car washes, shoe repair, and janitorial work. . . .

Although open-borders advocates say that these workers are simply taking jobs Americans don't want, studies show that the immigrants drive down wages of native-born workers and squeeze them out of certain industries. Harvard economists George Borjas and Lawrence Katz, for instance, estimate that low-wage immigration cuts the wages for the average native-born high school dropout by some 8 percent, or more than $1,200 a year. . . .

Consequently, as the waves of immigration continue, the sheer number of those competing for low-skilled service jobs makes economic progress difficult. A study of the impact of immigration on New York City's restaurant business, for instance, found that 60 percent of immigrant workers do not receive regular raises, while 70 percent had never been promoted. . . .

Similarly, immigration is also pushing some native-born workers out of jobs, as Kenyon College economists showed in the California nail-salon workforce. Over a 16-year period starting in the late 1980s, some 35,600 mostly Vietnamese immigrant women flooded into the industry, a mass migration that equaled the total number of jobs in the industry before the immigrants arrived.

Though the new workers created a labor surplus that led to lower prices, new services, and somewhat more demand, the economists estimate that as a result, 10,000 native-born workers either left the industry or never bothered entering it.

In many American industries, waves of low-wage workers have also retarded investments that might lead to modernization and efficiency. Farming, which employs a million immigrant laborers in California alone, is the prime case in point. Faced with a labor shortage in the early 1960s, when President Kennedy ended a 22-year-old guest-worker program that allowed 45,000 Mexican farmhands to cross over the border and harvest 2.2 million tons of California tomatoes for processed foods, farmers complained but swiftly automated, adopting a mechanical tomato-picking technology created more than a decade earlier. Today, just 5,000 better-paid workers—one-ninth the original workforce—harvest 12 million tons of tomatoes using the machines.

The savings prompted by low-wage migrants may even be minimal in crops not easily mechanized. Agricultural economists Wallace Huffman and Alan McCunn of Iowa State University have estimated that without illegal workers, the retail cost of fresh produce would increase only about 3 percent in the summer-fall season and less than 2 percent in the winter-spring season, because labor represents only a tiny percent of the retail price of produce and because without migrant workers, America would probably import more foreign fruits and vegetables. . . .

As foreign competition and mechanization shrink manufacturing and farmworker jobs, low-skilled immigrants are likely to wind up farther on the margins of our economy, where many already operate. For example, although only about 12 percent of construction workers are foreign-born, 100,000 to 300,000 illegal immigrants have carved a place for themselves as temporary workers on the fringes of the industry. In urban areas like New York and Los Angeles, these mostly male illegal immigrants gather on street corners, in empty lots, or in Home Depot parking lots to sell their labor by the hour or the day, for $7 to $11 an hour. . . .

Because so much of our legal and illegal immigrant labor is concentrated in such fringe, low-wage employment, its overall impact on our economy is extremely small. A 1997 National Academy of Sciences study estimated that immigration's net benefit to the American economy raises the average income of the native-born by only some $10 billion a year—about $120 per household. And that meager contribution is not the result of immigrants helping to build our essential industries or making us more competitive globally but instead merely delivering our pizzas and cutting our grass. Estimates by pro-immigration forces that foreign workers contribute much more to the economy, boosting annual gross domestic product by hundreds of billions of dollars, generally just tally what immigrants earn here, while ignoring the offsetting effect they have on the wages of native-born workers.

If the benefits of the current generation of migrants are small, the costs are large and growing because of America's vast range of social programs and the wide advocacy network that strives to hook low-earning legal and illegal immigrants into these programs. A 1998 National Academy of Sciences study found that more than 30 percent of California's foreign-born were on Medicaid—including 37 percent of all Hispanic households—compared with 14 percent of native-born households. The foreign-born were more than twice as likely as the native-born to be on welfare, and their children were nearly five times as likely to be in means-tested government lunch programs. Native-born households pay for much of this, the study found, because they earn more and pay higher taxes—and are more likely to comply with tax laws. Recent immigrants, by contrast, have much lower levels of income and tax compliance (another study estimated that only 56 percent of illegals in California have taxes deducted from their earnings, for instance). The study's conclusion: immigrant families cost each native-born household in California an additional $1,200 a year in taxes.

Immigration's bottom line has shifted so sharply that in a high-immigration state like California, native-born residents are paying up to ten times more in state and local taxes than immigrants generate in economic benefits. Moreover, the cost is only likely to grow as the foreign-born population—which has already mushroomed from about 9 percent of the U.S. population when the NAS studies were done in the late 1990s to about 12 percent today—keeps growing. . . . This sharp turnaround since the 1970s, when immigrants were less likely to be using the social programs of the Great Society than the native-born population, says Harvard economist Borjas, suggests that welfare and other social programs are a magnet drawing certain types of immigrants—nonworking women, children, and the elderly—and keeping them here when they run into difficulty.

Not only have the formal and informal networks helping immigrants tap into our social spending grown, but they also get plenty of assistance from advocacy groups financed by tax dollars, working to ensure that immigrants get their share of social spending. Thus, the Newark-based New Jersey Immigration Policy Network receives several hundred thousand government dollars annually to help doctors and hospitals increase immigrant enrollment in Jersey's subsidized health-care programs. Casa Maryland, operating in the greater Washington area, gets funding from nearly 20 federal, state, and local government agencies to run programs that "empower" immigrants to demand benefits and care from government and to "refer clients to government and private social service programs for which they and their families may be eligible." . . .

Almost certainly, immigrants' participation in our social welfare programs will increase over time, because so many are destined to struggle in our workforce. Despite our cherished view of immigrants as rapidly climbing the economic ladder, more and more of the new arrivals and their children face a lifetime of economic disadvantage, because they arrive here with low levels of education and with few work skills—shortcomings not easily overcome. Mexican immigrants, who are up to six times more likely to be high school dropouts than native-born Americans, not only earn substantially less than the native-born median, but the wage gap persists for decades after they've arrived. A study of the 2000 census data, for instance, shows that the cohort of Mexican immigrants between 25 and 34 who entered the United States in the late 1970s were earning 40 to 50 percent less than similarly aged native-born Americans in 1980, but 20 years later they had fallen even further behind their native-born counterparts. Today's Mexican immigrants between 25 and 34 have an even larger wage gap relative to the native-born population. Adjusting for other socioeconomic factors, Harvard's Borjas and Katz estimate that virtually this entire wage gap is attributable to low levels of education. . . .

One reason some ethnic groups make up so little ground concerns the transmission of what economists call "ethnic capital," or what we might call the influence of culture. More than previous generations, immigrants today tend to live concentrated in ethnic enclaves, and their children find their role models among their own group. Thus the children of today's Mexican immigrants are likely to live in a neighborhood where about 60 percent of men dropped out of high school and now do low-wage work, and where less than half of the population speak English fluently, which might explain why high school dropout rates among Americans of Mexican ancestry are two and a half times higher than dropout rates for all other native-born Americans, and why first-generation Mexican Americans do not move up the economic ladder nearly as quickly as the children of other immigrant groups.

In sharp contrast is the cultural capital transmitted by Asian immigrants to children growing up in predominantly Asian-American neighborhoods. More than 75 percent of Chinese immigrants and 98 percent of South Asian immigrants to the U.S. speak English fluently, while a mid-1990s study of immigrant households in California found that 37 percent of Asian immigrants were college graduates, compared with only 3.4 percent of Mexican immigrants. Thus, even an Asian-American child whose parents are high school dropouts is more likely to grow up in an environment that encourages him to stay in school and learn to speak English well, attributes that will serve him well in the job market. Not surprisingly, several studies have shown that Asian immigrants and their children earn substantially more than Mexican immigrants and their children.

Given these realities, several of the major immigration reforms now under consideration simply don't make economic sense—especially the guest-worker program favored by President Bush and the U.S. Senate. Careful economic research tells us that there is no significant shortfall of workers in essential American industries, desperately needing supplement from a massive guest-worker program. Those few industries now relying on cheap labor must focus more quickly on mechanization where possible. Meanwhile, the cost of paying legal workers already here a bit more to entice them to do such low-wage work as is needed will have a minimal impact on our economy.

The potential woes of a guest-worker program, moreover, far overshadow any economic benefit, given what we know about the long, troubled history of temporary-worker programs in developed countries. They have never stemmed illegal immigration, and the guest workers inevitably become permanent residents, competing with the native-born and forcing down wages. Our last guest-worker program with Mexico, begun during World War II to boost wartime manpower, grew larger in the postwar era, because employers who liked the cheap labor lobbied hard to keep it. By the mid-1950s, the number of guest workers reached seven times the annual limit during the war itself, while illegal immigration doubled, as the availability of cheap labor prompted employers to search for ever more of it rather than invest in mechanization or other productivity gains.

The economic and cultural consequences of guest-worker programs have been devastating in Europe, and we risk similar problems. When post–World War II Germany permitted its manufacturers to import workers from Turkey to man the assembly lines, industry's investment in productivity declined relative to such countries as Japan, which lacked ready access to cheap labor. When Germany finally ended the guest-worker program once it became economically unviable, most of the guest workers stayed on, having attained permanent-resident status. Since then, the descendants of these workers have been chronically underemployed and now have a crime rate double that of German youth. . . .

"Importing labor is far more complicated than importing other factors of production, such as commodities," write University of California at Davis professor Philip Martin, an expert on guest-worker programs, and Michael Teitelbaum, a former member of the U.S. Commission on Immigration Reform. "Migration involves human beings, with their own beliefs, politics, cultures, languages, loves, hates, histories, and families."

If low-wage immigration doesn't pay off for the United States, legalizing illegals already here makes as little sense as importing new rounds of guest workers. The Senate and President Bush, however, aim to start two-thirds of the 11 million undocumented aliens already in the country on a path to legalization, on the grounds that only thus can America assimilate them, and only through assimilation can they hope for economic success in the United States. But such arguments ignore the already poor economic performance of increasingly large segments of the *legal* immigrant population in the United States. Merely granting illegal aliens legal status won't suddenly catapult them up our mobility ladder, because it won't give them the skills and education to compete. . . .

If we do not legalize them, what can we do with 11 million illegals? Ship them back home? Their presence here is a fait accompli, the argument goes, and only legalization can bring them above ground, where they can assimilate. But that argument assumes that we have only two choices: to decriminalize or deport. But what happened after the first great migration suggests a third way: to end the economic incentives that keep them here. We could prompt a great remigration home if, first off, state and local governments in jurisdictions like New York and California would stop using their vast resources to aid illegal immigrants. Second, the federal government can take the tougher approach that it failed to take after the 1986 act. It can require employers to verify Social Security numbers and immigration status before hiring, so that we bar illegals from many jobs. It can deport those caught here. And it can refuse to give those who remain the same benefits as U.S. citizens. Such tough measures do work: as a recent Center for Immigration Studies report points out, when the federal government began deporting illegal Muslims after 9/11, many more illegals who knew they were likely to face more scrutiny voluntarily returned home.

If America is ever to make immigration work for our economy again, it must reject policies shaped by advocacy groups trying to turn immigration into the next civil rights cause or by a tiny minority of businesses seeking cheap labor subsidized by the taxpayers. Instead, we must look to other developed nations that have focused on luring workers who have skills that are in demand and who have the best chance of assimilating. Australia, for instance, gives preferences to workers grouped into four skilled categories: managers, professionals, associates of professionals, and skilled laborers. Using a straightforward "points calculator" to determine who gets in, Australia favors immigrants between the ages of 18 and 45 who speak English, have a post–high school degree or training in a trade, and have at least six months' work experience as everything from laboratory technicians to architects and surveyors to information-technology workers. Such an immigration policy goes far beyond America's employment-based immigration categories, like the H1-B visas, which account for about 10 percent of our legal immigration and essentially serve the needs of a few Silicon Valley industries.

Immigration reform must also tackle our family-preference visa program, which today accounts for two-thirds of all legal immigration and has helped create a 40-year waiting list. Lawmakers should narrow the family-preference visa program down to spouses and minor children of U.S. citizens and should exclude adult siblings and parents.

America benefits even today from many of its immigrants, from the Asian entrepreneurs who have helped revive inner-city Los Angeles business districts to Haitians and Jamaicans who have stabilized neighborhoods in Queens and Brooklyn to Indian programmers who have spurred so much innovation in places like Silicon Valley and Boston's Route 128. But increasingly over the last 25 years, such immigration has become the exception. It needs once again to become the rule.

STEVEN MALANGA is a contributing editor to City Journal and a senior fellow at the Manhattan Institute, which publishes *City Journal*. His primary area of focus is economic development within dense urban centers, with a particular emphasis on those areas in and surrounding New York and the Tri-State Area.

Diana Furchtgott-Roth

 **NO**

The Case for Immigration

It was raining in Washington last week, and vendors selling $5 and $10 umbrellas appeared on the streets. They had Hispanic accents, and were undoubtedly some of the unskilled immigrants that Steven Malanga referred to in his recent *City Journal* article, "How Unskilled Immigrants Hurt Our Economy."

I already had an umbrella. But the many purchasers of the umbrellas did not seem to notice that the economy was being hurt. Rather, they were glad of the opportunity to stay dry before their important meetings.

The *City Journal* article is worth a look because it reflects an attitude becoming more common these days in the debate. The article speaks approvingly of immigrants from Portugal, Asia, China, India, Haiti, and Jamaica. But it also makes it clear that we have too many Mexicans, a "flood of immigrants" who cause high unemployment rates among the unskilled. They work in shrinking industries, drive down wages of native-born Americans, cost millions in welfare, and retard America's technology.

These are serious charges indeed. Similar charges, that immigrants have caused native-born Americans to quit the labor market, have been made by Steven Camarota of the Center for Immigration Studies. But are they true?

Annual immigration is a tiny fraction of our labor force. The Pew Hispanic Center Report shows that annual immigration from all countries as a percent of the labor force has been declining since its recent peak in 1999.

Annual immigration in 1999 equaled 1% of the labor force—by 2005 it had declined to 0.8%. Hispanics, including undocumented workers, peaked in 2000 as a percent of the labor force at 0.5%, and by 2004 accounted for only 0.4% (0.3% for Mexicans) of the labor force.

Looking at unskilled workers, Hispanic immigration as a percent of the American unskilled labor force (defined as those without a high school diploma) peaked in 2000 at 6%, and was 5% in 2004 (4% for Mexicans). Five percent is not "floods of immigrants."

Mr. Malanga writes that America does not have a vast labor shortage because "unemployment among unskilled workers is high—about 30%." It isn't. In 2005, according to Bureau of Labor Statistics data, the unemployment rate for adults without a high school diploma was 7.6%. Last month it stood at 6.9%.

Data from a recent study by senior economist Pia Orrenius of the Dallas Federal Reserve Bank show that foreign-born Americans are more likely to work than native-born Americans. Leaving their countries by choice, they are naturally more risk-taking and entrepreneurial.

In 2005 the unemployment rate for native-born Americans was 5.2%, but for foreign-born it was more than half a percentage point lower, at 4.6%. For unskilled workers, although the total unemployment rate was 7.6%, the native-born rate was 9.1% and the foreign-born was much lower, at 5.7%.

According to Mr. Malanga, unskilled immigrants "work in shrinking industries where they force out native workers." However, data show otherwise. Low-skilled immigrants are disproportionately represented in the expanding service and construction sectors, with occupations such as janitors, gardeners, tailors, plasterers, and stucco masons. Manufacturing, the declining sector, employs few immigrants.

One myth repeated often is that immigrants depress wages of native-born Americans. As Professor Giovanni Peri of the University of California at Davis describes in a new National Bureau of Economic Analysis paper last month, immigrants are complements, rather than substitutes, for native-born workers. As such, they are not competing with native-born workers, but providing our economy with different skills.

Education levels of working immigrants form a U-shaped curve, with unusually high representation among adult low- and high-skilled. In contrast, the skills of native-born Americans form a bellshaped curve, with many B.A.s and high school diplomas but relatively few adult high school drop-outs or Ph.D.s

Low-skill immigrants come to be janitors and house-keepers, jobs native-born Americans typically don't want, but they aren't found as crossing guards and funeral service workers, low-skill jobs preferred by Americans. Similarly, high-skilled immigrants also take jobs Americans don't want. They are research scientists, dentists, and computer hardware and software engineers, but not lawyers, judges, or education administrators.

Because immigrants are complements to native-born workers, rather than substitutes, they help reduce economic bottlenecks, resulting in income gains. Mr. Peri's new study shows that immigrants raised the wages of the 90% of native-born Americans with at least a high school degree by 1% to 3% between 1990 and 2004. Those without a high school diploma lost about 1%, an amount that could be compensated from the gains of the others.

If immigrants affect any wages, it's those of prior immigrants, who compete for the same jobs. But we don't see immigrants protesting in the streets to keep others out, as we see homeowners in scenic locations demonstrating against additional development. Rather, some of the biggest proponents of greater immigration are the established immigrants themselves, who see America's boundless opportunities as outweighing negative wage effects.

Mr. Malanga cites a 1998 National Academy of Sciences study to say, "The foreign-born were more than twice as likely as the native-born to be on welfare." Yet this study contains estimates from 1995, more than a decade ago, and mentions programs such as Aid to Families with Dependent Children that no longer exist. Even so, the NAS study says that foreign-born households "are not more likely to use AFDC, SSI, or housing benefits."

The NAS study concludes that, since the foreign-born have more children, the "difference in education benefits accounts for nearly all of the relative deficit . . . at the local government level." Mr. Malanga, writing about how unskilled immigrants hurt the economy, would likely be in favor of these immigrants trying to educate their children, especially since these children will be contributing to his Social Security benefits.

Mr. Malanga suggests that the availability of low-wage immigrants retards investments in American technology. He cites agriculture as an example where machines to pick produce could be invented if labor were not available. Or, Mr. Malanga says, we could import produce from abroad at little additional cost.

Although consumers don't care where their food comes from, farmers certainly do. Farms provide income to farmers as well as to other native-born Americans employed in the industry as well as in trucking and distribution, just as immigrants in the construction industry have helped fuel the boom that sent employment of native-born construction workers to record levels. It makes little sense to send a whole economic sector to other countries just to avoid employing immigrants.

If unskilled immigrants don't hurt our economy, do they hurt our culture? City Journal editor Myron Magnet writes that Hispanics have "a group culture that devalues education and assimilation." Similar concerns about assimilation were made about Jews, Italians, Irish, Germans, Poles, and even Norwegians when they first came to America. All eventually assimilated.

Moreover, for those who are concerned with Spanish-speaking enclaves, a September 2006 paper by a professor at Princeton, Douglas Massey, shows that within two generations Mexican immigrants in California stop speaking Spanish at home, and within three generations they cease to know the language altogether. He concludes, "Like taxes and biological death, linguistic death seems to be a sure thing in the United States, even for Mexicans living in Los Angeles, a city with one of the largest Spanish-speaking urban populations in the world."

Legalizing the status of the illegal immigrants in America by providing a guest-worker program with a path to citizenship would produce additional gains to our economy. This is not the same as temporary worker programs in Germany, which did not have a path to citizenship, and so resulted in a disenfranchised class of workers.

With legal status, workers could move from the informal to the formal sector, and would pay more taxes. It would be easier to keep track of illegal financial transactions, reducing the potential for helping terrorists.

For over 200 years, American intellectual thought has included a small but influential literature advocating reduced immigration. The literature has spawned political parties such as the Know-Nothing Party in the mid-19th century and periodically led to the enactment of anti-immigrant laws. Immigrants, so the story goes, are bad for our economy and for our culture.

The greatness of America is not merely that we stand for freedom and economic prosperity for ourselves, but that we have consistently overcome arguments that would deny these same benefits to others.

Diana Furchtgott-Roth is a senior fellow at the Manhattan Institute. She is also a contributing editor of RealClearMarkets.com, and a columnist for the *Washington Examiner*, MarketWatch.com, and *Tax Notes*.

EXPLORING THE ISSUE

Do Unskilled Immigrants Hurt the American Economy?

Critical Thinking and Reflection

1. What might be the goals of an unskilled immigrant policy?
2. How might an unskilled immigrant policy be implemented in the United States?
3. What might be the costs to consumers, corporations, and the nation of an unskilled immigrant policy?
4. What is the likelihood that an enacted unskilled immigrant policy will lead to anticipated outcomes?
5. What does the future hold for immigration policy?.

Is There Common Ground?

One reason the issue of an unskilled immigrant policy is so contentious is that both sides can cite data in support of their position. While finding common ground on even basic aspects of this important management topic is difficult, there is consensus that an unskilled immigrant policy is a highly charged topic that will continue to be examined and debated for quite some time.

Additional Resources

Passel, J. S. (2005). "Estimates of the Size and Characteristics of the Undocumented Population," Pew Hispanic Center, March 21.

Tancredo, T. (2005). "Illegal Aliens Taking American Jobs," House of Representatives, November 17.

Internet References . . .

Immigration Quotas vs. Individual Rights: The Moral and Practical Case for Open Immigration

Binswanger, H. (2006). "Immigration Quotas vs. Individual Rights: The Moral and Practical Case for Open Immigration," *Capitalism Magazine*, April 2.

> **http://capmag.com/article.asp?ID=4620**

Immigration Law Should Reflect Our Dynamic Labor Market

Griswold, D. (2008). "Immigration Law Should Reflect Our Dynamic Labor Market," The Cato Institute, April 27.

> **www.cato.org/pub_display.php?pub_id=9360**

Q & A Guide to State Immigration Laws

Immigration Policy Center. (2012). "Q & A Guide to State Immigration Laws," February 16.

> **www.immigrationpolicy.org/special-reports /qa-guide-state-immigration-laws**

Amnesty for All Undocumented Immigrants and Full Labor Rights for All Workers!

Open World Conference of Workers, "Amnesty for All Undocumented Immigrants and Full Labor Rights for All Workers!" OWC Continuations Committee.

> **www.owcinfo.org/campaign/Amnesty.htm**

American Brain Drain

Wall Street Journal Opinion. (2007). "American Brain Drain," *Wall Street Journal Review and Outlook*, November 30.

> **http://online.wsj.com/article/SB119638963734709017 .html?mod=opinion_main_review_and_outlooks**

Selected, Edited, and with Issue Framing Material by:
Kathleen J. Barnes, *William Paterson University*
and
George E. Smith, *University of South Carolina, Beaufort*

ISSUE

Is Economic Globalization Good for Humankind?

YES: Paul A. Gigot and Guy Sorman, from "Foreword," The Heritage Foundation (2008)

NO: Branko Milanovic, from "Why Globalization Is in Trouble—Parts 1 and 2," *YaleGlobal Online* (2006)

Learning Outcomes
After reading this issue, you will be able to:
• Understand the positive and negative consequences of economic globalization.   • Understand both corporate and national motives driving economic globalization.   • Understand what policies might be implemented with regard to economic globalization.   • Appreciate the practical implications and limitations of economic globalization.

ISSUE SUMMARY

YES: Arguing that globalization is good for humankind are Paul A. Gigot and Guy Sorman. They outline seven ways in which globalization has positively impacted life and what needs to be done to further its advancement.

NO: Branko Milanovic, an economist with both the Carnegie Endowment for International Peace and the World Bank, is against globalization. Milanovic addresses several reasons for his views while emphasizing the incompatibility of globalization with the ages-old ethnic and religious traditions and values that characterize much of the world.

According to a leading international business textbook, globalization is "the inexorable integration of markets, nation-states, and technologies . . . in a way that is enabling individuals, corporations, and nation-states to reach around the world farther, faster, deeper, and cheaper than ever before" (Griffin and Pustay, 2010). Globalism is a phenomenon that has its roots in the rebuilding of Europe and Asia in the aftermath of World War II. As a measure of how powerful a phenomenon it has become, consider that the volume of international trade has increased over 3,000 percent since 1960! Most of this tremendous growth has occurred in the TRIAD, a free-trade market consisting of three regional trading blocs: Western Europe in its current form as the European Union, North America, and Asia (including Australia). Increasingly, however, the developing nations of the world are contributing to the expansion in world trade. Foreign investment has grown at a staggering rate as well: over three times faster than the world output of goods. In the early part of the twenty-first century, it is not a stretch to say that virtually all businesses in industrialized nations are impacted to some degree by globalization.

It seems pretty clear that globalization will continue to grow as a dominant force in international relations among countries, particularly as more Second and Third World countries open their borders to international trade and investment. What may be less clear, however, is whether or not this is a positive development. In other words, is economic globalization good for humankind?

Globalization invokes strong arguments and strong emotions from supporters on each side. Those who believe globalization is a beneficial force for humans have a plethora of reasons for their view. From an economic perspective, the spread of free trade and free markets across the globe has liberated hundreds of millions from poverty over the past 40 years. Studies on economic freedom consistently show that countries that embrace globalization are more economically free and, as a direct result, enjoy higher per capita wealth than countries that are more isolated economically. Supporters also note that the growth in globalization has been accompanied by a growth in democracy as well. Along with these two benefits, globalization enhances the cultures of those countries that embrace it.

Guy Sorman, one of the authors of the YES selection in this debate, points out: "Through popular culture, people from different backgrounds and nations discover one another, and their 'otherness' suddenly disappears." Increases in cultural tolerance and openness to different worldviews is part-and-parcel of globalization. A tangentially related benefit involves the spread of respect for the rights of women and minorities around the globe. Discrimination is incompatible with freedom and democracy, and the spread of globalization brings pressure to bear on governments to recognize and protect the rights of all their citizens.

Detractors of globalization raise several important points. Echoing anti-outsourcing advocates, they argue that globalization results in a loss of jobs due to competition with low-wage countries. Indeed, the major economic force driving the tremendous growth of the Indian and Chinese economies over the past 15 years is their competitive advantage of access to cheap labor. Many antiglobalization supporters argue that corporations are becoming too powerful politically and economically and believe that the search for overseas profits and markets is the primary cause.

Opponents also raise concerns over national safety and security issues. As the globe continues to shrink and the ease and speed of information exchange continues to increase, the likelihood of cyber-attacks and the theft of sensitive military, technological, and economic information is assumed to increase. The threat of terrorism has grown dramatically in the past 30 years due in large part, say the globalization critics, to the spread of globalization driven by the United States and other western, First-World civilizations. As the recent Swine Flu outbreak reminds us, the threat of a worldwide health pandemic grows larger the more integrated the world becomes.

YES ⤶

Paul A. Gigot and Guy Sorman

Foreword

I don't know who first used the word "globalization," but he was probably no friend of capitalism. The word is bureaucratic and implies that the world economy is subject to the control of some vast, nefarious force beyond human influence. The reality is that the world economy is enjoying its strongest run of prosperity in 40 years thanks to the greater ability of billions of individuals to make free choices in their own self-interest. The *Index of Economic Freedom* has been encouraging this trend for 14 years, and at the end of 2007, we can happily say it continues.

The world economy extended its multiyear run of 5 percent or so annual GDP growth this year, notwithstanding an American slowdown due mainly to the housing correction. As I write this, the U.S. economy seems to have survived the August credit crunch related to the collapse of the sub-prime mortgage market. The summer squall showed once again how interrelated financial markets have become, with sub-prime losses popping up around the world and even causing an old-fashioned bank run at Northern Rock in the United Kingdom.

The episode is naturally leading to soul-searching about the stability of this brave new world of global finance—including the spread of asset securitization, the rise of hedge funds, and an explosion in derivatives. This introspection ought to be healthy. The sub-prime fiasco has, at the very least, exposed the need for more careful vetting by investors, but regulators and bankers are also sure to examine the rules for transparency and capital requirements to prevent the spread of problems throughout the financial system. The event also shows the need for more careful driving by America's Federal Reserve, whose easy-money policy in the first half of this decade was the root cause of the housing boom and bust. The good news is that, at least so far, there hasn't been a regulatory overreaction that could stymie growth.

The irony of the year has been the shifting economic policy trends in America and France, of all places. The U.S. political debate is moving in a negative direction as "fairness" and income redistribution replace growth as the policy lodestar and proposals for tax increases proliferate. The Bush tax cuts of 2003 were crucial

to kicking the economy out of its post-9/11, post-dot.com doldrums. But they expire after 2010 and are in serious jeopardy. The free-trade agenda has also stalled as bilateral pacts with Latin America and South Korea face heavy going on Capitol Hill. The 2008 election will be as much a referendum on economic policy as on foreign policy.

Perhaps the rest of the world will have to teach America a policy lesson or two. As the *Index* shows, Europe overall has moved in a freer direction this decade. This is due in large part to reform in the former Eastern Europe, as well as to the policy competition caused by the success of the euro. With capital and people free to move and governments no longer able to inflate their way out of fiscal difficulty, the trend has been toward lower tax rates and labor market liberalization.

Miracle of miracles, even France has been mugged by this reality. Nicolas Sarkozy made the revival of the French economy a main theme of his successful campaign for president, and he has followed with proposals for what he called "a new social contract founded on work, merit and equal opportunity." We should all hope he succeeds—not merely to compensate for any slowdown in America, but for its own sake to help Europe break away from its self-imposed sense of diminished expectations. In any event, this policy churning in Europe shows how the ability to move capital freely across borders imposes a price on bad government decisions.

The larger point is that if we step back from the daily turmoil, we can see that we live in a remarkable era of prosperity and spreading freedom. Hundreds of millions of people are being lifted out of poverty around the world as global trade and investment expand and countries like India and China liberalize parts of their economies. The International Monetary Fund reported in early 2007 that every country in the world, save for a couple of small dictatorships, was growing. This prosperity can itself create discontent due to the rapidity of change, and it certainly poses a challenge to political leaders who are obliged to explain and manage its consequences. The *Index of Economic Freedom* exists to help in that explanation, and we hope readers continue to find it a source of comparative policy wisdom.

Globalization Is Making the World
a Better Place

What we call "globalization," one of the most powerful and positive forces ever to have arisen in the history of mankind, is redefining civilization as we know it. This is one of my hypotheses. To be more specific, I will try to describe what globalization is, its impact on world peace, and the freedom it brings from want, fear, and misery.

Globalization has six major characteristics: economic development, democracy, cultural enrichment, political and cultural norms, information, and internationalization of the rule of law.

Economic Development

Usually, globalization is described in terms of intensified commercial and trade exchanges, but it is about more than just trade, stock exchanges, and currencies. It is about people. What is significant today is that through globalization many nations are converging toward enhanced welfare.

This convergence is exemplified by the 800 million people who, in the past 30 years, have left poverty and misery behind. They have greater access to health care, schooling, and information. They have more choices, and their children will have even more choices. The absolutely remarkable part is that it happened not by accident but through a combination of good economic policy, technology, and management.

Of course, not all nations are following this path, but since the fall of the Berlin Wall, more and more are coming closer. Only Africa's nations have yet to join, but who would have hoped and predicted 30 years ago that China and India, with such rapidity and efficiency, would pull their people out of misery? There is no reason why Africa, when its turn comes, will not do the same. Convergence should be a source of hope for us all.

Democracy

In general, since 1989, the best system to improve the welfare of all people—not only economically, but also in terms of access to equality and freedom—appears to be democracy, the new international norm. As more and more countries turn democratic or converge toward democratic norms, respect for other cultures increases.

Democracy has guaranteed welfare far better than any dictatorship ever could. Even enlightened despots cannot bring the kind of safety democracy is bringing. Sometimes a trade-off between economic allotment and democracy occurs. Sometimes the economy grows more slowly because of democracy. Let it be that way.

Democracy brings values that are as important for the welfare of the human being as [the] economy is.

After all, as history shows, the chance of international war diminishes step by step any time a country moves from tyranny to democracy, as democracies do not war against one other. That more and more nations are turning democratic improves everyone's way of life.

Cultural Enrichment

Critics of globalization frequently charge that it results in an "Americanization of culture" and concomitant loss of identity and local cultural values. I would propose a more optimistic view, and that is that globalization leads to never-ending exchange of ideas, especially through popular culture, since it affects the greatest number of people.

Through popular culture, people from different backgrounds and nations discover one another, and their "otherness" suddenly disappears. For example, a popular Korean television sitcom now popular in Japan has shown its Japanese viewers that, like them, Koreans fall in love, feel despair, and harbor the same hopes and fears for themselves and for their children. This sitcom has transformed the image Japanese have of the Korean nation more profoundly than any number of diplomatic efforts and demonstrates that globalization can erode prejudices that have existed between neighboring countries for centuries.

Furthermore, this process of better understanding allows us to keep our identity and add new identities. The Koreans absorb a bit of the American culture, a bit of the French, a bit of other European societies. Perhaps they have become a different sort of Korean, but they remain Korean nonetheless. It is quite the illusion to think you can lose your identity. And it goes both ways. When you look at the success of cultural exports out of Korea—this so-called new wave through music, television, movies, and art—Korea becomes part of the identity of other people.

Now, as a Frenchman, I am a bit Korean myself. This is how globalization works. We do not lose our identity. We enter into the world that I call the world of multi-identity, and that is progress, not loss.

Political and Cultural Norms

One of the most significant transformations in terms of welfare for the people in the globalized world is the increased respect given to the rights of women and minorities. In many nations, to be a woman or to belong to a minority has not been easy. In the past 30 years, however, women and minorities everywhere have become better informed and have learned that the repression they suffered until very recently is not typical in a modern democracy.

Let us consider India, where a strong caste system historically has subjugated women and untouchables. Thanks to the globalization of democratic norms, these minorities are better protected; through various affirmative action policies, they can access the better jobs that traditionally were forbidden to them. This transformation has positive consequences for them, of course, and also creates better outcomes for their children's welfare and education. We are entering into a better world because of their improved status, thanks to the cultural and democratic exchanges generated by globalization.

Information

Through legacy media and, more and more, through the Internet and cellular phones, everyone today, even in authoritarian countries, is better informed. For one year, I lived in the poorest part of China, and I remember well how a farmer, in the most remote village, knew exactly what was happening not only in the next village, but also in Beijing and New York because of the Internet and his cellular phone. No government can stop information now. People know today that, as they say, "knowledge is power."

Now let us imagine if the genocide in Darfur had happened 20 or 30 years ago. The Darfur population would have been annihilated by the Sudanese government, and no one would have known. Today we all know about the genocide. The reason why the international community has been forced to intervene is because of the flood of information. Knowledge is proving to be the best protection for oppressed minorities and, thus, one of the most vital aspects of globalization.

Internationalization of the Rule of Law

Internationalization of rule of law, of course, has limitations. The institutions in charge of this emerging rule of law, whether the United Nations or the World Trade Organization, are criticized. They are not completely legitimate. They are certainly not perfectly democratic, but you cannot build a democratic organization with non-democratic governments. It becomes a trade-off.

In spite of all the weaknesses of international organizations, the emergence of a real international rule of law replaces the pure barbarism that existed before, which had consisted of the most powerful against the weak. Even though globalization cannot suppress war, it is remarkably efficient at containing war. If you examine the kinds of wars we have today, compared to the history of mankind, the number of victims and number of nations involved are very few. We are all safer because of both

this emerging rule of law and the flow of information provided by globalization.

Invented by Entrepreneurs

We also need to remember that globalization is not some historical accident but has been devised and built by those who wanted it. Diplomats did not invent it. Entrepreneurs did.

Let us look at Europe. After World War II, the Europeans discovered that they had been their own worst enemies. For 1,000 years, we were fighting each other. Why? We do not remember very well. Every 30 years, we went to war. The French killed the Germans. The Germans killed the French. When you try to explain this history to your children, they cannot understand. Diplomats and politicians from the 18th century onward unsuccessfully made plans to avoid this kind of civil war within Europe.

Then, in the 1940s, a businessman came along named Jean Monnet. His business was to sell cognac in the United States, and he was very good at it. The idea Jean Monnet had was that perhaps the unification process of Europe should not be started by diplomats. Maybe it should be started by business people. He proceeded to build the European Union on a foundation of commerce. He started with coal and steel in 1950, and it was through the liberation of that trade that he conceived the unification of Europe, which has played a crucial role in the globalization process.

Monnet's guiding principle was that commercial and financial ties would lead to political unification. The true basis of European solidarity has come through trade. Through this method, all of the benefits of globalization have been made possible, because free trade has been at the root level. An attack on free trade is an attack on both globalization and the welfare of the peoples of the world, so we must be very cautious when we discuss trade, as it is the essential key allowing the rest to happen.

None of this is to imply that trade is easy. In the case of Europe, it was made easier because all of the governments were democratic. It is much more complicated to build free trade with non-democratic governments, but because globalization starts with the construction of this materialistic solidarity, ideals must come afterwards.

Two Threats to Globalization

Perhaps what I have presented so far is too optimistic a picture of globalization, but I believe we have good reason to be upbeat. However, there are two threats to globalization that may be taken too lightly today.

Global epidemics. In terms of health care, we are more and more able to cope with the current illnesses of the world. Though Africa still poses a problem, through global efforts it will be possible in the years to come to reduce the major epidemics there: AIDS and malaria.

But new epidemics are threatening the world. If we remember what happened in China some years ago with the SARS epidemic, which was very short, and then the avian flu threat in 2005, you understand that there are new threats somewhere out there and that the modern world is not really prepared. One of the consequences of globalization is that people travel more, which means that viruses travel more and adapt.

Therefore, I think globalization should require the international community to develop ever more sophisticated systems to detect and cure the new epidemics that have been a negative consequence of globalization.

Terrorism. Although wars these days are more limited, new forms of warfare have emerged, which we call terrorism. Terrorism today can seem like a distant menace somewhere between the United States and the Middle East. Because of the global progress of the rule of law, however, violent groups know that it is no longer possible to wage war in the traditional way; therefore, people driven by ideological passions are increasingly tempted by terrorist methods as a way of implementing their agenda.

Those are the true negative aspects of globalization: epidemics and terrorism. Regretfully, we are too focused on the traditional problems like free trade. We are not focused enough on the future threats.

I wish globalization were more popular, but it is our fault if it is not. Perhaps we should use different words. "Globalization" is ugly. We should find a better word, and we should try to explain to the media and students that we are entering into a new civilization of welfare, progress, and happiness, because if they do not understand the beauty of globalization, they will not stand up for it when it is threatened.

Paul A. Gigot is the editor of *The Wall Street Journal* Editorial Page.

Guy Sorman is a French journalist and author.

Branko Milanovic

 **NO**

Why Globalization
Is in Trouble—Parts 1 and 2

Part I

Washington: Historically, the dominant power tends to support globalization as a way to increase the ambit of its influence, expand trade and gain economic advantage, co-opt new citizens and possibly show the advantages of its own pax. This was the case with the Roman, British and now American-led globalizations. But recently, the rich West—which saw globalization as a prelude to "the end of history"—is having second thoughts.

Two fears drive this unease with globalization: The first is a fear of job loss due to competition from low-wage countries. The second is the fear of ethnic and cultural dilution due to increased immigration.

The cause of the first fear is a fast reemergence on the world stage of China and India. For students of history, the rise of China and India is not a surprise. The two countries are just recapturing the ground lost during the 19th and most of the 20th century. Before the Industrial Revolution, China's and India's combined output accounted for one half of the world's total. Now, after a quarter-century of China's spectacular growth, and more than a decade of India's growth acceleration, the two countries contribute less than a fifth of total world output. Although their share is, in the long-term historical sense, still below what it used to be, it has nevertheless increased dramatically compared to where it was 30 years ago. The rise of the two Asian giants, reflected in their dynamic trade, large Chinese export surpluses and India's role as an outsourcing center and a potential leader in information technology, has made the West wonder whether it can compete with such hardworking, cheap, plentiful and yet relatively skilled labor.

While the fear of job loss is driven by fast economic growth of the two giants, the fear of immigration is, ironically, caused by the slow economic growth of the rest of the developing world. The people who try to reach the shores of Europe or cross from Mexico into the US come from the countries that have disastrously fallen behind Western Europe and the US during the last quarter century. In 1980, Mexico's real per-capita income, adjusted for the differential price level between Mexico and the US, was a third of that in the US. Today, the ratio is almost 4.5 to 1. The poor Africans who land daily on beaches of the Spanish Canary Islands come from

the countries that have seen no economic growth in 50 years. Take Ghana, a country often touted as an African success case: Around its independence, in 1957, its income was one half of Spain's; today, it is one tenth.

Immigration puts a similar pressure on low- or medium-skilled jobs in the West as do cheap imports from China and outsourcing to India. And indeed, wages of low- and medium-skilled workers in the rich countries have failed to keep pace with incomes of educated workers at the top of the pyramid. While the median US real wage has not risen in real terms over the last 25 years, real wages of the top 1 percent have more than doubled. The richest 1 percent of Americans today controls almost 20 percent of total US income, a proportion higher than at any time since the Roaring Twenties. The U-turn of inequality—a sharp increase that started during the Thatcher-Reagan era, after a long decline—has affected, to a varying extent, all Western countries.

But at stake is something more profound than a threat to jobs and stagnant wages in a few "exposed" sectors. After all, the West is no stranger to structural change. Ricardo in his "Principles" written in 1815 discusses labor dislocation "occasioned" by the introduction of machinery. The Western countries handled the decline of powerful industries like coal, textile and steel. Economists have never been sympathetic to the protection arguments of sunset industries: In an expanding economy, structural change is necessary and inevitable; jobs lost in one industry will reappear as new jobs in another industry.

The difference now is that the twin challenge undermines the consensus upon which the West's welfare state was built since World War II. To understand why, recall that the Western welfare states rest on two building blocks: those of ethnic and social solidarity. The first building block implies that one is willing to be taxed if certain that aid will flow to somebody who is ethnically or culturally similar. But once large stocks of immigrants with different, and not easily adaptable, social norms, arrive, that certainly is no longer. More immigrants will strain the already-tattered solidarity among citizens of rich European countries.

The second building block of the welfare state is class solidarity. For it to exist, there must be relatively similar economic conditions between classes so that one can reasonably expect that for social transfers paid out of his pocket today, he may be compensated—if the need arose—by a similar benefit in the future. If, for example, unemployment rates are relatively equal across skill levels, then the highly skilled will pay for unemployment benefits; but if unemployment rates are different, the highly skilled may opt out. As the income divide widens in the West between the rich and the highly educated who have done well, and the middle classes and the unskilled who are merely scraping by, the second building block on which welfare capitalism was built crumbles. Economic inequality also translates into a cultural divide. "Ethnic" migrants who fill the rungs of low-paid workers are not the only ones economically and culturally different from today's Western elites; the elites are also growing more different from their own poorer ethnic brethren.

So far reaching, these developments require an entirely new social contract, a redefinition of capitalism no less. Such fundamental changes are not easy to come by when the threat is subtle, continuous, incremental and far from dramatic in a daily sense. Difficult decisions can be postponed, and neither politicians nor the electorate have an appetite for change. A battle of attrition regarding who would bear the costs of adjustment ensues, and this is at the heart of Europe's present immobilism.

Why is the development of "new capitalism" and rethinking of the old social contract so much more difficult for Europe than for the US? First, for an obvious reason, because Europe's welfare state is much more extensive, more embedded in ordinary life, and its dismantlement is more socially disruptive. Second, because a low population growth—or in many countries, a decline—necessitates continuing large immigration. But, and this is the crux of the matter, Europe struggles more in absorbing immigrants than the US. Historically, of course, Europe was not a society of immigrants. Europeans were happy to receive foreign workers as long as they would do low-paying jobs and stay out of the way. This quasi-apartheid solution preserved immigrants' culture, which then, most famously in the Netherlands, was found to clash with some European values. Immigrants, more so their daughters and sons, were not happy to remain in subaltern jobs. And while Europe was good about welcoming them to its soccer and basketball teams, it was more stingy when it came allowing them to direct operating rooms or boardrooms.

The bottom line is that Europe needs no less than a social revolution: replacement of its welfare state, and acceptance that Germans, French or Italians of tomorrow will be much darker in their skin color, composed of individuals of various religions, and in many respects indeed a different people. As fusion of Frankish ethnicity and Latin culture created France, a similar Christiano-Islamic and Afro-European fusion may create new European nations, perhaps with a different outlook on life and social norms. No society can accomplish such epochal transformation quickly and painlessly.

Part II

Washington: In the rich world globalization had driven the wedge between social classes, while in the poor world, the main divide is between countries: those that adjusted to globalization and, in many areas, prospered and those that adjusted badly and, in many cases, collapsed.

Indeed the Third World was never a bloc the way that the first and second worlds were. But it was united by its opposition to colonialism and dislike for being used as a battlefield of the two then-dominant ideologies. As the Second World collapsed and globalization took off, the latter rationale evaporated, and a few countries, most notably India and China, accelerated their growth rates significantly, enjoying the fruits of freer trade and larger capital flows. And although these two countries adapted well to globalization, there is little doubt that their newfound relative prosperity opened many new fissure lines. Inequality between coastal and inland provinces, as well as between urban and rural areas, skyrocketed in China. So did, and perhaps by even more, inequality between Southern Indian states, where the hub cities of Mumbai, Chennai and Bangalore are located, and the slow-growing Northeast. For China, which still may face political transition to democracy, widening inequality between different parts of the country, could have disastrous consequences.

But another large group of Third World countries, from Latin America to Africa to former Communist countries, experienced a quarter century of decline or stagnation punctuated by civil wars, international conflicts and the plight of AIDS. While between 1980 and 2002, the rich countries grew, on average, by almost 2 percent per capita annually, the poorest 40 countries in the world had a combined growth rate of zero. For large swaths of Africa where about 200 million people live, the income level today is less than it was during the US presidency of John F. Kennedy.

For these countries the promised benefits of globalization never arrived. The vaunted Washington consensus policies brought no improvement for the masses, but rather a deterioration in the living conditions as key social services became privatized and more costly as was the case, for example, with water privatizations in Cochabamba, Bolivia, and Trinidad, electricity privatization in Argentina and Chad. They were often taken over by foreigners, and to add insult to injury, Western pundits arrived by jets, stayed in luxury hotels and hailed obvious worsening of economic and social conditions as a step toward better lives and international integration. For many people in Latin America and Africa, globalization appeared as new, more attractive label put on the old imperialism, or worse as a form of re-colonization. The left-wing reaction sweeping Latin America, from Mexico to Argentina, is a direct consequence of the fault lines opened by policies that were often designed to benefit Wall Street, not the people in the streets of Lima or Caracas.

Other Third World states—particularly those at the frontline of the battle between communism and capitalism, with ethnic animosities encouraged during the Cold War, efforts by Washington and Moscow to get the upper hand in the conflict—exploded in civil wars and social anomies. That part of the world associates globalization with disappointment (because Washington consensus never delivered), resentment (because others got ahead) and poverty, disease and war. In several sub-Saharan African countries, life expectancy at the turn of the 21st century is not only where it was in Europe almost two centuries ago but is getting worse. In Zimbabwe, between 1995 and 2003, life expectancy declined by 11 years to reach only 39 years.

Ideologies which proposed some economic betterment and offered self-respect to many people in Africa (from Kwame Nkrumah's African socialism to Julius Nyerere's "cooperative economy") and parts of the former Communist bloc (Tito's "labor management") all collapsed and have given way to self-serving oligarchies that justified their policies, not by calling on their own citizens, but by publishing excerpts from reports written by the World Bank and the International Monetary Fund.

In the Third World as a whole, globalization, at best, produced what Tocqueville, with a touch of aristocratic disdain, called a government of the commercially-minded middle classes, "a government without virtue and without greatness"; at worst, it produced governments of plutocrats or elites unconcerned about their own populations. Globalization thus appeared in the poorest and weakest countries at its roughest.

Perhaps the greatest casualty of the money-grubbing global capitalism was loss of self-respect among those who have failed economically—and they are preponderantly located in the poorest countries. The desperate African masses who want to flee their own countries leave not only because incomes are low and prospects bleak, but also because of a lack of confidence that either they or their governments, no matter who is in power, can change life for the better. This despondency and loss of self-respect is indeed a product of globalization. In the past one could feel slighted by fortune for having been born in a poor country, yet have as compensation a belief that other qualities mattered, that one's country offered the world something valuable, a different ideology, a different way of life. But none of that survives today.

The problem was, strangely, noticed by Friedrich Hayek. Market outcomes, Hayek argued, must not be presented as ethically just or unjust because the market is ethically neutral. But to buttress the case for global capitalism, its proponents insist in an almost Calvinist fashion that economic success is not only good in a purely material sense, but reveals some moral superiority. Thus winners are made to feel not only richer but morally superior, and the converse: The losers feel poor and are supposed to be ashamed of their failure. Many people do, but understandably not all take gladly to such judgment.

An interesting coincidence of interests emerges between the desperate masses and the rich in advanced countries. The latter, educated and with considerable property "interests," are, economically, often in favor of greater Third World competitiveness and migration since, either as investors abroad or consumers of cheap labor services at home, they benefit from low-wage labor. This unlikely coincidence of interest lends some superficial justification to the claims of George Bush and Tony Blair that the opponents of free-trade pacts work against the interests of the poor. The problem that the president and the prime minister fail to acknowledge, or perhaps even to realize, is that many of the policies urged by their governments on poor countries in the last two decades have indeed brought people to their current point of desperation.

Sandwiched between this unlikely "coalition" of the global top and the global bottom, are globalization's losers: the lower and middle classes in the West, and those in the "failed" states, not yet sufficiently desperate to board the boats to Europe or cross the US border at night. They too lost in terms of their national sovereignty and personal income. They may not gladly accept, though, that they are morally inferior. At first sight, they do not seem likely to derail globalization because their power is limited. Yet in a more interdependent world with an easy access to deadly weapons, politics of global resentment may find many followers.

BRANKO MILANOVIC is an economist with the Carnegie Endowment for International Peace. Milanovic's most recent book is *Worlds Apart: Measuring International and Global Inequality*.

EXPLORING THE ISSUE

Is Economic Globalization Good for Humankind?

Critical Thinking and Reflection

1. What might be the goals of an economic globalization policy for corporations and nations?
2. How might an economic globalization policy be implemented? Could such a policy be implemented on a global scale?
3. What is the likelihood that an enacted economic globalization policy will lead to anticipated outcomes?
4. What might be the costs to consumers, corporations, and countries of an economic globalization policy?
5. What does the future hold for an economic globalization policy?

Is There Common Ground?

One reason the issue of an economic globalization policy is so contentious is that both sides can easily cite data in support of their position. The underlying balancing act that appears to exist with this particular issue is that of balancing corporate profit motives with socially responsible business practices that truly address various societal needs. While finding common ground on even basic aspects of this topic is difficult, it is anticipated that discussions of an economic globalization policy will continue to be highly charged and ongoing for quite some time.

Additional Resources

Griffin, R. W. & Pustay, M. W. (2010). *International Business*, 6th ed., Prentice Hall.

Nikiforuk, A. (2007). *Pandemonium: How Globalization and Trade Are Putting the World at Risk*, University of Queensland Press.

Investor's Business Daily (2007). "The Backlash Against Globalization."

Stoylarov, G. (2009). "Globalization: Extending the Market and Human Well-Being," *The Freeman*, 59 (3).

Internet References . . .

Strength in Numbers for Globalization's Critics

Elsaeßer, C. (2007). "Strength in Numbers for Globalization's Critics," *Deutch Welle*, September 5.

www.dw-world.de/dw/article /0,2144,2473215,00.html

Findings of *Freedom in the World 2008*—Freedom in Retreat: Is the Tide Turning?

Puddington, A. (2008). "Findings of *Freedom in the World 2008*—Freedom in Retreat: Is the Tide Turning?" Freedom House.org.

www.freedomhouse.org/template .cfm?page=130&year=2008

Selected, Edited, and with Issue Framing Material by:
Kathleen J. Barnes, *William Paterson University*
and
George E. Smith, *University of South Carolina, Beaufort*

ISSUE

Are Protectionist Policies Beneficial to Business?

YES: Ha-Joon Chang, from "Protecting the Global Poor," *Prospect Magazine* (2007)

NO: Robert Krol, from "Trade, Protectionism, and the U.S. Economy: Examining the Evidence," The Cato Institute (2008)

Learning Outcomes
After reading this issue you will be able to: • Understand the positive and negative consequences of protectionist policies on American corporations.   • Understand how protectionist policies can be used as an effective corporate strategy.   • Understand what policies might be implemented to support an effective protectionist corporate strategy.   • Appreciate the practical implications of corporate protectionist strategy use in the workplace.

ISSUE SUMMARY

YES: In support of the idea that protectionist policies help business, Ha-Joon Chang focuses attention on developing industries in poor countries. Further, he describes and advocates historical protectionist policies from around the world.

NO: Robert Krol describes the findings of various economic studies of international trade. The areas that he surveys include the effect of trade on employment and wages as well of the costs of trade restrictions. He concludes that overall the benefits from protectionist policies are overshadowed by their negative effects.

It is understandable that a country would want to take care of its own citizens first. To this end, many countries adopt policies that prop up domestic industries and limit foreign organizations from engaging in business in their country. Generally speaking, such policies are typically labeled "protectionism." A formal definition of protectionism is the "National economic policies designed to restrict free trade and protect domestic industries from foreign competition" (Cavusgil, Knight, and Riesenberger, 2008, p. 620). Protectionist policies include governmental actions such as tariffs (taxes on imported goods), quotas (limits on the amount of goods that can be imported), subsidies (government support of certain domestic businesses or industries), and other policies like the "Buy American" requirements in the United States.

Let's take a look at a couple of broad examples. When foreign competitors in a particular industry operate with a lower cost basis, home governments will frequently provide funds (subsidies) to that industry in their own country to help the domestic

companies compete against foreign competitors. The ultimate goals of such policies are many and may include keeping specific domestic industries competitive, keeping the country's workers employed, and keeping them employed at higher wages than would be the case without subsidies. Another protectionist strategy is to assess tariffs on foreign goods. The addition of the tariff causes foreign competitors to charge higher prices than they would otherwise desire in order to remain profitable.

For a more concrete example, we can look at the U.S. steel industry. To address increasing fears that foreign steelmakers will increase market share in the United States, politicians and U.S. steel industry advocates want to implement economic stimulus legislation requiring that infrastructure projects in the United States use domestic steel (Hardy and Buley, 2009). Further, there is concern that market share increases from foreign competitors will hurt not only the steel industry, but also have negative effects on the environment. Consider the following comments from a union leader in the U.S. steel industry: "In congressional testimony in

March [2009], United Steelworkers boss Leo Gerard explained how unfettered trade in steel would both ship jobs abroad and make the world's pollution worse. Ton for ton, he said, Chinese steel leaves a carbon footprint three times as large as American steel" (Hardy and Buley, 2009).

Although many believe that protectionism may indeed afford some advantages for domestic business, opponents of protectionism argue that due to the interdependence of global trade and financial systems, these advantages are offset by many negative consequences (Kerr, 2009). For instance, an unintended, and unavoidable, consequence of subsidies and tariffs is higher prices for products available to consumers. Protectionist policies also tend to lower the overall quality of goods available and ultimately increase the tax burden on the general public.

Writing in the NO selection for this debate topic, Robert Krol describes the findings of various economic studies of international trade. Krol looks at the effect of trade on employment and wages as well as examining the costs of trade restrictions. From his research, he concludes that "Although international trade forces significant adjustments in an economy, as the evidence shows, the costs of international trade restrictions on the economy outweigh the limited benefits these restrictions bring to import-competing industries" (p. 10).

The opposing view, taken from *Prospect Magazine*, is provided by Ha-Joon Chang, who focuses attention on the benefits of protectionism for infant, or developing industries in poor countries. Chang describes and advocates historical protectionist policies from all around the world. Interestingly, the selection contains many examples taken from the histories of today's wealthiest countries. The point behind this approach is that history shows that for today's poorer nations to succeed, they need to be allowed to adopt regulations that protect their fledgling key industries.

YES ↵

Ha-Joon Chang

Protecting the Global Poor

Once upon a time, the leading car-maker of a developing country exported its first passenger cars to the US. Until then, the company had only made poor copies of cars made by richer countries. The car was just a cheap subcompact ("four wheels and an ashtray") but it was a big moment for the country and its exporters felt proud.

Unfortunately, the car failed. Most people thought it looked lousy, and were reluctant to spend serious money on a family car that came from a place where only second-rate products were made. The car had to be withdrawn from the US. This disaster led to a major debate among the country's citizens. Many argued that the company should have stuck to its original business of making simple textile machinery. After all, the country's biggest export item was silk. If the company could not make decent cars after 25 years of trying, there was no future for it. The government had given the car-maker every chance. It had ensured high profits for it through high tariffs and tough controls on foreign investment. Less than ten years earlier, it had even given public money to save the company from bankruptcy. So, the critics argued, foreign cars should now be let in freely and foreign car-makers, who had been kicked out 20 years before, allowed back again. Others disagreed. They argued that no country had ever got anywhere without developing "serious" industries like car production. They just needed more time.

The year was 1958 and the country was Japan. The company was Toyota, and the car was called the Toyopet. Toyota started out as a manufacturer of textile machinery and moved into car production in 1933. The Japanese government kicked out General Motors and Ford in 1939, and bailed out Toyota with money from the central bank in 1949. Today, Japanese cars are considered as "natural" as Scottish salmon or French wine, but less than 50 years ago, most people, including many Japanese, thought the Japanese car industry simply should not exist.

Half a century after the Toyopet debacle, Toyota's luxury brand Lexus has become an icon of globalisation, thanks to the American journalist Thomas Friedman's book *The Lexus and the Olive Tree*. The book owes its title to an epiphany that Friedman had in Japan in 1992. He had paid a visit to a Lexus factory, which deeply impressed him. On the bullet train back to Tokyo, he read yet another newspaper article about the troubles in the middle east, where he had been a correspondent. Then it hit him. He realised that "half the world seemed

to be . . . intent on building a better Lexus, dedicated to modernising, streamlining and privatising their economies in order to thrive in the system of globalisation. And half of the world—sometimes half the same country, sometimes half the same person—was still caught up in the fight over who owns which olive tree."

According to Friedman, countries in the olive-tree world will not be able to join the Lexus world unless they fit themselves into a particular set of economic policies he calls "the golden straitjacket." In describing the golden straitjacket, Friedman pretty much sums up today's neoliberal orthodoxy: countries should privatise state-owned enterprises, maintain low inflation, reduce the size of government, balance the budget, liberalise trade, deregulate foreign investment and capital markets, make the currency convertible, reduce corruption and privatise pensions. The golden straitjacket, Friedman argues, is the only clothing suitable for the harsh but exhilarating game of globalisation.

However, had the Japanese government followed the free-trade economists back in the early 1960s, there would have been no Lexus. Toyota today would at best be a junior partner to a western car manufacturer and Japan would have remained the third-rate industrial power it was in the 1960s—on the same level as Chile, Argentina and South Africa.

Had it just been Japan that became rich through the heretical policies of protection, subsidies and the restriction of foreign investment, the free-market champions might be able to dismiss it as the exception that proves the rule. But Japan is no exception. Practically all of today's developed countries, including Britain and the US, the supposed homes of the free market and free trade, have become rich on the basis of policy recipes that contradict today's orthodoxy.

In 1721, Robert Walpole, the first British prime minister, launched an industrial programme that protected and nurtured British manufacturers against superior competitors in the Low Countries, then the centre of European manufacturing. Walpole declared that "nothing so much contributes to promote the public wellbeing as the exportation of manufactured goods and the importation of foreign raw material." Between Walpole's time and the 1840s, when Britain started to reduce its tariffs (although it did not move to free trade until the 1860s), Britain's average industrial tariff rate was in the region of 40–50 percent, compared with 20 percent and 10 percent in France and Germany, respectively.

The US followed the British example. In fact, the first systematic argument that new industries in relatively backward economies need protection before they can compete with their foreign rivals—known as the "infant industry" argument—was developed by the first US treasury secretary, Alexander Hamilton. In 1789, Hamilton proposed a series of measures to achieve the industrialisation of his country, including protective tariffs, subsidies, import liberalisation of industrial inputs (so it wasn't blanket protection for everything), patents for inventions and the development of the banking system.

Hamilton was perfectly aware of the potential pitfalls of infant industry protection, and cautioned against taking these policies too far. He knew that just as some parents are overprotective, governments can cosset infant industries too much. And in the way that some children manipulate their parents into supporting them beyond childhood, there are industries that prolong government protection through clever lobbying. But the existence of dysfunctional families is hardly an argument against parenting itself. Likewise, the examples of bad protectionism merely tell us that the policy needs to be used wisely.

In recommending an infant industry programme for his young country, Hamilton, an impudent 35-year-old finance minister with only a liberal arts degree from a then second-rate college (King's College of New York, now Columbia University) was openly ignoring the advice of the world's most famous economist, Adam Smith. Like most European economists at the time, Smith advised the Americans not to develop manufacturing. He argued that any attempt to "stop the importation of European manufactures" would "obstruct . . . the progress of their country towards real wealth and greatness."

Many Americans—notably Thomas Jefferson, secretary of state at the time and Hamilton's arch-enemy—disagreed with Hamilton. They argued that it was better to import high-quality manufactured products from Europe with the proceeds that the country earned from agricultural exports than to try to produce second-rate manufactured goods. As a result, Congress only half-heartedly accepted Hamilton's recommendations—raising the average tariff rate from 5 percent to 12.5 percent.

In 1804, Hamilton was killed in a duel by the then vice-president Aaron Burr. Had he lived for another decade or so, he would have seen his programme adopted in full. Following the Anglo-American war in 1812, the US started shifting to a protectionist policy; by the 1820s, its average industrial tariff had risen to 40 percent. By the 1830s, America's average industrial tariff rate was the highest in the world and, except for a few brief periods, remained so until the second world war, at which point its manufacturing supremacy was absolute.

Britain and the US were not the only practitioners of infant industry protection. Virtually all of today's rich countries used policy measures to protect and nurture their infant industries. Even when the overall level of protection was relatively low, some strategic sectors could get very high protection. For example, in the late 19th and early 20th centuries, Germany, while maintaining a relatively moderate average industrial tariff rate (5–15 percent), accorded strong protection to industries like iron and steel. During the same period, Sweden provided high protection to its emerging engineering industries, although its average tariff rate was 15–20 percent. In the first half of the 20th century, Belgium maintained moderate levels of overall protection but heavily protected key textile sectors and the iron industry.

Tariffs were not the only tool of trade policy used by rich countries. When deemed necessary for the protection of infant industries, they banned imports or imposed import quotas. They also gave export subsidies—sometimes to all exports (Japan and Korea) but often to specific items (in the 18th century, Britain gave export subsidies to gunpowder, sailcloth, refined sugar and silk). Some of them also gave a rebate on the tariffs paid on the imported industrial inputs used for manufacturing export goods, in order to encourage such exports. Many believe that this measure was invented in Japan in the 1950s, but it was in fact invented in Britain in the 17th century.

It is not just in the realm of trade that the historical records of today's rich countries burst the bindings of Friedman's golden straitjacket. The history of controls on foreign investment tells a similar story. In the 19th century, the US placed restrictions on foreign investment in banking, shipping, mining and logging. The restrictions were particularly severe in banking; throughout the 19th century, non-resident shareholders could not even vote in a shareholders' meeting and only American citizens could become directors in a national (as opposed to state) bank.

Some countries went further than the US. Japan closed off most industries to foreign investment and imposed 49 percent ownership ceilings on the others until the 1970s. Korea basically followed this model until it was forced to liberalise after the 1997 financial crisis. Between the 1930s and the 1980s, Finland officially classified all firms with more than 20 percent foreign ownership as "dangerous enterprises." It was not that these countries were against foreign companies per se—after all, Korea actively courted foreign investment in export processing zones. They restricted foreign investors because they believed—rightly in my view—that there is nothing like learning how to do something yourself, even if it takes more time and effort.

The wealthy nations of today may support the privatisation of state-owned enterprises in developing countries, but many of them built their industries through state ownership. At the beginning of their industrialisation, Germany and Japan set up state-owned enterprises in key industries—textiles, steel and shipbuilding. In France, the reader may be surprised to learn that many household names—like Renault (cars), Alcatel (telecoms equipment), Thomson (electronics) and Elf Aquitaine (oil and gas)—have been state-owned enterprises. Finland, Austria and Norway also developed their industries through extensive state ownership after the second world war. Taiwan has achieved its economic "miracle" with a state sector more than one-and-a-half times the size of the international average, while Singapore's state sector is one of the largest in the world, and includes world-class companies like Singapore Airlines.

Of course, there were exceptions. The Netherlands and pre-first world war Switzerland did not adopt many tariffs or subsidies. But they did deviate from today's free-market orthodoxy in another, very important way—they refused to protect patents. Switzerland did not have patents until 1888 and did not protect chemical inventions until 1907. The Netherlands abolished its 1817 patent law in 1869, on the grounds that patents created artificial monopolies that went against the principle of free competition. It did not reintroduce a patent law until 1912, by which time Philips was firmly established as a leading producer of lightbulbs, whose production technology it "borrowed" from Thomas Edison.

Even countries that did have patent laws were lax about protecting intellectual property (IP) rights—especially those of foreigners. In most countries, including Britain, Austria, France and the US, patenting of imported inventions was explicitly allowed in the 19th century.

Despite this history of protection, subsidy and state ownership, the rich countries have been recommending to, or even forcing upon, developing countries policies that go directly against their own historical experience. For the past 25 years, rich countries have imposed trade liberalisation on many developing countries through IMF and World Bank loan conditions, as well as the conditions attached to their direct aid. The World Trade Organisation (WTO) does allow some tariff protection, especially for the poorest developing countries, but most developing countries have had to significantly reduce tariffs and other trade restrictions. Most subsidies have been banned by the WTO—except, of course, the ones that rich countries still use, such as on agriculture, and research and development. And while, of course, no poor country is obliged to accept foreign inward investment (and most receive none or very little), the IMF and the World Bank are always lobbying for more liberal foreign investment rules. The WTO has also tightened IP laws, asking all but the poorest developing countries to comply with US standards—which even many Americans consider excessive.

Why are they doing this? In 1841, Friedrich List, a German economist, criticised Britain for preaching free trade to other countries when she had achieved her economic supremacy through tariffs and subsidies. He accused the British of "kicking away the ladder" that they had climbed to reach the world's top economic position. Today, there are certainly some people in rich countries who preach free trade to poor countries in order to capture larger shares of the latter's markets and to pre-empt the emergence of possible competitors. They are saying, "Do as we say, not as we did," and act as bad samaritans, taking advantage of others in trouble. But what is more worrying is that many of today's free traders do not realise that they are hurting the developing countries with their policies. History is written by the victors, and it is human nature to reinterpret the past from the point of view of the present. As a result, the rich countries have gradually, if often sub-consciously, rewritten their own histories to make them more consistent with how they see themselves today, rather than as they really were.

But the truth is that free traders make the lives of those whom they are trying to help more difficult. The evidence for this is everywhere. Despite adopting supposedly "good" policies, like liberal foreign trade and investment and strong patent protection, many developing countries have actually been performing rather badly over the last two and a half decades. The annual per capita growth rate of the developing world has halved in this period, compared to the "bad old days" of protectionism and government intervention in the 1960s and the 1970s. Even this modest rate has been achieved only because the average includes China and India—two fast-growing giants, which have gradually liberalised their economies but have resolutely refused to put on Thomas Friedman's golden straitjacket.

Growth failure has been particularly noticeable in Latin America and Africa, where orthodox neoliberal programmes were implemented more thoroughly than in Asia. In the 1960s and the 1970s, per capita income in Latin America grew at 3.1 percent a year, slightly faster than the developing-country average. Brazil especially was growing almost as fast as the east Asian "miracle" economies. Since the 1980s, however, when the continent embraced neoliberalism, Latin America has been growing at less than a third of this rate. Even if we discount the 1980s as a decade of adjustment and look at the 1990s, we find that per capita income in the region grew at around half the rate of the "bad old days" (3.1 percent vs 1.7 percent). Between 2000 and 2005, the region has done even worse; it virtually stood still, with per capita income growing at only 0.6 percent a year. As for Africa, its per capita income grew relatively slowly even in the 1960s and the 1970s (1–2 percent a year). But since the 1980s, the region has seen a fall in living standards. There are, of course, many reasons for this failure, but it is nonetheless a damning indictment of the neoliberal orthodoxy, because most of the African economies have been practically run by the IMF and the World Bank over the past quarter of a century.

In pushing for free-market policies that make life more difficult for poor countries, the bad samaritans frequently deploy the rhetoric of the "level playing field." They argue that developing countries should not be allowed to use extra policy tools for protection, subsidies and regulation, as these constitute unfair competition. Who can disagree?

Well, we all should, if we want to build an international system that promotes economic development. A level playing field leads to unfair competition when the players are unequal. Most sports have strict separation by age and gender, while boxing, wrestling and weightlifting have weight classes, which are often divided very finely. How is it that we think a bout between people with more than a couple of kilos' weight difference is unfair, and yet we accept that the US and Honduras should compete economically on equal terms?

Global economic competition is a game of unequal players. It pits against each other countries that range from Switzerland to Swaziland. Consequently, it is only fair that we "tilt the playing field" in favour of the weaker countries. In practice, this means allowing them to protect and subsidise their producers more vigorously, and to put stricter regulations on foreign investment. These countries should also be allowed to protect IP rights less stringently, so that they can "borrow" ideas from richer countries. This will have the added benefit of making economic growth in poor countries more compatible with the need to fight global warming, as rich-country technologies tend to be far more energy-efficient.

I am not against markets, international trade or globalisation. And I acknowledge that WTO agreements contain "special and differential treatment" provisions which give poor country members certain rights, and which permit rich countries to treat developing countries more favourably than other rich WTO members. But these provisions are limited and generally just give poor countries longer time periods to liberalise their economic rules. The default position remains blind faith in indiscriminate free trade.

The best way to illustrate my general point is to look at my own native Korea—or, rather, to contrast the two bits that used to be one country until 1948. It is hard to believe today, but northern Korea used to be richer than the south. Japan developed the north industrially when it ruled the country from 1910–45. Even after the Japanese left, North Korea's industrial legacy enabled it to maintain its economic lead over South Korea well into the 1960s.

Today, South Korea is one of the world's industrial power-houses while North Korea languishes in poverty. Much of this is thanks to the fact that South Korea aggressively traded with the outside world and actively absorbed foreign technologies while North Korea pursued its doctrine of self-sufficiency. Through trade, South Korea learned about the existence of better technologies and earned the foreign currency to buy them. In its own way, North Korea has managed some technological feats. For example, it figured out a way to mass-produce vinalon, a synthetic fibre made out of limestone and anthracite, which has allowed it to be self-sufficient in clothing. But, overall, North Korea is technologically stuck in the past, with 1940s Japanese and 1950s Soviet technologies, while South Korea is one of the most technologically dynamic economies in the world.

In the end, economic development is about mastering advanced technologies. In theory, a country can develop such technologies on its own, but technological self-sufficiency quickly hits the wall, as seen in the North Korean case. This is why all successful cases of economic development have involved serious attempts to get hold of advanced foreign technologies. But in order to be able to import technologies from developed countries, developing nations need foreign currency to pay for them. Some of this foreign currency may be provided through foreign aid, but most has to be earned through exports. Without trade, therefore, there will be little technological progress and thus little economic development.

But there is a huge difference between saying that trade is essential for economic development and saying that free trade is best. It is this sleight of hand that free-trade economists have so effectively deployed against their opponents—if you are against free trade, they imply, you must be against trade itself, and so against economic progress.

As South Korea—together with Britain, the US, Japan, Taiwan and many others—shows, active participation in international trade does not require free trade. In the early stages of their development, these countries typically had tariff rates in the region of 30–50 percent. Likewise, the Korean experience shows that actively absorbing foreign technologies does not require a liberal foreign investment policy.

Indeed, had South Korea donned Friedman's golden straitjacket in the 1960s, it would still be exporting raw materials like tungsten ore and seaweed. The secret of its success lay in a mix of protection and open trade, of government regulation and free(ish) market, of active courting of foreign investment and draconian regulation of it, and of private enterprise and state control—with the areas of protection constantly changing as new infant industries were developed and old ones became internationally competitive. This is how almost all of today's rich countries became rich, and it is at the root of almost all recent success stories in the developing world.

Therefore, if they are genuinely to help developing countries develop through trade, wealthy countries need to accept asymmetric protectionism, as they used to between the 1950s and the 1970s. The global economic system should support the efforts of developing countries by allowing them to use more freely the tools of infant industry promotion—such as tariff protection, subsidies, foreign investment regulation and weak IP rights.

There are huge benefits from global integration if it is done in the right way, at the right speed. But if poor countries open up prematurely, the result will be negative. Globalisation is too important to be left to free-trade economists, whose policy advice has so ill served the developing world in the past 25 years.

HA-JOON CHANG *is one of the leading heterodox economists and institutional economists specializing in development economics. Currently a reader in the political economy of development at the University of Cambridge, Chang is the author of several widely discussed policy books, most notably 2002's* Kicking Away the Ladder: Development Strategy in Historical Perspective.

Robert Krol

 **NO**

Trade, Protectionism, and the U.S. Economy: Examining the Evidence

Introduction

America's trade with the rest of the world expanded significantly after World War II. U.S. goods (exports plus imports) increased from 9.2 percent of gross domestic product in 1960 to 28.6 percent in 2007. This expansion of international trade has benefited the United States and its trading partners considerably. The benefits include a higher standard of living, lower prices for consumers, improved efficiency in production, and a greater variety of goods.

The expansion of international trade raises concerns about the impact on domestic firms. In particular, many people fear that international trade reduces job opportunities for workers and depresses wages. These fears create political support for protectionist policies. However, international trade restrictions are costly to consumers as well as producers.

A recent survey found that 59 percent of Americans have a favorable view of international trade, although survey trends also indicate that a growing number of Americans now view international trade less favorably. When asked about their attitudes concerning the expansion of U.S. trade relations with the rest of the world, 36 percent thought it was "somewhat bad" or "very bad" in 2007 compared with 18 percent in 2002.

In this presidential election year, interest in the international trade views of the likely Democratic and Republican nominees is high. A meaningful way to determine the candidates' thinking on international trade is to look at their legislative voting records.

According to the Cato Institute's Center for Trade Policy Studies, Republican Sen. John McCain (R-AZ) voted against trade restrictions 88 percent of the time over his career. He is classified as a free trader based on his voting record. Sen. Barack Obama (D-IL) voted against trade barriers only 36 percent of the time. Clearly, the outcome of the November election could significantly affect future U.S. trade policy. Whether the United States continues to promote free trade will depend in part on who is elected president.

Opinion surveys and congressional voting records suggest Americans disagree strongly about the costs and benefits of international trade. This paper reviews empirical studies that examine the evidence on how international trade affects the economy. The goal of this paper is to discuss the evidence with respect to four important areas of international trade: the causes of expanded international trade, the benefits of trade, the impact of trade on employment and wages, and the cost of international trade restrictions.

The following points summarize the evidence from a survey of major research in the field:

- Comparative advantage remains the major driver of global trade flows.
- Income growth accounts for two-thirds of the growth in global trade in recent decades, trade liberalization accounts for one-quarter, and lower transportation costs make up the remainder.
- Trade expansion has fueled faster growth and raised incomes in countries that have liberalized. A 1-percentage-point gain in trade as a share of the economy raises per capita income by 1 percent. Global elimination of all barriers to trade in goods and services would raise global income by $2 trillion and U.S. income by almost $500 billion.
- Competition from trade delivers lower prices and more product variety to consumers. Americans are $300 billion better off today than they would be otherwise because of the greater product variety from imports.
- International trade directly affects only 15 percent of the U.S. workforce. Most job displacement occurs in sectors that are not engaged in global competition.
- While trade has probably caused a net loss of manufacturing jobs since 1979, those losses have been more than offset by employment gains in other sectors of the economy. Net payroll employment in the United States has grown by 36 million in the past two decades, along with a dramatic increase in imports of goods and services.
- Growing levels of trade do not explain most of the growing gap between wages earned by skilled and unskilled workers. The relative decline in unskilled wages is mainly caused by technological changes that reward greater skills. Demand for unskilled workers has been in relative decline

in all sectors of the economy, not just those exposed to trade.

- Trade barriers impose large, net costs on the U.S. economy. The cost to the economy per job saved in protected industries far exceeds the wages paid to workers in those jobs.
- Protectionism persists because small, homogeneous, and concentrated interests are better able to lobby the government than the large, heterogeneous, and dispersed mass of consumers.

Why Countries Trade

Comparative advantage remains the basis of international trade. Differences in production costs within countries determine much of the flow of goods and services across international borders. Economists use the term "comparative advantage" to indicate that a country has a cost advantage in producing certain goods relative to other goods that could be produced within that same country. In other words, what spurs trade and specialization is not the absolute cost advantage that one country's producers have over their competitors in another country, but the relative advantage they have compared to other sectors within their own country.

Consider the example of a more-developed Country A and a less-developed Country B. Country A may be able to produce t-shirts twice as efficiently as Country B; but if it can produce computers 10 times more efficiently, it will make economic sense for Country A to specialize in producing and exporting computers while importing t-shirts from Country B. Trade allows both countries to direct their internal resources—principally labor and capital—to those sectors where they are relatively more productive compared to other sectors in the domestic economy.

Comparative advantage can spring from multiple sources. A country can have a cost advantage in the production of a particular good because of superior production technology. This superiority can include better ways to organize the production process or a climate that allows the country to grow certain crops, such as bananas and mangos, more cheaply. It can also include greater investments in skilled labor and equipment that can result in a comparative advantage in such areas as computer software.

The United States has proportionately more skilled labor than unskilled labor compared with most countries. This makes the United States the low-cost producer for goods that rely on skilled labor and sophisticated machinery. Therefore, the United States exports high-tech manufactured goods that can be produced using relatively more skilled labor and imports shoes and apparel that are produced using a large amount of unskilled labor.

However, sometimes trade involves similar goods. For example, the United States both exports and imports golf clubs. This type of trade occurs in markets where businesses differentiate their products and experience declining average costs as production expands. In this setting, opening an economy to international trade increases the size of the market. Average costs fall, resulting in lower prices and a wider array of products being sold in each of the trading countries. Consumers can select from products produced by domestic as well as foreign firms. Lower prices and greater variety increase consumer welfare.

Global trade has expanded significantly since World War II for a number of reasons, including lower transportation and information costs, higher per capita income, and changes in government policies. The containerization of shipping has reduced loading times, improving efficiency, just as less expensive air transportation has increased international trade in perishable items. Improvements in information technology have made it less costly for consumers to determine the characteristics of products produced abroad. Information technology has also made it easier for producers to assess consumer preferences, allowing better customization of products and services for buyers in foreign markets. Income growth in developed countries and even in some less-developed countries has increased the demand for goods and services produced domestically as well as from abroad. Finally, trade restrictions have decreased significantly since World War II.

Evidence is now available that quantifies the relative contribution of these different factors to the growth of world trade. Scott Baier and Jeffrey Bergstrand attribute 67 percent of the increase in international trade to income growth, another 25 percent to tariff reductions, and the remaining 8 percent to falling transportation costs. Critics of trade blame trade agreements for spurring global competition, when in fact most trade growth simply stems from rising global incomes. A reversion to protectionism would not necessarily stop the growth of global trade, but it would sacrifice the considerable economic benefits of more open competition.

Benefits from International Trade

Since World War II, multilateral and unilateral tariff negotiations have reduced barriers to international trade. Several attempts have been made to quantify the resulting welfare gains to consumers and producers. In brief, trade leads to specialization based on comparative advantage, which lowers production costs, allowing for greater levels of output and, therefore, consumption. Individuals are able to purchase products at lower prices, resulting in higher real incomes and a higher standard of living. In addition, trade allows countries to import products that embody new technologies which are not produced at home.

One way to assess the gains from international trade is to compare the level of welfare (measured imperfectly by real per capita GDP) before and after trade restrictions are dropped. A dramatic example of this type of trade reform occurred in Japan during the early 1850s. For 200 years up until then, Japan had almost no economic or cultural contact with other countries. Then the Japanese government signed a treaty with the United States that was designed to shift the country from a no-trade to a free-trade regime in seven years. Daniel Bernhofen and John Brown estimate that, with the increase in international trade, Japan's real GDP was 8 percent higher by the end of the seven-year period than if the economy had remained closed. Furthermore, by opening its economy to the rest of the world, Japan was able to import capital goods, new technologies, and new production methods that promoted faster economic growth and even higher living standards over time.

In another historical episode, the United States closed its borders to international trade in 1807 when President Thomas Jefferson imposed a trade embargo to avoid conflicts with the warring British and French navies. Dartmouth economist Douglas Irwin estimates the embargo reduced U.S. GDP by about 5 percent in one year. Jefferson quickly ended the embargo because of the high economic cost it imposed on the country.

Research economists have used computer models of the economy to capture the industry adjustments and aggregate GDP gains from trade liberalization. Work by Drusilla Brown, Alan Deardorff, and Robert Stern represents this type of study. They estimate that a one-third reduction in agricultural, manufacturing, and service-sector trade restrictions worldwide would increase world GDP by $686 billion (measured in 1995 dollars) over a prereduction baseline. In the United States, GDP would rise 1.8 percent. If all trade barriers were eliminated, world GDP would increase by more than $2 trillion and U.S. GDP would be $497 billion, or 4.8 percent, higher than before liberalization.

Although the association between free trade and prosperity has been well documented, the correlation between international trade and increased per capita income has been difficult to illustrate—perhaps because countries with higher per capita income choose to trade more. In a well-known study, Jeffrey Frankel and David Romer examined the relationship between international trade and per capita income using 1985 data for a large cross-section of countries. To deal with the causality issue, Frankel and Romer used geographic variables correlated with international trade but not per capita income. This approach isolates the portion of international trade not caused by growth in per capita income. They found that, as the share of exports-plus-imports to GDP rises by 1 percentage point, per capita income increases by 2 percentage points.

However, Frankel and Romer's work has been criticized because the geographic variables they used may be correlated with other geographic factors that influence GDP. For example, distance from the equator correlates with per capita income, possibly invalidating the results. Marta Noguer and Marc Siscart used an improved specification to reestimate the relationship. Controlling for distance from the equator, they found that a 1-percentage-point increase in trade share raises per capita income by 1 percentage point. Noguer and Siscart concluded that trade does indeed raise a country's standard of living.

More recently, Romain Wacziarg and Karen Horn Welch examined the relationship between trade and economic growth for 133 countries over most of the post–World War II period. Using country case studies and trade policy indicators, they identified the year countries in the study liberalized their trade policies. They found that, on average, countries grew 1.5 percentage points faster per year following trade liberalization during the period 1950 to 1998. Focusing on a subgroup of countries that had at least eight years of data before and after liberalization, they found 54 percent of these countries grew faster. Of the remaining countries examined, 21 percent did not experience faster growth while 25 percent of the countries grew more slowly.

Wacziarg and Welch found that the countries that experienced faster economic growth maintained their liberalization polices while the others did not. Also, some of the countries that did not grow faster following trade liberalization experienced political instability and restrictive macroeconomic policies that hindered growth in the post-trade-liberalization period. Obviously, trade liberalization alone is not always enough to overcome other factors inhibiting growth.

Economists have also turned to individual factory-level data to better understand the connection between international trade and a country's standard of living. Looking at U.S. manufacturing data from 1987 to 1997, Andrew Bernard, J. Bradford Jensen, and Peter Schott found that a one-standard-deviation decrease in tariffs and transportation costs increased productivity growth by 0.2 percentage points per year, primarily as a result of a shift in production from low- to high-productivity plants. Many low-productivity plants closed. At the same time, however, exports from plants already exporting increased, and high-productivity plants that previously produced only for the domestic market entered the export market.

Daniel Trefler found productivity gains of 1.9 percent per year in Canadian manufacturing following the implementation of the 1989 free trade agreement with the United States. Average manufacturing employment fell by 5 percent in the seven years following the agreement. Those job losses were disproportionally in manufacturing plants that received the greatest tariff protection prior to the trade agreement. However, employment growth in more efficient manufacturing plants helped to reemploy displaced workers over time. These studies show that the short-run adjustment costs and job displacement associated with the closing of inefficient plants can be offset by greater productivity and higher standards of living in the longer-run.

These estimates of the gains from international trade probably underestimate the improvement in well-being that increased trade brings. Moving to freer international trade also increases the variety of goods and services individuals can choose from. If consumers value variety, then welfare improves in an open economy. This welfare gain may not show up in income data, but it does make people better off. In addition, greater variety in intermediate capital goods benefits producers. Better intermediate goods improve efficiency and speed productivity growth, resulting in a higher standard of living for workers.

Christian Broda and David Weinstein examined the benefits of greater import variety in the United States over the period 1972 to 2001. They estimated that the variety of international goods imported into the United States tripled over the period. One traditional measure of the welfare gain from international trade is the decline in prices as measured by an import price index. However, Broda and Weinstein point out that the United States' import price index is not adjusted for changes in variety. If greater variety increases a consumer's satisfaction and standard of living without raising prices, then consumers should be able to achieve the same level of welfare while spending less. When Broda and Weinstein adjusted the U.S. import price index for changes in variety, they estimated the U.S. welfare gain from a greater variety of imports to be approximately 2.8 percent of GDP, or $300 billion per year.

These empirical studies provide evidence that international trade raises income and productivity. They also show that the greater product variety brought about by expanding international trade improves welfare.

Trade's Effect on Employment

People concerned about trade worry that gains in productivity and product variety come at the expense of domestic employment. Yet, the evidence shows little relationship between greater imports and any change in aggregate employment. Over the past 20 years, U.S. *aggregate* net employment has increased from 102 million jobs to nearly 138 million jobs, while imports of goods and services have gone from a little over $500 billion to $2.35 trillion. As shown in Figure 1, employment tends to rise along with imports. Demographic trends, worker education and skill levels, labor-market regulations, and business-cycle developments—not trade—are the dominant factors influencing the overall level of employment and the unemployment rate in the U.S. economy.

International trade does have distributive effects. Although the country as a whole is better off, individual groups of workers or industries may be worse off. This occurs because, once a country opens itself up to international trade, import prices fall because of greater competition and export prices rise because producers can sell to a larger global market. Domestic production of import-competing goods contracts while production in export industries expands, changing the real earnings of inputs employed in these sectors.

What are the implications for the United States? As noted earlier, the United States exports goods that use relatively more skilled labor and imports goods that use relatively more unskilled labor. As the economy adjusts to changing trade patterns, the demand for skilled labor increases and the demand for unskilled labor decreases. Thus, as the United States opens its economy to greater international trade, real wages of skilled labor rise relative to the real wages of unskilled labor. Making matters more difficult for unskilled laborors, displaced workers may also experience a period of unemployment before they find a new job.

Researchers who investigate the impact of international trade on employment and wages find that, despite public rhetoric, international trade has a relatively small impact on wages and employment in the United States. Growth in wage inequality over the last 25 years has apparently been driven more by technological change than international trade.

Two facts shed some light on this general conclusion. First, international trade directly affects only 15 percent of the U.S. workforce. This suggests that international competition is an issue for

Figure 1

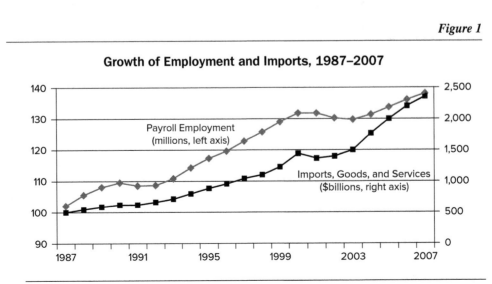

Growth of Employment and Imports, 1987–2007

Sources: Economic Report of the President, 2008; Bureau of Labor Statistics, and U.S. Department of Commerce.

only a minority of workers. Second, high rates of job loss occur in sectors of the economy that are not engaged in international trade, indicating that factors other than international trade play an important role in labor-market disruptions.

In addition, the decline in employment in the manufacturing sector has been driven primarily by greater labor productivity rather than by growth in international trade. The net employment impact of international trade on manufacturing is small because the United States is both an importer and exporter of manufactured goods.

In a series of studies, Lori Kletzer examined the impact of increased imports on gross U.S. industry employment. For industries most affected by imports, she estimated 7.45 million *gross* manufacturing jobs were lost between 1979 and 2001, or 28,219 per month. This represents a loss of 15 percent of all manufacturing jobs during the 22-year period.

Kletzer points out that data limitations make it difficult to determine if displaced workers have lost their jobs because of imports or for some other reason. Other factors, such as changes in technology or consumer tastes, can also result in job loss. For example, high labor-productivity growth has resulted in a long-run decline in manufacturing jobs—independent of foreign competition. These studies also ignore the jobs created from exporting or from the lower business costs that result from imports, which can expand employment in other sectors.

The more important finding is the *net* effect of imports and exports on employment. Economists at the Federal Reserve Bank of New York have estimated the number of workers needed to produce U.S. goods—imports and exports—with the difference representing the net number of jobs gained or lost in the goods sector because of international trade. Because imports are greater than exports, the calculation shows a net loss in jobs from trade. For the period 1997–2003, they found that net job loss from trade averaged 40,000 per month, or 2.4 percent of total employment. However, the study does not capture employment gains in other sectors, like services, which result from access to lower cost inputs and new technology embedded in imports. It is important to recognize that total net employment in the United States increased by 7.2 million jobs over this period, which indicates that job creation in nonmanufacturing sectors more than offset job losses in manufacturing.

Trade's Impact on Wages

A more contentious labor-market issue concerns the increase in wages of skilled workers relative to unskilled workers. Is this trend the result of changes in information technology, or is international trade to blame? Most studies conclude that international trade has played only a modest role in rising wage inequality. The empirical evidence suggests that skill-biased technological change has had a bigger impact.

First, the demand for skilled labor has increased relative to the demand for unskilled labor in most industries, even those not heavily engaged in international trade. If international trade were driving this trend, we would not observe high relative demand for skilled labor in all sectors, or in sectors that do not engage in significant international trade.

If international trade was driving the growing wage inequality between skilled and unskilled workers, then import prices of unskilled-labor-intensive goods should be declining over time and export prices of skilled-labor-intensive goods should be rising over time as trade expands. That is, import prices should decline as we replace higher-cost, domestically produced products with similar products produced at lower cost from countries that have a comparative advantage in those items. Similarly, export prices should be higher in foreign markets because those markets tend to be high-cost producers of the products we export due to our comparative advantage. Using aggregate export and import price indices, Robert Lawrence and Matthew Slaughter found this not to be the case over the 1979 to 1991 period. Their result is consistent with many (though not all) studies that take this approach. A few studies did find a shift in relative international prices in the 1970s, but they still concluded that the relative wage change was driven primarily by technological change rather than shifting international prices.

More recently, using a similar approach for the period 1981 to 2006, Robert Lawrence found a 12 percentage-point decline in the ratio of blue- to white-collar compensation which he attributed to greater international trade. Most of the decline occurred during the 1980s, a period of fairly stable import-to-export price ratios. The evidence from the 1980s is inconsistent with the theory that international trade is the primary driver of greater wage inequality.

Robert Feenstra and Gary Hanson argue that the outsourcing of less-skilled jobs does reduce demand for unskilled workers in the United States (lowering relative wages), but it is not the primary cause. They examined the impact of this type of outsourcing for 435 U.S. manufacturing industries from 1972 to 1990. For the 1972–1979 period, they found that changes in wage inequality were not related to outsourcing. For the 1979–1990 period, outsourcing appeared to explain about 15 percent of the increased wage inequality, while the introduction of computers explained 35 percent.

Expanding international trade can influence employment patterns and relative wages in an economy. The evidence reviewed in this paper indicates that trade is not the primary source of U.S. job displacement or wage inequality. Technological change and faster productivity growth play the dominant role in these developments.

Cost of Protectionism

Countries can influence international trade by using tariffs and quotas. The purpose of an import tariff is to reduce imports and expand domestic production in the protected industry. With higher output, industry profits and employment expand. However, that expansion comes at a cost. Domestic consumers pay more for products, and domestic resources are used less efficiently. Downstream industries that would use imported products as an input face higher costs, lowering output and employment in those industries.

Gary Hufbauer and Kimberly Elliott examined the welfare gains from the elimination of tariffs and other quantitative restrictions in 21 major sectors of the U.S. economy in the 1980s. Perhaps the most interesting and striking result they reported is their calculation of the consumer gains per job lost if the United States were to eliminate tariffs on an industry. They estimated the dollar cost savings for consumers relative to the total number of jobs lost due to the elimination of an international trade restriction. The average for all 21 sectors was $168,520 per job annually—far higher than the annual earnings of an individual worker. The dollar cost savings ranged from a high of more than $1 million per job in the ball bearings industry to a low of $96,532 per job in costume jewelry. For the sugar sector, the figure was $600,177 per job. For each job "saved," consumers paid three times the average wage in manufacturing. In other words, trade restrictions impose costs on consumers three times the gain to protected workers.

Why do these costly international trade restrictions remain in place? The simple explanation is that the benefits from these types of policies are concentrated in the affected labor force while the costs are spread out over the entire population of consumers.

Producers tend to be a small, relatively homogeneous group. Often they are geographically concentrated. As a result, the costs per person associated with organizing and lobbying for protection from imports are low. Because they form a small group, the benefits per person (higher profits and wages) from import protection are high. The benefit-cost ratio or payoff associated with lobbying government officials is high. Producers and workers find it worthwhile to organize in order to place political pressure on governments for protection from imports. Since elected officials are interested in reelection, they respond by providing protection in exchange for political support.

For consumers, the benefit-cost ratio per person is low. Consumers are a large, geographically diverse, heterogeneous group. As a result, the costs of organizing to lobby against international trade restrictions are high. Furthermore, although the total cost to consumers of these restrictions is high, the cost is typically low on a per-person basis. The benefit-cost ratio or payoff associated with lobbying elected officials is low. Consumers are less likely to expend the resources needed to generate political action in their favor. For example, in the sugar industry the benefits per producer for import

restrictions are more than $500,000 per year. For sugar consumers, although the total costs are high, the per-person cost comes to only $5 per year. Not surprisingly, sugar producers actively lobby for import protection and sugar consumers take few steps to oppose it, despite the high total cost to consumers.

Conclusion

International trade has expanded dramatically since World War II. Recent polls and political rhetoric suggest support for continued trade liberalization may be waning—and that is of concern. A movement away from the relatively open global trading system that is currently in place would impose significant economic costs on the United States and the rest of the world.

This paper has provided a comprehensive review of the important empirical studies that quantify the impact of trade on the economy. The evidence is clear: International trade raises a country's standard of living. Lower prices on imported products and greater product variety enhance consumer well-being. Specialization based on comparative advantage and increased competition from foreign businesses improves production efficiency, raising GDP. Firms also get access to foreign capital goods that often contain new technologies, further improving productivity.

Concerns over international trade often center on the effect on jobs and wages. The evidence shows trade can result in the displacement of workers in industries that must compete with imports. However, the impact is modest relative to overall employment growth. Although displaced workers do face adjustment costs, overall the United States has experienced robust total employment growth in the presence of expanded trade. Furthermore, studies show that international trade has a relatively small affect on wages. Greater wage inequality has been driven more by skill-biased technological change than by international trade.

Although international trade forces significant adjustments in an economy, as the evidence shows, the costs of international trade restrictions on the economy outweigh the limited benefits these restrictions bring to import-competing industries.

ROBERT KROL is a professor of economics at California State University, Northridge.

EXPLORING THE ISSUE

Are Protectionist Policies Beneficial to Business?

Critical Thinking and Reflection

1. What might be the tactics of a protectionist strategy?
2. How might a protectionist strategy be implemented in a corporation?
3. What might be the costs to consumers, corporations, and the nation of corporations following an unmitigated protectionist strategy?
4. What is the likelihood that an enacted protectionist strategy will lead to anticipated outcomes?
5. What does the future hold for industries following protectionist strategies?

Is There Common Ground?

One reason the issue of protectionist policies is so contentious is that both sides can easily cite data in support of their position. While finding common ground on basic aspects of this important management topic is difficult, there is consensus that protectionist policies are an important topic that will be debated for quite some time, especially in certain industries.

Additional Resources

Cavusgil, S. T., Knight, G. & Riesenberger, J. R. (2008). *International Business*, Pearson, p. 620.

Hardy, Q. & Buley, T. (2009). "The Greening of Trade Wars," *Forbes*, May 10, 2009, Forbes.com, p. 26.

Johnson, I. (2009). "World News: Foreign Businesses Say China Is Growing More Protectionist," *Wall Street Journal* (Eastern Edition), April 28, p. A8.

Kerr, W. A. (2009). "Recession, International Trade and the Fallacies of Composition," *The Estey Centre Journal of International Law and Trade Policy:* Special Section on Geographical Indicators, 10(1), pp. 1–11.

The Economist (2009). "Low Expectations Exceeded.

Internet Reference . . .

Buy American Is About Building Jobs, Not Protectionism

Connell, T. (2009). "Buy American Is About Building Jobs, Not Protectionism," *AFL-CIO NOW*, February 20.

http://blog.aflcio.org/2009/02/20/buy-american
-is-about-building-jobs-not-protectionism/

Selected, Edited, and with Issue Framing Material by:
Kathleen J. Barnes, *William Paterson University*
and
George E. Smith, *University of South Carolina, Beaufort*

ISSUE

Is Globalization Beneficial for Society?

YES: Stephen A. Baker and Robert A. Lawson, from "The Benefits of Globalization: An Economic Perspective," *Journal of Lutheran Ethics* (2002)

NO: Sergio Obeso, from "Globalization and Its Consequences for the Countries and People in Mexico and Latin America," *Kolping International* (Accessed 2012)

Learning Outcomes

After reading this issue, you will be able to:

- Define what globalization is.
- Identify and explain both positive and negative consequences of economic globalization.
- Understand why developing nations view globalization as a potential opportunity.
- Appreciate the challenges of pursuing a globalization agenda while attempting to retain a distinct and unique culture and political process.

ISSUE SUMMARY

YES: Professors Steven A. Baker and Robert A. Larson discuss the benefits of globalization for both developed and developing nations and peoples. While acknowledging that there are imperfections in the approach, they note that globalization can have a positive effect and can help nations and people successfully address the issue of poverty.

NO: Sergio Obeso, Archbishop Emeritus of Xalapa, presents his view of globalization's impact on the people of Mexico and Latin America. While he acknowledges that some benefits were derived from these practices and this process, Archbishop Obeso observes that there have been adverse consequences on local and regional cultures as well as other forms of regional and nationalistic expression (e.g., politics, religion, societal values).

According to the World Bank's, Is globalization a good or a bad thing? Does it benefit everybody or mainly the "banksters"? There have been many debates about globalization and inequalities, but what is the evidence?

Global inequalities started to rise with the Industrial Revolution, when a score of countries experienced much faster economic growth than the rest of the world. This gave them an advantage which they kept until the beginning of the globalization era. A "catching-up" phenomenon is now at play, with some of the poorest countries having emerged and turned into global engines of growth. It is too early to pass a definitive judgment, but it seems that inequality across countries has started to decline since the late 1990s. On the other hand, there is evidence that in some

countries globalization has been accompanied by an increase in inequalities—as recently raised by people as different as Pope Francis and President Obama.

Yet, in a recent paper, a World Bank researcher, Branko Milanovic, looked at the question from a different perspective—what if we forget for a moment about borders and measure inequality among individuals (not nations)? What if we do not compare, say, Poland to Germany, or rich and poor in Poland, but each person in the world to all others? Would we see global inequalities, those between the world's richest and poorest citizens regardless of where they live, on the rise or in decline? The study provides some interesting insights on the nature of inequality in the age of globalization.

As could be expected, it shows that the world remains a tremendously unequal place. Using a standard indicator (the Gini coefficient), global inequality is far greater than inequality within any country, even the most unequal ones. The gap between a poor person in India or Sub-Saharan Africa and the Western upper-class is an abyss.

The study also shows that the determinant factor of one's income is where one lives. The poorest five percent of Germans are richer than the wealthiest five percent of Ivoirians. In other words, social classes matter less than places of residence. The consequences are clear—either poor countries can develop their economies fast, or their people will be inclined to migrate to richer shores.

Maybe most interestingly, the study looks at the winners and losers of the globalization process—and unveils several unexpected facts. It is often assumed that there are two main groups who benefit from globalization—the "top 1 percent" and the "emerging middle class" in countries like China, India, etc. The numbers confirm these intuitions. But they also show that the income of the "emerging middle class" rose even faster than that of the top 1 percent. And that this "emerging middle class" accounts for about half of humankind. This is no small feat!

The study also shows that the people at the "global bottom" too have gained over the past decades, less than the "emerging middle class" but enough to reduce abject poverty dramatically (the exception is the poorest five percent of the world population, people who typically live in conflict-affected countries, and who have seen little benefits of a globalization process that has largely bypassed them). This is very encouraging.

In fact, the biggest losers of the globalization process may well be the "global upper middle class" (technically: those between the 75th and 90th percentile of income distribution), i.e., the poorest part of the population in Western European countries, the lower middle class in Central Europe. These groups have not lost out, but they have not seen their income rise in any meaningful manner over the past two decades while the rest of the world surged.

So what does it all mean for a country like Poland? In spite of common perceptions, Poland as a whole is already among the wealthiest countries in the world, even though of course not everybody in Poland is wealthy. The study highlights the need to accelerate economic growth, so as to increase as rapidly as possible the distance from the potentially swampy grounds of the "global upper middle class." It also suggests that continued policy action is needed to ensure that prosperity can be truly shared by all, that the gains of globalization are not captured by a "happy few," but on the contrary that all can take advantage of the opportunities offered by the globalization process, including those who earn the least. It highlights the importance of contributing to other countries' development to reduce the global inequalities which can be the seeds of geopolitical turmoil. And most importantly it provides a confirmation (with numbers!) that the world is indeed becoming a better place.

YES

Stephen A. Baker and Robert A. Lawson

The Benefits of Globalization: An Economic Perspective

Introduction

The process of globalization of the world economies has recently generated severe protests from many quarters, including on the pages of this journal (Moe-Lobeda, 2001; Yutzis, 2001). Among these critics, almost every social ill from poverty to pollution to pestilence seems to be caused by globalization and the evils of capitalism. In this paper we shall argue that the increased openness of economic life around the globe has generated great benefits to vast numbers of people. To be sure, not everybody has gained from globalization, or gained equally, but never have so many people in so many countries lived so well. Furthermore, we contend that globalization and the extension of freer markets to the world's people offer the best hope for sustained progress around the world. Government solutions of the sorts supported by those opposing globalization will consign millions of the world's poorest people to continued squalor.

What Is Globalization?

For the purpose of discussion, we use the term globalization to refer to the trend toward increased trade in goods and services, increased capital mobility, and increased/faster/cheaper communication and transportation.

Although there have been periods of significant international trade and investment, most notably in the years leading up to World War I, the recent trend towards greater openness began after World War II. Since 1947, The General Agreements on Tariffs and Trade (GATT) helped reduce barriers to trade and investment. GATT has now evolved into a World Trade Organization (WTO), which seeks to reduce barriers to trade and investment and resolve disputes. As a result of GATT and the natural reductions in the cost of transport, the volume of trade flowing around the globe has dramatically increased. Among 90 countries for which complete data were available between 1970 and 1998, there was a 394% increase in the total volume of imports and exports (in real terms). (World Bank, 2001.)

The Benefits of Trade

Economics teaches that voluntary trade is a positive-sum exercise. That is, people trade because they gain by trading—this is true for both the buyer and the seller. Notice that after buying something at a store, both parties to the exchange often say "thank you" because both parties have improved their situation in life through the exchange. To an economist, it is difficult to describe any voluntary trade with the term "exploitation." Most often, "exploitation" means someone is paid less (or is paying more) than he or she would like. Much of the literature on this subject that comes from a religious perspective (Duchrow, 1996) implicitly assumes, usually along Marxian lines, that all economic relationships are power relationships characterized by aggressors and victims. They assume that economic life is zero-sum, where there must be winners and losers. But the economist rejects this. In fact, voluntary economic arrangements are positive sum games with winners and winners (though it is true that some people may win more than others). The entire basis of economic life, unlike political life, is to better your own condition by doing good things for others. This principle was best espoused by Adam Smith (1776) himself with his famous "invisible hand" metaphor.

Furthermore, we would not expect the benefits of trade to stop at national borders. These borders were drawn for political reasons, not economic reasons. And it should be noted that countries do **not** trade. Only people trade; individuals gain by trading across national boundaries just as they gain from trade within a single country. Why should trade be good between Ohioans and Kentuckians, but harmful among people of different colors, between people who speak different languages, or because the people live under different political regimes? Much of the debate about international trade is characterized racism, nationalism, and talk of them and us. Again, religious thinkers must understand that trade between people is a fundamentally enriching exercise for all involved.

Trade Allows Specialization

The primary way in which trade works to improve our lives, and ironically the target of much criticism from opponents of globalization, is through specialization. International trade takes place when one group of people can produce a product cheaper than another group. For example even though it would be possible to grow oranges in Alaska (using greenhouses), Floridians can grow oranges far cheaper than Alaskans. By contrast, Alaskans produce salmon cheaper than Floridians could ever imagine. On the basis of these differences in costs of production, it makes sense for the people in

Florida to grow oranges and for Alaskans to produce salmon, and then for the Floridians to trade some of their oranges to the Alaskans for salmon. In so doing, both the Floridians and the Alaskans will have more oranges and more salmon than it would be possible to have if they each tried to produce both products. That is, their standards of living will improve through this specialization and trade.

An economic policy of self-sufficiency would cause Floridians to waste precious resources raising salmon themselves even though the salmon raised by Alaskans would be cheaper. Likewise, self-sufficiency would cause the Alaskans to build costly greenhouses to grow oranges instead of buying cheap Florida oranges.

This principle has been recognized by economists since the time of Adam Smith. Smith (1776) pointed out that Scotland could grow grapes and even make wine, but that this would take more resources than would be needed to pay for wine from other countries. This principle that specialization and trade leads to higher living standards is one of the most powerful, and least controversial, of all economic facts. And churches frequently back policies of sustainable development which incorporate principles of self-sufficiency into their design.

Ugandan farmers have found that they can earn money by producing flowers for Europe instead of continuing with subsistence farming. By doing this they can buy more food and clothing than if they try to produce what they consume for themselves. If we prevent Ugandan farmers selling flowers to Europe in the name of "sustainable development," we are condemning the people to hunger and poverty. As the Economist points out: Growing flowers is hard work, but no more so than subsistence farming, which is the alternative; and it pays better. (June 1 2002, p. 68)

We all know that the factory workers in poor countries do not get paid as much as workers in the U.S. We hear stories of children making soccer balls in Pakistan. We also read that workers rights and environmental regulations are not as well developed as in the U.S. We might remember that children worked on American farms and in American factories when the U.S. was in the early stages of development. Wages were low, pollution controls were weak, and workers rights were minimal. As the economy grew, these problems were reduced. Many countries of the world are in the early stages of development. They cannot afford to live up to the standards of a rich country. Globalization is the path to higher incomes, and with higher incomes comes the willingness and means to deal with environmental problems. Antweiler, Copeland and Taylor (2001) show that free trade is on net good for the environment.

Trade Restrictions

How would opponents of globalization have us slow globalization? The answer usually entails trade restrictions, or increased regulations related to labor standards, the environment, and so on. How do these

policies change the fundamental problem of low productivity? The answer is that they don't. Such policies may even make poor people poorer.

The problem facing the developing world is not free trade; the problem is that the international trade system is not free enough. Poor and rich countries alike often levy high tariffs to protect local, politically influential industries. Many Asian countries employ massive tariffs and quotas on automobiles to prop up a domestic car industry, for instance, even though it is cheaper to buy a car made in Japan or the U.S. When the people of a country are already poor, forcing them to pay more for imports reduces their real income further. Consumers are not the only group affected. Producers in poor countries are often hurt because tariffs raise the price of imported goods they use in the production process. While some producers do gain, the evidence clearly shows that overall production, including the production of exports, suffers when countries adopt isolationist policies. (See Krueger, 1985 and 1995.)

The U.S. is a part of the problem here as well. The recent 30% tariff on imported steel is a travesty. Similarly, the recent farm bill will provide billions of dollars of support to American farmers, encouraging them to overproduce food for export markets, thus harming farmers overseas. American tariffs or quotas on imported agricultural products that poor countries can produce, such as sugar, cotton, and peanuts, prevent people in poor countries from doing what they are good at. For example, export subsidies have pushed U.S. cotton exports to 35 percent of the world market in a product that is produced and exported by many poor countries. (IMF, 2002.)

It might be illuminating to ask: Who benefits from trade restrictions? Trade restrictions reduce competition and help inefficient domestic companies survive. American workers calling for restrictions on imports to promote better workers' rights in foreign lands may be more interested in protecting their own incomes than the rights of foreign workers. Where is the justice in a policy that impoverishes people in other countries in order to provide more money to comparatively rich American workers?

Small, poor countries cannot produce everything they need. If they are cut off from international trade, the people will be poorer and have a narrower range of goods. It is often suggested that poor countries cannot trade because they lack resources. Not every country can produce every good, but even a country with lots of people and no resources can enjoy a reasonable standard of living if it trades. For example, at the time that China regained sovereignty over Hong Kong, the median income in Hong Kong was higher than the median income in Britain. Hong Kong's only significant resource is its people. Japan's natural resources are insignificant compared with its population and their standard of living.

International Capital Flows

Poor (and rich) countries often need international investment to finance projects. International aid sometimes helps, but government-financed development projects have been a dismal failure. Unlike the critics of globalization, we do not believe that the failures of international aid are a reason to increase aid or to forgive debts. Foreign aid has propped up inefficient, often corrupt governments whose interventionist economic policies have led to so much misery. Even the World Bank (2002a, 2002b) has come to realize that building market-oriented institutions is critical if international aid efforts are to succeed.

Money flowing into a country may finance new projects directly, or enter the savings pool from where it can be borrowed and used to finance investments. If capital flows are restricted, fewer projects will be financed. It is that simple. And poor countries have little capital to begin with. Private capital flows to (developing are four natoins to five times larger) than official capital flows. Even if official flows were increased dramatically, private flows would be vital for poor countries. (See World Bank, 2002c.)

Concern about foreign ownership of capital is a red herring. In Marysville near Columbus, Ohio, (where we live) there is a Honda plant. It provides good non-union jobs for 6,500 people. No rich country would turn down the possibility of such a plant. Poor countries are desperate to attract such investments. People in rich countries may denounce multinational firms, but politicians of almost every party around the world recognize that these companies produce jobs and votes. Even the Cuban government is desperate for the country to be freed from restrictions so that it can attract more foreign investment. If multinationals are so detrimental to economic health, why does every country in the world seek their business?

We would never claim that all multinational companies at all times have behaved perfectly. Nor would we make that claim for the companies of any country. We do believe that investment by multinationals helps alleviate shortages of capital, spreads technology between countries, and provides employment and income for the workers.

Empirical Evidence

Numerous recent studies by economists (Vamvakidis, 2002; Bhagwati and Srinivasan, 2002) have shown that the pattern of economic progress around the globe reflects, among other things, a country's willingness to jump on the globalization train. Krueger (1995) makes a forceful case that globalization is important for developing nations. Recent evidence on global economic policy provided by Gwartney and Lawson (2002) provides powerful evidence of the benefits of trade. Gwartney and Lawson

rate countries' openness to foreign trade on a zero to ten scale based on a range of factors such as tariffs, quotas, and other trade restrictions.

Table 1 shows the basic relationship between trade openness and various measures of economic and social progress. The most open quartile of countries (i.e., the most open 25% of the world) had an average income level of $22,012 compared with the least free quartile of countries with a $3,402 average level of income. The rate of per capita economic growth is faster in open economies, with the top quartile growing at 1.95% per year in the 1990s and the bottom quartile growing at just 0.38%. Moreover, the prosperity that openness brings is shared throughout the income distribution. The poorest tenth of the population actually receives a larger share of national income in the most open economies than in the closed economies. Furthermore, the poorest tenth are much richer in more open economies than in less open economies. Contrary to the claims of globalization's opponents, there is simply no statistical evidence that globalization is contributing to a narrower distribution of income.

Economists are often unjustly accused of being interested only in money. This is certainly not true, but the image persists. In our table, we also present the relationship between the Gwartney and Lawson openness measure and other indicators of "social" progress. Table 1 also shows that infant mortality is much lower and life expectancy is over 14 years greater in more open economies compared with comparatively closed economies.

Another line of argument frequently advanced by opponents of globalization is that free trade may lead to higher incomes but it is a threat to democracy, as nations consider the interests of

Table 1

Openness to Foreign Trade and Measures of Economic and Social Progress

Trade Openness	Gross National Income per capita, US$, 2000	GDP per capita % growth, 1990–2000	Life Expectancy at Birth, 1999	Under Five Mortality per 1,000, 1999	Lowest 10% Share of Income	Lowest 10% Level of Income, US$, 2000
Top Quartile	$22,012	1.95	75.52	14.21	2.99	$6,401
Second Quartile	$8,453	1.66	68.82	32.82	2.43	$2,355
Third Quartile	$6,653	1.00	66.07	50.62	2.51	$1,624
Bottom Quartile	$3,402	0.38	56.93	124.37	2.51	$484

Table 2

Openness to Foreign Trade and Measures of Civil Liberties and Political Freedoms

Trade Openness	Freedom House Rating of Civil Liberties (1=Free . . . 7=Not Free)	Freedom House Rating of Political Freedom (1=Free . . . 7=Not Free)
Top Quartile	1.93	1.60
Second Quartile	3.07	2.39
Third Quartile	3.41	3.55
Bottom Quartile	4.11	3.96

global capital markets and multinationals instead of the interests of local citizens. We argue that the free flow of goods and services and with it the free flow of information is the best pro-democracy strategy one can employ. This is true for two reasons. First, openness leads to higher incomes, as we have shown above. And people with higher incomes often demand greater political and civil liberties. This dynamic has certainly played out in Taiwan and South Korea. Second, globalization increases the flow not just of goods and services around the globe but of information. When people in repressive societies find out about the political and civil freedoms in other places, they have a natural desire to want the same things for themselves. The fax machine may have done more to bring down the oppressive Soviet Union than all the ICBM's in the U.S. arsenal. Of course, this is why repressive political regimes try to restrict the citizenry's access to outside information.

Table 2 below shows the same trade openness measure from Gwartney and Lawson as it relates to the measures of political freedom and civil liberties constructed by Freedom House (2001). Clearly, more open economies also enjoy greater civil liberties and political freedoms. Anti-globalists who care about such matters are wrong to oppose free trade.

Conclusion

When we buy goods from people in poor countries we help them live. Restricting imports from such countries would deprive those people of the income that they need. The workers may be poorer than those in the U.S., but at least they have jobs, even if they are at low wages. Removing those jobs by restricting trade, when there are few other ways that the people can feed themselves, is tantamount to starving them. Is it not contradictory to say that we care about the material welfare of other people, and yet to argue for less trade, which reduces their material welfare?

You can contribute to Oxfam or buy a soccer ball from Pakistan. Either way you help feed a person. Given the unfortunate scarcity of altruism in our world, the former option is not likely to help much. But international trade has in fact lifted millions out of poverty. Anti-globalists who care about poverty should rethink their position.

References

Freedom House, 2001. Freedom in the world 2001-2002: *The Democracy Gap*. New York: Freedom House.

Gwartney, James and Robert Lawson, 2002. *Economic Freedom of the World*: 2002 Annual Report. Vancouver: The Fraser Institute.

IMF, 2001, *Market Access for Developing Countries' Exports*, report prepared by the staffs of the IMF and the World Bank, April 27, 2001. Available on line: http://www.imf.org/external/np/madc/eng/042701.pdf

International Monetary Fund, 2002. *Improving Market Access: Towards Greater Coherence Between trade and Aid*, IMF Issue Brief, March.

Krueger, Anne, 1995. *Trade Policies and Developing Nations*. Washington, DC: The Brookings Institution.

Krueger, Anne, "Import Substitution Versus Export Promotion," *Finance and Development*, 22, June 1985, pp. 20–23.

Moe-Lobeda, Cynthia, 2001. "Journey Between Worlds: Economic Globalization and Luther's God Indwelling Creation." *Journal of Lutheran Ethics*.

Oxfam, 2002. *Rigged Rules and Double Standards: trade globalization, and the fight against poverty*. http://www.maketradefair.com Accessed: June 17, 2002.

Smith, Adam, 1776, *An Inquiry into the Nature and Causes of the Wealth of Nations*, New York, Modern Library College Editions, Random House, 1995.

Vamvakidis, Athanasios, 2002. "How Robust is the Growth-Openness Connection: Historical Evidence." *Journal of Economic Growth* 7, 56–80.

World Bank, 2002a. *World Development Report 2002: Building Institutions for Markets*. New York: The World Bank and Oxford University Press.

World Bank, 2002b. *Globalization, Growth and Poverty: Building Inclusive World Economy*. New York: The World Bank and Oxford University Press.

World Bank, 2002c, *Global Development Finance: Financing the Poorest Countries, Analysis and Summary Tables*, Washington DC, The World Bank.

World Bank, 2001. *World Development Indicators 2001.* New York: The World Bank and Oxford University Press.

Yutzis, Mario Jorge, 2001. "The Argentine Crisis: Economy, Society and Ethics in Times of Globalization." *Journal of Lutheran Ethics*

STEPHEN A. BAKER is the Honors Program Director at Capital University in Columbus, OH.

ROBERT A. LAWSON is the George H. Moor Professor of Economics at the School of Management of Capital University in Columbus, OH.

Sergio Obeso

 **NO**

Globalization and Its Consequences for the Countries and People in Mexico and Latin America

1) Introduction

Our world today is characterized by rapid changes, which are reflected in all areas of human relationships and the exchange of ideas and goods of any kind, in scientific discoveries, technological innovations, in the various life styles, in values and in cultural expressions of any kind, as well as in art and religion. Every day we hear about and experience the consequences of a multi-dimensional phenomenon, the so called globalization.

Globalization undoubtedly brings new challenges to the social, political, and religious institutions of every country, because it has brought about new and complex social, economic, and political processes which, in turn, have accelerated conflicts inherited from earlier times and also created inequalities in the exchanges taking place, which impair the life and development process of people and the marginalized groups considerably.

For some time, numerous analyses have been available and wide-spread discussions are under way, just how much the phenomenon of globalization—while offering all countries opportunities for economic growth (but not development) on the one hand—means, on the other hand, an enormous risk of polarization between economic blocks and new forms of socio-political and cultural dependencies for the poorer countries.

Of course, this address does not intend to provide a scientific examination of such a broad scope of problems as presented by globalization; we would rather like to make a modest contribution of a more pastoral character against the background of some of the facts of our lives.

2) Globalization as a Process of Economic Integration

The nature of the globalization process is the integration of the world into one single economic system, the capitalistic one. The trans-national capital imposes its conditions, in order to complete its projects of economic development at the expense of human rights and the independence of sovereign nations. Mexico, like all the other Latin American countries, will be forced to curb its latitude in

deciding its own models of economic, social, political, and cultural development. In fact, Mexico has entered fully into the globalized economy when the country signed the eight free trade agreements, which affect 24 countries, and when it joined the World Trade Organization.

By doing so, Mexico took on a development model that is—with regard to the creation of economic wealth, economic growth, and new jobs—determined completely by the laws of free trade and fundamentally based on the export sector and the speculation of foreign capital.

Changing over from a national project to an economic model which is more and more dependent on decisions made abroad, resulted in an excessive growth of the manufacturing industry, while simultaneously forcing most of the small and intermediate companies into bankruptcy. At the same time, the national production chains were phased out, the foreign debt grew, and the emigration to the North and into the United States was encouraged.

The result of the population drain was the decline of rural regions with extremely negative consequences: agricultural production dropped and our country's dependency in the area of food provisions rose. Products which had formerly covered the domestic market, such as rice, corn, and beans, now have to be imported to meet national demands.

It is obvious that the export of semi-finished products as an alternative source of foreign exchange was not the best decision. Over the last decade, exporting companies were involved in only 3.4% of the jobs created on the national level, and for every exported dollar almost one and a half dollars were imported.

While it is true that the decline of the agricultural sector began already at the time when the country's industrialization was given preference, the government's specifically directed economic policies resulted in a growing number of small and intermediate production companies which had to close over the past 20 years.

In 1980, 12% of public expenditures went to the agricultural sector; in 1989 this had dropped to just under 5%. Added to this is the unfair competition of some countries, predominantly the USA, which raise the subsidies for their own agricultural products, while the Mexican government drops its subsidies or eliminates them altogether. And if Mexico—in spite of the laws of free trade—wants to protect a sector, for instance the producers of sugar cane with a 20% tax on products with a high fructose content, the US government takes an even harder position and threatens with import sanctions for Mexican products.

Regularly and in six-year cycles, this situation has led to a further rise in poverty, particularly in the rural regions and in the "Comunidades Indigenas". Careful estimates show that in Mexico at least 22 million people live below the poverty line. In contrast, the average income of the richest families, which make up 10% of the total population, has risen by more than 20% in the last four decades of the past century.

Poverty and unemployment were the two main reasons for the increase in emigration to the USA and Canada from Mexico as well as from other countries of Central America. This is illustrated by the example of Atzálan, a small community of in the province of Veracruz: From there, more than 6000 people, i.e. 12% of the total population, emigrated in one year. The negative consequences are well known: family relationships are disrupted, the fields neglected, the emigrants face great risks with regard to their lives and their health, etc. Furthermore, this phenomenon destroys the social cohesion of the population in their home communities, withdraws from them their most dynamic and productive forces, alienates them from their culture, upsets the balance of local and regional economies, and also takes the most capable people away from groups and institutions of the Church.

3) Globalization as Expression and Expansion of Neoliberalism in Latin America and Mexico

Neo-Liberalism, as understood and promoted in Latin America and Mexico, is not only an economic program but a model of development, which portrays the market as the ultimate value and elevates it to be the means, the method, and the objective of all human behaviour. It therefore seeks to integrate the lives of people, the behaviour of societies, and the political actions of governments into this broad framework of inter-dependencies.

The Mexican bishops, as well as other religious leaders in Latin America, have spoken out against this neo-liberal model, because it infringes on human rights and freedoms, limits the share of all people in the goods of the world, and hampers solidarity and healthy competition. (See Pastoral Letter of the Mexican Bishops' Conference 2000, # 323—330, and "Neo-Liberalism in Latin America", Universidad Iberoamericana de Mexico, 1997, pages 16 ff.)

Our rejection of Neo-Liberalism does not mean that we oppose the efficient use of the resources that are available to a society; we also do not want to limit the freedom of the individual, or speak out for state socialism. We do declare, however, that there are no absolute institutions which can fathom or guide the fate of

mankind. We emphasize that men and women, as human beings, cannot be pawns of the market, the state, or any other power or institution that wants to establish itself in a totalitarian way.

If we emphasize the negative consequences of globalization, we do not deny some of the positive results of internationalizing science, technology, and communication. We are well aware of the fact that progress in the area of medicine has made inroads on the decline of certain diseases and increased the average lifespan, and that rapid access to information has brought about the exchange of knowledge and skills in the areas of education, production, and employment.

We are also aware that, in catastrophic events, new means of transportation have made solidarity actions possible on the international level, etc. At the same time, however, we see with great sadness how much greed, consumerism, individualism, hedonism, and lack of solidarity are on the rise and affect ever increasing circles of the population.

Seen from an institutional perspective, globalization has had strong effects on social policies of the governments toward the weakest sections of the population, whose quality of life is being reduced through cuts in social spending in the areas of health, shelter, education, and support of the rural populations. The macro-economic criteria (low inflation rates, stable trade balances, recovery of public finances through new taxes, etc.) are given a higher priority than a balanced social development which takes everybody into consideration and gives all people the opportunity to grow as individuals and as communities, with long-term employment, adequate income, and living quarters and places for recreation which correspond to their cultural identity and are not dependent on the marketing of television and radio monopolies.

A further consequence which is often connected to an undiscriminating expansion of the markets is the decline of a country's social capital. This capital is based principally on local culture in all its peculiarities and manifold expressions, on knowledge accumulated over long periods of time, on education in all its forms and classifications, on natural resources, and on the diversity of species. This social capital is the result of active cooperation between society as a whole and the government, as long as both sides pursue the strengthening of social and political institutions in a peaceful collaboration based on mutual trust. This collaboration is required so that culture and productivity can be developed in all areas of human activity.

This social capital has declined in all our countries. The range of educational programs, the quality of raising children, and the awareness for social values is becoming increasingly more precarious. On average, more than half of Latin America's populations suffer from inferior education which subdues people's awareness instead of liberating people's development potential, an education system that puts more stock in obtaining a certificate that in an over-all education that kickstarts an individual's life as a whole. Illiteracy—the absolute as well as the functional one—still affects a high percentage of people over the age of 15. According to estimates, the illiteracy rate in Mexico is still 12%, and the number of inhabitants over 15 who have not completed elementary school was 34 million just 6 years ago.

We would be very naive if we claimed the greatest concern of our governments in Latin America to be the fate of the poor. That has not been the case for a long time and is now even less since, according to the free market norm, the poor are not profitable.

Because of neo-liberal policies, the state concerns itself less and less with the weaker sections of society, as it withdraws more and more from the assistance and development programs for the poor, even though public discussions introduce new projects with new names. In reality, social welfare is being privatized, the increase of social and cultural patrimony neglected, and the networkings of social-issue-related non-government-organizations weakened. The privatization of social welfare follows world strategies which do not benefit the poor but enhances the reputation of the multi-nationals.

4) Some of the Consequences of Globalization on Regional Cultures

It is a fact that lately a new evaluation of regional and local cultures has taken place in some of our countries, which resulted in a growing acceptance of inter-culturalism and the ethnic, societal, and social pluralism. Yet, the prospects for the future are discouraging because—in view of the trends promoted by marketing, the globalization of information, and the above-mentioned inferiority of education—this progress will not be consolidated.

It is not chauvinism when we claim that in our environment we see the gradual acceptance of mind-sets and patterns of behaviour which correspond to cultural norms that are foreign to our Latin American and Christian-Catholic way of thinking. By means of the ever-increasing speed of exchange between information technologies, entertainment, and product marketing, many characteristics of a consumer-oriented, hedonistic, and individualistic world view are gradually being forced upon us. At the same time, the individual characteristics of our culture are losing their image, particularly in the case of the "indigenas" and the people living in rural areas. Communal traditions, the active participation of all in important decision making processes, the exchange of gifts and tasks for the benefit of those who need them, and, above all, the deep conviction that God determines the personal life and the fate of mankind, all those are being lost more and more.

5) Other Side-Effects of Globalization

Without being the direct cause of it, globalization has brought about an acceleration and intensification of several problems from which this continent has suffered for several decades. Let us name a few

examples: the decreasing stability of family life; the increase of violence in all its forms; the discrimination of women; the destruction of the environment and the exploitation of natural resources; the intimidation of those who defend the human rights of such groups of farmers and "indegenas", who are not in agreement with the expansion plans of a rampant capitalism; the corruption of leaders induced to speak up for the government's policies favouring transnational companies; the unpunished freedoms with which gangs of drug dealers and kidnappers can operate; the almost natural acceptance of corruption; the kidnapping and rape of defenseless women; and, last but not least, the replacement of Christian spirituality and mysticism with pseudo-religious practices, which want to have nothing to do with Christian commitment in the fight against sin, in the practice of justice, in loving service to all who are our neighbours, notwithstanding all differences in race, colour, gender, or culture.

6) Conclusion and Call for Action

We have described some of the consequences of globalization and its connection to the neo-liberalistic development model which still predominates in all our countries. In view of these so very complex problems we cannot stop at pointing out the facts. We have to join together to take on these challenges, brought on by these circumstances, and we have to become aware of the fact that—notwithstanding all these threats from the outside and our own weaknesses—we do possess a potential full of opportunities to stand up for Jesus Christ's model of living and to enter into new ways of solidarity.

It would be naive to think that we could contribute to the solution of some of these problems by means of short-term or locally limited endeavours or projects. It is therefore urgently required that the meeting, in which we are now participating, brings us to the point where we think globally in order to then go forth and act locally and serve as members of our Church. The solidarity which makes it possible to face these challenges requires an open and continuously multi-lateral communication, in order to present analyses and alternatives which include us all, taking up topics such as emigration, protection of natural resources, export of our products under conditions of competition, enforcement of workers' rights in the manufacturing industry, adequate and factual information on actual and productive investment of economic and technological resources for a sustainable development, etc.

On the basis of our faith in Jesus Christ who became poor for us and an advocate for the poor, we ultimately must, as Christians and in solidarity with others, take on the co-responsibility and obligation, so that justice and peace for all and the preservation of creation become reality.

Sergio Obeso is Archbishop Emeritus of Xalapa, Veracruz having retired in August 2007.

EXPLORING THE ISSUE

Is Globalization Beneficial for Society?

Critical Thinking and Reflection

1. What can be done to protect developing nations from the potential traps of globalization?
2. Is economic or social betterment always an outcome of globalization?
3. What, if anything, should corporations do to protect developing nations and people from globalization?
4. Is globalization harmful or helpful?
5. Are there ways to maximize the benefits of globalization and minimize the potential harms?

Is There Common Ground?

Common ground does exist in this issue. First, there is agreement that globalization practices are here to stay. Second, despite concerns both sides of the argument concede that there are both potential positive and negative outcomes. The debate that exists here seemingly revolves around the issue of whether or not the potential risks and damage to society warrant the perpetuation of the practice as presently implemented.

As you have seen from the readings contained in this issue, both sides can make strong cases for their positions. There are two points to consider when thinking about where you personally stand on this issue. First, what is your personal view of business's role in society? What do you believe business "owes" society or should be doing to protect it. Second, how might your view potentially be altered if you were a citizen of one of the developing nations bearing the impact of globalization's effects?

Given the anticipated future expansion of global markets and the economy, this discussion and debate will continue for some time.

Additional Resources

Crafts, N. (2004). "Globalisation and Economic Growth: A Historical Perspective," *The World Economy,* pp. 45–58.

Dreher, A. & Gaston, N. (2008), "Has Globalization Increased Inequality?" *Review of International Economics,* pp. 516–536.

Nolan, P. (2008). "The Contradictions of Capitalist Globalization," in *Issues in Economic Development and Globalization: Essays in Honour of Akit Singh, Basingstroke,* Hampshire: NY, pp. 115–133.

Razak, M. A. (2001). "Globalization and Its Impact on Education and Culture," *World Journal of Islamic History and Civilization,* pp. 59–69.

Velasquez, M. (2000). "Globalization and the Failure of Ethics," *Business Ethics Quarterly,* January, pp. 343–352.

Weber, S., Barma, N., Kroenig, M. & Ratner, E. (2007). "How Globalization Went Bad," *Foreign Policy,* January/ February, pp. 48–54.

Internet References . . .

Globalisation: Good or Bad?

http://news.bbc.co.uk/2/hi/talking_point/1444930.stm

Globalisation: Negative Impacts of Globalisation

http://www.bbc.co.uk/schools/gcsebitesize/geography /globalisation/globalisation_rev5.shtml

Is Globalization a Good or a Bad Thing?

http://www.worldbank.org/en/news/opinion/2014/02/11 /is-globalization-a-good-or-a-bad-thing

The Good, the Bad, and the Ugly Side of Globalization

http://www.forbes.com/sites/panosmourdoukoutas /2011/09/10/the-good-the-bad-and-the-ugly-side-of -globalization/

Why Globalization is Good

http://www.forbes.com/forbes/2007/0416/064.html